The Gentlemen at ﹢

Policing Britain 1939-45

By the same author:

Police of the World
Police Vehicles of the World
European Strategic Alliances (translation)
Mission Incomprehensible

The Gentlemen at War

Policing Britain 1939-45

Roy Ingleton
MA, FIL, FITI

Cranborne Publications

Published 1994 by

CRANBORNE PUBLICATIONS
10 Cranborne Avenue,
Maidstone, Kent,
ME15 7EB

Telephone : (0622) 762039
Fax : (0622) 759132

Printed and bound in Great Britain by Pardy & Son (Printers) Ltd, Ringwood
Bureau output by Colin Powell, Bournemouth.

British Library Cataloguing-in-Publication Data
A catalogue record for this book is available from the British Library

ISBN 0 9523437 0 3

To Jo

Contents

Acknowledgements

It would be impossible for me to thank adequately all those kind persons - retired policemen and women, the wives, widows and families of those who served in the police during the Second World War - who provided the personal details which were so crucial to this work. Although the memory can play tricks - especially after half a century - policemen are trained and accustomed to remember facts without embellishment and there is no doubt that the personal experiences recounted reflect the truth very closely. The fact that they incorporate close similarities also makes them mutually supportive and corroborative.

Thanks are due to BBC Radio Kent and to Mr Charlie Chester, both of whom broadcast my appeal for information, and to the secretaries of the various branches of the National Association of Retired Police Officers (NARPO) and the Force Welfare officers who so kindly contacted their members with my appeal.

I am also indebted to Dorothy Sheridan for allowing me access to the Mass Observation Archives and for permitting me to quote from these sources (copyright the Trustees of the Mass-Observation Archive at the University of Sussex, reproduced by permission of the Curtis Brown Group Ltd, London)

Illustrations

All the photographs used in this book have been reproduced by kind permission of the Hulton Deutsch Collection with the following exceptions :

Cover photo :   The Central Office of Information
Page 190 :   Mrs Joan Salhurst
Page 388 :   Sport & General Press Agency

Introduction

*"All honour to the civil defence services of all
kinds ... who have helped our people through this
formidable ordeal, the like of which no civilised
community has ever been called upon to undergo.*

*"If I mention only one of them tonight –
namely, the police – it is because many tributes have
been paid already to the others. But the police have
been in it everywhere all the time. And, as a working-
woman wrote to me in a letter, "What gentlemen they
are".*

(Winston Churchill, in a broadcast
made on 9 February, 1942).

Despite Churchill's complimentary comments, half a century later
there has still been very little written about the work of the police in the
1939-45 war. The fire service, the wardens, the Home Guard – all have
had books devoted to them. And quite rightly so. But the vital role
played by the ubiquitous and omnipresent police men and women,
seems to have been largely ignored – possibly because their role was so
very wide-reaching. As Norman Longmate pointed out in his book,
How We Lived Then, there were surprisingly few films about Civil
Defence: a couple about the fire service and one on nursing but, of the
police, nothing. The British film-going public had to wait until after
the war for *The Blue Lamp*, introducing the celebrated Constable
Dixon, which dealt with post-war rather than wartime policing matters.
Where the police were portrayed in other films, they tended to be the
forelock-tugging, loyal servant of the public or the bumbling,
unimaginative detective, easily outsmarted by the upper-class amateur
sleuth.

This lack of publicity conceals the fact that, virtually overnight, the
functions and responsibilities of the police were widened and
completely changed. Policemen whose beats happened to include a
ghetto of Jews found themselves having to intern some good friends,

1

just because they happened to come from Germany (as refugees) or were Italians who had lived and worked in this country for a number of years. New organisations were formed (Wardens, Rescue, Home Guard, AFS), many of which had responsibilities which tended to overlap those of the police. No longer did the country copper in a quiet East Anglian town have just a little poaching to worry about; he now had a squadron of Flying Fortresses based on his "patch" with its full complement of attendant American servicemen.

The war produced dramatic shifts in the patterns of crime. Rationing, combined with severe shortages, resulted in a black market which was supplied by a whole army of pilferers as well as a few professional criminals. Almost everyone became a receiver of goods which had been stolen or had 'fallen off the back of a lorry' and traditional standards no longer applied. It also had a far-reaching effect on the morals and mores of the population and both the authorities and many members of the public were concerned that these were deteriorating. The absence of the indigenous menfolk and the influx of foreign troops were reflected in changes in moral behaviour, in increases in prostitution, sexual offences and vice in general. The war had a significant effect on police/public relations and fundamentally changed police attitudes and policing philosophies.

Those books and film scripts which have been written about what is generally referred to as the Home Front during the Second World War usually perpetuate the accepted images and myths and ignore or gloss over the more sordid and criminal aspects. They stress the concept of national unity and the mixing of social classes, the notion of heroism and good humour during the dangers of the Blitz and the plucky determination of the British people in the face of insuperable odds. More recently some historians have taken a critical look at these clichés and popular assumptions, highlighting the negative aspects of popular morale and drawing attention to the snobbish nature of the Establishment. They suggest that the war did not herald great changes in society but merely swept it along on a new course, reinforcing the old regime. Whilst acknowledging the changes in morality and possibly mentioning the changing crime trends, these academics seldom refer to the impact this had on those entrusted with enforcing those standards which the nation's conscience dictates: the police.

If one compares the nation in the 1930s with post-war Britain, with all its faults, one comes to the ineluctable fact that British society did, in fact undergo a great sea-change during those few years of the war. Among those institutions which were profoundly affected by the war, the British police service stands as a clear example and, with the benefit of hindsight, one can readily identify the changes and the determinant factors. From contemporary records and the memories of those who lived through those troubled times we can obtain a good impression of just what went on in the police during the Second World War.

Of course, not too much reliance should be placed on the uncorroborated evidence of those who played a part in this great turmoil since the memory can play tricks. This is understandable since the war was a cataclysmic experience for those who lived through it and people tend to remember what they want to remember about such times, rather than what is necessarily the truth. So horrific were some of the experiences that there was a natural tendency to suppress the memory of these. But, as more than one police witness to the events of the war years has discovered, these can be rescusitated by a simple incident, a word or phrase, or even an odour.

The chapters which follow therefore take a look at Britain from the police perspective and, at the same time, look more closely at the police service itself and the effects the war had on this great British institution.

1. The Storm Clouds Gather

No sooner had Neville Chamberlain finished his historic broadcast on that warm summer morning in September, 1939, informing the nation that '... a state of war exists between Great Britain and Germany ...' than Constable 77B Arthur Furness of the Newcastle City Police received orders to sound an air raid warning. Within seconds of the order being given, the eerie wailing of sirens was to be heard across the city, warning the apprehensive citizens of an imminent air attack. All traffic on the roads came to a halt as steel-helmeted policemen and wardens shepherded civilians into the nearest shelter.

A chilling scene, but one which was not confined to Newcastle: in London and all over the country, other policemen were throwing switches to sound the alarms, or taking to the streets, blowing lustily on their whistles and, in some cases, bearing cardboard notices on their chests advising the populace 'Air Raid Warning – Take Cover'.

The situation was not without its humour, however. Sergeant Grey of the Metropolitan Police on the Isle of Dogs remembers meeting one of his men coming towards him soon after this first sounding of the air raid siren, fully kitted out with his steel helmet, eye shield, gas-proof jacket and trousers, rubber boots and with his gas mask at the ready. It was a warm day and the unfortunate officer was perspiring freely. The sergeant gently led him back to the police station where a senior officer remarked, 'For goodness sake, Constable, you frighten me; God knows what you'd do to the public!'. Comical though this might seem in retrospect, this man was not alone and an air raid warden describes how

> *... already the streets were manned by War Reserve policemen in full gas clothing, consisting of oilskin coats and trousers, rubber boots, helmets and respirators, warning rattles in their hands[1]*

PC 506 Bert Ayers (Kent) recalls hurrying through the streets, frantically trying to blow his whistle without success as it was full of fluff!

In the event, this first alert proved to be a false alarm – an error of identification rather than an incursion by the Luftwaffe – but it does serve to illustrate the state of preparedness of the nation in general and the police in particular on the day that war was declared.

But this was quite a different body to the police force we know today. To the reader brought up on a diet of *Starsky and Hutch, The Sweeney* or *The Bill*, the idea of policemen riding around on bicycles, wearing placards round their neck and blowing whistles may seem faintly ludicrous and even bizarre. But it must be remembered that over half a century ago life was very different for everyone, not least the policeman. We are dealing with a period when most towns of any size had their own police force, as did even the smallest county; in 1938 there were no less than 58 county forces and 121 borough or city forces, as compared with a total of around forty today. With such a large number of forces, many were naturally very small. Oxfordshire, for example, had but 156 men and 2 women; there were no specialists, not even a criminal investigation department, although just before the outbreak of war and in response to Home Office exhortations a Special Branch officer had been appointed to each of the five divisions to deal with reports of Fifth Columnists. The retiring chief constable at this time advised his successor (a young 'Trenchard' man fresh from the Metropolitan Police) never to go to the office in the afternoon. *'Start as you mean to go on. The men don't want you about the place all the time. Your job is to recruit the right men and to maintain discipline. Let the Superintendents run the force'.*

Each of the 179 forces, no matter how small, had its own chief constable and one young detective constable from the county force, attending a course in Canterbury, was astonished to see the city's chief constable, in full dress uniform including sword and cocked hat with ostrich plumes, riding a bicycle down the main street!

The number and comparatively small size of the forces throughout the country meant that a system of mutual aid was essential and all forces were required to have a quota of men available to reinforce other forces which were experiencing public order problems, strikes or other difficulties. This system proved invaluable during the air raids on the cities outside London, although experience was to highlight the need to designate adequate facilities for incoming reinforcements. At Portsmouth, in January 1941, seven of the nine buildings which had been earmarked for this purpose were destroyed by enemy action and the other two rendered unusable.

In the years between the wars, the Depression, resulting from the Wall Street slump had caused widespread unemployment and stringent cut-backs in every walk of life. In September 1939 the strength of the police throughout the country was some 60,000 – around 1,800 less than the already inadequate establishment. In Lancashire, the Mounted Branch had been reduced by half and 50 supervisory ranks abolished, resulting in a total blockage of promotion for at least six years. The already minuscule policewomen's branch was reduced from 24 to 12. By 1940 the total number of regular police officers in the whole country had fallen still further, to 57,000 as a result of the recall of some of the younger men to the armed forces and reached an all-time low of 43,000 by 1944. However, by 1941, this hard core of regular officers had been supplemented by nearly 37,000 auxiliaries – special constables and police war reserves.

The pre-war lack of jobs and almost non-existent social benefits ensured that there were often 120 applicants for two vacancies and those who were successful had no alternative but to accept the sometimes appalling conditions and often draconian discipline. To even be considered, a prospective recruit had to be at least 5' 9" (in some forces the minimum was 6' 0"), of good build and character and with a sound education which included impeccable spelling and report writing. The pay was around £2.10.0. (£2.50), plus a rent allowance or free accommodation. The basic salary was similar to that received by most junior civil servants, train drivers and teachers but there was one very important difference which, more than any other, encouraged recruitment; the pension. A policeman could retire after 25 years with a half-pay pension or after 30 years with two-thirds of his salary whereas in most other jobs one had to soldier on until one reached the age of 65.

The reason for this apparently generous treatment was the fact that the police were equated with the armed forces. Although the official working hours were eight, they were required to make enquiries and carry out other duties outside those hours where necessary and they had to be available at all times, 24 hours a day, with no question of overtime payment. True, there was a system of 'time off' for overtime worked but this was always hard to get. There were a myriad of reasons why it was 'not in the interests of the service' to grant time off when it was requested. The policeman was entitled to one day off a week, provided the exigencies of the service did not prevent this being taken. Despite these exacting conditions and a strict discipline code, the attractions of the job meant there was no shortage of applicants.

Where a force sent its recruits to a training school (not invariably the case), recruits had to take it in turns to cook for the rest of the intake – sometimes with disastrous results. One 'survivor' from that period recalls that a fellow recruit calculated that, if one egg takes three minutes to boil, then 30 eggs must take 90 minutes! Every weekend at least four men had to be found guilty of some minor misdemeanour so that they could be 'confined to barracks' for the weekend in order to carry out certain domestic chores, such as cleaning the windows of the assistant chief constable's house. Where training was given it was often cursory and sometimes inexplicable. All recruits to one force had to learn the morse code, although nobody in the force used it!

Once satisfactorily through the initial training, the fledgling constables found other things to concern them. Single men usually lived in 'digs' or, in London and other large cities, in single men's quarters. The latter were run on rigid lines with a strict curfew imposed on those who were not on duty. Often the occupants of such accommodation were forbidden to be out after midnight (unless they were on duty), no matter how old they were.

Constable Freddie Pearce of the former Devon Constabulary (now the Devon & Cornwall Constabulary) recalls that, as the only single constable on his sub-division, he was required to sleep on the police station. Except on leave days he was expected to be in the building from 11pm onwards since the building was then otherwise unmanned. The sergeant also had his quarters there and covered on the constable's days off. The telephone was sited in the inspector's office, two doors away from the constable's bedroom. If it rang he was expected to answer it within five seconds, otherwise he would be recorded as absent, entailing a long explanation the next day. To wake up, leap from his bed and dash to the phone in such a short time almost defied human capacity but he managed it – sometimes only just. With such a start to his police career it is not surprising that Freddie Pearce went on to attain senior rank in the force after distinguished service in the army during the rest of the war.

Even those who were fortunate enough to be placed in lodgings had much to contend with, as Constable A Roberts of the West Riding Constabulary recalls:

> *I was the last to be delivered by the police furniture van that day. We left Wakefield (training centre) at 8 am and I was deposited at 7 pm. All constables had their uniform in a large wooden box with 'Bryant & May Matches' on the side, which we had to purchase from the wholesalers in Wakefield.*

Don Batty, another single policeman who joined in 1941 recalls that he and another recruit were found 'digs' in a two-up, two-down terrace house in Barnsley occupied by a miner's widow and her 19 year old daughter. Although the two policemen had not met until that day, they slept together in a double bed for the whole of their stay there.

> *There was no bathroom and washing and shaving operations were performed in the kitchen with the landlady frying the bacon and eggs at one's elbow and the daughter eating her breakfast at the kitchen table.*

The married man, if he was lucky, might eventually be allocated a police house or cottage but these had little in common with the modern post-war police house, especially in the rural areas. They often had no electricity and oil lamps were used to provide illumination on dark evenings while meals were cooked on a coal stove and water came from a well in the garden. One policeman from that era recalls that his wife was given an electric iron for a wedding present and had to wait seven years before she could use it! On the whole, police accommodation was very poor by modern standards, with no bathrooms or indoor sanitation. And yet, as Detective Constable Leonard Winter (West Riding) recalls, members of the force had to ask for permission to go to the public baths if these happened to be off their beat, as they usually were. When he had managed to save a modest amount, he tried to buy a pair of houses for £450 each, one to live in himself and the other to be let to the county authorities for occupation by another policeman, but permission was firmly refused. Policemen in the city and borough forces were usually permitted to buy their own houses but the wages paid meant that they could only afford a very basic type of accommodation of the 'two up, two down' type.

Even police stations were, on the whole, far from luxurious. In his memoirs[2], (Sir) Eric St. Johnston recalls that, on taking up his post as the new chief constable of Oxfordshire, he found the force headquarters to be in a nineteenth century militia barracks. The building was antiquated, dark, dismal and very badly furnished. On the ground floor there were offices for the chief constable and his deputy, a telephone room and two general offices, while on the first floor there were two further offices. There were no civilian clerks or typists and the general office contained just a few filing cabinets and a mahogany dining table with a typewriter, at which sat the Superintendent and two constable clerks.

Eric St. Johnston discovered that the situation out in the county was not much better. A new divisional police headquarters and court house had been built in Banbury just before the war and, while it had a pleasant aspect, being sympathetically built of Cotswold stone, the internal planning was appalling. The police office contained a very high Victorian counter at which a constable stood while another constable sat at a desk nearby. The Divisional Superintendent was sitting at another desk –

> *wearing a cap which looked like the kind worn by prison officers in Victorian stage melodramas. I suggested that we adjourn to his office. 'This is my office', he said, and when I replied that I thought it was the General Office, he told me there was only one police office in the whole building ... In a room immediately behind the General Office was a telephone booth, a gas cooker, a scrubbed and unpainted kitchen table ... and two benches. A policeman was frying some bacon on the cooker and was about to have a meal. 'This is the Charge Office', said the Superintendent, and I discovered that it was the only place where men could take their refreshments or where the single men who resided in the station, could sit when off duty... There was a staircase leading to the single men's quarters on the first floor. In each of the six rooms there was an iron bedstead and a chair. ... There was no linoleum nor any floor covering in any of the rooms.*

Most recruits to the police service before the war were single men whose courting prospects were severely restricted by the hours and duties they were called upon to perform. When the young constable eventually found his intended partner, he had to apply for permission to marry and the history and antecedents of the prospective bride were subjected to severe scrutiny. The wife of a policeman became an integral part of the police service, especially in the rural areas.

Although the basic tour of duty was restricted to eight hours, this was frequently broken up into so-called 'split shifts', such as 9 am – 1 pm and 7 pm to midnight, particularly in the country. Often no provision was made for any form of meal break and policemen in the Metropolitan Police carried their sandwiches behind them in a small black bag attached to their belt and ate these standing in a shop doorway. Many had their own secret hideaways where they could get a cup of hot tea (and sometimes something a little stronger!) but this was strictly unofficial and contrary to the disciplinary regulations. Woe betide any officer who was caught off his beat or 'idling and gossiping'.

The duties to be performed also had little in common with those which the police are called upon to exercise in the final decades of the Twentieth century and the level of recompense would cause most prospective recruits today to think twice about pursuing their application to join. Constable Roberts, the West Riding officer we met earlier recalls

> *Pay at the training school was £2.2.0 (£2.10p) but rose to £2.8.9 (£2.43) plus 21/6d (£1.07p) lodging allowance when we were posted to our beats. My landlady had had other policemen and she told me ... (on the day I arrived)...that I was to work 8pm to 12 midnight that day and she gave me a vague idea of the extent of my beat. On my very first day I worked from 8 am to 7 pm ... (moving in) ... and from 8 pm to 3 am ... (on the beat)... About 11 pm, a young woman ran up to me and said "Are you a policeman?". It seemed a boy of 13 had been knocked off his bike by a car and killed. I had no idea who or where my sergeant was and there was no telephone in the immediate vicinity. The driver of the car had been drinking but I had no idea where the doctor lived or where the public mortuary was, or even where to take the driver. The dead boy had no identification on him and nobody nearby knew him. Eventually took the body to a nearby mill and left it in the care of the nightwatchman. About 2 am, a dour inspector arrived on the scene and asked me what the hell all the fuss was about! The next day was spent, entirely unaided, taking various statements about the accident. The third day I was told to work 1 pm to 5 pm and 9 pm to 1 am but, at 9 am I*

*was told by a local millworker that the sergeant had phoned
and I was to get myself down to the sanatorium. There I found
an older man, bald and wearing a uniform shirt, sawing a
body open, who told me to get my uniform off and to saw the
skull off, ready for the pathologist. I later arranged for the
inquest to be opened and was shouted at by the Coroner – a
crusty old bachelor – because I hadn't got £2. to pay the
witnesses (I hadn't even got £1.!)*

This incident reflects the fact that the death toll on the roads was
alarmingly high in the between-war years but, such incidents apart,
police duties in these relatively untroubled times were, on the whole,
fairly mundane and low-key. The issuing and checking of various
licences and certificates took up a great deal of the time, as did the
serving of warrants and summonses. Traffic control and the enforcement of the still fairly novel Road Traffic Act of 1930 were prime
tasks. One pre-war police duty which was to have important
repercussions once war was declared was the requirement for
policemen to check on registered aliens, while even in those far-off
days, the IRA (or Sinn Fein, as it was often referred to) was a constant
source of aggravation. In the summer of 1939 there were a number of
terrorist outrages, including several in Coventry – soon to be hit so
tragically by the Luftwaffe – where a bomb in a tradesman's bicycle
killed five people and injured many more. The explosion was heard
across the city and many thought the war had actually started. But
even these callous murders had their positive side. They gave the
police and ambulance services a foretaste of what high explosives
could do to persons and property and what could be expected once war
was declared. One Coventry citizen said it was his desire to take some
positive action against those responsible and not a hatred of the Nazi
régime which led him to volunteer for the Special Constabulary.

Len Winter, the former detective in the West Riding Constabulary,
describes how a prominent resident of his area was suspected of being
an IRA target and the police provided protection for him, armed with
revolvers. One night this particular officer was on duty when he heard
a suspicious noise. He called out a challenge and, when there was no
response, he feared the worst and opened fire – and found he had killed
a deer! Fortunately the VIP was very pleased with the attention the
police gave him and used to invite some of them onto his yacht at

Cowes – a rare and unusual treat for these very ordinary men from generally humble backgrounds.

In the years preceding the outbreak of the Second World War, many of the inhabitants of these islands still had vivid memories of the Zeppelin raids of the previous conflict which had wreaked havoc and claimed the lives of many innocent civilians. More recently, the Spanish Civil War had been an object lesson in the use of air power to win battles and the strategic value of raids on non-military targets. Most people were convinced that the country would be subjected to immediate, heavy air raids, including the use of poison gas once war broke out.

This view was not confined to the man in the street. The Government had long been considering the possibilities and making preparations. With the ink on the 1919 Armistice barely dry, the Baldwin Government was determined not to be caught unprepared should a major war break out again. In 1927 a Home Office committee was formed whose task was to review the war-time organisation and duties of the police and to prepare air raid precautions – a concept subsequently to be hallowed in the initials ARP (a term which, by the end of 1941, had been largely superseded by that of 'Civil Defence'). This committee made no plans for any form of specialized air raid precautions service, the received opinion being that, where civil defence duties might arise which could not reasonably be regarded as an extension of the functions of an existing service, then these would fall on the Special Constabulary.

In the event, this committee fell into abeyance in the same year but, in 1935, four years before the outbreak of war, the European situation was regarded as sufficiently menacing to justify the reconstitution of this special committee to 'consider and advise on questions relative to the duties of the police in the event of war'. It is strange to think that, while the crowds were cheering and waving their flags in the celebrations of King George V's Silver Jubilee, a number of serious-minded gentlemen were sitting round a table in the Home Office discussing a future war; while policemen in London were good-naturedly lining the route of the procession and keeping the crowds in check, and while their provincial colleagues were keeping a paternal eye on the loyal festivities elsewhere, their role in quite different circumstances was being seriously discussed in secret by a group of politicians and senior civil servants.

The Government was very much alive to the possibility of invasion by a foreign power or large-scale civil unrest resulting from enemy action, especially if, as expected, poison gas were used. The War Emergency Legislation Committee discussed whether, in such circumstances, the nation should come under military control – some form of martial law – or whether some scheme of civilian control should be implemented. In the end it decided on the latter course of action. The organisation of this infant prodigy was deposited firmly in the lap of the Home Office as 'the recognised guardian of public safety', to be aided in its upbringing by its ubiquitous executive arm – the police.

One of the first tasks of the committee was the preparation of Police War Instructions, the initial copies being distributed to chief constables in 1935. These Instructions highlighted the role which Constable Furness and his colleagues would be called upon to play. Their contribution was to be vital to the nation's state of readiness and the police force became closely involved in the formation and organization of the various branches of the home civil defence structure. It was obvious from a very early stage that there was a need to organise air raid precautions on a national basis and that the police would be required to play a key role in the home defence organisation. They could bring to the task ready-made qualifications of a kind which no other body could offer; the protection of life and property and the maintenance of public order remains a primary function of the police as much in war as in peace-time. Their long tradition of public service and the nature of their training, their experience in handling people, both singly and in crowds, and in dealing with emergencies of various kinds were assets of inestimable value. Of perhaps even greater importance was the confidence of the public; through long habit people had become accustomed to looking to the policeman for a lead in frightening or perplexing situations and such situations seemed likely to occur with painful frequency in a country under attack from an external enemy. To the police was assigned a position in the front line of defence, especially in London and the South-East because of its proximity to the continent of Europe.

As long ago as 1917 air observer posts had been made a police responsibility and a network of such posts was set up in Kent and Sussex, manned by volunteers enroled as Special Constables. This network satisfactorily passed its first practical tests in the years between the wars and it was not until 1935 that an independent Observer Corps was created in the south-east (later to be extended nationwide).

The phase of war preparations which centred around air raid precautions may be taken as opening with the issue of the Home Office Circular of 9 July, 1935. This covered the protection of buildings against bombs, protection against gas, the employment of auxiliary police (First Police Reserves and Special Constables), the organisation of rescue parties and the warning of air attack (the Observer Corps ceasing to be part of the Special Constabulary on the outbreak of war). So far as training was concerned, the greatest emphasis was to be placed on coping with gas attacks.

It was with the issue of this Home Office Circular that the ARP proper could be said to have begun to exist, including arrangements for dealing with the unevacuated urban masses. Baldwin's Cabinet approved the sum of £100,000 to finance serious planning. Wing Commander E J Hodsoll, who had been the secretary of relevant committees since 1929, was appointed head of a separate ARP department at the Home Office, continuing the already-begun approaches which emphasised the delegation of authority through the central ministries down to local authorities. Hodsoll was raised to Inspector-General of ARP in early 1939 with a larger budget but a much wider range of responsibilities was devolved on the other ministries and local authorities.

The country was divided into 12 Civil Defence Regions, each under the nominal control of a Commissioner. These were retired service officers (like General Sir Hugh Elles in the south-west), academics (such as Sir Will Spens in East Anglia) or members of the aristocracy (Lord Harlech, Lord Trent, Lord Portal, the Earl of Dudley, the Earl of Airlie). In the event of the central government losing control due to enemy action or invasion, the United Kingdom would revert to a form of government by barons, not seen in this country for centuries. In 'normal' times, these Civil Defence Commissioners were to co-ordinate the work of the local authorities, the ARP service, the fire brigades, the police and the armed forces within their area.

It was assumed from the outset that there would be a very close relationship between any ARP organisation and the police although the Home Office was of the opinion that, in view of the onerous duties of a chief constable, he should not be responsible for air raid precautions in time of war. Initially, the chief constables of police forces outside London were nominated as the Chief ARP Officer for their force area. In London, the Commissioner of Police of the Metropolis was nominated the Chief Executive Officer with a co-ordinating role for the whole of the London and Home Counties Region, while the Clerk to the London County Council was made the Chief ARP Officer for the capital. It was generally accepted that chief constables would be responsible for the organisation of air raid precautions in peacetime, as well as assuming control over the service in an emergency.

Unfortunately, in order not to alarm the populace, most of these contingency plans and appointments were kept a closely guarded secret, with the result that the various local authorities were confused as to their functions and responsibilities in time of war. Consequently, in March 1939, following the Munich crisis when war with Nazi Germany had become a very real possibility, various county and borough councils were instructed to appoint an ARP Controller for their area, to act under the orders of the Government or the local Emergency Committee. Of these so-called 'scheme-making authorities', 120 nominated their county or town clerk while 70 gave the job to their chief constable. Most of the remainder (about 60 authorities) chose one of their elected representatives – a councillor or alderman. Warwickshire went completely out on a limb and, despite Home Office advice, decided to appoint one of its paid officers to organise and control the county's ARP services. An important and occasionally contentious provision was that these local ARP Controllers would have no control over the police or fire brigade (except, of course, where the Controller also happened to be the chief constable).

Once war was declared, these ARP Controllers were to be far and away the most important individuals in every air raid outside London. They ranked over all the other main service chiefs, including the chief warden, the chief medical officer, and the borough surveyor. Although police and fire brigades remained under their respective heads, their work was to be co-ordinated by the Controller.

It is recorded that where the chief constable was appointed the ARP Controller, he often injected a valuable drive and discipline into the local organisation. It must be added, however, that they sometimes introduced a rigidity which was far from universally favoured. This martial style of management was possibly due to the fact that many chief constables, especially in the shires, were former army or navy officers. Not until 1944 could the Police Review comment that the current advertisement for the post of chief constable of Durham County specified that 'applicants must have served in a senior rank in a United Kingdom police force', whereas previous advertisements had merely stated '... must have had at least 10 years police experience...' with no mention whether this might be in the United Kingdom, in India or in the Colonies. The magazine regarded this as a promising sign for the future.

In 1939 even London had only recently ceased to be under the command of Lord Trenchard, the 'father of the RAF' who had introduced the 'Trenchard Scheme' for the direct entry of selected candidates to senior rank in the force – a military-style officer class. Indeed, quite a number of the chief constables in post on the outbreak of the war were young 'Trenchard men'.

Where the chief constable was not the ARP Controller (ie. where the town or county clerk, a councillor or alderman had been appointed), police officers were often called upon to act as Deputy or Sub Controllers. The Wardens service was in the general charge of the chief constable in about 200 of the 250 scheme-making areas and the police were closely involved in the training of air raid wardens in almost every area. By April, 1939, there were, for example, 33,000 trained wardens available for duty in Lancashire alone, ready to man 3,000 warden posts.

A revised and consolidated version of the Police War Instructions was circulated in August, 1939, after the Home Office had decreed that all police officers should be properly trained in air raid precautions. At this stage a great many policemen had in fact received some measure of civil defence training and the value of this was noted at the time of the Munich Crisis. One problem which the civil defence planners had to cope with was the lack of reliable precedent. The raids on this country in the Great War had been sporadic and of little value in assessing the impact of full-scale air war on congested populations. In the event, the plans were well thought out and, if they erred at all, they tended to err on the side of over-caution. Among the great surprises of the war was the enemy's delay in striking at London from the air and his failure to use gas, his success with incendiary bombs and his failure to inflict casualties on the scale envisaged.

Until the beginning of the war, the fire brigade in some cities and boroughs came under the direct control of the police and formed part of the police service. But even where this was not the case, policemen had to be given some basic fire-fighting training, mainly involving the use of stirrup pumps to extinguish incendiary devices – one aspect of training which was to prove invaluable when the air raids eventually started. The police were involved in the siting of large static water tanks to supplement the water supply in the event of the water mains being breached and in the building of brick air raid shelters in most streets. In addition, the cellars of some large buildings were reinforced so that they could be used as shelters and the police were among those whose advice was sought in this matter.

In the final years leading up to the war, most policemen had received instruction in Air Raid Precautions as part of their initial training. They were given experience of tear gas and the effectiveness of their respirators against this type of comparatively innocuous gas. Full-scale training exercises were carried out, simulating the use of gas, in which personnel wearing the heavy gas protection suits had to pass through gas dispersal units – looking very much like a modern car wash – to remove any traces of mustard gas. All the ARP services practised rescuing injured and trapped victims with access roads blocked and water officially deemed to be unavailable. Many police officers attended courses to learn how to control an 'incident' while others became 'Bomb Reconnaissance Officers'. One constable who attended one of the latter type of course confessed that, although he was not worried about the possibility of unexploded bombs before going on the course, he was '...shit-scared afterwards!'

Certain officers were trained in specialist ARP duties and police ARP instructors were usually available to give advice and instruction to any voluntary, commercial or municipal organisation. It was probably these early contacts which were responsible for the excellent co-operation which existed throughout the emergency between all the various departments, services, organisations and the police. In Bradford, during the 1938 Munich crisis, no fewer than 50 police officers were employed in distributing and fitting gas masks, while four officers were seconded to full-time ARP duties – a situation which was replicated all across the country. A number of auxiliary police stations were set up in Bradford during 1939, each under the control of a First Police Reserve (about whom more later) to which the Special

Constabulary were to report when the air raid sirens sounded. The idea was that, in the event of a heavy raid destroying communications between the Town Hall and the suburbs, there would still be an organised police section in each of the six sub-divisions, with a base from which to operate.

And so, as the country plunged into war, for the second time in just over two decades, the police were, on the whole, as well-prepared as most and better prepared than many. In the week following the outbreak of war, the Police Review commented that, although the country was generally ill-prepared for war, the work done by the police had won the admiration and appreciation of the Home Office, especially its work in the formation and training of the air raid precaution services. By the time war was declared, the police could generally be said to be in a good state of readiness. They had been issued with gas masks and blue-painted steel helmets with the word 'POLICE' in white across the front (some of the more conscientious, or perhaps 'regimental', policemen polished their helmets with Ronuk floor polish!). In London and other likely targets, square brick shelters had been erected in every street and there were concrete-lined trenches in parks and open spaces. An orange-coloured booklet, entitled 'War Duty Hints' had been issued, the opening words being 'Not that we expect a war to take place...' Despite this, as a policeman who was serving in the East Riding of Yorkshire at the time recalls, many policemen and others made their own arrangements and he describes how he built a sort of 'grave' lined with thick wooden planks and with a rough bed and an old blanket over the doorway, the whole covered with an ornamental rockery. Later, proper shelters were built in his area and the famous Anderson and Morrison shelters were issued. Police stations and offices were sandbagged with just a slit to let light in, the bags filled by volunteers from the Boy Scouts and Girl Guide organisations. (These sandbags proved to have a limited life and, before a year was out, they became rotten and stinking and eventually collapsed). The familiar blue lights were removed 'for the duration'. At Chichester, the police station was equipped with steel shutters over the windows, to be lowered by pulleys when the air raid siren sounded, one of the policemen having to climb up outside the station to operate these.

Some forces were not as well-organised as others, however. Sir Eric St Johnston describes in his book[3] how, on arriving to take up his duties as the newly-appointed chief constable of Oxfordshire in July

1940, he discovered that the gas masks and protective clothing issued in bulk to the force in March 1939 were, Dunkirk and the threat of invasion notwithstanding, still lying in their original cartons, the gas masks not even assembled. He found the Home Office Circular, issued in November 1938, advising chief constables on the necessary preparations for war, had been endorsed by his predecessor, 'We do not want anything in Oxfordshire. Perhaps, however, we should get another typewriter'. This item of office equipment represented the whole of Oxfordshire's preparations to combat the expected invader, despite the fact that the previous chief constable was a former naval officer who had served with distinction in the Great War.

The main principles on which the organisation of the police was based in order to meet the developing situation may be summed up in three words : elasticity, decentralisation and co-operation. *Elasticity:* in war police activities are superimposed on peacetime activities and there is merely a change of emphasis. In war the police have to be prepared to switch from ordinary to extraordinary tasks at the drop of a hat (or a bomb!). *Decentralization:* policemen are trained to act on their own initiative and the only difference between war and peace in this respect is the need to master a great quantity of new Orders and Regulations designed to meet wartime conditions. *Co-operation:* the air defence organisation provided the police with a number of new, trained collaborators to whom special tasks were assigned. As in peacetime they had their old friends in the fire service. Wartime additions were Air Raid Wardens, Rescue Parties, Casualty Services and various semi-official voluntary organisations such as the WVS, the Boy Scouts and the YMCA, not to mention the Home Guard and the casual assistance provided by ordinary members of the public. It was the police who shouldered the responsibility of recruiting, training and organising not only the ARP personnel, but also the Auxiliary Fire Service and the Royal Observer Corps, at least in many places and during the initial phases. This early contact had the happy effect of forging close relations between the various services when the going got rough.

Poison gas had proved such an effective and deadly weapon in the Great War that most people were convinced that this would prove an irresistible temptation to any future aggressor. A gas-warfare training school was set up at Winterbourne Gunner and, later, at Easingwold in Yorkshire, where police and selected ARP personnel were trained in the measures to be taken to protect the populace in the event of this terrible weapon being brought into use. In fact, it was probably the efficiency of our anti-gas arrangements which convinced the enemy that the use of this weapon would be largely ineffective and, if it prompted retaliatory measures, could even be counter-productive since the German people were undoubtedly far less prepared for this type of warfare. More than three years before the war, the police in Kent had been instrumental in providing a one-day training course in anti-gas measures for 60 men and 40 women of the county's St John's Ambulance Brigade. This intensive and extensive course (held on a Sunday so as not to interfere with normal work) was held in Maidstone, while similar training for those from the eastern part of the county was given in Ramsgate. Those attending these courses were to be the future instructors who would initiate hundreds of others in the niceties of gas warfare.

George Whitcomb, who was serving in the Bradford City police at this time, comments that crawling about in smoke-filled tunnels, testing gas masks and learning about mustard gas provided a welcome change from the monotony of point duty and other mundane policing tasks. There seems little doubt that these exercises were not taken too seriously by many of the younger men but, fortunately, older and wiser heads prevailed.

Another form of air raid precaution was the introduction of a complete 'blackout'. This aspect will be covered more fully in later chapters but, in this, the immediate pre-war period, fifteen counties in the south of England took part in a test blackout over one Saturday night and Sunday morning in July, 1939. Sirens were sounded at intervals from 10 pm when the incidents arranged by each local authority began. Families screened their windows, motorists drove with only sidelights on, road beacons were covered with sacks and traffic lights were fitted with masks to deflect their light downwards. Some of the realism was lost when bad weather forced the RAF to abandon its part in the exercise but most of the other tests were completed without any problems. A few local difficulties were recorded, however, as Andrew Rootes describes in his book:

> *When the chief warden at Rolvenden (Kent) was told that his post had been bombed and that he had received head injuries affecting his reason, his protests were ignored as delusions and, in spite of his resistance, he was strapped to a stretcher*

and taken to the casualty station. All the lights were switched out at a dinner in Ramsgate, just as Captain H Balfour, the Under-Secretary of State for Air, rose to speak. A 'corpse' rang up Margate police station to report that his post had been blown up by a bomb, killing everyone inside. Another message said, "A bomb has fallen on the circus, killing an elephant. Send the ambulance". When a length of piping was thrown at a fire engine as it was passing through Margate, although no-one was injured, the police were rushed to the scene... and it was thought at first that the IRA might be involved.[4]

The (qualified) success of this test led to an event greater trial blackout being held in 26 counties, including London, the following month.

By February, 1939, in response to Home Office exhortations, most forces had set up an Air Raid Precautions Department, the principal function of which was to be the training of a new creature – the air raid warden. These departments varied greatly in size and scope, ranging from one or two (Plymouth City had appointed one chief inspector and one sergeant) to as many as 18 or 20 (Liverpool City had one superintendent, three inspectors, nine sergeants and five constables, while Essex County had one superintendent, seven inspectors and 12 sergeants). Many forces merely appointed a number of constables to the task (Bradford and East Suffolk, nine constables each, Cardiff 12 constables and the West Riding 16).

One of the first measures to be discussed when considering what form the air raid precautions should take was the provision of some kind of warning. In 1936 the Home Office asked chief constables in the South-east to compile a list of all those who should receive 'preliminary' or 'action' air raid warnings. As a result of this, it was decided that 'preliminary' warnings should be disseminated to the police, the fire brigades, ARP headquarters and certain strategically important and vulnerable factories. A colour coding system was devised, with the 'preliminary' warning being coded 'yellow', the cancellation of a preliminary warning being white, and the 'action' warning (raid imminent) was dubbed 'red'. The 'all-clear' or 'raiders passed' signal was designated 'green'. In the event of poison gas being used wooden rattles were to be used – the same method of

22

communication the police had employed a century or more previously! The police were entrusted with the task of organising a public warning system, using electrically-operated or hand-cranked sirens, and were given the job of operating these. Which is where Constable Furness and his colleagues came in. All siren points had to be manned 24 hours a day and, on hearing the warning, all police personnel, whether on or off duty, were required to report to the nearest police station, box or pillar and contact the Control Officer who, in one case at least, was installed in the police cells under the local police station. Even those men who had been on night duty were obliged to get up, get dressed and report to their station by bicycle or on foot. Often the 'All Clear' would have sounded before they reached the station and they would wearily turn back and try to get back to sleep. So disruptive was this requirement that it was soon discontinued.

The whole of the air raid precautions system was tested in a major exercise in the South-east region (under Commissioner Sir Auckland Geddes) in the summer of 1939, involving all the services in Kent and Sussex. The system was found to work well and the nation braced itself for the possibility of war.

In practice, however, it has to be admitted that the warning system was not as effective as it might have been. Nervous tension caused some policemen, firemen and factory employees to sound the sirens unnecessarily; mechanical defects, such as electrical short circuits, caused them to operate independently; bogus alarms made by telephone by 'unbalanced or malicious individuals' were responsible for other false alarms. A tendency on the part of the police and ARP officers – who might be able to see an attack developing but were incapable of judging accurately when the raiders had passed – to sound the sirens on their own initiative occasionally caused some problems. One such incident occurred in Folkestone in October, 1940, when German 'tip-and-run' raiders attacked the town, dropping bombs which caused considerable damage and casualties. Because of the speed of the attack, the sirens were not sounded and, as a result, the rescue parties failed to turn out. Because of the need for stand-by parties to be called to the scene of the attack, Inspector Dick Butcher ordered the sirens to be sounded. He was reported in the Folkestone Gazette as saying,

> *I gave orders for the siren to be sounded and asked permission afterwards. As it happened, permission was refused but the*

rescue parties were alerted and, as if to justify my action, there was a second tip-and-run raid almost immediately afterwards. ... I had my resignation written out all ready for the senior officers who came down from Tunbridge Wells but I was supported by Mr Beesley (the chief constable) who tore up my resignation[5].

No doubt the senior officers from Tunbridge Wells to whom Inspector Butcher referred were staff from the Regional Commissioner's Office. Fortunately, far from being given the 'Order of the Boot', his general competence and meritorious service later resulted in Inspector Butcher being awarded the British Empire Medal.

Constable Bill Cavey of the Metropolitan Police remembers a siren being affixed to the police box in the middle of the Wanstead Flats which, during the early war years, was permanently manned. On one occasion, being short-staffed, there was no-one to relieve the duty constable in the box and Constable Cavey volunteered to drive across to do so. Very weary after 18 long hours of continuous duty, he succumbed to fatigue while in the box and was awakened by the telephone ringing. The voice at the other end said 'Yellow warning' and, since the procedure was for the siren to be sounded only on receipt of a red warning, PC Cavey should have done nothing but await the next call. However, still half asleep, he switched the siren on. He immediately realized his error and switched it off. The telephone rang again and the station sergeant enquired, 'Did you hear a siren?'. 'Yes', replied our hero, 'but it was a long way off from here!' and his mistake was never discovered by his superiors (until now!).

R C Dyson, the son of a Leicestershire village constable and himself now a retired Metropolitan police officer, recalls that the authorities decided to instal the village siren on the roof of the house occupied by the family. This was duly located on a wooden platform in the roof valley, with an electrical lead running into the kitchen, fitted with a plug similar to the socket of an electric light bulb. Over the cooker there was a switchboard with a large circular switch to control the cooker, which turned clockwise. There were two 'on' positions (north and south) and two 'off' positions (east and west) with a low power bulb beside the switch to show when the cooker was switched on. The siren lead hung down close by and, when the alarm was to be sounded, this bulb was removed and the siren lead plugged in. Slowly turning the switch from point to point gave the rising and falling note required for the warning while leaving it in the 'on' position gave the continuous note required for the 'all clear'. One day young Master Dyson came into possession of an old wooden electrical plug and, for some inexplicable reason or perhaps due to the curiosity of the young, he inserted this into the socket above the cooker and switched it on. There was an enormous bang and blue smoke rose from the plug. It was soon established that he had fused all the lights in the house. The father was furious. What would happen if headquarters rang up to order the sounding of the siren? What could he say? He had no electrical knowledge at all and even the local handyman from next door declared himself baffled. By this time the poor village constable was beside himself, with visions of an air raid with no alarm given, the whole village razed to the ground, the inhabitants killed and himself solely responsible. Eventually, after what seemed an age, the local electrician turned up and quickly put things right. Happily, the apprehended disaster never occurred but one wonders what would have happened in the event of a power failure – a very possible event as later air raids showed. There was no provision for this or any form of back-up. If a 10 year old schoolboy could render the system inoperable, one wonders what the might of the Luftwaffe might have achieved!

Freddie Pearce (Devon) whom we met earlier and who slept in the police station, assumed additional responsibilities when war broke out. After numerous false alarms the day came when the first 'red' warning was given and it could not have come at a more inconvenient time. It was around midnight and, in the absence of the sergeant, his wife took the call and then, in her nightdress and dressing gown, went with the constable in his private car with the portable siren to the three points in the town where it had to be sounded. The siren had a very limited capacity and an unconvincing tone so no-one in the streets took any notice of the Sergeant's wife in her night attire with her slippered feet on the siren operating button. By the time they got back to the station the sergeant had returned and had received the all clear and so the two officers set off again to indicate, as best they could, that the Lufwaffe would not be visiting the town that night.

2. Closing the Gaps

With war imminent, the Government introduced compulsory National Service in the middle of 1939, under which all physically fit 20 and 21 year olds were required to serve 6 months in one of the Armed Forces. This had an immediate and marked effect on police recruitment. Although it had been agreed that the rights of any young police officer called to perform his National Service would be retained, most police authorities deferred the appointment of any candidates for recruitment until they had completed their period of military training. Another problem facing the authorities was the likelihood of depletion of the police force through the call-up of reservists to the colours. In 1939 nearly 3,000 policemen were ex-servicemen on the reserve list and thus liable for immediate call up in the event of war. This situation reflected the problems which had been experienced in both the Boer War, when 1,500 policemen with reserve commitments had been called up, and in 1914 when the Metropolitan Police alone lost 1,032 men from its strength of just over 22,000. In the provincial police forces 2,728 had been called up out of a total of 33,416.

It was anticipated that any future conflict would have a much more direct effect on the United Kingdom police forces since there was the very real likelihood that air raids would bring the war to this country, rather than being isolated in foreign lands. The need for a strong police force to maintain public order and prevent panic was clear and so it was agreed that reservists serving with the police force would not be recalled to the colours until at least three months after the mobilization of their units. Similarly, around 25% of the police strength was aged 25 or under and therefore, although not subject to recall as reservists, were liable to call up in the normal manner should a general mobilization be decreed, and it was agreed that these too should benefit from a three month deferment of call up.

In November 1939, the expected call up of policemen on the reserve list began. All former servicemen under 35 who had a reserve commitment were called up, leaving a large gap in the strength of the police to be filled by the auxiliaries whose role we shall be looking at later in this chapter. In addition, some policemen who were skilled craftsmen or tradesmen were directed into jobs where their old skills would be of great value to the war effort, such as the shipyards and the mines.

To avoid a further drain on the police resources, the Police and Firemen (Employment) Order, 1940 was passed the following June decreeing that the police and fire brigades were to be regarded as 'reserved occupations' and the posts frozen. All those presently serving in these organisations were required to continue to do so except in exceptional circumstances. No retirements or resignations were permitted and, for some police officers nearing their retirement, this was a catastrophe. Most accepted the situation with good grace, acknowledging the slogan 'there's a war on'. Others were not so phlegmatic and Eric St Johnston describes how he was suddenly posted to a new station where the Sub-Divisional Officer who was due for retirement had simply 'given up'. He did the bare minimum of work, taking no interest in seeing that the job was done well or that the men were properly supervised.

> *Moreover, he was in the habit of having drinking sessions with his cronies late at night in the police canteen, and on one or two occasions they had girl friends with them whom they had later taken home in police cars – on one occasion when no other transport was available, in the police van used to transport prisoners[1].*

This all very soon came to the notice of Scotland Yard and the officer and his cronies were all suspended from duty, pending disciplinary proceedings. Eric St Johnston was accordingly sent to take over the sub-division and get things back on to a proper footing once more.

A similar situation arose in Ulster where a young officer who was not permitted to resign (presumably to join the armed forces) just refused to do anything. He was prosecuted and served a term of imprisonment but eventually returned to the force where he became a respected and much thought of member of the force.

If, as everybody had expected, the bombs had rained down on the country in the autumn of 1939, with the use of gas and other horrific weapons, it would not have been excessive had the regular force been twice its actual size. The auxiliaries undoubtedly did their very competent best but they were to all intents and purposes untrained.

Had heavy air attacks come there would have been a terrific strain placed on the police defences, no matter how strong these auxiliaries were numerically.

However, as we now know, these understandable expectations were not fulfilled for nearly a year and it did not take the Authorities long to realize that quality was even more important than quantity and that with increasing efficiency due to training and experience, a numerically smaller force would suffice. And so a process of shedding began, which was continued, increasing rather than decreasing in momentum, throughout the whole of the war, regardless of air attacks. Beginning with certain auxiliaries, the process was extended to the regular force in the spring of 1941. Although the police force was still regarded as a reserved occupation, a limited number of men under a certain age were encouraged to apply for air crew duties with the RAF and the Fleet Air Arm. Within a few days 4,000 applications had been made to New Scotland Yard by Metropolitan officers and, in the event, some 800 regular officers left that force alone in the course of 1941. Many more were chafing at the bit, anxious to 'do their bit' and despairing at the bureaucracy which prevented them from joining the armed forces.

In the spring of 1941 the *Police Review* published a number of letters from such potential volunteers, drawing attention to the fact that many of their colleagues who had been recalled to the colours as reservists were now busy scrubbing floors or engaged in other menial tasks. It is true some reservists were released to rejoin their forces but the rule was that this concession was confined to those under the rank of Sergeant and who were not serving in the Military Police, a twin condition which effectively eliminated most former police officers. It has to be admitted that many of the prospective volunteers were inspired by the lack of promotion prospects in the police force. The freezing of retirements meant that the supervisory ranks were largely filled by men well above the age for active service and who looked as if they were going to be there for the duration. On the other hand, those who had joined the armed forces were often doing very well for themselves, holding commissioned or senior NCO rank. In fact, as we shall see later, many had serious doubts about returning to the police when the war was finally over.

By 1942 the threat of invasion had receded, air raids had decreased in number and ferocity and the nation was about to go on the offensive. It was therefore decided to make cut-backs in the general civil defence services and to release some 7,000 young volunteers from the police for duty in the armed forces (not necessarily for flying duties), provided such applications conformed to certain conditions and that the vacancies so created were filled by part-timers. As a result, all regular police officers under 25 and auxiliaries under 30 (subsequently raised to 30 and 35 respectively) were 'dereserved'. This situation caused serious concern to be expressed by many police authorities as police duties in the United Kingdom were not getting any easier, especially now that the United States troops were arriving in this country in ever-increasing numbers.

In May 1943, when a further relaxation was sought, the Ministry of Home Security agreed that '... *those services in which bodily vigour and staying power are needed should be the last to be affected by the further sacrifice'*. It was further decreed that young women in the police and fire service should be retained as far as possible and that no further regular police should be allowed to leave nor any police auxiliaries under the age of 35.

By September 1944 the war situation had improved sufficiently for substantial reductions to be made in the civil defence forces other than those in London and the south-east (ie the Civil Defence Regions based on London, Tunbridge Wells, Reading and Cambridge). The later extension of such cut-backs to these areas represented the virtual winding-up of the civil defence service. By the end of the year nearly 4,000 Metropolitan regulars and 8,000 auxiliaries had joined the Armed Forces, with a similar number from the provincial forces.

This depletion of the force through conscription and volunteers had numerous and far-reaching effects. Recruits in the earlier years found that their training period had been reduced from 16 weeks to 11 weeks but these were perhaps the lucky ones; soon there was to be virtually no recruitment whatsoever as all young men were conscripted into the armed forces. As we have seen, the denial of the right to retire led to a serious blockage in promotions and caused some officers, perhaps already fatigued after thirty years of pounding a beat, to lose interest in the job and become mere uniform carriers. In London, it had been the peacetime practice to post the younger, single men to the inner city areas, moving the more experienced and married men to the outer, more relaxed areas. With the loss of so many young men, many older married men found themselves back in the thick of things. PC Bill Cavey, with nearly 20 years service and who had been happily stationed in the comparatively quiet London borough of Leytonstone found himself back at Bow, just in time for the Blitz. Although normally a driver, there was no such vacancy at Bow and so he had to be content with motorcycle patrol duties, which was at least an improvement on pounding a beat.

Despite the many losses from the police ranks, it is a fact that, in some areas, mass evacuation coupled with the mobilization of nearly all the younger men, meant that towns had virtually died and the police had very little to do. In the first year of the war, the population of Broadstairs in Kent dropped from 20,000 to around 800 while in nearby Birchington it was estimated that 90% of the properties in the town were unoccupied. The whole town was policed by one sergeant and three constables, with assistance from the Special Constabulary. This situation was reflected in a number of areas in the vulnerable south-east. However, these displaced persons had to settle somewhere else, whether in military camps, factories or evacuee reception areas where they added to the problems of the police in these places.

Although there was a virtual moratorium on recruiting for the regular police, coupled with the loss of many of the younger officers, this is not to say that the police force as a whole was drastically reduced. The shortfall was more than made up (at least numerically) by the various auxiliaries which have been mentioned previously. These fell into three categories; the First Police Reserve, the Special Constabulary, and the Police War Reserve, to which must be added the Police Auxiliary Messenger Service and the Womens' Auxiliary Police Corps. The latter will be covered more fully in a later chapter and, for now we shall concentrate on the other types of auxiliary.

In the years leading up to the Great War there was a very real possibility of a revolution in this country and so in 1911, following the threat of a railway strike, the Home Secretary, Winston Churchill, instructed the Commissioner of the Metropolitan Police to engage up to 3,000 'trustworthy men, including pensioners and persons having disciplined training and that these should do regular duty with your force'. This was followed by a Home Office Circular, recommending all provincial police authorities to follow suit. Plans were therefore made for the creation of two police reserve organisations. The First Reserve was to be made up of former police and army personnel who would be accustomed to discipline and thus qualified for police work. They were to be taken on for a limited engagement on the same terms and conditions as the regular force and would wear uniform. They would be paid a retainer and would receive proper pay when called up, rather like the Territorial Army. The Second Police Reserve would consist of those suitable persons who were ready and willing to be sworn in as special constables.

Considerable doubts were expressed as to whether former army personnel had much to offer and this aspect of the First Police Reserve was soon dropped. Most Chief Constables were lukewarm to the whole idea and felt they should be able to rely on the military to come to their aid in times of civil disorder and strife (the war scenario was not foreseen at this stage).

Nevertheless, the plan was proceeded with and a considerable number of police pensioners expressed their willingness to turn out for duty, should the need arise. They were to be paid a yearly retainer of £1 and had to attend two drills per week for six weeks and then one drill per month thereafter. Payment was at the rate of 1/- (5p) per drill. Those who were recalled to full-time duty were to be paid 4/- (20p) a day. These ex-policemen were used extensively in the Great War, with considerable success.

The scheme fell largely into abeyance in the between-wars years but the political situation in the 1930s led to it being revived and a number of FPRs were mobilised during the Munich crisis of September, 1938. In Kent 200 police pensioners had been enroled as First Police Reserves by the outbreak of war. The previous police experience held by these men was of great value, especially as the laws and policing had changed little over the years. The main pieces of legislation dated from mid-Victorian times (The Malicious Damage Act, 1860, the Larceny Act, 1860) or even earlier (The Vagrancy Act, 1824) while the 1913 Larceny Act was a rare piece of new legislation. Only the 1930 Road Traffic Act and the 1936 Public Order Act were possibly outside the experience of this stalwart band of volunteers. In view of their age and experience, most of these police pensioners were employed as station officers or placed in charge of small out-stations with a number of specials or Police War Reserves under their direct control. In one case at least a First Police Reserve, who had returned to his former Cambridgeshire village beat on the call-up of the local sergeant, had to take over the sergeant's duties until the end of the war when the sergeant lost his life on active service – one of the first casualties.

Being former colleagues, they were readily accepted by the serving regular officers, although their age was sometimes a problem. The son of one such Reserve officer remembers that his father joined the police (in Bristol) in 1898 and, apart from 3 years in the Grenadier Guards during the Boer War, continued to serve in that force until his retirement as a sergeant in 1929. He was recalled from the reserve in 1939 when he was 63 and served until he reached the mandatory retiring age of 65 in December, 1941. This example would seem to be somewhat exceptional as the normal maximum age for recruitment to the First Police Reserve was 58, later reduced to 57, although one Metropolitan officer wrote about a former sergeant who was recalled and describes him as

> *... pushing 68. He never appeared to have shaved and wore boots with a one-inch sole. A well-liked liability.*

In common with the other auxiliaries and the ARP personnel, First Police Reserves were paid £3 a week but, since they also had their police pension, they were generally better off than most.

The majority of these retired policemen had been on active service during the First World War, many in the trenches in France, and so war was not new to them. Consequently, their experiences made them much less blasé about the threat than some of their younger colleagues.

Freddie Pearce, who was a young constable in Devon at the time, describes these invaluable assistants in the following terms:

> *They were a delightful group, three being in my immediate area, who all did their utmost in often trying circumstances. One had been out 16 years, another 12, whilst the youngest, a former sergeant whose son had just been appointed a chief constable, only 10 years. All of them found an eight hour tour of duty a bit arduous and all three expressed very positive doubts about the amount of detail required in reports, as compared to the time before their retirement. All of them became adroit at press-ganging me to "get down what is needed" by means of the station typewriter. Often the details I was given were brief in the extreme but the finished product was always described as excellent when they came to read and sign it, though they often indicated they liked my frequent bits*

of embellishment. One of them, who had a very witty approach to report writing, often told a long story about how he finally satisfied his superiors over an accident report, returned to him on several occasion for further details to be added, by finally endorsing it, "Sir, words fail me. Please see new sketch". Without exception, these three old officers gave excellent service and I was always inclined to accept that they were much more dedicated to the job than were the civilians recruited as Police War Reserves, most of whom seemed to be more concerned with keeping their former occupations partially maintained in their spare time.

The age of these men was a distinct disadvantage and one, PC Thomas Moon of Kent, aged 65, died from natural causes whilst on duty and his body was was found by two special constables. It was perhaps this age factor which deterred Cornwall from employing any First Police Reserves.

As the years went by, more and more of these 'old soldiers' took definitive retirement and, by the end of the war, their numbers had dropped to almost vanishing point. Some, however, continued to serve long after the war was ended and a handful were still 'in harness' in the 1950s. During the time they were employed the permitted differences in the conditions of the First Police Reserve in different forces, and comparisons drawn at various times between the conditions of this Reserve and those of the paid special constables, led to innumerable representations to the Home Office from one body or another.

The Special Constabulary formed the basis of the second police reserve which was also used in both world wars. The Special Constables Act of 1831 provided for the employment of special constables, without pay, where riot, tumult or disorder had occurred or was anticipated. In 1914, this Act was amended to cover their use in time of war for the duration of hostilities. Under the provisions of this Act, it was possible to pay special constables a reasonable allowance (the amount is not specified) where they were employed regularly, half of this being met by the Home Office, the remainder from local funds.

The later Municipal Corporations Act of 1882 required that a sufficient number of men should be nominated each year to serve as special constables if called upon. In practice, specials appointed under this Act were of limited value until they had receive some training and experience. The Act also provided for the payment of special constables who were employed on a regular duty or call-out basis. The specified amount which could be paid was very parsimonious and therefore it became the practice during the 1914-18 war to appoint specials under the 1831 Act. The implementation of this scheme in 1914 provoked strong resistance from the trades union movement which anticipated these auxiliaries being used for strike-breaking purposes.

The Special Constabulary was deployed throughout the 1920s and 1930s and rendered valuable service during the General Strike when across the country, the total strength of the Special Constabulary rose from 80,000 to 226,000 in the course of 10 days. In London, where there had been around 8,000 specials, 56,000 were mobilised. In general, however, the organisation of these volunteers was very haphazard and, in places, chaotic and so, in the early 1930s, steps were taken to reorganise the service and to weed out the large amount of dead wood, particularly in London. This was generally very successful and the Commander in Chief of the Metropolitan Special Constabulary was able to report in 1937 that there were now nearly 8,000 active special constables in the capital, of whom 43% were serving under the new conditions. This number grew as the war became imminent, reaching a peak in August 1939 when there were over 12,000 active specials in London. Because of call-up and other commitments, this number declined and, by the following December, had dropped to just over 9,000, made up of some 4,000 full-time officers and 5,000 part-timers.

Of course, London was not alone in reorganising its Special Constabulary and putting it on a war footing. Following the Munich crisis in September 1938, the recruitment and training of specials was stepped up across the whole country, although in some forces they had already been fully mobilised in response to the Sinn Fein bombing campaigns of 1934-1939. In February, 1939, the Government appealed to men 'of sound physique and health and of good character' to offer themselves for National Service in an emergency as special constables.

An Order in Council on 28 September, 1939 provided for the employment of special constables on a full-time basis on a salary of £3. per week, the same rate as that fixed for full-time ARP volunteers but higher than the weekly pay of a regular officer on Scale B salary (the lower scale of pay paid to new recruits as an economy measure, introduced in 1931)! Since the Government regarded the newly-formed Police War Reserve as the appropriate body for whole-time police volunteers to join, the effect of this order was limited to those special constables who had been appointed prior to its issue. The whole wage bill (including the cost of the Police War Reserves, part-time specials and the Womens Auxiliary Police Corps) was to be met by the Government. We shall be looking at the Police War Reserves later in this chapter but, as these too were full-time paid auxiliaries, many forces, such as Surrey, followed the Home Office line and plumped for this option instead of appointing full-time special constables. In the Metropolitan Police, however, an appeal for volunteers to enrol for full-time work with the force resulted in over 5,000 applicants from the Special Constabulary who were over 30 years of age being taken on full-time, enroled '... for the preservation of the public peace and the protection of the inhabitants and the security of property'. Indeed, later on it was not unusual for Police War Reserves to apply to become full-time specials. Of those special constables who did not sign on for full-time work, a large number (nearly 6,000) joined the Armed Forces. The remainder, many of whom were excluded from active service through age or physical fitness, constituted the war-time force of part-time special constables.

Full-time specials were regarded as being in a reserved occupation if they were over 30 years of age. They were expected to attend specific training classes alongside their regular colleagues and later to go out on duty with them, assisting in the day-to-day policing of London as well as undertaking duties associated with war-time incidents[2]. It is of interest in these days, when it is not uncommon to see regular police officers wearing spectacles, that a number of applicants for the full-time Special Constabulary were rejected on the grounds of eye-sight and others for lack of height. The number of full-time specials gradually dropped as the war progressed until, by 1944, there were just 607.

The situation in the provinces varied widely. In Portsmouth a Special Constabulary had been formed primarily for air raid precaution duties and a transport section, consisting of both full-time and part-time units was created. 186 specials were recruited in Bolton and, in 1938, over 1,250 specials in Essex had undergone an ARP course, out of a total strength of just over 2,000. In Derbyshire the specials formed a mounted section of 12 men using their own horses. Eric St. Johnston, however, describes how, on taking up his post as the new Chief Constable of Oxfordshire, he found that :

> *Although there were about a thousand Special Constables in Oxfordshire when I assumed command, they were virtually untrained and none had been issued with uniform or organised on a county basis. All had the rank of constable and wore only arm bands with here and there a peaked cap of First World War vintage. ... Eventually, uniformed and well-trained, they gave valuable service where it was most needed, especially in mounting guard at places vulnerable to sabotage. ... The regular police owe them a great debt of gratitude for their assistance and good comradeship.*

The latter comment is reflected in the views of Ted Maidment who eventually retired from the East Riding force as a superintendent, but served as a constable and (later) a sergeant during the war. He describes how ;

> *The specials worked like Trojans and the comradeship between "them and us" was never so close, either before or after. Perhaps this was mainly due to the dangers we faced together.*

Frank Butler, a special constable in the City of London force, described the day war broke out in graphic terms:

> *On September 3rd, 1939, I reported for duty at 10.45 am. The station ... was crowded. There was a good muster of Specials and War Reserves ... It was a bit chaotic as we specials had to be issued with steel helmets and gas masks ... We heard the Prime Minister's announcement that the country was at war, followed by the Inspector's order, 'Get those men on the streets at once'. The sirens were screaming overhead.*

The age limit for specials on entry was 20, lowered to 18 in 1940. There was no upper age limit, although most forces followed the Metropolitan Police practice of transferring specials over the age of 50 to an Auxiliary or Reserve section, only performing duty in exceptional circumstances. The demands made by the Armed Forces meant that, by 1940, part-time recruits to the Special Constabulary had to be between the ages of 41 and 55 unless they were definitely in a reserved occupation and thus not liable for call up. In London, all part-time specials were required to perform 8 hours duty each week and 40 hours every month, including 2 night duties. They were employed on most of the usual policing duties, many of which are described later in this book. Initially specials worked under the close supervision of a regular officer but, as time went on and the shortage of regular policemen grew more acute, they worked entirely unsupervised, often with great distinction. However, by 1944 the need had declined to such an extent that they were becoming underused.

Although most of the urban areas and larger conurbations reported excellent recruitment to the Special Constabulary, this was not always the case in the rural areas, where farm workers were already working long hours on the land and were reluctant to give up the very little free time they had to become a voluntary policeman – or an air raid warden, for that matter. Paradoxically, the Special Constabulary was particularly well supported in Devon, being several times the strength of the regular force. Such was the enthusiasm of these part-time policemen that, in one small town, it was not unusual to find eight or ten turning out for duty every time the siren sounded, which could occur twice a night. They came from all walks of life, including two bank managers, three company directors and an auctioneer, as well as many from more mundane occupations.

The part-time specials fared better than their counterparts in the First World War as regulations were passed enabling them to qualify for refreshment and uniform allowances and travelling expenses. A Home Office Circular issued in November 1939 set out the conditions for cash allowances for motor vehicles, travelling, bicycles and refreshments, the cost being met in part by the Government through an Exchequer grant[3]. It appears, however, that the implications of this had not been fully thought through. The Chief Constable of Bolton (Lancashire) drew attention to the fact that he had a mobile unit consisting of 100 part-time specials who covered about 5,000 miles on patrol each month. If paid at the specified rates, they would be entitled to a total of between £700 and £800 each year, while specials who used their cars to drive to and from duty averaged 3,000 miles each month at a cost of £400 to £500 per annum. The Watch Committee agreed that they should be supplied with petrol from the police pump rather than be paid an allowance[4].

For a long time, many specials were not supplied with a uniform,

38

the Police Review reporting in April, 1940 that only around 10% had been so equipped, the sole concession to uniformity of the remainder being a raincoat, an armband, a cap and a steel helmet. The latter were heavy and uncomfortable to wear for long periods and so, in the City of London, specials who had them were permitted to wear peaked caps when travelling to and from duty, the use of the steel helmet being reserved to those times when they were actually on duty. They were later permitted to cease wearing them on day duty, leaving them at the police station to be collected should the need arise. In October, 1940, presumably to avoid the scandal of specials falling sick through lack of proper protective clothing, a Home Office Circular was issued instructing Chief Constables to provide their specials with winter coats and linings. The boot allowance was also increased to 1/- a week[5]. Despite this instruction, letters to the Police Review in January, 1941 were still complaining about the lack of proper uniform for many auxiliaries.

In his book on the Metropolitan Police at War, the former Secretary to the force, H M Howgrave-Graham describes how –

> *... there were many unaccustomed sights in London during those early days. One ... was that of men in plain clothes with tin hats, armlets, whistles and, of course, the inevitable respirator, doing duty as constables, generally in company with regular officer.*
>
> *However, it was not long before they were properly clothed and equipped, and all that people then noticed was that the average height of the force seemed to have dropped a bit and that the new kind of Bobby wore a flat hat instead of a helmet.*[6]

Arthur Marshall, who served in Sheffield throughout the Blitz on that city in December, 1940, remembers with amusement the sight of the Sub-Commandant of the Special Constabulary, one of the city's leading solicitors, lying in a semi-prone position on the floor beneath the large office table in the police station. Two female telephone operators took it in turns to crawl from under the telephone cabinet to take incoming calls and relay them to the Sub-Commandant who nonchalantly recorded incidents in the Telephone Message Book as they were reported.

When an Oxford City councillor opined that 'one pensioned

policeman is worth a dozen special constables', this was seen as a grave slur on the Special Constabulary although one Chief Constable supported this point of view, admitting that if he could get 50 pensioners to serve in the First Police Reserve, he would welcome them. But the Chief Constable of Birmingham reported that a number of the pensioners who had been re-engaged by him were physically unable to stand up to the work. To make up the deficit he was taking on a number of full-time specials, preference being given to '... cricketers and footballers because they are physically fit'.

When the Chief Constable of Kent applied to his Standing Joint Committee (the police authority for the force) for £43,000 for uniforms for his Special Constabulary, the Committee voted the money in less than eight minutes, most of this time being taken up by members jostling to get on their feet to pay tribute to the Kent Special Constabulary.

There appears to be little evidence that relations between the regular officers and the part-time specials were anything but amicable, although some specials felt that their competence was underrated. One complained that as soon as he spied trouble and sent to the sergeant for instructions, he would be transferred elsewhere and a regular officer sent to deal with the matter. It is of course possible that the fact that he felt the need to send for instructions was taken as indicating a lack of confidence, if not a lack of competence. Certainly there seems to be no sign that co-operation between the regular police officers and the auxiliaries was lacking to any serious extent, unlike certain other sections of the Civil Defence organisation. The Ministry of Home Security's Research and Experiments Department concluded, for example, that in Birmingham during the Blitz on that town, '... relations between certain sections of the Civil Defence services, notably the Fire Brigade and the Auxiliary Fire Service, left much to be desired'[7].

Of course, then as now, there was some reluctance amongst members of the regular force to accept the specials. Bill Cavey, the former Metropolitan Police constable, remembers that some of the new recruits to this body were of doubtful character; one was a former organ grinder and the constable was most unwilling to let him into the mysteries of the policeman's craft, such as the use of pieces of paper and cotton across doors and gates to reveal whether anyone had opened them since they were last checked. Another Metropolitan officer, in an unpublished account of his war experiences, held in the Imperial War Museum, describes how recruiting for the specials was slow in the East End. Men who rose at 6.30 am and worked manually until 5.30 pm to keep their families had little time for any form of part-time activity, except the odd pint. Such volunteers as there were tended to be dockers or other manual labourers. One applicant was a street hawker who went around with a pony and cart, selling market rejects – over-ripe fruit, limp greens, bruised potatoes, etc. He was a bit of a character, 'four-foot nothing in his boots', a true Cockney who always wore an over-large greatcoat which swept the ground. He had a small, pinched face and a big moustache. He was always dirty and stank, possibly because he slept with his pony. The sergeant took his name and promised to let him know (which he conveniently 'forgot' to do). Despite this rejection, during the Blitz this little man was always to be found at the scene of any bombing incident on the Isle of Dogs, still in his long coat, scrabbling in the debris to look for survivors.

> *I looked up one night from a wrecked piano and what was underneath it and there he was, covered in dirt and dust and enjoying every bit of the grand job he was doing'[8].*

Sadie Ward, in her book about the war in the countryside, notes that young or inexperienced new guardians of the law were likely to be met with resentment by villagers, one of whom commented,

> *The Specials are very grand with dark blue coats, rubber boots, a tin hat with letters in white paint and lots of power to keep us in order. They are enjoying their power, often the first they have had in their lives.[9]*

One correspondent describes how his father was in charge of a contingent of special constables in a village just outside Leicester. One of these was quite small and, noticing a light showing on a council estate in the village, knocked on the door which was opened by a very large man who demanded, 'What do you want?'. The nervous special replied, 'Er, – can you tell me the time, please?'

The understandable timidity of some special constables in the face of ordinary police duties forms the subject of a number of other tales. Joan Salhurst, one of the rare regular policewomen performing duty in those days, tells of how she was scheduled to make a routine patrol of the coloured US soldiers' quarters in Bristol. Although she normally made this tour on her own, on one occasion she was allocated a special constable to accompany her and found him to be :

> ... *an elderly, terrified, pint-sized man who asked if we really needed to do this patrol. I assured him from my lofty height of 5 foot 11 inches that I would make sure no harm came to him.*

At this time women special constables were something of a rarity, if not an anomaly. A few Chief Constables had appointed women to the Special Constabulary prior to the invention of the Women's Auxiliary Police Corps but this was generally discouraged by the Home Office, not on any specific legal grounds (though the Home Office at this time had doubts on this aspect also) but because of doubts as to the suitability of women for special constabulary duties which were traditionally associated with civil disturbances[10].

These doubts were felt by others and a letter to the *Daily Mail*, quoted in the *Police Review*, expressed the concern of at least one special:

> *When I enroled as a special constable I felt that I had at least volunteered for a man's job. From the Daily Mail I am surprised and almost disgusted to see that Bolton has just appointed its first woman special constable. Is there nothing sacred to man? For my part, I shall not attend any lectures or instruction classes at which there are women[11].*

It must be added that subsequent correspondence in the columns of the *Police Review* was by and large totally opposed to this chauvinistic point of view and supported the use of women in this manner.

We shall be looking at the role of women in the war-time police in a later chapter but, in the meantime, we come to the third type of police auxiliary – the Police War Reserve. This body was conceived in 1938 at a specific war-time measure. Anticipating that the First and Second (Special Constabulary) Police Reserves would be incapable of filling the gaps left by policemen called for active service in the Armed Forces and providing the sort of augmented police service which enemy action in this country would demand, it was decided to create a Police War Reserve. It was widely believed that, if air raids started in earnest as soon as war was declared, a police force more than twice the peacetime size would not be excessive and the Chief Constables throughout the country called for the establishment of a war reserve of nearly 30,000 men. Many forces accordingly, and with Government blessing, began to form Police War Reserves during the course of 1938 and 1939.

It will be recalled that the original proposal was to enlist ex-servicemen and other men used to discipline but without previous police experience into the First Police Reserve. One of the objections to this was the fact that they would then be paid the same as a regular officer, and this was regarded as unacceptable. The Police War Reserve, which would be pleased to take on volunteers of this calibre, was therefore aligned with ARP rates of pay and received £3 per week, the same as the full-time specials. Formed initially in the Metropolitan Police, the scheme was rapidly extended elsewhere. To begin with, only men over 30 who were not in reserved occupations were accepted and, although recruits to the Police War Reserve were initially all volunteers (it has to be admitted that service in that body – a reserved occupation – was seen by some as a preferable alternative to being called up for the Army), the 1941 National Service Act gave a person due for call up the option of joining some full-time branch of the ARP service. It was even decided that suitable candidates could be directed into this service if this was felt desirable and the Act made it clear that the Police War Reserve was included under this general umbrella of ARP services. The introduction of compulsion became a serious bone of contention and caused great resentment among the gallant volunteers of 1939 and 1940. As one very senior police officer has since commented,

> *The difficulty with police work is that it needs men who want to do the job. It is unwise – indeed, unsafe – to have men in police uniform with police powers who do not want to be police officers. Conscripts will not do: we must have volunteers*[12].

The linking of Police War Reserve conditions and pay with the Civil Defence services also created problems. Early in 1940, for instance, The Commissioner of the Metropolitan Police, faced with the serious levels of wastage from the Police War Reserve (paralleled if not exceeded by wastage in the Auxiliary Fire Service at the time) urged that these men who were working alongside the regular constables, doing full tours of duty including nights, should have their conditions brought nearer to those of the regular police. This was opposed by the Civil Defence side and Sir John Anderson decided against the proposal, holding that the parallelism with the Civil Defence services must be maintained. The grievance did not go away, however, and did much to compel the Government to agree to the formation of an Auxiliary Police Association towards the end of 1941, which was empowered to consider matters affecting their welfare and efficiency. As late as 1944 the Association was asking the Home Office to go to arbitration to settle various questions relating to their pay and conditions of service. The idea of breaking free from the Civil Defence conditions (and so, indirectly, with Army rates) had been quietly dropped as a result of a substantial pay increase awarded to the Army. Pay was also a source of ill-feeling between some regulars and their auxiliary colleagues; the latter received the same pay but were not subject to the same stringent discipline and restrictions.

The type of man recruited to the Police War Reserve varied, some being well-educated and of above-average intelligence, others were less well-endowed in this respect. One Police War Reserve in Kent is described by his own son as 'an unlikely volunteer'. He was the proprietor of two ladies hairdressing salons in which he continued to work on his days off, often foregoing sleep to do so. It was not unusual for a reserve constable to retain an interest in his former trade or profession and this was a frequent source of complaint on the part of the regular officers, especially as the latter were strictly forbidden to take any form of additional employment to boost their meagre income. Where the War Reserve was himself unable to continue to follow his peacetime occupation he could sometimes turn to his family. Norman Longmate describes how a former commercial traveller, who became a wartime constable in Coventry, still admires the courage of his wife who, never having driven before, agreed to 'try and keep a little of my connection together till after the war' and, after a couple of runs round the square, she drove throughout the war, dodging the bomb holes and with their six-month old son in a carry cot[13].

Many auxiliaries were totally unaccustomed to any discipline, certainly of the rigid type to which the police were subject in those days, and this did not endear them to their regular colleagues, especially the supervisory officers. Don Batty, a former sergeant in the

Barnsley County Borough force recalls an incident in that town, where it was the practice (as in some other towns) for the sergeant to attract the attention of the patrolling constable at night by rapping his steel-ferruled nightstick on the kerb. On this occasion the constable the sergeant wanted to contact was a War Reserve and, being unable to see him, the sergeant went through the time-hallowed process of rapping his stick. The correct process was for the constable concerned to flash his torch to indicate his whereabouts but this time there was no response. Fearing some misfortune had occurred to the inexperienced PWR, the sergeant proceeded up the street, flashing his torch into all the shop doorways until finally it illuminated the missing constable, standing well back in a shop doorway. 'Why didn't ya' flash ya' light?' asked the irate sergeant. 'Nay, sergeant', replied the other, 'Thee's looking for me, I'm not looking for thee'. The unfortunate constable was very quickly disabused of his understanding of the situation.

As the inspector at Chelsea, Eric St Johnston had to recruit very quickly 250 War Reserves and, among those he recruited were the whole of the Chelsea and Fulham football teams, but 'they did not prove very amenable to discipline and we soon got rid of most of them'[14]. Other War Reservists were dismissed quite early on when it was discovered that they were members of the British Union of Fascists, only very cursory checks being made as to their suitability before they were enroled. According to a divisional station sergeant serving at Epping at the outbreak of the war, there was resentment that fully-trained and disciplined regular officers were being replaced by amateurs. The sergeant was in charge of sifting applications from aspiring Police War Reservists sent by the local employment exchange. One, a 'beefy Irishman', was set to work trench digging. Four days later a warrant was received for his arrest for non-payment of maintenance:

> *We hung onto him until he had finished building the trenches, then brought him into the police station, gave him a good meal, and arrested him!*[15].

Their efficiency also a bit like the curate's egg – good in parts. At the beginning of 1940 the *Police Review* reported that one PWR had arrested a man for being drunk in charge and had then instructed him to drive to the nearest police station![16]. A suggestion made as early as 1944 that these Police War Reserves should be retained after the war met with a great many adverse comments. There were frequent complaints that these amateur and ill-trained policemen had to be 'carried' by their regular colleagues and even by some of the more experienced special constables, especially where the inevitable paperwork was concerned. Curiously enough, a measure of police experience did not always help; one 'country copper' describes one of his war-time assistants, who had served in the Indian Police, as being more of a liability than an asset, unlike his non-police colleague who made himself very useful.

In other areas, these mature recruits to the police service were readily accepted by their colleagues since they were usually well-known locals 'doing their bit' and their local knowledge was a useful asset to the force. Some, like the actor Lockwood West (father of Timothy West) were also invaluable when it came to organising much-needed Christmas entertainment in Bristol. Quite a number of former special constables saw joining the Police War Reserve as a means of offering their services full-time and a number were commended for their excellent work during air raids.

The widow of one former Police War Reserve tells how her late husband, then employed as a insurance agent, used to go into town every Thursday to pay in his week's takings – Thursday being chosen as it was the day before pay day and none of his clients would have any money for him to collect that day. One Thursday in the Spring of 1941, when he was 38 years of age, he was very late coming home and his wife was beginning to worry that he had fallen off his bicycle or some other misfortune had befallen him. When he did eventually return home he announced to his astonished wife that he had joined the police! His wife was appalled; he had never discussed this possibility with her before and she couldn't understand why he didn't wait to be called up. But, as he explained, by volunteering for the police, he could remain at home with her. He had spent the day sitting the War Reserve entrance examination and had to return the next day for a medical. The wife, who worked in a local shop, was astonished a week later when a fellow worker told her she had seen her husband, in police uniform, patrolling the main street. He had been issued with a uniform and sent out, without any training whatsoever, to patrol the town's main shopping area. He was later given some basic training – about two hours each week. In due course, being a qualified motor cyclist, he was given the task of delivering dispatches from County Hall in Maidstone to Winston Churchill's private home at Chartwell. Like a number of other Police War Reservists, this volunteer found the work to his liking and stayed on after the war as a regular policeman and eventually retired at the age of 60, having worked the last ten years as the night duty telephone operator at the headquarters of the Kent County Constabulary.

The employment of these diverse police auxiliaries was essential to the running of the police service. In September, 1939, the various forces throughout the country had a combined strength of around 60,000, which was nearly 2,000 below that authorised. By March, 1940, despite mobilisation and the recall of reservists to the colours, the picture had in fact improved, partly due to the continued recruitment of suitable candidates over 25 years of age. It was further enhanced by the existence of over 190,000 auxiliaries – First Police Reserves, Special Constables (full- and part-time), Police War Reserves and Women's Auxiliary Police Corps. There were wide variations in the numbers of auxiliaries employed but, overall, they averaged 49% of the regular force in the counties and 22% in the boroughs and cities. The numbers reached a peak of over 194,000 in 1941.

By 1945, when the Civil Defence services were being rapidly scaled down, the number of police personnel was :

Regular policemen with less than 30 years service	38,739
Regular policewomen	416
Regular policemen due for retirement	2,717
First Police Reserve	2,061
Police War Reserve	14,412
Full-time Special Constables	732
Women's Auxiliary Police Corps	3,702
Total :	62,779

The total strength was therefore not far below the pre-war establishment of men – 63,388 – but was largely made up of auxiliaries, many of whom had been conscripted and would leave as soon as they were permitted. Not all did, as we have seen, and a number of the more dedicated and competent reservists were invited to transfer to the regular force after the war. Some of the First Police Reserve also remained in the ranks for a good ten years after hostilities had ceased. The fact that they were permitted – indeed, often encouraged – to remain with the police in some capacity or other is a testament to their undoubted efficiency and effectiveness. Like many serving on the Home Front, they had little to show for their efforts apart from their memories and the ribbon of the Defence Medal. Some, because of their age and general health, were even to be deprived of the opportunity to reflect very long on these small blessings.

In the years leading up to the war, some Chief Constables, anticipating the loss of many of their younger constables to the Armed Forces, set about recruiting youths as civilian clerks. Their role was to perform messenger duties, both inside the police stations and outside, either on foot or using the ubiquitous bicycle, and also to do some odd jobs around the police station, such as making tea and even a little typing. Once war broke out, the existence of these lads was generally recognised and augmented by the formation of a Police Auxiliary Messenger Service. Many of these young men – little more than boys, in fact – displayed extreme courage under enemy attack, dodging the bombs and the shrapnel on their bicycles to deliver vital messages where telephone communication had broken down or was overloaded. Like most civil defence organisations, the Police Auxiliary Messenger Service was disbanded at the end of the war. Most of those who were old enough and met the other physical and personal requirements joined the post-war police service as recruit constables but many forces were anxious to retain the services of these very useful – and cheap – young men and continued to employ 'boy clerks' for a number of years after the cessation of hostilities.

Once again, this ad hoc arrangement was soon officially recognised and the Police Cadet Corps was formed in the decade following the end of the war, although now the Cadets were seen as a valuable source of recruitment to the regular force which was suffering in the face of competition from industry, rather than just a source of cheap labour.

And so the police service became once more a full-time professional body, denuded of virtually all the ageing First Police Reserves, while most of the Police War Reserves had returned to their pre-war employment. The members of the Women's Auxiliary Police Service either joined the regular force, took employment as civilian drivers or simply married and gave up any form of employment. Only the Special Constabulary remained as a reserve force, albeit now entirely part-time. They were at last all provided with a suitable uniform and received regular training for their important role and remain today an indispensible part of the modern police service.

3. The Defence of the Realm

How the war was going to affect the British citizen as an individual one could only guess in 1939, and the role of the police was equally unclear. The received opinion in police circles was that the war work of the British police forces in their corporate capacity would continue to fall within the wide limits traditionally set by the protection of life and property and the maintenance of public order. In the event, this viewpoint proved to be largely correct. The bases of police organisation to meet the conditions of war were twofold; firstly the force had to aim for a flexible organisation which, while it would provide for a concentration on war work, would equally facilitate the performance of its duties in periods of comparative quiet. Secondly, flexibility demanded a wide delegation of responsibility. Local officers had to consider all the many and varied problems which might arise in areas as dissimilar as Birmingham and Brighton and had to lay their plans on the basis of heavy damage resulting in disrupted communications and the consequent lack of control from above. Fortunately, the British policeman, unlike his counterparts in the Armed Forces, had traditionally been expected to work largely alone and on his own initiative and was accustomed to doing just that.

But the war brought a very heavy burden. Colonel G H R Halland, one of His Majesty's Inspectors of Constabulary, noted in his 1938/39 report the growing tendency to dump all sorts of extra duties on the police – 'the outcome of the confidence placed on the efficiency and reliability of the police, although a contributory factor is doubtless the desire to avoid the trouble and expense of setting up other suitable agencies'. This tendency is naturally intensified in time of war. Some of these duties were a natural extension of peacetime policing tasks, such as the control of traffic, keeping roads clear for essential traffic, setting up diversions, etc. In addition, the police are often the first on the scene of an incident and take the first steps in rescue, searching debris and vehicles for survivors, evacuation of the occupants of damaged or threatened properties. Some of the wartime police duties were, however, entirely new and often overlapped those of air raid wardens.

As we have seen, air raid precaution training and other war-related police duties began well before the declaration of hostilities and in the summer of 1939 policemen could be found, going from place to place, earmarking commercial vehicles and motorcycles in good condition and less than three years old for subsequent requisition. The only exemptions were cattle trucks which would be needed for the agricultural war effort. The normal peacetime checks on aliens living in this country were also stepped up but the real impetus did not come until the declaration of war.

Sir Arthur Dixon[1] listed some of these wartime duties :

– enforcing lighting restrictions,

– enforcing security measures

– the display of mobilisation posters

– arranging for the billeting of troops (often at short notice)

– assisting in the detention of enemy merchant ships in British ports

– supervising the movements of aliens

– issuing air raid warnings

– providing guards for vulnerable points

– the enrolment of the various types of police reservists

– the protection of police stations with sandbags, etc.

– training in anti-gas precautions.

And, although householders were actively discouraged from hoarding food supplies, stocks of tinned food were held at police stations in case of emergency.

To this list must be added the multitude of jobs arising out of the introduction of the Defence Regulations, such as those relating to the blackout, vehicle lighting, identity cards, wireless sets in cars, prohibited noises, football crowds, pigeons and other animals, kites and fireworks. In this chapter we look more closely at some of these extraneous duties which were thrust upon an already hard-pressed and short-handed police force in the early days of the war.

The British police force, unlike many of its continental cousins, does not have at its disposal a gendarmerie or similar military strong arm and, in the event of serious civil unrest, it had always been understood that the civic authorities would call in the military, as indeed they did on numerous occasions in the 19th and early 20th centuries. It was assumed by many people (who should have known better) that the same would apply during a war. If the police were overstretched, the military would help out, especially in garrison towns and naval ports, and this in fact happened in some places, but many functions which the Armed Services could have fulfilled in Portsmouth and in Southampton, for example, fell upon an overloaded police force. What is curious is the narrow spectrum of authority delegated to the Army in Portsmouth; no special role was allocated in advance and sometime no role at all afterwards, despite dire needs. No clear-cut plan existed and there was plenty of jealousy.

Because of the demands made upon them and the additional problems which the anticipated air raids were expected to bring, the working conditions in most forces underwent a radical change. The right to a rest day each week was suspended in September 1939 and, although the normal eight-hour period of duty was not officially affected, the right to time off in recompense for overtime worked was also discontinued where the total period of duty performed was less than 12 hours. There was, of course, no question of payment for this overtime.

Like the Civil Service, police constables earning less than 95/- (£4.75) a week (which was most of them) were granted a war bonus of between 2/6 (12½p) and 5/- (25p), called a Supplementary Allowance. In view of the loss of overtime, a War Duty Allowance of 4/- (20p.) and 3/- (15p.) was paid to sergeants and constables respectively in August, 1940 and was increased periodically throughout the war.

The police authorities were quick to seize upon this change in conditions and many forces immediately imposed a 12 hour day. In Kent, for example, personnel worked six hours on the beat and six hours on reserve duty in the station, whilst in Sheffield the system was eight hours on the beat and four hours inside. This was applied for only three months before more normal shift duties were resumed.

A similar situation applied in Lancashire where the 12 hour day proved unworkable since it meant men could not change shifts and the system was soon abandoned.

Nevertheless, the hours of duty performed continued to be well in excess of the pre-war 48 hour week and the Police Review commented that these were often unjustified by circumstances :

> ... *the Police are quite willing to go on with the job right round the clock if need be in an emergency, but they consider that they are entitled to keep to their regulation hours when circumstances permit*[2].

In another force, there were complaints that constables who had been on 2 pm to 10 pm shift were required to remain at the police station one night each week. They were not required for duty and beds were provided for them. The men maintained, quite reasonably, that in an air raid it was better for the police to be dispersed rather than gathered together in one place where they could all become casualties.

In Bow, in the East End of London, qualified drivers were so thin on the ground that those who could drive were required to sleep on the station, working no set tour of duty, but turning out whenever the siren sounded. In fact, in London, the families of many policemen had been evacuated and the men only went home to get a change of clothing and to check that their homes were still standing before returning to the station to continue their work.

In the country, the practice of flexible working hours continued. Although the rural constable was still required to be on duty at set times (often split shifts with a four hour break between two four hour tours of duty) he had always accepted that he was never really off duty and that he had to deal with any matters which might arise on his 'patch', regardless of the time of day or night. For him, the war made very little difference to his patten of work and he was proud of his status in the village and the respect afforded him by the locals.

The original requirement for policemen to report for duty whenever the air raid siren sounded was another onerous commitment. There could be as many as 18 alerts in a single day, each one necessitating off-duty officers getting dressed in their uniform and making their way, usually by bicycle, to the police station. Often the 'all clear' sounded even before they got there and they had to wend their weary way home again. The disruption was such that this instruction was soon abandoned.

Eventually the weekly rest day was restored to give the exhausted officers something of a break but this was often coupled with a requirement to remain within the police division. Since regulations prohibited an officer from frequenting a public house in his own division, this meant that, even on their days off, they could not have a drink in a pub. Dennis Vorley, who was a constable in West Sussex at the time, tells how a married colleague bought a barrel of beer and, when they had cycled home, they would both go to his house for a glass of beer and a game of darts. Constable Roberts, of the West Riding force remembers how, out for a walk with his fiancé, he was stopped by his inspector who told him to turn back as he was on the point of leaving his prescribed area.

The specials too were working flat out and the Walthamstow Occurrence Book records a special constable reporting his inability to undertake duty at present (May, 1940) owing to his working 8 am to 8 pm seven days a week on Government work. He expressed his willingness however to report for duty during his non-working time if required.

There is no doubt there was plenty for the police to do in the first few months of the war. Gas masks been issued to both the population at large and the various civil defence services and the recipients had to be instructed in their use. Although the newly formed ARP service was closely involved in this, much of the work fell on the police who organised instructional sessions, often at the local pub. Police stations had to be strengthened with balks of timber and sandbags, the windows either blanked off or criss-crossed with adhesive tape to limit the effects of flying glass. Exercises were organised in conjunction with the other civil defence organisations – wardens, rescue units, fire-watchers, first aiders, ambulance drivers, stretcher bearers, damage control units – with varying degrees of success.

The Metropolitan Police ordered that its police boxes should be manned at all times and these became a home from home for many policemen in the early months as the nation awaited the anticipated air strike. This task often fell to reservists, some of whom, thanks to their previous occupation still owned a car (something few regular policemen could afford) and it was not unusual to see the duty constable seated comfortably in his private car within earshot of the box's telephone bell. Even the less fortunate members of the force occasionally arranged for their families to join them for a picnic tea beside the box on fine days. This wasteful use of scarce manpower was soon abandoned and the boxes were only manned when there was an alert.

The control of vehicles has always been one of the principal tasks of the police and their responsibilities in this respect were increased by wartime legislation. In order to prevent an invading army from making use of British transport, as the Germans had done in France and Belgium, regulations were introduced which demanded that any motor vehicle left unattended should be immobilised, usually by the removal of the rotor arm. The police were empowered to immobilise any vehicle they found whose driver had failed to take the necessary precautions and this usually took the form of deflating the tyres or ripping out the ignition leads. In addition to suffering considerable inconvenience as a result of these drastic measures, many drivers were prosecuted, with fines up to £50 being imposed.

Vehicle lighting was another important area of concern, with only very reduced lighting being permitted. The strict enforcement of lighting regulations even during the Blitz had its humorous side as described by a Sheffield policeman:

> *When we were going down Attercliffe Road this copper comes out and he signals us down because our lights were out. Half the bloody street was on fire!*[3]

An ARP messenger had a similar experience in London :

> *There was a raid on ... and fires burning some distance off. It was possible to read a newspaper unaided... it was very difficult to obtain batteries ... so as it was so bright I switched off my lights (and) as the road was deserted I rode along the wrong side of the road. After a couple of hundred yards a voice shouted 'Stop!' and a policeman appeared. 'Do you realise you have no lights on your bicycle?' At that moment we heard a bomb falling and fell flat on the ground. ... We got up, dusted ourselves down (and) he continued, 'And do you know you were riding on the wrong side of the road?'. Another bomb whistled down ... we got up and for the next two minutes or so I was given a lecture on the correct way of riding a bike at night.*[4]

Another task which fell on the police in respect of motor vehicles arose out of Home Office Circular 826,862/1 of 12 March, 1940, which requested that the police provide lists of any dumps of scrap cars which would be of use to the Iron and Steel Control organisation.

After the fall of Dunkirk in June 1940 the greater part of the Army was to be found licking its wounds in Britain and preparing for the next stage in the conflict, while the RAF was urgently preparing both men and aircraft for the expected aerial onslaught. This concentration of the military on these small islands created great pressures on accommodation and one of the early tasks of the police was to locate billets for servicemen and others engaged on essential war work, a task which was to continue for virtually the whole of the war.

This possibility had been foreseen well before hostilities broke out and, in 1937, an extensive review was carried out of any possible billets for the military and their horses (Home Office Circular 480,566/23 of 8/1/37). In addition, a Central Register of Accommodation was drawn up of premises suitable for requisitioning for purposes other than the billeting of individuals, since it was reasonably assumed that there would be a need for government departments to leave London and for storage centres to be located throughout the country. The police were closely involved in this exercise, working in conjunction with both the local authority and the military.

The power to commandeer premises for the billeting of troops arose mainly from the Army and Air Force Acts which required the occupiers of 'victualling houses' to provide accommodation for members of these two services. In times of emergency this power is extended to cover the occupiers of public buildings, private dwellings, warehouses, barns, etc., subject to certain statutory exceptions. The Government had the authority, under these Acts, to issue Orders, requiring chief constables execute billeting requisitions to cause the occupiers of suitable premises to provide billets for such officers and men (and women) of the Armed Forces together with their horses and such vehicles as are specified in the requisition. In practice the task was usually delegated down to any constable but, in one case where a householder refused to comply and was convicted, the High Court later ruled that, as there was no evidence that the chief constable had given the constable any directions as to the selection of these particular billets, the law had not been complied with and quashed the conviction. It would obviously be quite impracticable for a chief constable to give his personal attention to the selection of every billet in a residential property and the law was changed in 1941 to give chief constables the power to authorise any constable to execute billeting requisitions.

This right of the military to require billets was later extended to United States and Commonwealth forces and it was reported in December 1943 that the police had been asked to find billets for 5,300 US troops in Manchester alone, all of which had been found 'without difficulty'.

Bert Ayers, the constable policing the Romney Marsh (Kent) in the early part of the war recalls requisitioning Noel Coward's former home at Goldenhurst Farm, Aldington, for use as the headquarters of 138 Brigade. At the same time, a detachment of the Royal Ulster Rifles was found accommodation in Ruckinge school – unused since most of the children had been evacuated. Bert Ayers remembers these Irishmen as being 'very rough'. On the other hand, when his colleague, Tom Longhurst, had to find accommodation for the WAAFs staffing a listening post near Sittingbourne, he had no difficulty at all as the villagers were only too willing to help.

The very real threat of invasion meant that a great many buildings and installations, deemed to be 'vulnerable points' had to be guarded. Some were placed in the care of the military or Home Guard but, in all, 1,300 became a police responsibility. These included water towers, oil refineries and storage areas, gas works, electricity power stations and certain private factories, as well as some dock installations. This task alone kept nearly 11,000 men fully occupied, 7,000 of whom were special constables. Grave doubts were expressed as to whether 4,000 regular officers, even supplemented by the war reserves, could be spared for the remaining places and there were suggestions that all this work should be entrusted to special constables. However, it was clear that some premises were not suitable for manning by specials, especially part-timers, because of their remote location.

Some of these 'vulnerable points' were curious places. Police War Reserve Constable Norman Buchanan, a peacetime hairdresser used to the delicate aroma of the oils and unguents of his trade, found himself guarding a sewer outlet discharging much less aromatic substances into the Thames, not to mention the occasional rat. He occupied his time during the long, monotonous tours of duty painting flowers!

A more typical example of the sort of location the police were called upon to supervise was Belfast docks. Normally the task of the Harbour Police, this latter body of men was quickly absorbed into the

Royal Ulster Constabulary which then assumed responsibility for the whole of the extensive dock area. One very unpopular job associated with the harbour was performing duty at the dockyard gates for eight hours with the coal dust from the discharging coal boats getting into one's eyes, ears, mouth and lungs. There was no dodging this unpleasant task as every vehicle going in and out had to be stopped and examined and the passes of all personnel checked carefully. Not only was there a very real danger of infiltration and sabotage by enemy agents, but the IRA were still very active both in Ireland and on the mainland and, in 1939, had carried out a number of callous, violent outrages against the civilian population of Great Britain.

Even where the military assumed responsibility for guarding their own installations, the police found that their duties took them frequently to these places. Sometimes these visits could be fraught with danger as the young, often ill-trained sentries were extremely jumpy, especially at night. On one occasion the local police sergeant was forced to arrest the sentry at Manston airfield!

Apart from fixed guards at these vulnerable points, the police in the south-east and in certain other areas also had the onerous task of looking after the great many unoccupied premises whose owners had fled the expected invasion or aerial bombardment. Private houses, offices, shops, factories – all had been left, often still furnished and complete with stocks and equipment, making a tempting target for the light fingered.

Richard Crane[5] describes how, in the chaotic days just before the fall of Dunkirk, he was approached by his chief inspector, accompanied by an English-speaking Frenchman who had just come across the Channel with a large lorry, its tarpaulin cover securely lashed down. Constable Crane's job was to find a safe parking place for the vehicle overnight and to keep guard over it until the morning. He was issued with a Service revolver and went with the Frenchman and the lorry to an all-night garage where, to conceal the vehicle at the rear of the premises, all the other cars and vans had to be moved and then replaced around the guarded truck. Happily, the night passed without incident and the lorry with its mysterious load was driven off early the next morning. Although Richard Crane never discovered just what he had been so assiduously guarding all night, it was strongly rumoured that it was a large consignment of gold, brought over to escape the advancing German army. Certainly the precautions taken would seem to support this theory.

Quite early in the war the Metropolitan Police was called upon to undertake a somewhat unusual task; the protection of Government stores in the area occupied by the British Expeditionary Force in France. A special force of detectives from New Scotland was formed, consisting of seven detective sergeants and 11 detective constables, all under the command of Superintendent C E Campion, formerly in charge of the Criminal Record Office, and was speedily dispatched to France. Superintendent Campion was given the rank of major but, sadly, he became one of the first police casualties of the war and was killed in France in May, 1940.

The lack of civil defence volunteers in the early days meant that the police also had to assume some of the tasks which, by rights, were incument upon the ARP Wardens, such as shelter duty. Bob Stewart, a constable in Broadstairs at the time, remembers how each constable was responsible for an underground shelter to which he had to report whenever the siren went, whether he was on or off duty, day or night.

Naturally, whenever the police were called out or had to report for duty because of an alert, they were expected to be properly dressed at all times. Fortunately, perhaps, the 'dog collar' type of tunic then worn did not call for the wearing of a uniform shirt with a separate collar and tie and cuff links, all of which were extremely time-consuming, as those who were still serving when the first of the open-neck tunics came into use in the 1950s discovered. Even senior officers had their uniform problems. Eric St Johnston, as we learned earlier, was appointed chief constable of Oxfordshire at the beginning of the war. Within days of taking up his appointment he had to go to Bicester to meet King George VI who was making a tour of bomber stations in the county.

> *Owing to the suddenness of my appointment I had no time to obtain a uniform and didn't possess even a bowler hat. Everyone wore uniform ... so I stood out in my civilian attire and wearing a black homburg ... on the way (to Bicester airfield) the King asked (Air Chief Marshal) Portal who I was and when Portal told him, he asked 'Why isn't he in uniform?' Portal replied that he was prepared to answer for the sins of Bomber Command but not for those of the police[6].*

Later during the visit, the new chief constable was invited to explain himself to the King, which he did. There was a sequel some six months later when the King, this time accompanied by Queen Elizabeth, came to visit a school near Henley-on-Thames. As the King greeted St Johnston, this time in uniform, he said 'Hello Chief Constable. I'm glad to see the uniform fits well!'

The police service has always been something of a dustbin, being allocated all those jobs which no-one else wanted to take on and this was especially noticeable in the smaller borough and city forces. The local council, as represented by the Watch Committee, kept a close eye on the council's finances and so used their policemen for all sorts of jobs which had very little connection with traditional police duties. For example, it is not generally appreciated that, in many of the borough and city forces, the police and fire services were combined, the fire tenders being manned by policemen. Although this practice gradually died out, it still remained in some forces until the formation of the National Fire Service. Even more common was the use of policemen to provide an ambulance service. In the early days the ambulance was nothing more than a sort of stretcher on wheels, used as much to bring in drunks as injured persons. By the time the war had begun, however, most if not all forces who still retained this duty were equipped with motorised ambulances.

The police have, of course, always had dealings with corpses, especially those arising from accidental circumstances or those whose demise was sudden or associated with suspicious circumstances. The Coroner's Officer was always a policeman, either on a full-time basis or appointed *ad hoc* to deal with a specific death. As such, they had to attend any post mortem examination or autopsy, often being called upon to physically assist the pathologist. Any unfortunate officer whose beat included an infirmary or old people's home could expect to attend more than his fair share of post mortem examinations and inquests and have to carry out all the multifarious enquiries connected with the latter. This role was to take on an even greater significance once enemy action became more intense, as we shall see in a later chapter.

At least the mainland police were spared having to enforce orders and decrees pronounced by the enemy, a fate which befell the police in the Channel Islands. This particularly distressing state of affairs has been amply covered in other works and it is not the function of this book to examine this particular phenomenon. Suffice it to quote one small example; in July 1941 notices were displayed throughout the Guernsey, offering a £25 reward (a substantial sum in those days, equal to a couple of months' pay)

> *... to the person who first gives to the Inspector of Police information leading to the conviction of anyone (not already discovered) for the offence of marking on any gate, wall or other place whatsoever visible to the public the letter V or any other sign or word or words calculated to offend the German authorities or soldiers.*

Much more of a 'proper' police duty was the removal of all MI5's Registry of Files from their temporary headquarters in Wormwood Scrubs prison to Blenheim under conditions of the strictest security. Documents assumed a vital importance during the war, especially those classified as secret and which enemy agents would be delighted to get a sight of. When a rural constable, placidly cycling around his 'patch' in the autumn of 1942 found a number of military maps, all marked 'TOP SECRET', the resulting consternation can well be imagined. These particular maps showed a stretch of coastline with place names in Arabic or French and a number of red lines running across the map with numbers attached to them. These were promptly handed in to police headquarters from where they were transferred to MI5. In all, following an extensive search, 28 of a set of 33 maps were found and handed over to the authorities by the police. It later transpired that these maps had been improperly packed and lost from a vehicle taking them from Cheltenham to London and showed details of the landing beaches to be used in Operation Torch, the invasion of North Africa, which took place the following November. A similar instance of unbelievable carelessness occurred in East Anglia where Special Constable Fred Dansie, sheltering in a pub doorway one stormy winter's night, stumbled over a bulky briefcase. This proved to contain maps and blueprints of the entire coastal radar network which the authorities were more than pleased to receive back.

The police were often privy to highly secret information, although they did not always appreciate the import of this. Just one example of this was the use of the Kent police to put a *cordon sanitaire* around an area of the north Kent coast in order to maintain complete secrecy for rehearsals for the famous Dam Busters raid. In the spring of 1943 an area of one square mile east of Herne Bay was cordoned off and two long poles were erected on the sea wall, the distance between the poles representing the width of the dam. During the trials, watched by various 'boffins' and senior RAF officers, including Wing Commander Guy Gibson, accompanied as always by his dog, Nigger, specks in the distance would resolve into Lancaster bombers flying 60 feet above the water. The aim was to drop their dummy bombs and endeavour to bounce them between the posts. On one occasion the bomb struck a breakwater which deflected it and those watching from some 200 yards away had to throw themselves flat as the bomb whistled over their heads. Fortunately it was not armed but, since it weighed around five tons, it would have given a nasty headache to anyone in the way!

The emphasis which most published reports place on the Blitz and other enemy action which was directed principally at the major centres of population and industry, tends to overlook the role of the rural community in the war, including the part played by the 'country copper', so often unfairly and inaccurately depicted as a bumbling oaf, with a mental capacity little above that of the village idiot. In fact, almost all rural officers began their police careers in the towns and were only given responsibility for a rural beat when they had proved their reliability and ability to work largely unsupervised. Most had passed the necessary examinations for promotion to sergeant and many had attended a detectives' course since, in some isolated areas, they had little support from the CID and the whole of their beat was very much their personal responsibility.

The rural constable can be likened to a 'chief constable' in microcosm; where the real chief constable reported his activities to the chairman of the Watch Committee or the county police authority, the country policeman worked in close contact with his local community leaders – the doctor, the vicar, the schoolmaster and especially the 'squire' where such existed. PC Bert Ayers, responsible for a large part of the Romney Marsh in Kent was expected to report each Sunday morning to the Lord of the Manor at Bilsington Priory to let him know what was going on in the area. This peacetime practice was not abandoned during the war and formed yet another of the 'normal' police duties which the rural officer had to perform in addition to his new wartime tasks. The need for efficient farming meant that there could be no relaxation in the enforcement of the Diseases of Animals

Acts and, in fact, there were a number of outbreaks of foot and mouth disease during the war years which, had they not been confined through strict police supervision, could have proved disastrous to the nation's food production. One Oxfordshire farmer's wife describes how, finding the local police superintendent outside the farmhouse one night, fully anticipated that she was in trouble for not complying with the blackout regulations. Instead, he had come with the innocent, bucolic enquiry, 'Would you mind asking your husband to let us know when he starts sheep dipping?'[7]. Such was the importance attached to this aspect of rural policing that country officers were given an allowance of 1/- (5p) a week for the purchase of paste to stick up various notices, many of which related to Diseases of Animals, although wartime regulations resulted in a considerable increase in the volume of bill-sticking work to be performed.

Even enemy action had sometimes to take second place behind the needs of the natural inhabitants of the countryside. One Kent beekeeper who was transporting his hives to pollinate a fruit orchard one night found his lorry held up by a long queue of halted vehicles due to an unexploded bomb on the road. The policeman controlling the traffic was informed that there was likely to be another incident any minute with something akin to an unexploded bomb at the other end of the queue; with the coming of the early morning light there would be several thousand inquisitive bees exploring the neighbourhood. The policeman, employing the discretion for which the British police is renowned, decided the bomb represented less of a risk than the bees and allowed the lorry to jump the queue[8].

Gipsies and 'travellers' have always been a problem for the police in the rural areas and the war made no difference to this. Indeed, the problem was exacerbated by the requirement for all persons of a certain age to register for National Service. This, of course, included these nomads who were unwilling to report to the Labour Exchange as required and so had to be rounded up and taken there by the police. Having been compelled to register, they would subsequently be required to attend for medical examination and the whole process of tracing them and conveying them to the medical centre had to be repeated. If found fit and then called for military service, it was a sure bet that they would have disappeared once more by the time their call-up papers had been issued. On the whole a great deal of valuable police time was occupied in this manner, all for very little result.

Fortunately the police in general saw the gipsy as a nuisance rather than a threat, unlike many other folk. Many a farmer who had lost a few chickens preferred to blame a mythical fox rather than the gipsies encamped nearby, for fear of the 'Gipsies Curse'. Superstition was still very strong in the country and Constable 'Buck' Taylor, who patrolled a large country beat on the North Downs during the war, remembers trying to convince one countrywoman whose husband had died in the bath that he was indeed dead, a fact she refused to accept because '... the dog 'asn't 'owled yet so 'e can't be'. Apparently it was a well-known fact that whenever a man died, his dog would begin to howl!

The need for a concentrated effort by farmers to produce more and more food resulted in the formation of County War Agriculture Committees to ensure that the best possible use was made of all agricultural land. Farmers were given explicit instructions as to what they were to do with their land and failure to do so could result in draconian measures being taken. Sadie Ward, in her book on the War in the Countryside[9] describes how there were cases of these Committees abusing their powers which extended to the right to take possession of farms deemed to be unproductive and to cultivate them directly for the duration of the war and for five years thereafter. Thus, in May 1941, a farmer in Malmsbury was given only six days to leave his land on the grounds of under-production, despite having farmed it successfully for 35 years. Shortly afterwards a Yorkshire farmer was forcibly ejected from his holding for not carrying out the East Riding Committee's instruction on manuring.

Just how harsh this procedure could be is shown in the following eviction order issued to a dairy farmer in Buckinghamshire in 1942:

(1) If by Friday November 20, 1942, you have not vacated the holding, the Executive Committee, *with the assistance of the police,* will remove the furniture from the dwelling house and place it either in one room of the house or in one of the farm buildings, where it will remain at your risk.

(2) The Committee will remove the farm implements into one of the farm buildings where they will remain once again at your risk.

(3)   The Executive Committee will ... requisition any livestock which
may be found on the holding. Such livestock will be conveyed to
Aylesbury and sold in the market. The proceeds of such sale will
be held against your claim for compensation.

The phrase in (my) italics shows that the police were obliged to play
a part in these distressing evictions, often of farmers with whom they
had worked for many years and with whom thay had shared a glass of
beer in the local pub.

Paradoxically, if some farmers were being evicted, and possibly
having to go to live in the town, the population of certain country areas
was being greatly augmented as town dwellers fled to what they saw as
safer areas. Oxfordshire, for example, saw its population grow from
120,000 to over 200,000 almost overnight. This sort of increase was
not reflected by any increase in police strengths and the officers in the
county were hard-pressed to cope.

But the biggest population explosions came with the arrival of the
US troops in 1942. East Anglia and the East Midlands were
particularly hard hit with new airfields springing up almost everywhere
to take the US Army Air Corps men and planes and this phenomenon
will be examined in another chapter. For their part, the chief constables
increasingly found themselves dealing directly with the Home Office
and other Governmental departments. They were required to submit
daily reports to their Regional Headquarters on the local situation.
These reports were expected to include :

(i)   public order and morale
(ii)   the Mutual Aid (later Regional Reinforcement) scheme
(iii)   requests for military assistance
(iv)   police casualties and damage to police property through
enemy action
(v)   the general situation.

These reports were combined with reports from other sources and
used by the Ministry of Information to create the Home Intelligence
Reports for the information of the War Cabinet.

The concept of Mutual Aid (item (ii) of the chief constables'
reports) is an important one. Given the comparatively small size of

many police forces at the time and the fact that war duties meant that there would be a lack of military support in times of difficulty or public disorder, it was essential that the various police forces should be in a position to aid each other. This system really came into its own during the Blitz and the Baedeker raids where reinforcements from less-troubled areas were sent to relieve the exhausted policemen in the hard-hit towns and cities. Edgar Storer, of the Walsall Borough Police recalls:

When Coventry was bombed the first time a call came to our force for 25 men within 12 hours. I was one of them. We paraded at 5 am with two blankets and a ration of ships' biscuits and cheese and were bussed to Coventry, about 25 miles away. When we reached the outskirts we found roads blocked by craters or house debris. Telephone wires were down and rescue work was going on and, in one instance, we got out to help the injured. We had to detour several times but we eventually reached the Police Social Club where we had been instructed to report. We were joined by a contingent from the Stoke-on-Trent Police and were told this would be our billet for the duration of our stay. Part of the roof was missing, there was no water and the centre was a shambles, still burning. Many of us slept on the billiard tables. Nothing in the city seemed to be standing and rescue work was going on everywhere. We were briefed at the Police Headquarters; we were to work during the daytime only but would be turned out at other times if needed. There were no cooking facilities but we had brought our own camping stove and paraffin. We had to appoint our own cook but he had nothing to cook. The only drink was beer from the odd hotel which was still open and so for two days we lived on ships' biscuits and beer. We patrolled during daylight and assisted with rescue where required. We also went out at night as there was nothing else to do. In spite of the damage there was practically no looting and the remarkable thing was people went about almost as though nothing had happened. The second night the bombers returned and we had a first hand experience of that episode. We spent two weeks there before being replaced by another unit.

Norman Longmate, in another of his excellent books[10], describes how many Coventry people found that the policeman in their road the morning after the raid was more likely to ask them the way than the reverse, for that morning 100 policemen were also sent from Birmingham and 50 more from both Shropshire and Worcestershire, with another 100 held in readiness in Staffordshire. The main role occupied by the local Coventry officers tended to be as guides for the rescue parties, ambulance crews and firemen, as well as for their out-of-town colleagues.

George Whitcomb, then serving with the Bradford City Police, had a similar experience when a contingent from his force was sent to Sheffield, which had just been devastated by the Luftwaffe, where they were billeted in the Town Hall basement. Feeding these additional mouths soon became a problem and so the City Fathers gave permission for one of the municipal deer in the local park to be slaughtered. This would be a formidable task for the average policeman but the Bradford unit was fortunate in including a former butcher in their number and he set about the task quietly and efficiently. The detachment fed royally on venison for the next few days.

Great Yarmouth was another small town which suffered badly in the air raids, to the extent that, after the worst attacks in 1941, the exhausted Borough Policemen had to be replaced by men from Norfolk County to let them have some well-earned rest. A variation of the mutual aid scheme was the arrangement, introduced in March 1941, when the police in the heavily-raided areas had been under severe stress for some time, for policemen from one force to be exchanged with volunteers from another force. Men so seconded were attested to their new force but their parent force retained responsibility for pay, etc. There were plenty of offers to help but no very great inclination to accept the offers. A number of officers did, however, take advantage of the scheme to send their wives and families to quieter areas. The chief constable of Exeter, already on a personal secondment to Southampton, arranged for an exchange between the two forces to give the Southampton men a rest in 1941. Of course, no-one was aware that, before long, Exeter itself would be hard hit in the so-called Baedeker raids.

Similarly, in the run up to the Normandy landings, extra police were drafted in to the coastal areas to help with the colossal amount of road traffic and other troop movements. For example, 60 officers from Durham, Northumberland and Newcastle City were sent to Kent where they gave valuable assistance, and similar contingents were sent to other police forces in the south and east. At times, whole stretches of road had to be closed to allow the transport of fuselages and wings for large bomber aircraft.

But perhaps the greatest single influence on policing, especially in the early part of the war, was the introduction of the Defence (General) Regulations 1939 which imposed all sorts of restrictions and obligations on the populace at large, all of which had to be enforced by the police. As early as August, 1939, an Emergency Powers (Defence) Act had been passed, enabling the government to make these Regulations, which they lost no time in doing. The Government was clearly of the opinion that it was necessary to use some of the weapons of tyranny to fight tyranny. The hallowed concept of *habeas corpus* was promptly consigned to the dustbin and, overnight, Britain became a totalitarian state for the duration.

> *The State had power to take possession of almost any property or undertaking, from a horse to a hotel, from a motor boat to a railway... It had authority to lock up without trial any person whose detention appeared desirable for the public safety. It could prevent people from holding processions or demonstrations or putting out flags. It could pack them off home by a stated hour. It could designate protected premises or areas and exclude any persons... from them.... It could extinguish the lamps of lighthouses. It could direct farmers what crops to grow and tell landowners what trees to fell... It could amend or suspend any Act of Parliament at whim. It could punish with 14 years penal servitude 'any omission on the part of a person to do anything which he is under a duty, either to the public, or to any person, to do' (which could have covered a refusal by a typist to make the tea)*[11]

In two weeks in 1939, more emergency laws were passed than in the whole of the first year of the previous war. The haste with which these regulations were prepared was reflected in the wide and often vague terms in which they were couched. Typical examples of these hastily-made regulations include :

Regulation 18B : the infamous power to detain or impose restrictions on anyone with a view to preventing acts prejudicial to public safety or the defence of the realm. The object of this Regulation was, in the Home Secretary's words, 'to provide for the custody on security grounds of persons against whom it is not practicable to bring criminal proceedings'. By the spring of 1940 a number of leading Fascists, including one Member of Parliament, Capt. H M Ramsay, and two former MPs, Sir Oswald Moseley and John Becket, had been detained under this regulation and incarcerated in Brixton Prison.

Regulation 39A and 39B(1) : causing disaffection amongst members of HM Forces or influencing public opinion in a manner prejudicial to the defence of the realm or the efficient prosecution of the war. (In June 1940, a newsvendor in Putney High Street wrote 'FRENCH TRAGEDY IF NO HELP COMES' on his placard. A young man was heard to say 'It's bloody near sedition' and watching police caused the offending placard to be removed).

Regulation 39B(2) : the power to restrict the publication of documents, etc., (in other words, censorship).

Regulation 39E : the power to prevent the holding of meetings, processions, etc

Regulation 88B : the power to stop and search any vehicle

Regulation 88C : the general power of arrest without warrant

All of these made a considerable contribution to the range of problems which required the vigilance of the police or occupied their time and attention as well as increasing their powers. During the so-called 'Phoney War' leading up to the time of Dunkirk, the Labour opposition had an opportunity to challenge aspects of these Regulations and, as a result, the wording of many was amended and the powers reduced in scope. The highly contentious Regulation 18b was amended to apply only to persons who were of hostile origins or association, and persons who had recently been concerned in acts prejudicial to public safety or who were in preparation or instigation of such acts. Another Regulation which was modified was that which forbade anyone to impair the working or movement of vehicles, vessels, machinery or apparatus intended for the use of the Services. There were objections that this regulation could be used against strikers (which some MPs thought was a good thing) and an exception was made to persons taking part in legitimate strike action. In fact, despite calls to 'pull together' for the good of the war effort, strikes were never banned or effectively controlled and a number of strikes were called during the war notwithstanding the nation's perilous position.

Other Defence Regulations which affected the police included those dealing with evacuation (Reg.21), billeting (Reg.22), lighting (Reg.24), clearing premises in the vicinity of an unexploded bomb (Reg.25) and restrictions on firearms and explosives (Reg. 34). This latter regulation had near tragic consequences in Southport when a large quantity of fireworks stored in the police station 'for the duration' were accidently set alight and entirely destroyed, causing considerable damage to the building and injuring two officers. The use of 'sirens, hooters, whistles, rattles, bells, horns, gongs or similar instruments' was prohibited, as was the flying of kites, model aircraft and balloons. The use of rattles was restricted to giving warning of gas attack and the ringing of hand-bells meant a gas 'all clear'. The latter restriction probably signalled the definitive end of the muffin man. Police whistles, as we saw earlier, were used to supplement sirens in giving warning of imminent air raids and a pensioner in Fareham became an early victim of this prohibition. Involved in a bitter dispute and feeling in need of police protection he blew a whistle, causing women to rush about screaming and 200 troops being ordered to take shelter. The continued existence of a privileged class can be gauged from the fact that the authorities warned Lord Brocket's agent that the blowing of whistles by beaters during a pheasant shoot 'should be kept to the minimum'. To begin with the ringing of church bells was exempt from this regulation but a second order did not specifically exclude church bells with the result that the police in some areas imposed a ban on ringing them. However, the confusion was finally resolved in June 1940 when the ringing of church bells was expressly proscribed, and their use reserved for warning of invasion. One 70 year old rector in Lincolnshire was blissfully unaware of the prohibition and was sentenced to a month in jail for ringing his bell. He later appealed and was released after spending 12 days 'inside'.

Regulation 42 gave chief constables the power to close premises which were being used for certain undesirable purposes or, in certain circumstances, clubs and premises used for entertainment, amusement, games or sport. Regulation 79 required anyone finding anything apparently dropped from an aircraft or any missile, to hand it to or report it to the police. This caused a lot of problems for the police, not least being the recognition of various items and what should be done with them. Michael Wise recalls how, as a young schoolboy playing in a field in Kent, he was delighted one day to find a trench covered in corrugated iron. Inside there were several parts of a Messerschmitt ME109, some of which he gleefully gathered to add to his own collection. However, he abandoned any further search when he saw a 250lb HE bomb (young boys in those days had an extensive knowledge of arms and ammunition). He reported his find to Ashford police station where he was taken to a store of anti-personnel bombs, in order that he might identify what he had found. He had great difficulty in convincing the station officer that what he had found was an ordinary high explosive bomb – a munition which was not represented in the police collection. Discretion proving the better part of valour, young Michael never went back to look at the cache and has no knowledge of what happened to it.

In the interests of morale, a further regulation (39BA) created the offence of publishing any statement or report likely to cause alarm or despondency. All cases under this particular regulation had to be reported to the Director of Public Prosecutions and many prosecutions did, in fact, result.

Other provisions of the Defence Regulations were incorporated into the Official Secrets Act, such as :

* Personation of a police officer or an officer in the service of the government or making or supplying any military or similar badge or uniform (Reg.1);
* Aiding the enemy or sabotage (Reg.2);
* Passing on information which might be useful to the enemy (Reg.3);
* Aiding or communicating with persons believed to be assisting the enemy (Reg.4);
* Taking photographs in a Restricted Area. It was also an offence to take pictures or make sketches of military equipment, vessels, aircraft, bomb damage, camps, oil stores, reservoirs and gasometers as well as of 'an assembly of persons... any injured person... any riotous or disorderly assembly...' (Reg.5);

Loitering near premises, vehicles, vessels or aircraft in His Majesty's Service was also forbidden and there was concern that this power might be used against young women hanging around military establishments for their sweethearts or to pick up a serviceman. The *Police Review* also suggested that its readers should not use these emergency regulations to expel courting couples from air raid shelters);

* Making signals prejudicial to the security of the realm (Reg.7);
* The unauthorised use of wireless telegraphy apparatus or carrier pigeons (Regs. 8 and 9).

The jittery state of the country in 1940 meant that the police were very much occupied in dealing with reports of illicit radio transmitters, or alleged signals being given to the enemy – invariably false alarms but made with good intent. The public in general were quick to report anything they regarded as suspicious – a marked change from the usual Englishman's attitude of keeping his nose out of anything which did not directly concern him. Richard Crane, whom we met earlier, had his attention drawn, in 1940, to a man in a foreign uniform who was taking photographs in the vicinity of Folkestone Harbour. The photographer, who was accompanied by an Englishwoman, proved to be a French naval officer on leave who claimed to be taking photos of the fishermen. Since he did not have a permit to take pictures of this kind, the policeman seized the film.

Much of the south and east coasts were designated 'Defence Areas' whilst specific vulnerable places were deemed 'Protected Places' or 'Protected Areas' (later augmented by the designation of 'Regulated Areas' for military training). People were forbidden to travel to Defence areas for the purpose of holiday or pleasure and only certain categories of persons were deemed authorised to enter and remain in a Defence area. These included those having genuine business in the area, those attending weddings or funerals or visiting sick or aged relatives, those visiting persons in HM Forces, persons returning home after working away or visiting their holiday home to carry out essential repairs or maintenance, as well as cricket and football teams (but no other sport!). All train arrivals were met and the passengers checked and, although the police had no power to permit or to forbid entry into a designated Defence Area, persons coming into it were subjected to searching enquiries as to their business and any persons there without good cause could be removed or prosecuted.

R Douglas Brown[12] describes how the whole of the East Anglian coastal belt, from Southend to King's Lynn, was declared a Defence Area in 1940. Efforts to have all but essential workers evacuated from the whole area were rejected by the War Cabinet and the effect was simply to prohibit holiday makers from entering an area extending 20 miles inland from the Wash to the Thames. As might be expected, there were some bizarre, typically British results. When a Norfolk girl, living and working outside the area, went to visit her parents she was told by the police that she would have to leave at once (a decision later overturned). Meanwhile, it was agreed that gentlemen sportsmen should be admitted to take part in shoots on the large estates, once more emphasising how the regulations could be interpreted to suit a certain section of the community.

East Anglia was not, of course, alone in being made a Defence Area; in fact the whole of the coastline, up to 20 miles inland, from the Wash to Rye in Sussex was so designated in June 1940. This area was later extended northwards to Berwick-on-Tweed and westwards to Dorset and parts of South Wales. The enforcement of these orders varied considerably from place to place. There were many tales of unauthorised visitors being met by the police and escorted onto the next train out of the area but Norman Longmate records how a Glasgow woman, eager to see her recently-torpedoed son after two years absence, found no difficulty in entering Portsmouth, although she was caught by a random check on identity cards while queuing for the sale of bomb-damaged goods. She was ordered by a policeman to leave Portsmouth at once but no-one bothered her and she stayed another two days[13].

In all Defence Areas sea-front hotels were requisitioned, machine guns sprouted from piers, bathing was prohibited, barbed wire sprung up everywhere and curfews were imposed. Roads adjacent to the sea-front were patrolled at night by soldiers with fixed bayonets. Policemen on night duty, going about their normal business, were often startled by a voice calling out, 'Who goes there?' and then being confronted by two or three soldiers with their rifles at the ready. One long-suffering policeman was heard to reply, 'Put that bloody thing away before you kill somebody' – a not unnatural reaction since many of these soldiers were young, inexperienced and often scared stiff of the totally dark, strange environment in which they found themselves.

Some Regional Commissioners even went so far as to impose a form of curfew in 1940, directing that 'No person shall be out of doors between one hour after sunset and one hour before sunrise without such cause as will satisfy any police officer in uniform, or any member of HM Forces in uniform and being both urgent and sufficient'. Such restrictions seldom lasted more than a few months. Population movements were monitored by the police and a survey was made of all civilians still residing in the coastal areas with a view to their enforced evacuation should the need arise.

In the event, only in the more stringently controlled 'Protected Areas' were the regulations really troublesome and by early 1944 these included virtually the whole of East Suffolk and large part of all the other south-eastern counties. Identity cards had to be carried in these areas at all times and cameras, field glasses and telescopes were forbidden without a permit. One young unmarried girl living and working in London found she could still spend her holidays at her mother's house in Sheringham, Norfolk, since this was still deemed to be her home, whilst her married sister had to get police permission. Even then, the latter's stay was restricted and, during one visit, the local policeman came to the house to tell her that her time was up and that she must go home. Later on many areas were designated 'Regulated Areas' into which entry was prohibited without a permit but even this had its amusing side. One courting couple returning from a meadow to their car were stopped by the police and told sternly, 'You've been in a prohibited area.' 'Oh no he hasn't,' said the young lady indignantly!

The compilation of a National Register and the issue of registration cards were necessary features in the organisation of the country for war. Without them the whole business of call-ups and rationing would have been unworkable. It was also of immense value as a security measure. The 1939 National Registration Act provided the necessary authorisation for the compilation of the Register and returns were collected from all places in which people passed the night of 29 September 1939. The police had the task of collecting particulars of tramps, vagrants and others without a fixed abode, or those who had elected to spend the night other than at their home.

Section 6 of the Act provided for the issue of National Identity

Cards to the whole of the population. In addition to the normal, buff coloured card, a special green card, complete with photograph and all the details normally to be found on a passport, was issued under the Official Secrets Act for those who had a need to enter prohibited places while a similar, blue card was issued to members of the Civil Defence General Services. A special buff identity card, with the endorsement 'Police' was issued to all police officers, including special constables. A constable in uniform (and certain other official persons) had the power to demand the production of identity cards but, curiously enough, there was no penalty for failure to do so provided the offender produced it at a police station within two clear days. A special form, NR/HO/1, was provided for issue to persons unable to produce their card on demand.

Road blocks were set up and manned by Local Defence Volunteers, empowered to examine the identity cards of all travellers, including initially the police. These part-time soldiers, especially in rural areas, were not backward in exercising this right to treat the local constable as a suspect and the police, who had taken on a great many additional responsibilities in connection with the enrolment and equipping of the Local Defence Volunteers, felt themselves ill-rewarded for their pains. Eventually a compromise was reached. The LDV was still empowered to compel a police officer to prove his identity but the police officers was given similar powers in respect of the LDV. Although this compromise, worthy of Lewis Carroll, might be expected to increase the friction between the two organisations, it does appear to have worked satisfactorily in most cases.

It was not only the overenthusiastic Home Guard (as the LDV were later to be called) which caused difficulties; sometimes one's own police colleagues could make things difficult, as Constable Gardner from Essex discovered. As the proud father of the bride, he was travelling with his daughter and her two page boys to the church in Upminster in the summer of 1941 when the car, resplendent in all its wedding ribbon and horseshoes, was stopped by a zealous policeman who demanded the production of the occupants' identity cards. At first Constable Gardner suspected a stunt pulled by mischievous colleagues but discovered that the other policeman, who did not know him, was in deadly earnest. He apparently thought it perfectly feasible for the Germans, in the guise of a middle-aged man, a young girl and two schoolboys, to be be moving about the countryside disguised as a wedding party.

All in all, however, although a good many stolen or forged cards found their way into circulation, the issue of Identity Cards was seen by the police as useful in tracing and identifying deserters, call-up dodgers and common criminals. Indeed, their continued use after the war would have been welcomed by the police. However, the public were not entirely at one with the police in this respect and it is interesting to see that, even in 1944, letters were being written to 'The Times' deploring the fact that identity cards were apparently going to remain valid until 1960 and decrying this threat to civil liberties. Other correspondents rehearsed the well-known riposte that only those with something to hide need fear the requirement to have some form of official identification. And the debate goes on fifty years later!

In 1940, the very real threat of invasion made the spreading of rumours highly undesirable. The offence of 'Spreading statements relating to war matters likely to cause alarm' was used to combat the propagation of false information, while the offence of 'Giving information likely to be useful to the enemy' covered cases where the unpleasant story was in fact true. The offence under the 1936 Public Order Act of using threatening, abusive or insulting words and behaviour likely to provoke a breach of the peace could also be invoked in suitable cases. Public houses, the focus of good comradeship and conversation now became security minded and the Morning Advertiser reported that 50,000 inns and licensed premises were co-operating to suppress the 'Chatterbugs' and that 'many thousands' had given useful information to the police.

As might be expected, this opportunity to 'grass' on ones neighbour was gleefully exploited by those who had an axe to grind or a supposed slight to avenge. Many of the reports came from harbourers of old grudges, from haters of Irishmen or Jews, xenophobes, political extremists, pompous petty officials as well as those who were just paranoid. Unfortunately, there seems ample evidence to suggest that, all too often, the police and the judiciary failed to use their commonsense in assessing the value of these reports, as the reader will see when we cover this aspect in more detail in a later chapter.

The Mass Observation organisation collated details of a number of prosecutions for the former offence, covering such diverse subjects as Allied military movements (35), fifth columnists (31), air raids (18),

German military movements (17), parachutists (15), Allied VIPs (14), Compulsory measures to be enforced (14), ARP and gas attacks (13), new defence measures (12), foreign aid for the Allies from US, Turkey, Russia, etc. (10), radio broadcasts (9), spies (8), suspicious nuns (8), new weapons (7), peace declarations (5). Many of these rumours were spread by people simply trying to appear important, coupled with a natural tendency to exaggerate for the sake of effect. This could prove irksome to the more rational listener such as the writer of a letter to *Woman's Own* on 16 July 1943, who asked:

> *How can I stop gossip? In a recent air raid on our town the casualty list was three ... but I hear women telling the most ghastly stories of hundreds of people killed and they seem annoyed when I burst in and tell them to go and look at the list in the Town Hall.*

One aspect of the air raid precautions had an immediate and universal effect: the blackout. In anticipation of the outbreak of war, tests were carried out as early as the spring of 1938, during which full blackout precautions were practised. Chief Constables issued requests that '... all windows, skylights, glass doors, etc in private houses, shops, garages, factories, etc may, in the area and during the period indicated, be completely screened so that no light is visible from the outside. All illuminated advertisements, signs and external lights of all kinds should be extinguished. Vehicles on the roads should only use frosted side and rear lights unless shaded by one thickness of tissue paper'. Once war was declared, orders couched in similar but more mandatory terms were issued. Even hand torches had to be covered with a paper filter to reduce the light emitted (although many police officers proved loth to enforce the law against the ordinary working man hurrying home from work who was perhaps a little careless with his torch; in the event the shortage of batteries did more to ensure the observance of the regulations than any police action.

But, all in all, these lighting restrictions had a very real and dramatic effect on everyone. The blackout was probably the greatest single source of discontent, at least in the months before the Blitz. In a Gallup Poll published in January 1940, no fewer than 18% of the interviewees claimed to have suffered injury as a direct or indirect result of the blackout. Most serious were the road accidents which we shall be looking at in a later chapter but injuries were also incurred by tripping over the kerb or walking into obstacles such as the surface shelters which had sprung up in many streets. Anyone who ventured outside at night experienced at first hand the physical sensation of blindness and those who lived through the period are unlikely to forget the nightly irritation of blacking out the house, using paper, cloth or specially made boards. For the owners of shops, hotels and other public buildings the task was extremely onerous and expensive.

The cry, 'Put that light out!' was soon to be heard across the land, sometimes uttered in an official manner by a warden or police officer, sometimes a trifle officiously by an ordinary passer by who felt it his duty to see that the regulations were properly obeyed. The cry seldom specified which light and where it was to be found, so all those within earshot hastened to check that their precautions were adequate and were not the cause of this peremptory order. Old ladies tumbled from their beds to look for badly drawn curtains while angry men complained vociferously about the disturbance of their rest. Nevertheless, the cry continued like a cracked gramophone record until the offending light was doused. There is no doubt that the majority of the citizens of the United Kingdom took the blackout very seriously, at least in the early stages of the war, and anyone who contravened it would get very little sympathy from his fellows. Indeed, blatant breaches of the regulations were enough to start a small riot.

It was primarily, of course, the police who had to enforce the blackout regulations. For once, the man on the beat had the assistance of a new colleague – the warden – but, whilst a warden could request the extinguishing of a light, only the police had the power to order a light to be extinguished or dimmed. Both the police and the wardens became thoroughly unpopular for their excessive zeal in tracking down minor breaches of the regulations – an unpopularity which was to endure until the bombing raids brought about a better feeling of camaraderie and mutual suffering. The wardens still had very little to do and their paid idleness annoyed the rest of the population – an annoyance which was aggravated by their preoccupation with breaches of the blackout. In Oxford alone, in October 1939, there were 40 cases brought before the courts in one week, a city on which, as it happened, not a single bomb was to fall. A girl in Bournemouth, a town filled with evacuated businessmen and wealthy refugees, absent-mindedly switched on the light before pulling her bedroom curtains. Instantly the doorbell rang and a policeman pushed past her, taking the stairs two at a time, and switched off the light. She was subsequently fined five shilling for this offence. Even the clergy found their Christian charity sorely tried and a rector from near Bletchley, challenged for showing a light visible 20 yards away, shouted at the special constable who had brought it to his attention, 'Go away you brute, you scoundrel', an outburst which cost him a £3 fine. A Walthamstow man, returning home from performing his ARP duty, found two special constables on their hands and knees outside his front door, discussing whether the light showing was too bright, so engrossed in their work that they failed to notice when he joined them on the doorstep. A Yorkshire farmer was approached by the police about a bright light which appeared over his farm each night and had to point out that this was in fact the evening star. Elsewhere, complaints about lights showing turned out to be the reflection of the full moon in a fully blacked-out window.

It was not always easy for the law-enforcement authorities, either. A Shropshire special constable who was also the village grocer, found that the first five people he had to report were customers of his shop. One of these,a motorist who had driven down the main street with his headlights full on, threatened the special that, if he were booked, his wife would never come into his shop again. Fortunately the special lived up to the best traditions of the British police and did his duty 'without fear, favour, malice or ill-will' and promptly reported the obstreperous motorist with obstruction and the use of foul language.

It is possible that, on occasions, the police and wardens were more in search of company to relieve the monotony of their long nightly vigil than seeking promotion. The night sister at a Nottingham hospital was puzzled when, night after night, the same policeman came to complain about a non-existent chink of light around 4 am. The mystery was solved when he enquired, rather pointedly, 'You do make a pot of tea about now, don't you?'.

Chief constables were appointed 'Outside Lighting Officers' and could authorise a certain amount of outside lighting. These included any street lighting and that required at railway stations, wharves, shipyards and similar installations, described as 'aids to movement'. In East Yorkshire, the chief constable decreed that such lighting should be blue in colour and not exceeding 25 watts. The bulb should be shrouded so that there was only a narrow shaft of light, directed towards the ground. Ted Maidment describes how, as a young constable in that force,

> *I would use one of the Jowett vans used for ARP work loaded up with boxes of blue bulbs and as many 'Nutalls' mint tins as I could gather together. I bored a one inch diameter hole in the bottom of each tin and pained the tin matt black inside and out. These I fitted to the bulb socket and that completed the project. It was no use leaving it to the people on the spot to do this; it was urgent and had to be done then, not sometime, perhaps. I remember fixing one of these lamps outside the offices of the East Yorkshire Bus depot in Bridlington. They never took it down after the war and it remained in place for years and was always painted matt black, even when everything else was painted in the bus company's colours of yellow and white.*

Large blocks of flats or tenements also presented particular problems. How did one locate in the long winding passages of a 10 storey building containing 600 or 700 separate flats the bright beam of light so plainly visible from the street below? A rather dramatic instance occurred in Soho in the winter of 1940-41 when the street was suddenly brilliantly illuminated by a large neon sign on the building housing the offices of a film company. This beacon caused much excitement and an indignant crowd soon assembled and angry voices raised. But the light blazed on. When the police arrived they found that the building was unoccupied so they had to break in, only to find themselves confronted with a complex electrical system. There was only one solution; cut the wires and go on cutting wires until the light was extinguished. The cause of this dramatic incident proved to be an electrician who had unwittingly reconnected the automatic timing device used in peacetime and which had been by-passed for over a year.

Despite all these efforts, when the chief constable of Portsmouth was taken up in an aeroplane over his city one night in the autumn of 1941, he was amazed at the amount of light which was showing, especially from inadequately obscured skylights. Letters to *The Times* in the early days of the war commented that:

> *Many "lights o' London" are still showing despite the drastic blackout regulations. From the roof garden of my house – one*

81

of the highest in the West End – .... I still see many top-storey lights which are difficult to detect from the street... In the interests of every Londoner I invite any police officer to visit my roof garden after blackout time to locate some of the offenders (9.9.1939).

Such was the importance afforded these regulations that some officers found they were becoming obsessed with their strict enforcement. The tale is told in London of two policemen friends, known respectively as Tubby and Lofty, who had occasion to search a bombed house in which it was believed the owners were trapped. Lofty undertook to examine what remained of the upper floors, while Tubby busied himself burrowing in the lower regions. Eventually Lofty came down to rejoin his companion who cried, 'Blimey, Lofty, you've left the lights on up there'. So up went Lofty again to switch off the offending light, only to realise on reaching ground level once again that they were surrounded by blazing buildings which completely outshone the pale glimmer from the 40 watt bulb he had struggled to extinguish.

It was, in fact, the enforcement of these particular regulations which led to the first police casualty of the war. In September, 1939, with the war only a matter of hours old, Constable Southworth of the Metropolitan Police was on duty in Harley Street when he saw a light shining from the top of a building. Unable to get any response from the occupant, he decided to climb up the front of the building to extinguish the light himself. He successfully gained access to the building by climbing onto a balcony and smashing a window. However, he was unable to get any further due to the interior doors being securely locked. Undeterred, he went back onto the balcony and began to continue his climb towards the fourth floor where the light was still shining out. He had nearly climbed as far as the fourth floor when he lost his grip and fell to his death.

Other police officers adopted less perilous means of enforcing the blackout when they were unable to rouse the occupant, or where the premises were unoccupied. In Winchester, Sergeant Rice made a small hole in the corner of the window frame and, borrowing an air gun, shot out the offending light bulb. This idea was copied by Constable Banks in Hastings who shot out two bulbs in a butcher's shop via a ventilator.

A constable in Folkestone, lacking an airgun, resorted to paper and paste and, climbing a borrowed ladder, successfully blacked out the window with these materials. Others, less circumspect, forced double-locked doors, causing extensive damage.

Sometimes the enforcement of the blackout regulations proved dangerous because of other factors. In Worthing, the police attending a house where a light was showing had hot water poured over them by the lady occupant. They eventually had to force an entry to put the light out. The offender was fined £25 – a substantial sum in those days. In Grays (Essex) in early 1941, three constables were taking a body to the mortuary on a hand ambulance when they were mown down by an Army lorry, killing one of the constables. Their only illumination was one torch and another constable pushing his cycle on the offside of the cart. At the subsequent inquest, the Coroner commented that 'This contraption, which must have come out of a museum, was being perambulated in a most improper manner'. Other policemen demonstrated a respect for law and order way above and beyond the call of duty, as exemplified by Inspector Tom Arnold of Nottingham who, being told by a passer-by that he was showing a light from his bedroom at the police station, promptly reported himself and was subsequently fined 10/- (50p) by the court.

Other offenders were not so public-spirited although their excuses deserved full marks for originality. An architect in Woking claimed a starling had flown into his house and switched on the light. Another man claimed that gun fire had caused an ornament to tilt and switch on the light. A Manchester employer pleaded that a conscientious objector employee had refused to put up the blackout boards. A Birmingham man claimed not to realise that he had to black out the back as well as the front of his house. But if some citizens were cavalier in their attitude to the blackout, others were not slow in condemning their fellows whom they suspected of using lights of some form or another to signal to the enemy and this became especially marked once the air raids started. Hitler's airborne navigators appeared to be credited with supernatural powers in their ability to pin point a target from the single torch or a cigarette but no amount of ridicule could prevent such allegations being made and a foreign resident of Kensington was accused of making signals to enemy aircraft, the evidence being based on the porter's statement that he had been seen on his balcony, smoking a cigar in a curious manner, '...

puffing hard to make a big light and pointing it at the sky'. When there was a partial relaxation of the blackout towards the end of 1941, public opinion was very mixed (it was finally lifted in September, 1944).

If the blackout was a major inconvenience to the residents of the British Isles, it was even more traumatic for the many foreign troops who began to arrive on these shores. Many a Canadian soldier, for example, was maimed or killed on the British roads in motor accidents. The motorcycle dispatch riders were especially vulnerable and men spoke grimly of Brookwood Cemetery as 'the DR's holding unit'. Soldiers, confused by the total darkness, stepped out of trains on the wrong side, often sustaining severe injury. Ralph Ingersoll, an American living in London in the early days of the war, wrote:

> *My hotel in London had a black, revolving door. I think I shall always remember the sensation of its spinning me out into the dark. One second you are in a cheerful, normally lighted hotel lobby ... next – just as if you had fallen through a trap door – you are in pitch black... Your eyes are unused to such complete darkness and see nothing. You put your hands out and you feel – outside most hotel doors – sandbags. Or the coats of unidentified people. That first night the three aviators and I stood together for a few minutes getting used to it. My memory is of the clatter and echo of people walking ... Presently the footsteps made some sense. Clearly there was a squad of soldiers in hobnailed boots somewhere about, some women walking slowly on high heels, some men moving briskly. Swish! Swish! That would be two motor cars passing. The motors had hardly any lights – one headlight blacked out, the other fitted with a slotted hood that threw a tiny flashlight beam a few feet ahead of it on the pavement. And red tail lights. But popped out into blackout for the first time, these lights didn't register for a few seconds... The last day I was in England I caused a near riot because I had the window open, woke up in the middle of the night and turned the light on for 30 seconds to see what time it was... A policeman spotted the light and was for waking up the whole hotel to find out who had made it. I learned of this at breakfast the next morning without letting on...*[14]

But to the police, the biggest drawback associated with the blackout was the cover it provided for all sorts of illegal and immoral activity. Almost anything could happen in the blackout and a great deal did, especially damage to shop windows, cigarette machines etc. One constable describes how he purchased a pair of boots with crêpe soles (uncommon in those days) so that he could move around both unseen and unheard. The blackout provided cover for all sorts of escapades, some innocent, some less so. The opportunity for pranks did not escape the attention of the police, who were not adverse to a joke to relieve the curious combination of stress and boredom. In Bradford, in the early hours of the morning, a sergeant and a constable were standing between two sets of sandbags erected as buttresses against the wall of the Town Hall when they heard the sound of approaching clogs. A man accidently collided with a fire hydrant pedestal and swore loudly and articulately. The sergeant, hidden from view in the dark, imitated a female voice and called out, 'Now then, now then. If you hadn't been drinking you would have seen where you were going'. The man, still smarting and assuming his accuser to be a charwoman, grunted, 'Ya silly bitch, I'm awa' to me work!' and limped away muttering about the stupidity of the female sex.

What with the blackout and the public's fear of what the war might bring, the first few months of the war were no time to be other than British. There always had been a number of foreigners living in Great Britain – referred to officially as 'aliens' – and their number was quickly and substantially augmented by refugees from the Nazis, especially those of the Jewish faith. Prior to the war, all aliens had to be registered with the police and their admission to the country was strictly controlled. It was therefore a comparatively simple process to place further restrictions on their movements and their possession of motor vehicles or other equipment which might be used to aid the enemy, although this did add considerably to the burden placed on the police force. For one newly-appointed special constable, war duties began in the early hours of 3 September, 1939, before the official announcement of the commencement of hostilities, when he had to tour local farms in his part of Shropshire to warn German farm labourers that they must not travel further than three miles without police permission.

One problem was the fact that the policy towards aliens constantly changed, partly as a result of public pressure and partly in sympathy with the progress of the war and the advance or retirement of the threat of invasion. On the outbreak of the war a number of Germans living in Great Britain, some of whom undoubtedly had Nazi sympathies, were interned and sent to a camp in Essex. Shortly afterwards tribunals across the country began to examine the cases of all 'enemy' aliens – those of German or Austrian origin. In the first few months 37,000 enemy alien cases were heard in London alone. The tribunals sorted the subjects into three categories: 'A' for those considered positively dangerous and who must be interned; 'B' for those who should be subject to restrictions but not actually interned; and 'C' for harmless persons allowed unrestricted freedom. The latter category covered those who had lived in the country for many years and were of good character together with the many refugees who had fled across the Channel to escape Nazism.

By the spring of 1940 73,800 cases had been heard, of which under 600 were recommended for internment, being seen as a positive threat to the nation, whilst nearly 7,000 were placed in 'Category B', which implied that there remained doubts as to their certain reliability. But the vast majority – over 64,000 were placed in Category 'C', most of whom were classified as refugees. Those interned under Category 'A' were housed in the vast Olympia building in London before being moved in the autumn to the Butlin's Holiday Camp at Clacton-on-Sea. Here the camp was apparently run by the inmates themselves with a full-blooded Nazi baron being elected camp leader.

But the pendulum swung violently the other way as invasion became more likely and imminent. A general sweep up of enemy aliens was ordered in May, 1940 and it fell to the police to make the collection. Following the fall of Holland, and in response to the alarming stories of Fifth Column activities in that country brought back by the fleeing British ambassador the Netherlands, Sir Nevile Bland, the British government put aside all inhibitions and ordered that all able-bodied male Germans and Austrians between 16 and 60 living in the south-east and east of the country should be interned. Even academics were not exempt and A D F Gow describes how the Cambridge police called at the university halls of residence and took a large number of male enemy aliens by car to the Guildhall, from whence they were taken to an internment camp by bus[15]. Elsewhere in the region similar action was being taken. 16 Germans and Austrians were arrested in Norwich and a further 18 elsewhere in

Norfolk. 175 aliens were detained in Kent including a doctor in practice there. In Tunbridge Wells 20 more were rounded up, quietly and without fuss, as demonstrated by the fact that, when two men were removed from a church in the town, the officiating priest was unaware what had happened until after the service. The SU carburettor works in West Yorkshire were German owned and so provided a rich source of 'enemy' aliens. In Kent, Bunce Court, near Sittingbourne, had been the centre for International Jewry for a number of years and housed many Jewish refugees, mostly intellectuals. The males residing at this centre did not escape the great round-up and many later lost their lives on the ill-fated Arandora Star. Later, the local constable had to serve a notice on Miss Essinger, the owner, to vacate the premises (which by now only housed a number of girls and children) within 24 hours. Miss Essinger, a leading figure in the Jewish community, had friends in high places however, and the order was quickly cancelled. The occupants later left on their own accord and the house was taken over by the RAMC who built an underground dressing station there.

By the 16 May, 1940, all Category B aliens had been taken into custody and, shortly afterwards, all women in this category, with their children were similarly rounded up. They were removed, in the first instance to an unfinished housing estate at Huyton, near Liverpool, which was surrounded with barbed wire. There was no furniture or soap, towels and toilet paper were in short supply and heavy rain rapidly transformed the camp into a sea of mud. Despite the fact that most of the men were over 50 years of age and many were ailing, medical supplies were in short supply. The inflexible manner in which the regulations were enforced is illustrated by a letter to *The Times* on 17 July, 1940 :

> *... Dr X, a German official of importance with Social Democrat views, left the service and came to this country soon after Hitler attained power. He sent his son to the Leys School, Cambridge. The father gave no occasion for suspicion. The son, who had only lived in Germany for 11 months since his birth, obtained a scholarship ... at Brasenose College, Oxford. The father was recently interned near Liverpool. The son, who was waiting to go up to Oxford, was first interned there and then sent to the Isle of Man. With him was another 17 year old boy from the same school. The headmaster ... made application to the Home Office asking for*

reconsideration. On July 4th, both boys were shipped to Canada. The father, now interned, asked if he might be sent to join the boy. He was told that his ultimate destination was not fixed. He might be sent to Australia. He is still in the camp.

As the situation in Europe worsened in the days leading up to Dunkirk, chief constables were informed that they could now intern any Category 'C' alien whose reliability seemed doubtful, while Italy's entry into the war on the side of the Germans created an extensive new category of enemy alien. There were around 19,000 Italians living in Britain, most of whom were involved with the catering industry, from West End restaurants to ice cream parlours. From being well-liked and accepted members of the community, they became overnight the target for a growing number of xenophobes. Several hundred were sent to what was probably the worst of the quickly improvised camps – a derelict cotton mill in Bury, Lancashire. According to Angus Calder, '...*it was filthy; its roof let in the rain. Food was bad, sanitation appalling. Some blankets were verminous. Rats scuttled among the remains of the mill machinery*'[16]. However, it has to be admitted that the police were able to take advantage of the new requirements to detain a number of Italians who were strongly suspected of criminal activities but against whom there was insufficient evidence to bring formal charges: petty gangsters, pimps, race course thugs and others of that ilk.

At first, public opinion was firmly behind this policy but, as news of the treatment of these aliens became known, this changed and became one of regret, especially when the *Arandora Star* was torpedoed whilst carrying over 1,000 aliens to Canada, many of whom lost their lives. The victims included an Italian merchant who had spent all his adult life in Scotland and whose family were serving in the British forces and who loathed Mussolini; Zangiacomi and Maggi of the Ritz hotel and Zavattoni from the Savoy, as well as a prominent engineer, P M Salerni, who had been doing important work on behalf of the British aircraft industry and who had lived in Britain most of his life, were other victims.

Bowing to public pressure, the War Cabinet agreed to the release of all aliens who were known to be actively hostile to the Axis regimes and, at the same time, responsibility for the internment camps was transferred from the War Office to the Home Office. The biggest concentration of these was now .on the Isle of Man which had become virtually a prison island. In due course the police became involved, at least partially, in the running of these camps and the *Police Review* of 8 May, 1942, reported that the commandant of the Fascist Camp at Peel was a Metropolitan Police superintendent.

At the same time as the Category B aliens were interned, the movements of all remaining aliens were restricted. They were forbidden to possess a bicycle or motor vehicle, boat or aircraft without police permission and they were confined to their place of residence between 10.30 pm and 6 am (12 midnight and 6 am in London). These restrictions were sometimes enforced with what can only be described as desperate severity. For example, a female servant was prosecuted for leaving her place of residence during an air raid to go to a shelter. The police told her that she should take shelter under the stairs, although they agreed that she could leave the house if it caught fire!

For the police, things were also complicated by changes of status. Friendly aliens suddenly became enemy aliens (as when Italy entered the war on the side of Nazi Germany); groups or individuals previously restricted became derestricted and vice versa. Restrictions were placed on places of residence and on the possession of certain articles such as cameras, cars, field glasses, maps, wireless sets, etc. It was the job of senior police officers to grant exemptions in specified circumstances. As we have seen, certain parts of the country were placed 'out of bounds' to aliens and those living in these areas had to be evicted, again with the help of the police.

Although the general internment policy was relaxed as time went on, the process of internment continued throughout the war in what were seen as justifiable cases. Leonard Winter, the detective inspector from West Riding, had to escort a German lady from Yorkshire to Holloway prison in London at a later stage in the war, taking along his wife as unpaid chaperone. As it was not possible to return to the north the same day, he attempted to find a hotel room in London but they all claimed to be full. At one hotel, having just been refused a room, he was infuriated when some GIs arrived with their 'floozies' and were immediately given rooms. Only by 'kicking up a stink' as he describes it was he able to get a room.

Some readers may be surprised to learn that, even during the darkest days of the war, there were still civilian airlines flying in to Britain from neutral countries such as Switzerland, Portugal and Sweden, many containing some of the more affluent refugees from the German advances. The Dutch national airline, KLM, had a twice weekly flight from Lisbon to Bristol and there were similar flights from Sweden to Leuchars air base in Scotland. On arrival all passengers were closely questioned as to their origins and intentions and any 'enemy' aliens were held for full questioning, usually in London, where they had to be taken under police escort. The men were mostly taken to one of the male prisons in the capital. The women were taken to Balham where a secure house had been set up. The refugees who used this route included some well-known names, including one reputed to be carrying valuable securities valued at over a million pounds. It is claimed that a spy was deliberately allowed into the country via this route so that his activities could be kept under observation before being eventually rounded up, tried and sentenced to death.

Some aliens entered the country by less orthodox routes. Eric St Johnston tells how one of his constables, Francis Cowan, came across a naked man standing in the gateway to a field one dark night in May, 1941, while he was cycling home. The man, Patrick Murphy, told the officer that he had come from Southern Ireland to Liverpool, evading all the stringent checks and restrictions, intending to get a job. In Liverpool he had met up with some other Irishmen who said they were going to London where they could find work for him too. On the way, Murphy recognised one of his companions as a man with a record of violence and he eventually plucked up courage to ask what job they were intending to do. He was told that they planned to loot bombed buildings, using him as a look-out. Murphy protested that he would do no such thing, whereupon a pistol was produced, the car stopped and Murphy was told to strip. He was pushed out of the car stark naked and had to take cover in the field where he was found. As an illegal immigrant, he was held in custody before being sent back to Ireland. Every effort was made to check his story but without success. The violent man was identified as being known to the police but no trace of him was ever found in this country. The truth or otherwise of Murphy's tale will probably never be known.

Although most of the restrictions were aimed at those aliens who might reasonably be regarded as possible spies or saboteurs, even 'friendly' aliens, such as Americans, were not free of restrictions.

They, too, had to register with the police (as they had before the war) and carry an Alien's Registration Certificate. Ralph Ingersoll, the American journalist described his experience of the registration process in his book[17]:

> *I asked the liveried (hotel) doorman and the taxi driver whom he called where the nearest police station was – or the one that aliens should register at. This sounded like a simple question, but it wasn't. It appeared that the right police station had been bombed out the day before yesterday... the traffic officer on the corner confirmed the bombing out but did not know where the police station had gone... the station that had been hit had been a new one ...(and) he suggested that possibly they had gone back to the original quarters. He proved to be correct. The place of registration was no ordinary police station but temporary quarters consisting of a long counter behind which six or eight extremely busy policemen sat facing equally busy and much more anxious aliens ... Behind the policemen were tier upon tier of files over which half a dozen more policemen were climbing ... A mourners' bench ran along the remaining wall and I was seated at one end to await my turn... I was almost at the top of the line when the first air raid came. I did not hear the siren ... A policeman from the street simply stuck his head in the door and blew loudly on a police whistle. I jumped a mile. The room was suddenly still. The sergeant in the middle of the counter chanted in a monotonous voice without looking up: "An air raid alarm has been sounded. There is a shelter underneath this building. The man at the door will show you the way to it. If you do not choose to go to the shelter we will carry on". Nobody went. ... What the police got [from me] were the particulars of my passport, where I intended to live, what I intended to do and where I intended to go. What I got was a small cardboard folder about 3" by 4" in which my picture was presently pasted ... and another, slightly smaller cardboard folder called an identity card, and a food-ration book.*

But with the fall of Dunkirk in June 1940, the situation became increasingly grave as the nation awaited fearfully the next stage – the invasion of Britain.

4. Waiting for "Operation Sealion"

By the summer of 1940, most of Europe had fallen to the irresistible German army and air force. Of the Allies, only Britain and her Empire remained and the mother country was under extreme pressure. There seemed little doubt that it was only a matter of time before an invading horde would set foot on the shores of England and the nation braced itself for the onslaught.

The Chiefs of Staff stated that there was no guarantee that the country could hold out as long as '... *the present quasi-peacetime organisation continued.'* They advocated that the country should become a fortress and, in particular (i) operational control over the police and other civil defence forces should be removed from the local authorities and vested in the Ministry of Home Security and exercised via the Regional Commissioners; (ii) all enemy aliens and doubtful persons should be rounded up; (iii) in order not to impede troop movements, there should be a prohibition on evacuations and the movement of refugees. As we saw in the last chapter, the second recommendation was largely adopted and, although the first recommendation was not entirely followed, there was a measure of rationalisation of the police service, including the amalgamation of a number of forces and a measure of control was exercised by the police liaison officer at the Regional Headquarters.

A code word, 'Cromwell', was chosen to indicate that an invasion was imminent but, in the event, many could not remember whether the code word meant that the invasion had started or was about to take place. On one occasion when the word was passed, troops began blowing up bridges, the Home Guard rang the church bells and general confusion reigned for some time, before order was eventually restored.

Letters to the press suggested the enrolment of the motoring organisations, the AA and the RAC, to help to counter invading parachutists, apparently ignoring the fact that most of these patrolmen had been, or would shortly be called up to serve in the armed forces.

One likely area for a seaborne landing was the flat area on the Kent and Sussex coast known as the Romney Marsh. Constable Bert Ayers who policed a large part of the Marshes at the time recalls attending a highly confidential demonstration of an anti-invasion device which consisted of pouring oil onto the surface of the sea and igniting it as the enemy approached. Such was the secrecy surrounding this demonstration, which was attended by Winston Churchill and other VIPs, that not even the local fire brigade were informed, the demonstration team bringing their own firefighters.

This was not the only secret to which PC Ayers was privy. On one occasion, prowling through Ruckinge Woods on the look-out for poachers, he came across what he describes as a truncated tree which had been made to pivot, thus providing access to a small chamber underneath. He reported his find to the police emergency department at Ashford but was later told to forget what he had seen and never to mention it. He assumes it was for use by resistance groups after the invasion.

It is not surprising that the nation as a whole was extremely jumpy at this time, every unusual event being associated with the invasion. Reports of parachutists were widespread and a report received by the police in Bangor, North Wales was treated very seriously. The inspector attended in person and confirmed that there was a large white billowing parachute at the first floor of the local hotel. Reinforcements were rushed to the scene, only to find that the 'parachutist' was a very large lady who, trying to get into her room without disturbing the proprietors of the hotel, had become firmly stuck. There were red faces all round, especially when the unfortunate lady was recognised as Tessie O'Shea, the entertainer.

All over the country, inexperienced watchers were convinced that the white puffs of anti-aircraft fire were billowing parachutes while perfectly natural phenomena were seen as something sinister, as George Lewis, a former constable with the Worcester City Police recalls:

> *On a cold winter's day, towards the end of 1943, I stood in a shop doorway trying to find some protection from a bitterly cold wind. It was about 10.30 am and too cold for a visit from my sergeant. As I stood gloomily contemplating my sanity in joining the police force, I was disturbed from my reverie by a patrol car pulling up with a squeal of brakes on the other side of the road. An inspector was sitting in the front passenger*

seat with a constable driving and another sitting in the back of the vehicle. They all appeared somewhat agitated, waving their arms in my direction and shouting and beckoning me to join them.

As I ambled across the road to find out what all the excitement was about, the rear door suddenly opened and a voice said, 'Get in, you bloody fool', the door being slammed on my ankle before I had time to gain the seat and the car sped off at high speed across the river bridge. Cursing with the pain, I timidly asked the inspector what it was all about. 'Parachutists', he snarled, and then added, 'Old Powick Bridge'. This bridge figured largely in the Civil War of 1651 and spans the River Teme on the south-west side of the city. On our arrival there we were met by an employee of the nearby laundry.

'False alarm', he said, laconically. 'A chap called at the laundry and asked us to call the police but they weren't parachutists; there's the culprits'. Looking in the direction of his pointing finger we saw four large white swans serenely gliding on the waters of the Teme. 'Bit of a wild goose chase, Sir', I ventured. The inspector's reply was unprintable.

However serious the situation, the British are noted for their penchant for black humour and the policeman is no different from the rest.

In the early days of the war, no clear role had been defined for the police in the event of invasion. In the towns, the concentration was on the action to be taken in the event of air attack, while in the country it was widely assumed that the peacetime triumvirate of policeman, doctor and vicar would look after the villagers, whatever happened. Gradually a more systematic organisation was devised and major towns were designated 'Nodal Points'. Those which came under Class A were expected to hold out against the invader for seven days; those in Classes B and C for two days. It was decided that an invasion triumvirate should be set up in each Nodal Point, consisting of a representative of the military (often an officer in the Home Guard), a senior police officer and a representative of the local authority. In Kent, the Category A Nodal Points were Canterbury, Chatham, Deal, Dover, Faversham, Folkestone, Maidstone, Margate, Ramsgate,

Sittingbourne, Tunbridge Wells and Tonbridge. Various Home Office Circulars stressed that, in the event of an invasion, the most important function of the police in and around the area of operations, would probably be to control any movement of the civil population, to prevent them from hampering the armed force. Forces were to arrange to have public address systems and motorcycle patrols and messengers (possibly special constables using their own vehicles).

In response to this, the Chief Constable of Maidstone, Mr Henry Vann, issued an instruction to his force that, as thousands of people were expected to try to leave their homes and head for the country in the event of an invasion, the police must be prepared to use force if necessary to prevent this. He went on:

> *Unless an ordered evacuation is effected some time before an invasion is imminent, and this is very unlikely, there will be no evacuation of the civil population. It is of paramount importance that when a crisis arises the public must remain where they are and any attempt at panic evacuation must be stopped, if necessary by force, regrettable though this course may be.*

Maidstone, like other towns in this category, had an outer perimeter and an inner circle – the 'keep' – which would have been the last line of defence. It was Government policy that, when an attack was imminent, the local police headquarters should be moved into the defended area, preferably the keep, as the military commander and the Invasion Committee would be reliant on the police for information.

Invasion Committees were set up in many villages to decide who was to do what once the enemy arrived on these shores. Their function was to run the parish if it were cut off and they included the Home Guard commander, the first aid services and the senior warden, with the chairman of the parish council in the chair. The police were invited in an advisory capacity.

A Mass Observation researcher described a meeting held in Great Bookham, Surrey, village hall in August, 1942

> *A local resident informed the well-attended meeting that, in the event of invasion, a triumvirate would be set up with himself, Lieutenant N of the Home Guard and Sergeant G of the local police as members. The police would give instructions*

regarding street leaders. Lieutenant N said the main task of the public was to keep out of the way of the military. 'Don't leave the area to go to work'. Sergeant G addressed the meeting, reading his speech word for word and very deliberately. 'Everyone should obey the police. Police may be distinguished from Fifth Columnists by their warrant card with photo – but at such a time you would be unlikely to have an opportunity to check a constable's bona fides. Get to know your local police'. (This raised the biggest laugh of the evening). 'I don't mean what you mean; I mean get to know them by using your powers of observation'.

Later comments included, 'Fancy having that man (Sergeant G) giving orders. Why choose the most unpopular man in the district?' (by a female aged 25).

The same organisation reported that the populace in general widely expected the invasion to take place but viewed the prospect calmly – possibly unduly complacently.

In July, 1940, the Home Office directed that;

The Police are not part of the Armed Forces of the Crown and therefore, in the event of a landing and effective occupation of an area by the enemy ... should not use arms nor carry arms in the occupied area. In the event of a landing by isolated parties who do not form part of an occupying force, and whose objective is ... to attack civilians, destroy property and cause confusion or devastation, ... the police ... are (not) debarred from resisting and, if possible, destroying the enemy ...

What clearly did concern many people was the possibility of an 'enemy within' – a Fifth Column – and enemy agents. The term 'Fifth Column' dates from the Spanish Civil War when General Franco's forces were closing in on Madrid from four directions. In a broadcast on 4 October 1936, General Mola, one of Franco's principal lieutenants, caused widespread alarm among the occupants of the besieged city by declaring that, in addition to the four columns in the field, he had a fifth column in Madrid itself, made up of sympathizers to the Nationalist cause.

As a weapon of psychological warfare, the term was impressively efficient. It created mistrust and suspicion, not just of obvious foreigners, but of one's own neighbour and any stranger. The odd comment, an unusual absence, an after-dark visitor, an unusual pastime, a beard, dark glasses – all were grounds for the deepest suspicion. The journalist, Cyril Connolly experienced this at first hand while sitting late one night in an Oxford hotel. He was suddenly accosted by a military policeman and accused of taking an undue interest in the conversation of a group of service officers talking nearby. The fact that he possessed a passport issued in Vienna did little to help, nor did the fact that he admitted being the editor of a literary magazine. In the end, after an inquisition conducted by eight policemen, only his impeccable background (Eton and Balliol) saved him from further embarrassment. Researchers found that the public, when asked to define a fifth columnist, saw them as 'Communists, Pacifists, Fascists' or else as 'Aliens and Traitors'. Intellectuals and writers were especially suspect, particularly if they held somewhat extremist political views. One such sufferer was the editor of the Co-operative movement's paper, the *Citizen*. In July 1940 his home was invaded by five plain clothes policemen who produced a search warrant and proceeded to ransack his house for an hour and a half. Nothing incriminating was found and it transpired that they were acting 'on information received', which was regarded by the authorities as justifying an immediate search. He was not, of course, permitted to know who had 'informed' on him.

Anyone expounding defeatist or pro-Nazi views was quickly denounced. The vicar of a Lincolnshire village was loudly proclaiming the advantages of National Socialism in the local butcher's shop, which incensed the butcher whose son was a Lancaster pilot (and was subsequently killed in action). The butcher frog marched the offending cleric to the police station, demanding that the village sergeant lock him up. The vicar's activities were officially investigated and he was interned for the duration under Regulation 18B.

The chief constable of every police force had a list of those persons in his area he proposed to arrest the moment invasion became imminent. When Eric St Johnston took over as chief constable of Oxfordshire in 1940 he asked to see the 'lock-up' list and was shown a document with three names on it, the first one being Unity Mitford, the sister-in-law of Sir Oswald Mosley. The new chief constable asked the detective inspector for the files relating to this entry and was told,

'Well, it's Unity Mitford, Sir. Hitler's girl friend. Of course we must lock her up'. St. Johnston replied that he was well aware of the stories which had been circulated about this lady and accepted that she might have been Hitler's mistress but he had no hard evidence of this fact and wanted to know on what evidence it was proposed that she should be interned. The detective inspector could only repeat that it was common knowledge that she was Hitler's girl friend and clearly felt that this was sufficient.

The new chief constable did not share this view and was surprised that no file on Miss Mitford existed in Oxford. However, he was sure that the appropriate authorities in London would have one but discovered that they, in turn, had assumed that Oxfordshire would have one. St Johnston decided to start a file and obtained newspaper cuttings from an agency and then arranged to meet her father, Lord Redesdale. Lord Redesdale opened the conversation by saying, 'Chief constable, my daughter Unity has been front page news in the national press for four years, yet you are the first official who has had the courtesy to come to discuss the matter with her father. I shall be delighted to help in any way I can'.

As a result of what he learned from Lord Redesdale and following discussions with Miss Mitford's neurologist, she was struck off the list of suspects, although St Johnston admits that whether he was correct in so doing is a matter of opinion. Certainly he had no doubt that, had the invasion taken place, he may have had to take Miss Mitford into custody for her own protection, such was the public's antipathy toward her.

Eric St Johnston's connections with the Mitford family did not stop there. In 1943 Sir Oswald Mosley and his wife, the former Diana Freeman-Mitford, the sister of Unity, were released from detention in Holloway prison on the grounds of Sir Oswald's ill-health. They were required to live with Pamela Jackson, another of the Mitford sisters, in Barford St John in the north of Oxfordshire where they were kept under close police supervision and forbidden to leave the house without the chief constable's permission. A constable was detailed to live in the house, more as protection from the press than to ensure security.

Further evidence of the suspicious attitude of the average Briton was gained by a representative of the Mass Observation organisation who visited East Suffolk soon after a German plane had crashed there and reported :

> *The atmosphere at the Butley Oyster pub was tense with suspicion. ... At Eyke there were groups of women talking in the streets and they turned and stared suspiciously at me. The atmosphere was so difficult, almost hostile, that I left.*[1]

That idea that the Germans were using Fifth Columnists was supported by the apparent ease with which they had been able to take country after country in Europe, often with little more than a token struggle. It was the view of both the man in the street and the authorities that there was undoubtedly some form of Fifth Column in Great Britain. The wireless transmitter, the aeroplane and the trained parachutist had all greatly enhanced the ability of a traitor to cause harm to his country or render aid to its enemies; the opportunities for sabotage were legion. With the advantage of hindsight, it is possible to say that, in fact, cases of treason or other Fifth Column activity were rare and usually quickly detected. One case involved a cipher clerk at the American Embassy, Tyler Kent, the aristocratic and anti-Semite daughter of a Russian admiral, Anna Wolkoff, and a Member of Parliament, Captain A H Maule Ramsay, who had served with distinction in the Great War but who held extreme right-wing political views. These three were all members of the 'Right Club', an anti-Jewish organisation of no great importance which Ramsay had founded. However, Kent, by virtue of his employment, was privy to confidential information, including messages which passed between Winston Churchill and President Roosevelt, of which he made copies. Some of these were forwarded by Wolkoff to an acquaintance in the Italian Embassy from where they found their way into German hands. Both Kent and Wolkoff were arrested in May, 1940 and subsequently sentenced to seven and ten years imprisonment respectively. There was insufficient evidence to prove that Ramsay was actively involved in the leaks but he was interned under Regulation 18B until the end of the war.

Another Fifth Columnist was a warrant officer in the British Army. Bert Ayers, the Romney Marsh constable we met earlier, received information that WO Latham was touring the churches in the area, ostensibly because of an interest in ecclesiastical architecture. He had visited the aristocratic occupant of Bilsington Priory on a number of occasions in the course of his tour. Constable Ayers's instructions were to apprehend Latham but not to question him. Care was to be exercised as it was believed that Latham was armed. Constable Ayers therefore telephoned all the various vicars and rectors, asking to be informed if Latham put in an appearance and made a similar request to Mr Bellman, the butler at the Priory. Sure enough, Mr Bellman rang back shortly afterwards to say that Latham was there. He was advised to do nothing which might alarm or forewarn Latham but to try to get the female staff off the premises and to summon the assistance of a gamekeeper (with shotgun) if possible. This being one occasion when the trusty rural constable's bicycle was an inadequate means of transport, Constable Ayers called upon the proprietor of a local garage to drive him to the Priory. When they arrived, he gave his truncheon to the driver (his only weapon) and told him to cover the front of the building while he went round the back. Inside, the butler told them that Latham was having a bath, after which he would be changing into some clothing belonging to the owner's son, as his own was soiled. Constable Ayers decided to lie in wait in the downstairs cloaks cupboard and, as Latham walked past some time later, he jumped out and grabbed him. He admits that he was so scared that he nearly strangled his prisoner! Latham was tried by court martial in Chelsea barracks, the details of which were kept secret. However, it was clear that he had been in the pay of the Nazis for some years.

The obvious candidates for suspicion were known Fascists and, given Russia's alliance with Germany, members of the Communist party, although General Ironside did not help matters by saying,

> *My experience is that the gentlemen who are the best behaved and the most sleek are those who are doing the mischief. We cannot be too sure of anybody.*

In fact, anyone with a foreign sounding name was a target for suspicion, especially if they committed some minor peccadillo. Odile Lesley had an unpleasant experience because of this:

> *I came home one night to the flat where I lived in Hampstead and found that the police had broken in. They started to interrogate me in an awful sort of way, saying things like, 'You're an enemy agent, you're a fifth columnist, who's paying*

101

you?' And this interrogation seemed to go on for such a long, long time, until I realised what had happened. I had left a light on without drawing the blackout curtains and, of course, it was shining out like a beacon across the Heath which, to them, was a signal to the enemy... Eventually I did convince them that I was not an enemy agent, it was a pure accident and I was just fined £2 at the local magistrates' court. But the outcome of it was that many of the neighbours shunned us for quite some time, whispering, 'Look, fifth column', which was to me so dreadful because nobody was more anti-Nazi than I was.

One researcher experienced difficulties in Ilford where he stopped and questioned an old, poorly-dressed man as part of a Mass Observation survey. A woman passing by reported the incident to the police and a Police War Reserve constable interrogated him, obviously suspecting him of being a spy. The constable appeared to be satisfied with the researcher's explanation but was unsure what he should do next, so he was invited to go with the constable and another officer to the police station. He was eventually released with an apology, and it seemed that the two main factors arousing suspicion had been the fact that (a) he was not working in his own area, and (b) being bored he had played noughts and crosses with himself, which was suspected of being some sort of code.

In the years since Hitler had come to power, bringing his particular brand of National Socialism to Germany, numerous refugees, fleeing the excesses of Nazi policies, had arrived on these shores and it would have been simple to infiltrate a few spies or fellow-travellers amongst these – a sort of Trojan horse. The flood of refugees from the low countries and France in 1940 was of such magnitude that it was impossible to carry out meaningful checks of their reliability, although the police and security services did their best. Freddie Pearce, as a constable in Devon, tells how he was put in charge of a platoon of troops and set up a road block to check possible infiltrators but admits it did not produce any noticeable results.

In November, 1940, MI5 issued all police forces with a guide to the points to look for when dealing with possible enemy agents, based on their practical experience. These included:

1. A clean identity card with an old date
2. Passports issued in Luxembourg
3. Pink (Traveller's) ration books with a CA number (unused since June of that year)
4. Writing the figure 7 in the continental fashion
5. Writing addresses in the continental manner
6. Comparison of official documents – ration book, identity card, etc.
7. Clothing of foreign cut.
8. Foreign accents
9. Possession of large sums in cash
10. Possession of Pyramidon
11. Carrying a heavy suitcase (could contain a radio)
12. Lack of local knowledge
13. Possession of large-scale maps.

A further document issued to the police described the type of wireless used by enemy agents, suggesting that a device using wireless telegraphy (Morse) was much more likely than one employing radio telephony (speech).

The nation had become gripped by a form of spy fever – an obsession from which even the Government was not immune. It was not helped by further wild statements by the Commander-in-Chief Home Forces, General Ironside, who complained that ;

> ... *it is extraordinary how we get circumstantial reports of Fifth Column and yet we have never been able to get anything worth having. One is persuaded that it hardly exists. And yet there is signalling going on all over the place and we cannot get any evidence.*

It was this sort of paranoia that led to the passing of the infamous Regulation 18B and the internment of all manner of innocent people, simply because they originated from Germany or Austria and, later, Italy. The Vice-Admiral in command at Dover reported to the Admiralty that there were :

> ... *indications of numerous acts of sabotage and fifth column*

103

activity in Dover, eg. communications leakages, fixed defences sabotage, second-hand cars purchased at fantastic prices and left at various parking places.

This report proved to be based on inaccurate information but was typical of many similar accounts being circulated. General Ironside told LDV commanders that there were examples of people preparing aerodromes in this country, but this statement too failed to survive scrutiny of the information on which it was presumably based. Eventually the General was quietly removed from his post, being made a Field Marshal 'for his distinguished services'. Similar reports passed from person to person, from government department to government department, from the police to the military and vice versa. Police stations were inundated with reports of suspicious activities; flashing lights, poisoned sweets, bridges blown up, tyres punctured, telephone lines cut, convoys misdirected – whenever something went wrong the hand of the Fifth Column was detected, rather than Sod's Law. Most of these reports proved to be either inaccurate, incorrect or to relate to perfectly harmless and legitimate activities. Barbara Nixon[2] tells how, as an ARP warden in London in 1940, she received a message that a German parachutist had landed in Garton Square and that a search was to be made for him.

> *The police turned out with revolvers and made a ring around the area; everyone seemed to be taking it very seriously and BB and I searched back gardens. I immediately fell off a wall and hurt myself and began to think the proceedings were ridiculous. Even provided there had really been a parachutist, if he were an airman, he would probably have broken at least a leg on a chimney pot and, in any case, would not fight; and if he were a genuine parachutist, a Fifth Columnist, he would have come down dressed as a warden and we should have directed him very politely to the next borough.... We decided that looking for parachutists [during an air raid] was a wholly ridiculous proceeding – and abandoned it.*

There was a good deal of sense in this attitude. The countryside around the capital obviously presented a much safer landing point for enemy agents. A parachutist landing in London would run the considerable risk of fouling trolley bus cables or striking rooftops and chimney pots. Despite this, when a barrage balloon broke loose in London and was followed by the crew to a rooftop some distance away, they were stopped by police and Home Guards who told them that there were 12 German parachutists on the roof with automatic weapons and they had to contact their squadron headquarters before they could retrieve their property.

In an effort to confuse malevolent new arrivals, it was ordered that all signposts in the country were to be removed and all milestones up-rooted. The names of streets, railway stations and village signboards were to be removed or rendered illegible.

As Peter Fleming reveals[3], the twin fears of airborne attack and treachery were essentially complementary to each other. Without the traitor to succour him, guide him to his objective and further his purpose by cutting telephone wires, spreading rumours and initiating bogus telephone messages, the parachutist was not, in the general opinion, likely to achieve a great deal. (The reliance by Allied agents on local Resistance groups later in the war would tend to reinforce this opinion). Based much more on Munchausenian tales than on reliable fact were the many rumours that the Germans were in the habit (no pun intended) of parachuting in dressed as nuns, nurses, monks and tramcar conductors, even though these were propagated by no less a personage than the Dutch Foreign Minister (*The Times*, 22 May 1940).

The possibility of infiltrators adopting some form of disguise prompted the authorities to issue an official pamphlet which enjoined the populace to '*know your policemen and ARP wardens by sight. If you keep your heads you can also tell whether a military officer is really British or is only pretending to be so*'. This entreaty appears to ignore the ease with which the uniform of a British officer could be obtained from a specialist tailor, and also the increasing number of friendly, Allied troops of foreign origin, including Poles, Czechs, Frenchmen, Belgians and Dutchmen who would be wearing British officer's uniform.

Such was the extent of the spy fever which raged through the country in 1940 that the Ministry of Home Security was forced to appeal to police and wardens to do more to verify reports of suspects before passing them on. It complained,

The number of unsubstantiated reports of parachute landings which have reached the Home Security War Room is such as to be likely to cause serious dislocation to the War Room machinery in the event of genuine attempts by the Germans to land troops by planes or parachutes.

The fear of parachuted enemy agents was fuelled by the practice adopted by the Germans in the low countries of dropping empty parachutes behind the Allied lines. The ploy was repeated in August 1940, at the very beginning of the Battle of Britain, when the Luftwaffe dropped nearly 100 parachutes, together with radio transmitters and maps, at various points in Yorkshire, the Midlands and the Scottish lowlands. The subterfuge was disclosed by the fact that no tracks could be found leading away from these items of equipment where they had fallen in fields of standing crops. However, it does seem that not all such finds were mere propaganda devices. An Express Message sent by the Buckinghamshire Police to all police forces in the country on 3 November, 1940 stated that :

Enemy parachute landing at 12.00 on 3/11/40. Complete enemy parachute with harness, overalls and flying helmet was found, neatly folded and placed under a hedge at Haversham, Bucks. Parachute was wet but clothing inside was dry and it appears that it may have been dropped during the past 2 or 3 days. Inside the parachute was a paper wrapping 'Chocolate – Made in Belgium' .... Parachute has without doubt been used and the parachutist landed uninjured and is still at large. There is no trace of any crashed aircraft and the parachutist was without doubt deliberately dropped.

Another spy scare arose in rural Norfolk where the officer commanding an airfield near the Wash reported that German planes changed direction overhead and that a nearby radar station was being jammed. Suspicion fell on an electrical engineer in a nearby small town who was known to have appeared on the same platform as Sir Oswald Mosley. The police had had a six-inch map of the area handed in to them, on which had been marked what appeared to be the bearing of the radar station. This map was found to belong to the electrician's brother. The evidence was damning and the houses of the two men were raided by the police with soldiers surrounding them to give covering fire if necessary. The local chief constable and the Army commander rushed up the garden paths and hammered on the front doors. In the electrical contractor's house they found a small box, carefully concealed.

> *It was locked; we asked the engineer for the key. He astonished us by saying that he had never seen it in his life. This appeared to be an obvious lie. The policemen fiddled with the lock and ultimately got it open. They gave a yelp, and handed it to me in triumph. There, inside, was an induction coil, some wire, and some crocodile clips ... There were some instructions inside the lid. I read them and realised that this was an electrical hair remover. His wife, a modest woman, had bought it for her personal use and had been practising a mild deception on her husband.[4]*

In fact, all the seemingly damning clues were similarly demolished and perfectly rational explanations were found for all the happenings.

In Oxfordshire, reports were received of a parachute landing in the summer of 1940 and a full-scale search was mounted by police and Canadian troops. The security officer on the Canadian General's staff attended the scene and, on the way, saw a young man of rough appearance and wearing military uniform, sitting under a hedge. The officer told him he suspected him of having been dropped from an enemy aircraft and, to his surprise, the young man readily admitted this. He was taken to the Headquarters of the Canadian forces and closely interrogated. The suspect claimed to be a Welshman who had been captured at Dunkirk and, as he was an ardent Welsh Nationalist, he had been recruited for training as a saboteur. He said another Welshman had been dropped with him and that his orders were to contact Mr James Florey of Manor Farm, Hardwick, near Witney, who would provide further instructions and equipment. Some German refugees working on the farm were in on the plan and would help. The Canadians promptly raided the farm and discovered that there were indeed some German refugees working there. The police inspector, although a little late coming into the enquiry, arrived at the farm before the Canadians and had no difficulty in arresting the three German male workers and the German woman who cooked for them. Unaware of this development, the officer commanding the Canadian raiding party was surprised at the lack of resistance but went on to occupy the farmhouse nonetheless. Mr Florey, his wife and all the other occupants of the farm were taken into custody by the soldiers. When the police inspector presented himself at the Canadian Army headquarters, he was promptly arrested by the over-suspicious security officer who decided that he too must be one of the gang. He was only rescued by the timely intervention of a colonel from MI5 who had heard by chance that a man claiming to be a detective was in custody. To add to the confusion, a young cyclist was arrested as the second saboteur because, when questioned, his name was revealed to be the same as that given by the first suspect. Like the inspector, the youth was rescued from captivity, this time by a police officer who knew him as a local butcher's assistant. Interrogated at length, the first suspect stuck to his story but, by now, only the Canadians were prepared to believe him. His clothing was all current British Army issue and he had no identity documents or any money or other articles of value on him. It seemed most unlikely that the Germans would drop an agent into this country so poorly equipped. Eventually he confessed to being no more than an Army deserter who had once worked for Mr Florey and had made up the cock-and-bull story about being dropped from a Junkers aircraft. He was soon identified by one of his NCOs and explained that he was so aggrieved by the rough handling he had received from the Canadian security officer who had picked him up and who had made up his mind that he had caught a dangerous spy, that the deserter decided, with the aid of a little local knowledge and considerable inventiveness, to reinforce the lieutenant's fixation. The Floreys were released after spending the night in close custody and returned to their farm to discover that some of their property had been stolen by the occupying troops and a great deal of damage had been done. It was this incident which finally convinced the Home Office that the county chief constable was not exercising sufficient control and he was quietly advised to retire.

A somewhat similar situation arose in Lincolnshire when a farmer who occupied an isolated farm near Wragby rang the local police sergeant, Sam Rounce, to say that he had seen what he believed to be German troops advancing stealthily towards his farmhouse and would the sergeant please come. Wasting no time the sergeant telephoned the army camp in Wragby where a liberty truck had just returned with a load of soldiers from a night out in Lincoln. Pausing only to collect their weapons, the troops, scenting a little excitement and action, climbed back aboard the truck and drove off at high speed towards the threatened farm. Once there they discovered, to their disappointment, that the enemy troops were in fact members of another company of their own regiment. By the time the troops from Wragby had arrived, however, under the instructions of a zealous lieutenant, the other soldiers had broken into the farmhouse and interrogated the farmer about the telephone call he had just made. He did not let on that it was to the police but claimed to be calling the vet about a sick animal. It is not clear why the officer felt the farmer to be under suspicion, although it may have been connected with the fact that he employed, like many other farmers in that time of labour shortages, a number of conscientious objectors who had been directed to work on the land. Sergeant Rounce was quickly able to disabuse the young lieutenant who was extremely embarrassed by the incident. It did not appear to have affected the army officer's subsequent career, however, as he went on to become a Queen's Counsel, a Member of Parliament, a member of the Cabinet and ultimately a peer of the Realm.

In another instance, reports began to come in from a number of points in Monmouthshire that parachutists had been seen dropping on the mountains. A number of search parties were sent out to look for them and the district was in a state of agitation until the police discovered that the whole affair was no more than a device employed by some miners to get the afternoon off.

Some other spy scares proved to be equally groundless. On one occasion, the Woolwich police brought in a very glamorous female 'spy' who had been seen making notes while travelling backwards and forwards across the River Thames on the Woolwich ferry. The police matron who was called to attend to this lady (there were no police women there at that time) very quickly discovered, to her embarrassment, that the 'lady' was in fact a very masculine stevedore with transvestite tendencies. The notes 'she' had been seen jotting down were not, in fact, military secrets intended for the enemy but a record of 'her' dates.

It is nevertheless true that, in September 1940, a number of spies were sent to the United Kingdom, all of whom were taken prisoner by the British authorities. The quality of these early infiltrators was poor; they were incompletely trained and seem to have been sent on what was virtually a suicide mission, although there was always a possibility that, if the invasion of England, 'Operation Sealion', had been put into effect fairly quickly, there was a chance that some of them might have survived.

Typical of these were the four agents sent across the Channel from Le Touquet on 2 September, 1940 in a fishing vessel. They were instructed to work in pairs and one couple landed on the beach near Hythe (Kent) early the next morning with a wireless set and an elementary code. By 5.30 am the same day they had both been challenged and taken into custody by army sentries. Both men were of Dutch nationality and were completely untrained. Their sole qualification appears to have been the fact that they had both committed some criminal offence which made them susceptible to blackmail by the German authorities. Neither had an adequate command of English and one was of distinctly Oriental appearance, due to his having a Japanese mother. It was the latter who was found by an astonished sentry, wandering around with a pair of binoculars and a spare pair of shoes slung around his neck.

The other pair consisted of a German, Jose Rudolf Waldberg, who spoke fluent French but no English and a man of doubtful origins, Carl Heinrich Meier, who claimed to be Dutch and who, alone among the four, had a good command of English. This pair landed at Dungeness (not far from Hythe), between Lade Coastguard Station and the Pilot Inn. Being very thirsty, Meier attempted to buy cider at a public house in Lydd before opening time. It was pointed out to him that it was not possible to buy intoxicating liquor until 10 o'clock and the barmaid suggested they he could have look at the nearby church while he waited. Meanwhile, the licensee, Mr C Cole, rang the Lydd police office to voice his suspicions. The officer in charge, Sergeant Joseph Tye, detailed a constable to investigate but, before he could do so, Meier was brought to the office by a local resident, accompanied by an army corporal.

'Who are you and where have you come from?' asked Sergeant Tye.

'I am a Dutch subject and have just landed on the beach in a small boat', replied Meier. 'I have come from France. I have left a sack of food in a boat on the beach. I can show you the boat'.

So the sergeant drove him to Dungeness where he pointed out a large boat on the beach. A search of the boat failed to disclose the sack but, shortly afterwards they saw a local walking along the beach carrying a sack which Meier claimed was the one he had hidden in the boat. Joseph Tye took possession of the sack which he found contained bread, canned food, biscuits, brandy, chocolate, sugar and cigarettes. (It is not clear whether the local man intended to hand the sack in to the police. However, given the contents and the strict rationing then in force, the temptation to apply the law of 'finders keeper' would have been very strong). Sergeant Tye reported the matter to his immediate superior, Inspector Hadlow, who told him to bring the suspect to Seabrook Police Station, where the other two agents were already in custody.

In the early hours of the next morning, 4 September, Sergeant Tye received a telephone call from the inspector, instructing him to take part in a full-scale search of the area as it was now clear that another man was still at large and that they were indeed enemy agents. In the early morning light a large party of police and soldiers began to comb the area but found nothing until Sergeant Tye spied a man walking along the beach who appeared to fit the description of the wanted man. On being hailed, this man, who was indeed Waldberg, came up to the policeman and asked, in French, to speak to an English officer. Taking no chances, the sergeant lost no time in searching Waldberg for weapons but did not find any. He did find, however, a compass. Using his smattering of French, Sergeant Tye asked Waldberg where he had spent the night and the latter indicated a large tree by the beach, around 400 yards from the Lydd-Dungeness road. By this time other members of the search party had arrived and they all went to the place indicated by Waldberg. There they found that the tree's branches came down nearly to the ground, forming a kind of room. In the fork of the tree there were two suitcases together with two black leather cases, one of which was found to contain a wireless transmitter/receiver and the other batteries and a Morse key. There was also an aerial in the tree and it transpired that Waldberg had already sent some messages to his base in France. Copies of some of these messages survived and were used in evidence against him at his trial. The information they contained was brief and of no operational value.

It appeared that their instructions were to move about among the people, listening in trains and buses, in cafes and in the streets for any careless talk (given the poor command of English possessed by at least three of the four, one wonders how successful this would have been). They were instructed to pick up as much military information as possible, especially that regarding airfields, troop concentrations and other defences, passing it by radio each evening. Their obvious lack of training and competence may be partially explained by the fact that they had been told to expect the invasion in about two weeks and they merely had to avoid capture for this comparatively short period of time – something they manifestly failed to do.

All four spies were tried *in camera* at the Old Bailey where one of the blackmailed Dutchmen was acquitted. The remaining three were found guilty and were hanged in Pentonville Prison in December 1940.

Other spies were infiltrated into the country in September, 1940 – a popular month for the practice, it would seem. Amongst these were two men and a woman who were landed on the coast of Scotland in a rubber dinghy, having been dropped off from a flying boat from Norway. They were very quickly arrested and found to possess a list of airfields in East Anglia. Another couple arrived by parachute, one in Oxford and one in Cambridge. The first was a young Finn, Goesta Caroli, who was arrested almost immediately, interrogated and successfully 'turned' by MI5. When the second spy, Wulf Dietrich Schmidt, a Dane, arrived two weeks later, Caroli was able to warn the British of his arrival. Schmidt, who had spent some time with Caroli in a Hamburg hotel prior to their being dropped, was flown over in a Heinkel by the same pilot as had dropped Caroli. Unfortunately things went wrong from the beginning for the hapless Dane. As he jumped his wristwatch caught on something, damaging the watch and injuring his wrist. He landed on a road and sprained his ankle. His parachute was caught up in some telephone wires and he had difficulty in tearing it down. The next morning he went into the nearest village and was picked up there by the police a few hours later. Schmidt too was turned and continued to work for the British for the rest of the war.

At least one other spy worked in the Cambridge area in 1940. This was a Dutchman, Jan Willen Ter Braak who was dropped by parachute near Amersham, Buckinghamshire, on 3 October 1940. (It is interesting to compare this fact with the information contained in the police Express Message referred to above, relating to what would seem to be a further arrival about a month later). As well as the usual wireless transmitter, money and a pistol, Ter Braak carried Red Cross letters addressed to refugees living in England which were intended to provide him with a contact list. It appears that he was unable to establish contact with another agent already working in the area and, running short of money and without the coupons necessary to obtain food, he crept into an air raid shelter in Cambridge where he was found shot dead in April, 1941, apparently having committed suicide, although reports of the occurrence were suppressed at the time.

Another spy, this time a Dane, was dropped in Buckinghamshire on 6 September, 1940, with instructions to report on the effect of the Blitz on Birmingham, a town which he knew well, having spent some time living there with an English family in Kings Heath to improve his English. He was easily picked up by the police as, on landing, the strap holding his wireless transmitter snapped and the apparatus hit him on the head, causing mild concussion.

Other enemy agents were already working in this country prior to the outbreak of the war but mostly left once hostilities commenced. Bob Stewart, who was a constable at Broadstairs when the war began, remembers that a German lawyer, Dr Albert Tester, lived in a house just below the North Foreland lighthouse, with his wife and five children. He was a good friend of William Joyce (Lord Haw-Haw) who often came to stay with him and it is believed that he was a leading figure in the Gestapo and would have assumed an important position in the county in the event of a German occupation. Once war was declared, orders were given for Dr Tester to be interned with the other enemy aliens but, when Constable Stewart went with other officers to the house to execute the order, he found the quarry had fled. A check of Ramsgate harbour revealed that his sailing yacht had also gone; Dr Tester had returned to the Fatherland. It is known that he was ultimately shot and killed in Rumania by the advancing Russian troops in 1944 after crashing through a road barrier.

Even before this, in the summer of 1935, another German citizen going under the name of Dr Hermann Goertz had arrived in England for a holiday. He was presently joined by a young German girl, Marianne Emig, whom he described as his niece. Goertz purchased a powerful motorcycle and the two of them roamed the English country side, stopping occasionally for Dr Goertz to set up his easel and make some sketches of the countryside. But it was no coincidence that these countryside scenes always seemed to include an RAF station. From Mildenhall, Suffolk, the couple moved to Broadstairs in Kent which is close to the RAF station at Manston. They rented a bungalow in the town for a six-week stay but, before this was up, the owner of the bungalow received a telegram from Dover, saying the couple were going to Germany for a few days and would she take care of his 'combination' and photo. This was followed by a similar postcard from Ostend, making a similar request. When the couple failed to return at the end of the tenancy, the owner went to check the inventory and found the photo but could not find the motorcycle. Fearing it had been stolen she called the police and Special Branch officers searched the bungalow. They found a pair of dirty white overalls which they realised were the 'combination' referred to in the telegram and postcard. A small camera in one of the pockets of the overalls was found to contain photographs of airfields and aircraft. They also found a number of Dr Goertz's well-executed sketches, all of which showed defence installations. As a result a warrant was issued for his arrest, should he ever return to this country.

Somewhat surprisingly, he did return and was arrested at Harwich as he landed. He was tried for offences against the Official Secrets Act at the Old Bailey and was sentenced to four years imprisonment. With remission, he was released from Maidstone prison just before the war started and returned to Germany. But his story does not end there; having made contact with a number of IRA terrorists while in prison, he was parachuted into Ireland in May 1940 to work on an IRA-backed invasion of England. He was arrested in Dublin and interned for the rest of the war. Dr Goertz poisoned himself in May, 1947 when told he was being repatriated to Germany; why he did so has never been explained.

As Norman Longmate asserts[5], if there were any undetected German spies in Britain they remained undiscovered even after the war and instances of careless talk, such as the lack of security displayed by the Canadians about their impending involvement in the Dieppe raid, do not appear to have resulted in any response on the part on the enemy. The agents which were discovered were, as we have seen, poorly-trained and ill-equipped but this does not detract from the efforts of the police and security services who apprehended them, not least of whom were the members of the police Special Branch. Formed as the Special Irish Branch to deal with Irish terrorists, its role rapidly developed to embrace all forms of terrorist and subversive activity. Although its activities are shrouded in secrecy and covered by the Official Secrets Act, there is little doubt that this branch of the police did a vital yet unpublicised and largely undramatic job in the apprehension of enemy agents, the internment of possible enemy sympathizers under Regulation 18B, the screening of refugees, the guarding of important personages – both British and foreign – and a wide variety of other sensitive investigations.

With the threat of air raids and, later, the very real possibility of invasion, it is understandable that there would be a migration from those areas deemed to be at risk. Evacuation of children and certain categories of adults from what were thought to be prime target areas was first put in motion soon after the outbreak of war, having been conceived as early as 1938. At the beginning of the war, even the police horses were evacuated from central London to Cheshunt. This initial evacuation was short-lived as the war went into its 'phoney' phase. There were no air raids and no gas attacks and so, by the end of the year, there was a steady trickle of evacuees returning home to London and other cities.

It was the second threat, the possibility of invasion, which prompted the next, bigger wave of evacuations. In May and June, 1940 there was a large scale evacuation from areas along the south and east coasts as well as from the capital. The thinking behind this was two-fold; firstly there was the simple humanitarian aspect that women and children and the aged and infirm should not have to face the ravages of invasion. Secondly there was the strategic consideration; note had already been taken of how the refugees on the roads of continental Europe had impeded the war machine and the military in this country were anxious this should not occur in Britain. The roads must be kept free for military traffic.

Children in the area (and this included a number of children who had been evacuated there from London during the first evacuation scheme) were to be evacuated, principally to Wales. This was not a compulsory evacuation but it was very heavily encouraged and the authorities were disappointed to discover later that large numbers of children still remained and were soon constituting something of a social problem since all State schools in the area were closed. Many women wished to remain with their menfolk, come what may, and they were reluctant to break up the family unit by sending the children away to live with strangers. Nevertheless, some 213,000 unaccompanied children were evacuated during May, June and July. The Government also introduced a scheme for 'assisted private evacuation' to help those

115

non-essential adults and small children who wished to leave the coastal belt. By mid-July, nearly half the population of the East Anglian coastal towns and roughly two-fifths of the inhabitants of the Kent seaside resorts had left for safer parts. For example, Folkestone, with a peacetime population of around 45,000 (augmented by holiday makers in the summer season) was reduced to a mere 9,000. Those who remained were warned that, in the event of invasion, they would be expected to stay put until further orders were given[6]. It was also decreed that the police in these areas should remain in sufficient numbers to do whatever had to be done and any surplus withdrawn to other areas. Those remaining in the areas under threat should, so far as was possible, be over military age.

Although the public remaining in these areas were told to 'stay put' in the event of an invasion, notices were nonetheless prepared for display in certain areas advising the population that, in the event of attack, everyone other than those who had been specifically instructed to stay, would be evacuated. Mothers with young children, schoolchildren, the aged and infirm, those with no occupation or who were retired were advised to leave without delay. A further notice advised residents to 'make preparations now to ensure that you could leave at short notice'. This excluded specified essential personnel (police, fire, ARP, doctors, local government officers, civil servants, employees of banks, transport undertakings and public utilities or those involved in food supply and distribution.

As usual, the police were very closely involved in the evacuation process, both at the point of departure and in the reception areas. In Oxford, the police were warned to expect 1,500 young children from Kent in the early hours of the morning. The train had to be met, buses organised and billets found for all – no easy task but one which was nevertheless accomplished without fuss or drama. These evacuees were a motley bunch and could be an embarrassment, as Eric St Johnston discovered. As the Chief Constable of Oxfordshire, he was walking through Oxford, in full uniform and with two important local dignitaries, when he heard his name being called. On turning, he saw:

> ... *a whole motley collection of London cockneys. They were the Huggins family who had for generations kept street stalls ... selling fruit and vegetables. The younger ones were true London barrow boys and they had been a confounded nuisance to me at Walham Green for their stalls and barrows*

overran the roadway and obstructed the traffic, while there was running warfare between the family and the police. But on this occasion all faces were wreathed in smiles and I was surrounded by the family shaking me by the hand. '... we'd read you'd become a top cop. We always knew you'd get on. Good luck to yer' ... I was very touched but my two companions wondered whether I had the right sort of friends.

Of these evacuated families, some were what might be called problem families whose behaviour was often quoted as being typical and exaggerated into the bargain. Freddie Pearce recalls that an elderly Devon constable was employed virtually full-time on resolving differences between the two parties, differences which could sometimes lead to violent disputes. A sergeant in the Special Constabulary, responsible for billeting over a large area of West Cumberland, had two problem mothers to deal with. No sooner had they and their large brood of virtually uncontrollable children been placed with a farming family than the poor hosts were pleading for them to be found alternative accommodation. The sergeant used his initiative and commandeered a vacant cottage with views across the magnificent Cumbrian countryside. He borrowed cooking utensils and the local farmers contributed coal, vegetables and other food and moved the families in. But within ten days the women were begging to be sent home, complaining that '...them bloody 'ills drive me crackers every time I look at them'. On their departure the bedding was found to be verminous and filthy and the sergeant had to burn the lot. None of the fresh vegetables had been used, only the tinned food which they had been supplied with. Small wonder that the job of billeting officer was often regarded as 'the most hated job'. However, the Mass Observation reports for the autumn of 1940 noted that there were no serious problems either way and several chief constables had commented on the absence of profiteering on the part of the hosts.

Once the Blitz started there were many more wanting to leave the target areas. Sergeant H F Grey writes of one lady with three children and two suitcases who went to Millwall Police Station at the height of the bombing, seeking help, as she had been bombed out of her home. The sergeant detailed one of the War Reserve constables to escort her to the railway station but, in the event, he travelled with her all the way to Iver in Buckinghamshire. None of them was asked to pay any fare[7].

Also in London, Geoffrey Taylor, who was a traffic patrol constable in the East End tells how he, with a dozen other policemen, paraded at 6 am after a particularly heavy raid in September, 1940 when they were sent on motor cycles to North Woolwich which had been badly hit. Their job was to escort bus loads of children and a few parents and teachers to Epping Forest where they were left among the trees, some crying for their parents, others white faced and bewildered. The police escorts went back and forth many times until late in the evening and moved thousands of people, many of whom were now homeless and possessing just what they stood up in.

> *It was fortunate that the weather was warm and dry and my last recollection of these children as I rode out of the trees into the setting sun was of two little girls, about eight years of age and obviously twins, holding hands and crying profusely with large tears falling down their cheeks. I have wondered many times since what happened to these children, some of them now orphans and unable to understand what had suddenly happened to them. As far as I could see there were no facilities made for them and indeed no time to do so, but I suppose they were evacuated out of London eventually.*

Although the Government's fear of refugees blocking the roads never came to pass, there is no doubt that, during the heavy raids on some provincial cities, the sight of those fleeing the devastation came very close to it. After the first taste of the Luftwaffe's Blitzkrieg, there began a mass exodus of many of the inhabitants of these cities. As the Ministry of Home Security Weekly Appreciation Report for 22 November 1940 stated, 'A certain number of people left Coventry and police took steps to deal with them in the surrounding districts'. Some left in an orderly manner and made their own arrangements to stay with friends and relatives in the country but a sizeable minority simply dropped everything and fled. The migration from Coventry began while the raid was still at its height and a special constable watched them walking away from the city centre, some with children but others with just a suitcase and their family pets, including canaries and budgerigars in their cages. One War Reserve policeman describes how

> *People were pouring out of Coventry on anything they could find, even hand carts and horses and carts',*

118

while he was trying to remove his own family.

These raids produced a further evacuation phenomena – the 'trekkers'. Instead of moving right away from the target areas, people began to move to the surrounding countryside each night, returning the next morning to take up their usual occupations, if they still had a job to go to! Bus companies began advertising special services to cater for these 'trekkers', some of whom quickly hired cottages from locals or took a room in which they passed the night sleeping uncomfortably but safely in a chair. Those fortunate enough to possess cars (and the necessary petrol) would drive out of town and sleep in their vehicles.

Waller and Vaughan-Rees describe the experiences of some of these 'trekkers' in their book[8].

> *People began moving out of the town for the night, sleeping in cars, huts, tents in the country. It was a sight to remember, crowds of people in cars leaving by exit roads. In the morning the ARP activities were much hampered as the roads were often jammed with people returning to the town* (John H Smith, Bristol).
>
> *... in the farm kitchen there was a row of chairs against the wall where exhausted people used to come during the Blitz and hire a chair for the night ...* (Barbara Waller, Plymouth).
>
> *When we arrived at our digs we were amazed to find the doors open and no one in the house and the roof was off. We slept the night there and then we went to the police again. We found no one in the streets and written in chalk or white paint was this message in large letters – THIS WAY TO THE HILLS – on the pavement. The police told us everyone had fled and dumped their house keys on them ...* (Mary Joy Miller, Belfast).

These brief references to the police give an indication of the multitude of tasks that the police, the universal 'uncles', were expected to take on as well as their normal tasks and the extra ones imposed by the war. Deserted and unlocked houses were obviously a prime target for looters and it will also be evident that the movements of these 'refugees' created considerable problems for the police from the point of view of traffic control when they were already working under impossibly difficult conditions.

In 1940, even the Prime Minister was undecided just how the civil population (including the police) should react in the event of invasion.

He did not contemplate or encourage fighting by persons not in the armed forces but he was not prepared to forbid it. He was worried about the role of the police; he thought it would be intolerable if they were to prevent the public from resisting the enemy. Should they be withdrawn with the last troops?

By the middle of 1941 a much more robust attitude towards a possible invasion could be detected, especially as far as the police role was concerned. The adoption of a 'stand firm' policy for the civil population, rather than mass evacuation was linked to a general quickening of national determination as exemplified by the raising and training of the Home Guard. A new Home Office Memorandum issued on 6 June 1942 replaced the earlier Memorandum referred to above, striking a much more positive note. It decreed that the primary role of the police was to carry out the functions for which it was organised and equipped and:

> *... so far as is consistent with this, the police in any area not in effective occupation by the enemy should not hesitate to use firearms and any other forcible means to deal with enemy marauders, saboteurs, etc. and ... should hinder and frustrate the enemy by every means ...*

If required by the military authorities to assist, it would be their duty:

> *... to answer wholeheartedly any call, however exacting, which may be made. In this matter ... the police are specially qualified to provide an example and leadership to the general body of private citizens.*

Where a threatened area was to be cleared, the police were expected to:

(1) remove the civil population

(2) watch out for persons trying to remain

(3) watch out for Fifth Column activities (posters, alarmist reports, false news, use of load hailers, etc.)

(4) assist the military to remove or destroy articles of use to the enemy (vehicles, horses, fire appliances, fuel, explosives, wireless sets, food, records – including police records).

(5) restrict means of communication (telephones/telegraphs, railways, docks, jetties, etc.). Police stations were regarded

as important lines of communication and, in London at least, the police were instructed that the station was to be held at all costs.

With the detailed anti-invasion plans written up and the civil defence services being rapidly reorganized, a series of full-scale invasion exercises were held in 1942 in every vulnerable town, involving the armed forces, the police, the Home Guard and every section of the civil defence organisation, as well as the public utilities, transport services, hospitals and communications systems, etc.

Some of these exercises – or 'tests', as they were known – were a little too realistic. The *Police Review* for 24 April, 1942, reported that, in some cases, serious damage to property and some personal injuries had resulted. In one exercise, involving the storming of a police station in Stoke-on-Trent, the Home Guard had smashed windows with their rifles and one of them had put a bayonet through a door, just missing one of the constables. A special constable was injured and lost two days work for which he was claiming compensation. This incident followed a similar one in Southend-on-Sea in which the military had caused serious damage to the police station (serious in that the station had to carry on its normal work during and after the exercise), and one member of the force had the lobe of his ear blown off by a tommy gun fired at him at close range.

For those familiar with the American or Continental police systems, it may seem curious that, even in a war situation, the police in Britain were not armed, at least not on a regular basis. The Government decided to equip all police forces with firearms and to increase the number of weapons available. Although there was no intention to create a combatant force, it was felt some policemen should be armed for their own protection and when on certain guard duties. Chief Constables had discretion whether to issue weapons to those who were detailed to guard the various vulnerable points, in which case they would be issued with either a .303 Lee Enfield or .300 Ross rifle or a service revolver. There was never any question however of there being a general issue of arms. The police had seldom received any firearms training; those who had previously served in one of the Armed Forces possessed a degree of competence but one wonders just how effective some of the others would have been, had they been required to make use of these unfamiliar weapons.

Some police patrol cars carried a rifle and a stock of somewhat elderly weapons was kept at most police stations for emergencies. Bill Cavey tells how there was a flurry of excitement at Bow police station in London when the 'look-out' rushed into the station crying, 'Parachutists!'. The armoury was quickly opened and rifles issued to the eager constables who rushed out to deal with the enemy. However, the parachutes proved to be supporting land mines, some of which dropped nearby, blowing in the shutters of the police station windows. Nevertheless, the duty inspector was well pleased with the way his men had responded and said that, had there been parachutists, his men would have been ready for them. Unfortunately, as was pointed out to him, no ammunition had been issued and the weapons would therefore have been of very limited use!

During the long hot summer of 1940, as the Royal Air Force was seeking to repel the enemy in the air by day, a call was received at Walthamstow police station that an enemy Zeppelin was off-loading troops to the north of Nazeing, Essex, under cover of darkness. The information was treated seriously and a van-load of police officers, armed with rifles, set off, calling at Chingford and Waltham Abbey on the way to collect extra 'troops' for the task ahead. The briefing was to take place on the road to Nazeing. No further reports had been received from the area concerned as the police van sped northwards towards its encounter with the might of the Wehrmacht. It was as they approached the scene that one of the officers, realising that something was missing from his unfamiliar rifle, spoke up from the gloomy interior of the van, asking the inspector in charge to pass along the ammunition. It was only then that the others realised that, not only were they all carrying unloaded weapons, but that no one had thought to pick any ammunition up. The idea of repelling the German military machine with nothing more lethal than the police issue truncheon really doesn't bear thinking about. Fortunately the débâcle was not as serious as it might have been; in the early morning light the Zeppelin disgorging hundreds of well-armed and highly-trained shock troops turned out to be just a partially-deflated stray barrage balloon. If nothing else, this incident amply illustrates the folly of relying on wholly untrained men, armed with unfamiliar weapons to defend the nation.

It is in fact a wonder that not more damage was done by the relative ineptitude of the police 'marksmen'. Time and again untrained and inexperienced police anti-parachutists were to be found crawling around various open spaces in search of these phantom enemies, weapons at the ready. Any cattle or sheep wandering in the area were in mortal peril from trigger-happy constabularies.

War Reserve Constable Norman Buchanan, the peacetime ladies hairdresser in Gravesend was, on the face of it, an unlikely choice for the issue of a deadly firearm but nevertheless, having been given a modicum of training, he had been issued with a revolver as he was occasionally sent in one of the Kent force's open MG patrol cars to look for a German airman who had been shot down. On one occasion he came upon a German airman who was pointing a pistol at him and, fearing he was about to be gunned down, was on the point of firing first when he realised that the pistol was being proffered butt-first in token of surrender. The airman was, in fact, a mere lad of 16 or 17 and was crying with the shock of his forced arrival on British soil.

Sergeant Grey from Millwall records how one time he and others went in search of reported parachutists without any success and, to relieve the tension and get a little target practice, took pot shots at the chimney of an empty house. Despite the fact that an air raid was in progress at the time, an anti-aircraft battery heard the shots and reported them to the police station. The quick-witted sergeant assured the worried military that the shots were undoubtedly fired by over-enthusiastic Home Guards and that he would ensure the appropriate action was taken.

This unfamiliarity with firearms often had repercussions where the police came into contact with downed enemy airmen. George Bland who was serving in the West Riding Constabulary at the time recalls an occasion when a German airman was brought to the police station (on the back of a police motorcycle!). The superintendent was called and duly arrived, resplendent in his uniform frock coat. The airman's Luger pistol was a source of great interest and was handed round the assembled policemen, one of whom inadvertently pulled the trigger. The bullet ricocheted around the parade room, knocking off lumps of plaster but fortunately missed all those present, including the puce-complexioned superintendent. The culprit was quickly made to appreciate the error of his ways. In fact, many tales are told of inexperienced policemen narrowly avoiding shooting their colleagues through mishandling their own or other people's weapons.

As more weapons and time became available, steps were taken wherever possible to offer some firearms training. A number of Kent policemen were sent to the ranges at the School of Musketry at Hythe where they at least learned to handle their weapons safely, even if they did not become crack shots. In London, some officers were taken to the docks to practise firing their .300 rifles with just five rounds each. Practice ceased when one tried to fire a .303 tracer round and jammed his weapon. In other areas, like East Yorkshire, the police were given firearms training by the military but never had any weapons issued. A writer to the *Police Review*[9] claimed that he could quote the instance of a police authority which had not issued a single firearm to men on outside protection duties, nor provided any small arms instruction.

The police were not the only ones whose unfamiliarity with firearms gave cause for concern. One Essex officer recalls that the commander of the local Home Guard was the local publican who, on one occasion, turned up at the officer's lodgings in full uniform, complete with a service revolver. This was at a time when the public were being encouraged to surrender any unlawfully held firearms under a general amnesty and, knowing that the publican was not the holder of a firearms certificate, the officer asked to examine it and, once it was in his hands, promptly confiscated it as he was sure the publican was the type of man who, in a crisis, would shoot first and ask questions afterwards. They still remained friends after this episode!

It has to be admitted, however, that the police themselves were not always as law-abiding as they might have been. Eileen Hanna, whose mother was the police matron at Woolwich Police Station, remembers one young constable, in the very early days of the war, buying himself an air pistol. Anxious to try it out, he embarked upon some practice from an upstairs window, using a metal advertising panel across the road as the target. The sound of the pellets hitting this resulted in complete panic with people hurling themselves to the ground, convinced that Hitler's Blitzkrieg had started!

If the British police avoided carrying firearms, this was not the case with our American allies, who appeared to find it necessary to carry their weapons in England, even when off duty. It became a popular pastime wherever the GIs were stationed to watch them collect their monthly payroll from the local bank. Norman Longmate[10] describes how:

> ... *the inhabitants of the small East Anglian town of*

Waiting for "Operation Sealion"

Halesworth, where there was rarely any crime more serious than riding a bicycle without a lamp, were highly diverted at the arrival of a jeep in the sleepy market place, followed by a couple of MPs jumping out and standing guard with revolvers at the ready while two more went in to draw the money....

A British detective sergeant recollects a similar scene at Carfax in the centre of peaceful academic Oxford, where he came upon four burly Military Policemen stationed around a bank entrance

... covering the inoffensive but intrigued population with sub-machine guns ... "I was told they were collecting the payroll".

The same officer (was) ... on duty at the police station (when) a Top Sergeant arrived and asked casually for a couple of armed Gmen to attend on the following day at the American-occupied Churchill Hospital when two months' pay was to be issued to his newly-arrived unit. They could muster, he explained shamefacedly, not a single firearm between them, their arms having been on a ship which had been lost. ... although unable to muster any Gmen, the British sergeant did discover a 'rather rusty revolver', which he carried conspicuously as the pay was issued. (Fortunately no pay snatch was attempted; he had no ammunition for the gun).

How different from the British armed forces! When John Thompson was serving at Minster (Kent) – a beat which covered Manston airfield – he was shown the stock of pikes held by the RAF police which the Defence Minister apparently believed to be a formidable weapon and proof against the machine guns and artillery used by the enemy!

Gradually, of course, the supply of firearms improved and all the Armed Forces were properly and suitably equipped to face the expected onslaught from across the Channel and even the police had access to a few weapons, albeit often of very ancient provenance. Rifles which had seen service on the Somme or even at Rorke's Drift found their way into the police armouries (if such a term can be used to describe what was usually simply a locked wooden cupboard) and it is perhaps fortunate that seldom if ever were the police called upon to use these weapons in anger.

125

5. Transports of Delight

One aspect of life on which the war had an immediate, significant and lasting effect was the traffic on the roads. Even before the declaration of war, the authorities had prepared plans for the requisition of vehicles suitable for military or other essential use. Although the actual requisition was the job of an Impressment Officer, the police were required to attend whenever a vehicle was to be requisitioned to ensure that there was no breach of the peace occasioned by irate vehicle owners.

This aspect had only a limited effect, however, and the first real change was the introduction of petrol rationing almost as soon as the war started. Petrol reserved for essential commercial use was dyed red, although it was an open secret that the dye could be removed by pouring the petrol through the filter of a gas mask (although it is not clear what effect this had on the efficacy of the respirator). All car owners were given a basic ration, sufficient for around 100 miles a month, supplemented where they could show that they had a genuine and essential need for additional supplies. Petrol hoarding was banned but, despite the very real dangers, was widely practised by storing supplies in all sorts of unsuitable containers, including bath tubs and kitchen coppers.

The careful conservation of precious petrol meant that cars were used only where necessary and that all the seats were filled if this proved practicable. Gradually, however, reduced rations and the scarcity of tyres and spare parts meant that many a cherished motor car was soon lovingly tucked away in its garage for the duration, propped on bricks or wood blocks to preserve the tyres. The final blow came in March, 1942 when the basic petrol ration was completely suspended. Apart from buses (working reduced schedules and often stopping completely at 9.45 pm), taxis (restricted to a distance of five miles from the borough boundary in many towns) and a few commercial vehicles, the military now had the roads to themselves, which was perhaps just as well as the standard of driving of some of these ill-trained service drivers left much to be desired. The suspension of the driving test also meant that the few new civilian drivers were often equally incompetent.

The reduced number of buses available meant that a fairer system of boarding than the pre-war free-for-all had to be devised and queuing became mandatory – another wartime measure which has found a permanent place in our lifestyles.

When the air raids on London first started all traffic used to come to a halt while the drivers and passengers sought shelter but this quickly proved impracticable as it hindered the movement of essential vehicles. Buses would therefore travel more or less normally although this had its dangers as is shown by an incident at Palmers Green where a bus was caught in the blast of two bombs at the same time and the crew and 47 passengers all perished. Special Sergeant Frank Butler was travelling on a bus at the height of the London Blitz when a bus inspector whispered something to the conductress. When he had gone she approached the policeman and told him that the inspector had used the word purple and asked what this might mean. The officer knew very well that this confidential code word meant that an air raid was imminent in that area but, as the other passengers were listening intently, he simply told the conductress to let her driver know. The latter promptly switched off all his lights and put his foot down in an attempt to get out of the area as soon as possible.

With the ending of the basic petrol ration, any driver could be stopped by the police and required to prove that his journey was essential and that he was travelling by the shortest possible route. One business man who deviated from his set route for about three-quarters of a mile to go home for lunch was convicted of a breach of this regulation. Sergeant Bill Henley of Mark Cross was supervising a late night road check during this period when one of the constables stopped a van which was crammed with young girls in their best outfits. The driver explained that he had been to a dance and the girls had missed their last bus home. Feeling sorry for them and not wishing to see them walk the several miles to their home village in the dark, he had deviated from his route so as to give them a lift. He protested that he was doing a public service and the young constable was inclined to be lenient with him. The sergeant then took a hand and, drawing on his extensive local knowledge, told the driver that they had not missed the last bus. The driver protested that this was not so and an argument looked set to begin when the the bus in question came wheezing up the hill, ample testimony to the mendacity of the van driver who was promptly booked for the offence.

On another occasion, the same officer was at a road check when a young driver admitted that he had made a small detour to take his fiancé home. Because the driver was honest and the distance involved was very small, the sergeant let him go with a caution, adding, 'And I suggest you turn left at the top of the hill and go that way; there's another road check on the other road.'

The actor-composer, Ivor Novello was less fortunate and spent four weeks in jail for travelling between the London theatre which was staging his musical comedy, *The Dancing Years,* and his home in Berkshire. A farmer in Wales managed to circumvent the regulations by using the fuel allocated for his trucks and tractors and, to fend off any awkward questions, kept a piece of work for the blacksmith permanently in his car, the smithy being next door to the pub. In many areas horses and horse-drawn vehicles, already obsolescent, experienced a sudden revival and it was not uncommon in some places to see the country doctor making his rounds on a sturdy hunter, a sight not seen for a generation. One doctor even managed to persuade the Inland Revenue to agree a tax allowance of £90 a year for the keep of his horse.

Immediately prior to the war there were some 2,000,000 private cars and 400,000 motorcycles on the road and there were still 1,400,000 cars a year later but, after the suspension of the basic ration, the number of cars dropped to 700,000 rapidly ageing and deteriorating private cars and around 125,000 motorcycles. With the invasion scare at its height, the police in the coastal areas were ordered to immobilise all vehicles in the area in the event of a landing by the enemy – if necessary by permanent, drastic steps.

The lack of transport, both private and public, placed a severe strain on those working odd hours, which included most of the civil defence services as well as the police. One special constable in Yorkshire remembers how he had to walk home, a distance of over three miles, carrying a steel helmet, gas mask, handcuffs, truncheon and a heavy overcoat after performing a full shift of police work. Bicycles, already a popular means of transport for the working classes, gained an unprecedented popularity, although this form of locomotion also suffered from a lack of spare parts and tyres. Batteries, too, were in short supply and often meant that the trusty Raleigh or BSA had to be left at home at night, just when it was most needed.

The lack of transport had some other consequences, as a former

Metropolitan policeman recalls. One night, around 1 am he was on motor patrol in the East End of London, when he saw an off-duty colleague walking towards him.

We stopped, and asked him what he was doing and he told us he was a member of the police golf team which had been playing a team from Hainault. They had had a good match and had spent a long time in the '19th' afterwards. As there was no public transport, a member of the opposing team had offered to run him and another constable home. On the way, however, it was obvious that the driver was very much under the influence and the first constable asked to get out. The other one stayed with the car. Some time later, a bus driver reported a car being driven 'all over the place'. We attended and found the car concerned was the one from the golf club and it had been involved in an accident. The off-duty policeman passenger was still there so I told him to scarper while we arrested the driver for being drunk in charge. At the station no mention was made of the passenger but, in court, the defending solicitor questioned us about the passenger which the driver claimed had been with him. Not wishing to commit perjury we agreed that there had been a passenger but said that while we were escorting the driver to the police car, the passenger had absconded (which was not a lie because that is exactly what we told him to do). The court accepted the story and duly convicted the driver but our superiors were very suspicious and questioned us closely. We stuck to our story and, although the powers-that-be had a pretty good idea as to what had gone on, we heard no more about it.

The next, far-reaching effect which the war had on road traffic was the introduction of the blackout. Arduous and dangerous for the pedestrian, the blackout was a nightmare for the motorist. Originally all street lighting was extinguished and, although sharp corners, kerbs, steps and car running boards and mudguards had been painted white, and tree trunks encircled by three painted white rings, people still collided with them or fell over them or were knocked down by them. Motorists were instructed that only heavily masked sidelights were allowed to be shown; red rear lights were permitted but the number plate light had to be blanked off or removed. Those who were driving in unfamiliar towns were at an added disadvantage, as A G Street wrote concerning a visit he made to Birmingham in November, 1939:

> *I saw my intended hotel quite close three times, but could not manage to get my car to its front door. After half-an-hour's vain driving, I cast myself on to the bosom of a stalwart policeman, admitting that I was just one poor silly chump from the south. He cheered me a trifle by telling me that I was not the only one, and gave me fool-proof directions which I was able to follow to a successful conclusion. I later learned the classic story of one poor motorist who drove helplessly around and round a square in Birmingham until King Edward the Seventh leaned down from his pedestal and said, 'Do you mind asking a policeman how to get out of this? You are making my mother on the other side of the square quite giddy'*[1].

The police had still to try to control the traffic, now driven by virtually blind motorists and various ingenious solutions were proffered to make the constable on point duty visible to drivers. In Brighton, experiments were carried out with a coat and helmet treated with a special paint. The rays from two ultra-violet lights were played on him and it is reported that he was perfectly visible to motorists but 'invisible to raiding airmen'. In Salford, the police invented an aluminium device which fitted onto the top of a normal police helmet, with the word 'POLICE' in large letters. A 4 volt battery in the officer's pocket provided the power to illuminate the sign at night, while the constable held a torch with red and green filters to direct the traffic. This some-what Heath-Robinson affair does not appear to have caught on!

By January 1940, one person in five had had some sort of blackout-related accident and Winston Churchill took time off from directing the Admiralty to suggest that some modified form of lighting would save lives, alleviate depression and reduce crime. As a result, very dim street lighting was restored at crossroads and other danger spots and motorists were permitted to use the offside headlamp provided it was fitted with the official pattern mask, which has been described as similar to a black cocoa tin with three shielded slits cut in the end. Traffic lights were all masked and the police often switched them off altogether during the blackout hours, leaving the few motorists on the roads to sort themselves out as best they could. Despite these difficulties, some

131

motorists doused even these inadequate lights during a 'red' alert, resulting in at least one fatal accident.

The poor lighting imposed a great strain on drivers, especially those working long hours in the dark, such as bus drivers. It was not un-common for a bus to leave the road entirely and end up in a field. On one such occasion, the traffic policeman called to attend the scene did not endear himself to the driver by asking if he had thought of volunteering for the Tank Corps. In a number of cities the trams and trolley buses, scheduled for replacement by petrol-engined buses, were given a reprieve, although the silent approach of the latter was an additional hazard in the blackout.

Speed was restricted to 20 mph after dark as a result of the dramatic increase in road accidents (but proved very difficult to enforce). Although the actual number of accidents which occurred during the early war years was fewer than pre-war, the consequences were much more deadly. In 1939/40 there were 8,400 road deaths, many of which occurred during the blackout while in 1940/41 the number rose to over 10,000. It is estimated that for every two persons killed through enemy action, one was killed on the roads. The Police Review quotes 926 fatal accidents in Nov 1939 (313 more than the same month the previous year), mostly pedestrians and mainly because of the blackout.

The number of accidents meant that the new War Reserve constables had to learn very quickly how to deal with such incidents, often under extremely trying circumstances. For one such officer, one of his first accidents was nearly his last. While taking the particulars of two vehicles involved in an accident in the blackout, neither showing lights on police instructions, he was so engrossed in his job that he didn't hear or ignored the sound of a falling bomb until a nearby Home Guard, a veteran of the Great War, grabbed him and pulled him into the ditch.

The speed limit and blackout did not always stop reckless driving as Police War Reserve Constable Norman Buchanan found. On motor patrol duty near Gravesend (Kent) he was instructed to watch out for and stop a Wolseley car travelling at high speed along the A2 road from London. The vehicle was easy to spot because of the distinctive illuminated Wolseley badge on the radiator but the driver refused to obey his signal to stop and sped on, eventually crashing in Rochester. The driver, who was killed in the crash, was no thief or 'joy-rider' but simply a young serviceman late back from leave.

But perhaps the biggest traffic problems came with the arrival of the American troops in 1942. Many lacked real driving skills and the practice of driving on the left-hand side of the road was completely alien to them. Norman Longmate[2] describes how one young Cambridge girl's first sight of a GI was nearly her last. Approaching her car as she drove along the Newmarket road came 'the biggest truck, driven by the biggest black man' she had ever seen, roaring straight towards her on the wrong side of the road. Since he had obviously not learned the English rule of the road, she prudently forgot it herself and nipped to the other side of the road and a collision was averted.

There are many tales told about these visitors from 'across the Pond', their large trucks and ubiquitous Jeeps and one lasting impression of them seems to have been their love of speed. Norman Longmate goes on to describe one Hampshire woman's experience:

> *They would drive up to my HQ at full steam only to brake at the entrance in a cloud of dust and a scream of tyres and, before the engine's flywheel had ceased revolving, the dispatch rider would be halfway up the steps of the building to deliver what would, as likely as not, be of minor importance and seldom urgent*[3].

In view of the danger of vehicles being used by unauthorised persons, such as spies and invading Germans, the Motor Vehicles (Control) Order, 1940, required motorists to immobilise their vehicles. The first safeguard was to close all windows, remove the ignition key and lock the doors. Although there was little point in locking the doors of an open-topped car, some policemen insisted on this being done. In fact, so poor were the locking devices on cars of that era that a short length of tubing or even, in some cases, a strong wrist, was sufficient to force the handle to open the car. To compensate for this, drivers were required to further immobilise their vehicles by removing part of the mechanism – usually the rotor arm or the HT lead to the distributor. The instructions issued to the Metropolitan Police were that, if an insecure vehicle was discovered, they were to try to locate the owner, leaving the vehicle in charge of another officer, and to use any reasonable means to prevent the vehicle from being driven away or else remove it to a police station. Officers were not to interfere with the mechanism unless no other means were available. Under normal circumstances, no police officer should resort to 'extreme measures' without the aid of a skilled police mechanic. These 'extreme measures' did not extend to the deflating of tyres – a fairly common practice in some parts and, as anyone who has had to inflate four tyres from dead flat using just an inefficient hand pump will appreciate, was an salutary deterrent. For anyone who had already taken adequate steps to immobilise his vehicle, this was highly annoying and it is recorded that one irate motorist actually managed to get the police to inflate his tyres for him after they had unjustly let them down in Holborn. The Dunlop tyre company issued a card which stated, 'This vehicle is immobilised, There is no need to deflate the tyres.' But the police did not always accept this assurance.

Eric St Johnston tells of how this Order had amusingly embarrassing consequences when, in November 1941, as Chief Constable of Oxfordshire, he attended a reception for General de Gaulle at Balliol college, in company with Charles Fox, the Chief Constable of Oxford City. On leaving they saw Lord Nuffield sitting at the wheel of the small Morris car he normally drove. He kept pressing the starter but to no avail and so the two policemen offered to help. 'Just give me a push,' said the noble Lord, 'It will start in a moment'. And so the inhabitants of Oxford were treated to the rare sight of two chief constables, in full uniform, pushing the leading British car manufacturer in a small family saloon along the Broad. All to no avail.

Suddenly Lord Nuffield slammed on the brakes and explained, 'Oh, I know, it's all your fault. You have advised us to immobilise our cars. I've got a secret switch', and pressing a switch underneath his seat, he started the car and drove away with a wave of his hand.

Other embarrassing situations resulted from a lack of mechanical knowledge or simply a lack of commonsense. The history of the Oldham Borough Police[4] records an incident in which a special constable, on patrol in the town centre, noticed an unusually large number of cars near the town's principal hotel, where a party was evidently in progress. He began to check these vehicles to ensure that they had been properly immobilised and, as it turned out, many of the guests had completely overlooked this requirement. So the constable methodically went about removing the rotor arms.

One by one the small items of equipment were removed from the car engines and dropped into the constable's pockets. Then he took the lot back to police headquarters and left them there to be collected by the owners. The party at (the hotel) ended at midnight. Those guests who had forgotten to remove the rotor arms from their cars struggled for some time to get their vehicles started before learning that they would have to collect the missing items from police headquarters. Unfortunately, the rotor arms had not been marked with any means of identification by the special constable, and it was some considerable time before the last guest could begin his weary journey home. And one guest, unaware of the special constable's diligent attention to duty, pushed his car past the police station and the full length of the High Street before discovering he had no rotor arm in the vehicle.

In 1940, with the invasion scare at its height, Sir Will Spens, the Regional Commissioner for East Anglia, issued an order that no private car might use any road within five miles of the main coastal towns unless they held a special permit. Cars without a permit had either to be removed from the area altogether or effectively immobilised. In the latter case, parts removed from vehicles had to be handed over to the police to be delivered to a special store in Bedford for safe keeping. Spens further ordered that all small craft had to be immobilised. They were taken from the water and removed to a safe distance inland. A night-time curfew was imposed within a five mile wide coastal strip from one end of the Region to the other. Towns and villages were excluded. as was traffic on A and B class roads.

Travel was rendered even more perilous by the requirement under the Removal of Direction Signs Order, 1940, to uproot or obliterate all signposts, milestones and place names from the roadsides in order to confuse the enemy. Whether or not this would have had the intended effect of creating confusion among the German invaders or parachutists is not known, but it certainly had that effect on native travellers, once they left familiar surroundings. It is never amusing to lose one's way and when this is coupled with a serious lack of fuel, the results can be, and often were, disastrous. The public were advised not to respond to any enquiries for directions or to tell anyone where they were. Correspondence in The Times raised the question what one should do if asked the way by a motorist, the suggested answer being to ask the motorist for his identity card. This ignored, however, the fact that people had been warned never to show their identity card to unauthorised persons. Ralph Ingersoll gives a very illuminating description of this phenomenon as it affected a non-British visitor:

> *[Our trip] was half-way over before we noticed the most characteristic thing of all: the complete absence of clues as to where we were. At the crossroads there are no signposts whatever, but this is only the beginning. In each town wherever, on a sign or the glass window of a store front, the name of the town or the county might have been revealed it was carefully painted out. Even the commercial vans on the road had addresses and telephone numbers conspicuously painted out. England's roads are complicated things. Later, even when I was driving with officers who had grown up in the country, we were continually getting lost or stopping every little while to ask directions of a passerby. I always found that directions were cheerfully given but I was told this co-operation was simply evidence that the September invasion scare had passed[5].*

There is some indication that the removal of place names did cause a degree of confusion. A report from an enemy agent working on the south coast referred to 'the area Tunbridge Wells to Beachy Head'. The *Abwehr* made a note on this report to the effect that '... Tunbridge, which lies on the railway line from Hastings to London, must, according to the sense of the report, also lie on the coast'. But, in fact, both Tonbridge and Tunbridge Wells lie some thirty miles from the coast and it is possible that the agent was confused by the fact that the owner of the post office and general stores in Camber (on the coast near to Hastings) was named Tunbridge and the sign over his shop read 'TUNBRIDGE – POST OFFICE AND STORES', the name of the village beneath this being deleted.

The drivers of military vehicles found a number of ways to circumvent this problem. One was to look at the manhole covers in the roadway which often bore the name of the nearest town. Telephone kiosks also had their uses as no one had thought to remove the label giving the location of the kiosk for emergency use.

However, the general introduction of the white line painted down the centre of the carriageway, previously an exception, was a boon and one which endured after the war had ended.

Enemy action only added to the problems of those travelling on the roads and railways of Britain. Craters big enough to hold a double-decker bus appeared in some roads and the debris from bombed buildings formed an impenetrable barrier across road and rail. Not all road users appreciated the problems facing the police and transport undertakings. On Tuesday, 13 May, 1941, one of the London dailies published an article headed 'BLITZ TRAFFIC CHAOS – WHY?'. A reporter, who had presumably spent a fairly comfortable night in some outer suburb complained bitterly that, on the Monday, his car had been diverted several times and that 'complete routes from one side of London to the other were never clearly defined'.

'Who,' he asked, 'was responsible for this muddle? Little had been done. Speedy transport is the life-blood of London.' – and a good deal more to the same effect. To those who had been in the middle of it, to those who had looked out over London in the early hours after the heavy raid of Saturday/Sunday 10/11 May and had seen major fires in all directions, too many to count, burning fiercely, to the police and wardens, to the fire service and demolition parties who had toiled through the Saturday night, all day Sunday and all through the Sunday night, this was a bit too much[6]. In fact, on the Sunday morning all the bridges over the Thames were closed for some reason or another – hoses, fires, dangerous structures, unexploded bombs, etc. No traffic had been able to move in the City at all and several vital traffic junctions, like the Elephant and Castle and Gardiner's Corner had been impassable. All Southern Railway terminii had been closed.

For the police, one of the major responsibilities during and after a raid was the devising and signing alternative routes. This was difficult where there was extensive damage; a route might be usable for a few hundred yards or a mile or so but would be no good to a person wanting to get right through. It was obviously impossible to indicate the necessary information on hundreds of diversion boards and, in retrospect, it is remarkable how quickly traffic was got moving again after some of the heavy raids. Much of the credit must go to the indefatigable police motorcyclists who sallied forth in the small hours to plan routes around obstructions and danger points. Close to the more devastated areas the police would set up interrogation lay-bys to which they could direct doubtful vehicles while they checked on their business, without interrupting the flow of legitimate traffic.

London was, of course, not the only city to be brought to a near standstill by enemy action, nor was it simply a question of ordinary workers going about their normal business. Some Coventry 'trekkers' were so desperate to leave town, that one Morris Minor van is reported to have hit an unlit bomb crater at speed. Its front wheels went into the crater and the car turned a complete somersault, landing on all four wheel on the other side. The occupants were merely dazed and soon recovered sufficiently to resume their hasty flight. Meanwhile, others were trying to get in but such was the ferocity of some raids that even emergency vehicles were unable to get through. An auxiliary fireman from Birmingham was one of many firefighters who were sent to Coventry during the devastating raids on that city:

> *As we approached Coventry at speed I noticed people waving us down. This I ignored as often on our way to a fire we had been stopped by someone whose garden shed was on fire. But the nearer we got the more urgent the waves got. I eventually stopped behind another vehicle and was approached by a policeman... He cried as he said, 'You may as well go back, mate, you can't get in.' We stayed until 2 am and like the others we then returned home. No one spoke and I think someone was sick*[7].

It was, of course, a primary police task under these circumstances to try to prevent non-essential vehicles from travelling in the raided areas. This meant stopping everything which was not obviously an emergency vehicle and turning back any which had no urgent business in the area. Naturally, this did not always please those who were on legitimate business but were not obviously so, like the airman who was engaged in conveying operational messages around the district. He found himself being repeatedly stopped by policemen with red torches, although he was invariably waved on once the officer saw that he was an airman and in an official car. Nevertheless, his patience began to wear thin and, when he was stopped for the sixth time, he drew his service revolver and waved it at the policeman who rapidly signalled him to carry on.

> *'So I said, "I'll flash my light the next time so get out of my way, I'm in a bloody hurry,' Needless to say I was not stopped again*[8].

No doubt the policeman was left reflecting on the utter bloody-mindedness of people who consider that they and/or their mission transcends everything else and places them above ordinary mortals and, had he not got his hands full with much more vital matters, would undoubtedly have conveyed this to the impatient and self-important airman.

As the war progressed and the Second Front became imminent, the whole of Britain became akin to a huge military camp. Troops and their equipment were on the move from one end of the country to another, especially towards the marshalling areas in the south of the country. Military vehicles, driven by soldiers strange to the area, often not even British since much of the invasion force was to consist of Americans, needed guidance and this task, like so many others, fell on the police. One such was Constable Tom Longhurst of Kent who, on an ex-WD Indian motorcycle, spent every night for several weeks escorting convoys along the A2 road, from Faversham, where he relieved another police escort, to Rainham, where he in turn handed his charges over to an officer from the next division. As soon as one convoy was duly handed over, the escorts returned to their starting point to meet the next one.

On one occasion Tom Longhurst was wending his way back to Faversham to meet his next clutch of 'chicks' when he came upon the convoy parked beside the road, taking up much of the opposite carriageway. As he approached these vehicles, another lorry came towards him at high speed, without lights and on the wrong side of the road, forcing him off the road. Cursing the reckless driver roundly and comprehensively, Tom Longhust remounted his machine and led the waiting convoy westwards towards Rainham. On the way they came across another convoy, stationary at the side of the road, with a great deal of bustle and activity in evidence. On stopping to see what had occurred, he found that the same rogue lorry had run down and killed a Canadian soldier who was crossing the road to relieve himself in the bushes at the side of the road. The lorry made no attempt to stop and was never traced.

Another constable engaged on similar duties was Geoffrey Taylor of the Metropolitan Police. One of his duties was to help escort the daily military convoys through the East End of London on a motor cycle, usually riding well ahead to warn oncoming traffic or holding up vehicles at crossroads and other junctions or danger spots. He and his colleagues would leapfrog up and down the convoy, changing places from front to rear and back again so that the convoy could maintain the regulation speed of 15 mph. This speed limit would be ignored when the escorted lorry contained unexploded bombs or mines and the sight of a military vehicle flying a red flag and escorted by two police 'speed-cops', all travelling at high speed, was enough to ensure that all other traffic kept well clear. Often the police motorcyclists would be aided by military dispatch riders or MPs in their task of keeping the convoy together. Some of the drivers were ATS girls with very little experience and it is all credit to them that they managed as well as they did, especially in the dark.

Philip Chignell, who kept a comprehensive diary at this time, quotes in his entry for 9 December, 1941 :

> *One fatal casualty so far ... our own army lorries have knocked down more lamp posts. You just knock one down, look round and laugh and drive on. Later a policeman comes along and stands by the fallen post, chivvying choirboys and the like away until two men come along with spades and a barrow. The post is removed ... one man remains behind to fill up the hole where the post stood ...* [9].

So far as the police themselves were concerned, motor vehicles were still something of a novelty in the 1930s. In Oxfordshire there were no traffic patrol cars, the only vehicles the force possessed were six Hillman Minx cars, one for each division and one for use by Headquarters personnel. Lancashire were experimenting with 'courtesy cops' in an effort to reduce the tremendous slaughter on the roads and to enforce the provisions of the 1930 Road Traffic Act. Certain other forces had taken similar, tentative steps towards mechanisation, especially those county forces which had a trunk road running through their area. Several forces set up a small Traffic Division or Mobile Section; in the East Riding of Yorkshire for example, there was a Traffic Patrol car located at each main police station – about 10 in all – which were used for all sorts of duties where a car was needed. By 1944 the Chief Constable was reported as seeking authority to purchase 17 patrol cars, by means of which he claimed 18 constables could do the work of

30 previously. He had not intended to implement this scheme until after the war was over but lack of manpower had forced his hand. By 1941, the chief constable of Northamptonshire was reported as proposing to introduce a 'courtesy' patrol scheme in order to improve the standard of road behaviour and to bring about a reduction in the number of accidents. He proposed that these vehicles, which would be clearly marked as police cars, should be crewed by uniformed members of the Women's Auxiliary Police Corps, accompanied by a police officer as observer.

In Kent, the Traffic Division was created in 1930 and equipped with one Rover saloon and 19 motorcycles at a total cost of just over £1,300. This 'fleet' was supplemented in 1933 by two open-topped MG sports cars, the drivers of which were much envied. Similar vehicles were used by other forces, such as West Sussex, even though these two-seaters with a soft-top and no boot were not very practical for police work. As the war progressed and regular policemen became thinner on the ground, these cherished cars were handed over to the War Reserves to use, much of whose work consisted of ferrying prisoners (including prisoners of war) to the local prison for processing and for general dispatch runs. Air raids proved an additional hazard to road users and War Reserve Constable Norman Buchanan was not very popular when he drove his smart new MG into a bomb crater which had suddenly appeared in the road he was travelling on near Gravesend.

A similar situation existed in Waltham Abbey (Metropolitan Police) where, on the outbreak of the war, the station was supplied with its first car, a Wolseley 14. Little thought had been given to the availability of drivers and only one sergeant and one constable held driving licences. The arrival of Police War Reserves eased matters since three of these were drivers and were able to share in the driving. Being unused to the luxury of a car, the supervisory staff at the station tended to use it for administrative purposes rather than patrol. At least it saved the inspector from getting wet when he wanted to visit his constables on the beat.

Although many city and borough forces lacked any kind of motor vehicle, a few (Bradford, Sheffield, etc.) used some small cars for patrol work, often the ubiquitous Morris 8 tourer.

The most novel aspect was the use of females to drive police cars – an unheard of state of affairs in most forces – but the introduction of the

WAPC and the increase in the number of policewomen meant that the force had a completely new source of possible drivers to add to the War Reserves. WAPC Darlington was one sworn auxiliary who was detailed for motor patrol duties in Stafford. She tells how 'all the ladies who could drive' (about a dozen in all) were allocated this type of work, enforcing speed limits and escorting the many abnormally wide loads.

During the war, production of civilian cars was extremely limited and the whole output was earmarked for the police and other essential services. Such vehicles as found their way into police garages were, understandably, carefully nurtured and the drivers were expected to cherish them. Constable Bill Cavey and his partner in the Metropolitan Police were among those lucky officers who had the use of a brand new patrol car, in their case a large Ford V8 complete with bell and public address equipment and just 15 to 20 miles on the 'clock'. One day they were ordered to the Wandsworth flats where there had been reports of a 'flasher' – a man indecently exposing himself. On arrival they saw a man talking to two little girls who then went with him across the flats to a railway cutting where they disappeared from view. Constable Cavey jumped from the car and ran to the cutting where he was just in time to see the man lifting the skirt of one of the girls. He shouted and the man made off towards the woods. The driver of the patrol car, seeing this, set of across the grass in the shining new car to assist and Bill Cavey caught the man just as he was about to disappear into the woods. The car arrived almost simultaneously, braked, skidded on the grass and glided into a large and very prickly hawthorn tree. The whole front of the car was badly scratched but, fortunately, as they had a prisoner, no disciplinary action was taken against the driver.

Later, the same crew in the same car, with an additional observer in the back, were hurrying to an incident when the car hit a poorly-filled trench which had been excavated by one of the public utilities. The excellent springing of this quality car took the shock but, when the Bill Cavey in the front passenger seat turned to speak to the observer in the back, he found he was lying unconscious, having struck his head on the ash roof bar to which the roof lining was attached. Luckily, he soon recovered with nothing worse than a headache.

Over-enthusiastic drivers were not the only hazard which faced police vehicles:

> *On a particularly nasty night a van was sent out to do a job*

142

which should have taken only a short time. The hours went by but the van did not return and no one had seen it. At last, after about three hours, the driver walked into the office, saluted smartly and handed in a small piece of paper. It was the revenue licence. 'All that's left of the van, Sergeant.' He explained that he had left the van for a short time and on return had found only a large hole – no sign of the van except the revenue licence fluttering gently amongst the rubble[10].

The lack of experienced officers through call-up meant that it often became necessary to group two or even more rural beats together and make them the responsibility of just one constable. In the East Riding of Yorkshire this meant that each constable had an enormous area to cover and, to enable him to get around his greatly enlarged 'patch', the force's Traffic Sergeant was sent all over the country accompanied by a Ministry of Transport agent, to locate and buy some small, second-hand cars for their use. He managed to find a dozen suitable cars and then had to teach the rural men to drive – not an easy task as few of them were motor- minded.

As time went on, the availability of vehicles for police purposes was restricted more by the lack of petrol, oil and tyres than by a lack of vehicles themselves. Mileage had to be kept to a minimum and, in the Metropolitan Police, the total mileage covered during each of the war years was about half that covered in 1939.

In common with the rest of the working classes, bicycles were the principal means of transport for most policemen, both to get to and from work and also, where the beat was designated a 'cycle beat', to cover his designated area. Although some WAPCs were lucky enough to be allocated to motor patrol duties, others were not so fortunate, as Agnes Cook discovered:

Cupar was a farming town with a market every Tuesday when the farmers brought their goods to market to sell and exchange. I remember one day trying to cycle to my digs through a flock of sheep. My greatcoat caught in the bike chain and down I went amongst the sheep who couldn't have cared less and just milled around while I tried to rescue what was left of my dignity. Since it was a small town everyone knew everyone else and the story of my "downfall" reached my landlady before I got home[11].

Even the US 'Army of Occupation' took to this novel (for them) means of locomotion which was ideal for getting around on the vast airfields used by their B17 Flying Fortresses. Although many had never ridden a bicycle before and looked upon them more as toys, the roads of East Anglia were quickly filled with gum-chewing, cigar-smoking figures in khaki drab, usually riding on the wrong side of the road. To the local policeman the sight of a group of these extrovert young men acting as an unofficial trick-cycling team in the main street of his village was a problem he had never encountered before and made another addition to his repertoire of 'war duties.'

It was normal for a rural constable to rely entirely on his trusty bicycle and there was very little likelihood of any motorised assistance from the neighbouring town section. Even quite remote places had to be visited by bicycle; one constable told his superior that a certain large house on his beat was 'A good ten minutes walk on a bike!' Questioned as to this curious assessment it transpired that, in fact, the house in question was up a steep hill up which no one in their right minds would try to ride a heavy, single-geared police bicycle so it was indeed 'ten minutes walk (with a bike)'.

In many cases the sergeant too was reliant on a bicycle to get around his section although in some larger sections the sergeant was entrusted with a small car (the sergeant at Wragby in Lincolnshire was the proud possessor of a Standard 8 allocated to him to supervise his five constables on their large rural beats and in which he picked up many a downed enemy airman). Some other sergeants, like Bill Henley at Mark Cross (Sussex), used their own motor cars for duty purposes, for which they received petrol money (and coupons).

With the declaration of war and the anticipated explosion in police duties related to civil defence and general war matters, some positive steps had to be taken to improve the mechanisation of the police but this took a long while to filter down to the man on the country beat. Constable Leslie Taylor claims to have clocked up over 7,000 miles on his bicycle every year patrolling his rural beat on the North Downs, a feat made all the harder because of the lack of new tyres and inner tubes. His colleague, Constable Bert Ayers on the Romney Marsh had more luck in that his chief constable gave him permission to buy and use his own motor cycle, for which a petrol allowance would be given. As most of the best machines had been requisitioned for the army, the best he could do was a rather ancient BSA Gold Star, which he later traded in for a better Matchless machine. His colleague, Tom Longhust was perhaps luckier in that he was issued with a machine – an ex-WD Indian, with hand gearchange and a foot clutch, to use, as we saw earlier, in escorting military convoys towards the latter part of the war.

Further north, in the West Riding of Yorkshire, motor cycles were also to the fore and one constable surprised his colleagues by turning up at the police station with a German airman riding on the pillion of his Norton motorcycle. He had scoured some 100 square miles of desolate countryside looking for the crew of a downed Luftwaffe plane, one of a number which had been raiding the Avro works in Yeadon, where the Halifax bombers were being made. On locating the hapless German, the constable disarmed him and gallantly offered him a lift to captivity – an offer the airman could not refuse!

Bill Cavey, who was involved in the unfortunate incident with the new police car on the Wandsworth flats, had been posted to Bow from quieter Leytonstone at the beginning of the war because the loss of the younger men to the armed forces meant that the inner-city areas were very much depleted. However, on arrival he found that there was no vacancy for a driver and so he was put on motorcycle duties, using an Ariel Square Four and only later did he have the considerable benefit of a comfortable car.

Leslie Clarke who was stationed in an Essex village was another motorcycle owner. One night considerable damage was caused to property in the village by enemy action and all the telephones were put out of order. Having to make a report to his Divisional Headquarters three miles away, he set off on his motorcycle.

On arrival, I found the place in darkness and several lads coming out from under tables. They had also had bombs in the vicinity and all telephones were down. I was told to take a report to the County Headquarters at Chelmsford, about 15 miles away. I was nearly out of petrol and told the Super I needed some to make the journey. He nearly blew his nut, suggesting that I was taking advantage of an air raid to get force petrol. I made the journey but I cannot say I enjoyed it, driving in the dark with a mask on the headlight, giving me only a few feet of vision in front[12].

With the lack of fuel and tyres for cars, motorcycles became the most common form of official police transport throughout the whole of the war and performed great service in escorting convoys, abnormal loads and general message delivery duties. Dennis Vorley was a constable in West Sussex during the early war years (before volunteering for flying duties with the RAF) and considered himself fortunate to be chosen for Mobile duties, using a Triumph Speed Twin motor cycle, His main task was to stand by at the police station and, after a raid, sally forth to find out where the bombs had dropped and report back the location, damage and casualties. Since the machines were not equipped with radio, this had to be done in person or by telephone.

When those on foot patrol needed to get to another part of their beat in a hurry, their usual means of transport was a bus or tram. They were expected to pay their fare and it was a disciplinary offence not to do so, but few conductors asked for the money; they knew they would be only too pleased to have a policeman riding with them when they were operating a late night service. In some remote places it was common practice to hand official reports to the bus driver for delivery to the police station. In Harrogate, on court days, a tram made the rounds of the police stations, picking up prisoners and conveying them to the court house as there was no alternative means of transport.

During the Blitz, policemen were happy to use any form of transport they could. Sergeant Grey was working on the Isle of Dogs but lived across the River Thames and, during the worst of the London Blitz experienced great difficulty in getting to his home. His usual route was through the Greenwich Tunnel but this was flooded and, with others, he tried to get a lift on the Thames Police launch. At first the skipper refused to take them but later relented and, laden to the gunwales with policemen and their bicycles, the launch set off across the river. The reason for the skipper's reluctance soon became apparent:

> *The river was alive with hazards, the tide was driving London-wards, carrying anything that would float with it; huge 5 ton rolls of newsprint, rafts of 12 x 4 timbers from riverside timber wharves, crates, boxes, flotsam, junk, oil drums, jars and wicker work. The river stank to high heaven*[13]

If the transport available to the police in the Thirties and Forties was less than adequate by modern standards, the communications systems were even more archaic. Wireless was virtually unknown and few vehicles were equipped with this modern phenomenon, even though the first trials had taken place some 15 years earlier in London. By the early 1930s several forces were conducting experiments with wireless telegraphy (Morse), including Nottingham, Lancashire, West Riding and Brighton, while the Lancashire force first introduced radio in 1936 (2 cars) and, by 1940 had 140 cars so equipped. The Lancashire cars proved invaluable during the raids on Liverpool when, with the whole of the city's telephone system out of action, all top-level communications had to be passed through the cars' radios.

In London the Metropolitan Police were continuing with their trials; the wireless cars had a crew of three – driver, detective and wireless operator, while those which had yet to be equipped with wireless had to make regular contact points at a pre-arranged telephone kiosk or police box. Profiting from this lack of supervision, at least one Metropolitan policeman remembers spending time on his allotment while his colleagues remained with the car, giving him a 'toot' if a message came for them.

By 1939 two high frequency bands had been allocated for police and fire brigade use but those wireless sets which were available were unreliable and prone to 'black spots'. Not until 1940 did the Home Office make VHF radio channels available to city and borough forces with at least 75,000 inhabitants. The possibilities for the county forces at that time were not very promising and, on the whole, few police vehicles had been fitted with any form of radio communication by the outbreak of war. Some did have a public address system which was used extensively to warn of impending air raids.

Telephones were little better and some stations in certain remote rural areas lacked even this necessity of modern life. In 1935 the police station in Barmouth (Merioneth) had no electricity, no telephone and there was no police car in the whole force. Once the Blitz started there were to be many urban police stations which found themselves in a similar position, even if this was only temporary. Sergeant Walter Groom of the Coventry City Police was on duty at the central police station during the Blitz on that city and remembers :

... telephones gradually going out of order, lights coming up on the screen which said, 'That is out', 'This is out', eventually most of them were out'. Soon everybody was relying on an older, more reliable method of communication, the human messenger. 'We had messages coming in from the air raid wardens, Special Constables and all sorts of people, which we recorded and sent down to the Control Room below', remembers Mr Groom. ... In the Control Room the emergency lighting had been punctiliously tested every night but when ... it was needed in earnest it lasted one Special Constable ... remembers, 'for about ten minutes. We rustled up a hurricane lamp while a policeman was sent out for candles', the results adding a curiously bizarre touch to the scene for 'he eventually returned with some coloured, twisted fancy candles "borrowed" as he put it, from a piano shop'. ... before ten o'clock only two phones out of eighteen were still working'[14].

The public telephone service, manually operated, was the subject of many complaints. Long distance calls had to be made via 'Trunks' which was notoriously lax in responding (or overworked) and a wait of two hours for a response was not unusual. The American troops were highly critical of the British telephone system (they had yet to learn that it was infinitely better than any of the Continental systems!) and their newspaper, the Stars and Stripes carried a cartoon in 1944 which depicted British telephone operators filing aboard an aircraft with the caption, 'We're dropping them over enemy territory to disrupt communications.'

The Metropolitan Police was one of the few forces which had installed a system of direct telephone lines between the various sub-divisional stations and the headquarters at New Scotland Yard. Other forces were still trying to get the necessary funding from their police authority for this extremely valuable means of communication by the time war broke out.

The rural policeman was very much reliant on the public telephone system, both the instrument installed in his police house and the public telephone boxes. Leslie Taylor was on duty on his rural Kent 'patch' when the enemy made a raid on a decoy airfield close by. He hurried to the scene to establish the extent of the damage and if there were any casualties and, in due course, made his report to headquarters, using the telephone in the village shop. A couple of days later his chief constable visited the scene and queried why use had not been made of the public telephone kiosk nearby, using the 'transfer charge' system. To emphasise his point, the chief constable demonstrated to the small crowd of villagers which had collected by putting his 2d in the box and then, once he had established his connection, pressing Button B to retrieve his money. To this gentleman's consternation he got back not 2d but 4d and, in order not to be seen to profit from the transaction, said he would put the excess in the Red Cross tin. However, the highly amused constable told his superior that the money belonged to the Postmaster General and this would be stealing! The chief constable's visit to the scene was abruptly curtailed as he decided he had pressing business elsewhere.

At the rural offices, the lengthy absences of the village Bobby meant that the indefatigable wife had to act as an unpaid human answering machine, often taking down lengthy police messages for her husband's attention on his return. One Lincolnshire wife thought herself extremely fortunate when a special constable was allocated to the office to help with the telephone answering. Unfortunately, this gentleman had had no experience with telephones at all and would religiously replace the receiver 'to prevent the electricity being wasted' while he went through to ask the policeman's wife what he should do about a particular telephoned query, thus cutting off the exasperated caller.

Although few private houses had telephones installed, it was felt that, where those which had became unoccupied through the owners having evacuated, arrangements should be made for the telephone to be disconnected 'to deny telephone communication to the invading enemy'. The police were required to inform the GPO of any houses which they knew to be empty and in which there was, or might be, a telephone.

Even verbal communication was not free from difficulties. When Special Sergeant Frank Butler returned from attending a fire at the premises of a famous cosmetics manufacturer he was asked by the chief inspector where the fire was and was only able to give his superior fairly vague directions. A War Reserve Constable, obviously an educated man, volunteered that the fire was at a scent manufacturers and gave the name in impeccable French. The chief inspector promptly rounded on him, 'Cut out the ******* French. How do you spell it?' and wrote the name at the other officer's dictation. 'Oh, you mean Boo Joys,' he cried triumphantly, when he had finished writing. 'Now I know where we are.'

A novel form of police communication was introduced with the coming of the war; carrier pigeons. Cheshire was one of the first forces to introduce this ancient but still effective means of communication in 1940. Lancashire was also quickly on the scene, as was the West Riding force which built up its flock until it had 4,000 homing birds flying from more than 200 lofts. The Government took elaborate steps to control the use of long-distance pigeons for this sort of purpose and any person finding a pigeon, alive or dead, with an identification mark or message attached was instructed to hand it over at once to a policeman, making no attempt to read or decode any message it might be carrying. For mere wood pigeons, however, there was no mercy. Not only was pigeon pie a welcome addition to the meagre meat rations, they were regarded as pests which destroyed valuable crops and the authorities had the right to send 'authorised persons' (which in the event could well be policemen) onto any private land to destroy these and other pests. Should a homing pigeon be brought down by a farmer by accident, the *Shooting Times* advised the culprit to take any message attached to it to the nearest police station.

> *'Whether this should be done anonymously or not we prefer to leave to the good sense of the shooter as we do not know in what position he would find himself.'*

Pigeons were not the only creatures the police had to contend with. There was considerable concern as to the effect which air raids would have on domestic animals and horses and the police were authorised to destroy any animals without the owner's consent if injured through 'hostile attack'. Quite early on, the police in Kent and elsewhere had the unenviable task of arranging the destruction of dogs which had attached themselves to refugees and servicemen returning from the Continent. Because of the danger of hysterical animals running amok and for reasons of hygiene, pets were not allowed in public shelters, a fact which prompted many pet owners to remain outside themselves, rather than be separated from their canine and feline friends. Hard as this policy may seem, there was soon good evidence of the effect the raids had on animals.

Every evening for a week when the siren sounded, a large brown dog rushed wildly through our square and down the hill, its tail between its legs, howling as it went. ... But on the seventh night it did not appear: either the police or a bomb splinter must have caught it. Fortunately, the majority of dogs had been evacuated or destroyed, but sometimes one would howl for hours in an empty house, thereby adding considerably to our nervous discomfort[15].

There were, of course, no restrictions on people taking their pets into their own shelters; in fact, Constable John Thompson recalls that his Cocker spaniel was always the first into the family Morrison indoor shelter (a form of steel table with mesh sides) – except on the one occasion a carefully saved 6d box of chocolates had been inadvertently left outside!

Some pets were more than capable of taking care of themselves, one cat staying up the chimney of his Birmingham home for several days. Norman Longmate describes how Tony, a black and white Persian was cuddled by his owner during the Coventry Blitz:

When the raids started she 'bent over him every time we heard the sound of bombs falling' but finally, distressed by his 'horrible, frightening cries', put him outside. 'He slunk away with his stomach touching the ground [and] I spent the following hours worrying about him.' Tony, however, ... turned up next morning 'sitting in the garden washing his face and lived to a ripe old age'[16].

Tony showed his contempt of the Germans by using a nearby bomb crater as his lavatory. Another kitten, Chloe, was found leaping in the air and patting at pieces of charred paper which were floating from the direction of bombed houses and later did not let enemy action prevent her from forming a liaison with another cat and producing four kittens. Other cats were to be seen, after the Coventry raids, sitting on the windowsills of their burned-out homes, waiting for their owners to return home, apparently unperturbed by the event of the previous night. In London, Barbara Nixon[17] writes of hundreds of bombed-out cats slinking through the debris, hunting rodents and raiding garbage cans. Others had been simply turned out to fend for themselves when their owners were evacuated. A few cat lovers collected these scavenging moggies and fed and cared for them but many others had to be rounded up by police and RSPCA to be put down – a difficult task as they had grown wild and cunning.

Cats in the country were generally more fortunate, although one policeman's cat, which had taken to curling up in a large yew tree outside the police station, nearly lost several of its nine lives when it decided to drop out of the tree one dark and windy night, landing on his master's shoulders and nearly giving him a heart attack.

'Man's best friend' also had his experiences and the tale is told of the man who arrived at a Coventry mobile canteen 'near to starvation and with hardly any flesh left on his fingers', begging a drink for his bedraggled small terrier. His own needs were of secondary importance. It transpired that the man, a plumber, had returned home during an air raid to fetch his precious tools and was followed by his faithful dog. Both had been buried in the building and had escaped by the plumber digging them both out with his bare hands[18].

Early in the war the Metropolitan Police horses were removed from central London and quartered on the outskirts but they were soon returned to most of their normal stables, those at Great Scotland Yard and Bow being regarded as unsuitable because of the heavy glass roofs. Fortunately, the training of these animals inured them against loud and unexpected noises and, where stables were damaged in air raids, the horses would patiently wait to be released and then walk away as if nothing had happened. Their riders, accustomed to dealing with these animals, performed useful work in incidents where privately owned horses were trapped or injured. In the case of serious injuries they were able to put the animals out of their misery with their revolvers.

Animals' panic is almost as infectious as that of human beings. ... Few people realise how many horses are kept in London. On the night of the City fire, a large firm of carters caught alight along with all the surrounding streets, and the two stablemen, with one or two volunteers, led 200 horses to safety[19].

The example quoted above by Barbara Nixon, an ARP warden throughout the Blitz on London, is but one of many. On numerous occasions, horses were led from city stables to safety by policemen and other civil defence workers. In Birmingham, the stables in Suffolk

Street caught alight and the horses were trapped. Many willing hands arrived in response to a call for help and found the heavy shire horses stamping about in fright. The only way to get them out was to put sacks over their eyes and lead them through the burning building and, with a sharp slap on the rump, set them off down the street. Here there was further confusion as, in the heat of the moment, the helpers had forgotten to remove the sacks and the horses were unable to see where they were going. Not all horses were as lucky.

> *... a man came out of [a badly fire-damaged building] leading a horse. The animal looked terrified and the man was having trouble controlling it. ... I asked him 'Where did you get that horse?' and he said 'Over there', pointing to this particular building. This aroused my curiosity and off I went to have a look inside. To reach the upper floor I had to walk up a cobblestone ramp; the heat was so bad I could feel it through the soles of my top boots. I was not prepared for the sight that greeted me on reaching the first floor; it looked like a huge room and down either side was a range of stalls and, at the far end was what I think was called a loose box ... Lying on the floor down the centre of the room was what looked like huge joints of roast meat. It took a little while for me to realise I was looking at a row of dead horses that had had no chance of escape and had been burned alive. I am not ashamed to admit it was the only time during the war years that I just stood and cried*[20].

Sid Lowe, a young soldier who happened to be in Coventry during the Blitz on that city recalls a terrifying scene:

> *Through the haze and heat came several horses at full gallop, screaming dogs too, trying to scramble on the backs of the horses. They passed my by on either side as I stood rooted to the ground. Flames flickered on the horses manes, tails on fire. One dog wholly on fire screaming in my ear as it brushed my shoulder trying to leap on to a horse ... this was pure hell, another world ...*[21].

Although some horses were upset by the noise of bombs and guns, others took it in their stride, like the gelding who was turned out in a field in a very unhealthy part of Kent. Whenever there was a dogfight, he would simply trot across to the side of the field and stand under the hedge until it was all over.

Animals belonging to troops were another problem as they often had to be left when the unit was hurriedly moved out, possibly abroad, or where their owners had failed to return from a bombing raid. In parts of Suffolk the number of animals running wild became a serious problem for the police. Attacks on sheep and poultry were commonplace and eventually the US troops were forbidden to keep pets, especially as some aircrews had brought in somewhat exotic animals, such as parrots, monkeys and even a small bear and a donkey.

Special Sergeant Frank Butler was returning home from attending the scene of a bombing incident in London when he came across a pet rabbit which had obviously escaped or been blown from its hutch. He picked it up and took it home with the intention of taking care of it but discovered that it had a broken leg and, in the absence of any vet, reluctantly handed it over to a neighbour who promptly dispatched it and made preparations for an enjoyable lunch.

Farm animals have always been subject to police supervision and remain so today. Most rural policemen are also appointed inspectors under the Diseases of Animals Acts and are responsible for the enforcement of Foot and Mouth orders, and those relating to Swine Fever, Anthrax and other serious veterinary diseases. Regular inspections have to be made to ensure that sheep are regularly dipped in a suitable solution to destroy lice and ticks and to prevent infection while any outbreak of a serious veterinary disease means that the infected farm has to be isolated and any livestock which has been taken to market is traced and destroyed.

During the war, cattle and other livestock represented an extremely valuable food resource and the containment of diseases was of prime importance if they were not to sweep through the country in an unstoppable epidemic. The burning of diseased carcases was yet another of the many extraneous duties accepted by the police as it was vital that checks were made to ensure that the job was done properly and thoroughly.

The stress of war affected different farm animals in different ways; a herd of pigs is reported to have slept peacefully in a bombed slaughterhouse while the roof was blown off. Cows, on the other hand seem to have reacted by producing less milk. When a stick of bombs dropped on a Sussex farm it blew the door of the bull's pen off its hinges and presented an opportunity which the bovine occupant was quick to put to good use and he was last seen heading at a lumbering trot for the nearest herd of cows. Meanwhile, Sergeant Bill Henley, accompanied by a couple of special constables, was combing the fields around the farm to try to locate some of the other bombs in the stick which had not exploded on impact. The news of the bull's escape was conveyed to them by the worried farmer but, deciding that a little thing like a loose bull should not interrupt their duty, they carried on, not without a little trepidation. It was while the sergeant was leading his men in single file across a muddy field that one of them slipped and, reaching out to try to steady himself, grabbed the sergeant's hips. What with the possibility of unexploded bombs and the nagging fear of a rampaging bull, nerves were somewhat stretched and, convinced that the bull had somehow sneaked up behind him, the good sergeant broke all records for the 100 yards sprint to the nearest gate, much to the amusement of his colleagues.

Even wild animals occasionally came to the attention of the police. A report of a small, round, shiny object, apparently moving under its own volition through a London suburb brought two Metropolitan constables to the scene to investigate. The understandably apprehensive officers quickly located this new secret weapon which was indeed demonstrating a surprising degree of mobility. After watching it from a safe distance for some time the constables decided that it did not seem to be in imminent danger of exploding and cautiously approached to investigate the phenomenon more closely. As they did so they discovered that the object was nothing more sinister than a hedgehog which had got its foreparts wedged in a tin can and was moving backwards in a desperate attempt to extricate itself from its confinement.

'Clever little beast that,' said one constable to the other. 'Carries his own Anderson shelter about with him.' And proceeded to assist the little beast to escape from its unusual and unintentional form of protection against air raids.

6. The New Partners

... the Police had to make contact and arrange co-operation with the various Civil Defence Services, some of which, like the Wardens Service, were new ventures altogether, and to get a clear picture of where reports should and should not (to avoid congestion) be sent, to whom sufferers and enquirers should be directed, how wide an area must be evacuated ... how to obtain assistance quickly from the various public utility services and so on almost ad infinitum.[1]

The above quotation from an article written by the then Commissioner of the Metropolitan Police, Sir Philip Game, emphasises how, for the police, accustomed over a century to working on their own with only occasional assistance from the military and having a close but clearly defined relationship with the fire brigades, the war brought a novel concept; the introduction of other civil personnel, the tasks of whom sometimes cut across or ran parallel to those of the police. Originally formed under the generic title of Air Raid Precautions, this body soon became known as the Civil Defence services and embraced air raid wardens, light and heavy rescue units, firewatchers, stretcher parties, ambulance drivers/attendants, first-aiders, messenger boys, etc. Most of these were part-time volunteers, whom J B Priestley regarded as 'militant citizens' and the seed corn of a new democracy.

More than two years before the outbreak of war plans had been made for the recruitment of air raid wardens and the police were given a fundamental role in their training and organisation. By April, 1939, over 33,000 wardens had been enrolled in Lancashire alone and allocated to cover 3,000 wardens' posts. The wardens' section was conceived to work closely with the police and, outside London (where the particular complexities of local government prevented this) the chief constable of the borough or city was usually also the Chief Warden and the whole Civil Defence service was largely structured around the police force. In London, the Chief Warden for a borough would often be a retired military man. Each borough or similar area would be divided into districts, under a district warden, and these districts further divided into posts. The posts, in turn, were broken down into five or six sectors, each covered by between three and six wardens under a senior warden.

An official circular stated in 1937 that:

> *The general idea of an air raid warden is that he should be a responsible member of the public, chosen to be a leader and adviser of his neighbours in a small area, a street or a small group of streets, in which he is known and respected.*[2]

The perceptive reader will note a certain interesting similarity to the modern Neighbourhood Watch schemes and, although in practice the system often fell short of this ideal, the essential element was the fact that it was *local*. The wardens, in particular, comprised some 16% women, most were part-timers who came on duty after their normal work, much as the special constables did (and still do). They were predominantly middle-aged or elderly and, despite the problems of recruiting in mainly working class areas, where the inhabitants were often involved in heavy labour, they were mostly found to be working class. To begin with, relations between the police and the wardens were cool and somewhat distant, the former fearing the latter were trying to usurp some of their traditional emergency roles. In particular, their involvement in the enforcement of the blackout regulations in the early months of the war was often seen as cutting across the work of the police. Some chief constables were of the view that the wardens' duties only commenced once the siren had sounded, whereupon they should request householders to extinguish any visible lights. At other times they should report offending lights to the police for action as they lacked the coercive powers of the police[3].

In the light of experience some wardens, especially those in London, felt that it would have been better had they been organised on a national basis since they were of the opinion that their 'leaders' were not up to the job. Few local government officers or elected members of that era were capable of running an organisation comprising around 1,000 members under very trying times. Some quite unsuitable persons (unsuitable in respect of their training, qualifications and leadership qualities) had been appointed to many of the positions at the top of the service locally on political grounds or through sheer nepotism.

Nevertheless, when at the beginning of the war the London wardens were asked to vote whether they wished to come under the police or the local authority, they accepted the latter's assurances that their organisation would be more democratic under local government control and the local authority easily won the day. Apart from anything else, in the working class districts the police were not regarded merely as someone who controlled traffic and helped old ladies across the road, but as the true adversaries of the working class, especially by those who were inclined to be somewhat cavalier in their respect of the law. Had the London wardens come under the Metropolitan Police they would undoubtedly have benefitted from a far more efficient organisation but, in certain areas, they would probably have lost that friendly relationship they built up with the public and which became their chief asset.

The Government decided at a very early stage that the wardens should not, as was mooted in some quarters including the House of Commons, be sworn in as special constables even though, outside London, Chief Constables would normally be responsible for their organisation in peacetime and their control in time of war. Much was left to the discretion of the so-called scheme-making authorities, many of whom dragged their feet because of financial considerations. The monetary implications were finally settled by the Air Raid Precautions Act of 1937. An article entitled 'ARP Today', in *The Times* dated 19 December, 1938, remarked that the best ARP schemes which then existed were those which had been directed by the police or by officials working in close collaboration with them, but this state of affairs was exceptional.

The combined Civil Defence services all came under a local ARP Controller who was nominated by the local authority and who was 'empowered to take immediate executive action' over any aspect of civil defence. This Controller could be the local authority's own chief officer, such as the Town or County Clerk, the local Chief Constable, or an elected member of the local authority. Once war began, they were far and away the most important individuals in every raid outside London, They ranked over the other main service chiefs, including the chief warden, the chief medical officer and the borough surveyor. Although the police and fire brigades remained under their respective chief officers, their role was co-ordinated by the Controller.

It was considered that, whenever an incident occurred, a senior police officer would be the best person to take charge and assume responsibility for the general direction of the other services, whose own officers would be present to relay the necessary instructions. This senior police officer should establish an Incident Officer's Post and report its existence and location to the ARP Controller as well as to his police superiors. He was to be responsible for intelligence, for determining the priority of operations and for seeing that regular progress reports were made to the appropriate centres and to the proper police station.

In the London region and in a few others, selected wardens were trained to take charge of all ARP operations (excluding the fighting of fires which remained the responsibility of the fire brigade) at any major incident. Their job was to see that the necessary services were present, that vehicles were conveniently parked, that parties did not impede each other and that the Control Centre was kept informed of progress[4]. It soon became clear however that the ARP Incident Officer's position vis-à-vis the police would have to be clarified:

> *If the police appeared there would be an unedifying argument – between the officer of the law and the senior warden over who had the right to control the incident. The policeman would say that the ultimate responsibility was his; the warden would argue that the police knew nothing of Civil Defence; while the effective leader of the operation might well be the chief man of the rescue team ... The policeman would probably have his way. It was over two years before this problem was settled[5].*

In practice, where there were sufficient senior police officers trained in the duty the arrangement worked well, but where a local constable attempted to oust from control a more capable warden the interference was resented. Nevertheless, in May, 1940, it was made clear that the police, who had statutory duties and the power of enforcement, should take general charge of the situation and make every effort to maintain public order and the control of traffic. The ARP Incident Officer was to confine himself to supervising the ARP General services. In practice this meant that the police kept the outer ring within which the Incident Officer directed the operations of the ARP services and a Fire Officer those of the National and Auxiliary Fire Services.

By the spring of 1943 the police seem to have been convinced that those in charge of civil defence, at any rate in the Regions, were anxious to keep them away from the position of Incident Officer. On the other hand, the ARP services were saying that in some Regions the police had refused to allow civil defence personnel to undergo incident control instruction and that wardens had been ordered off the site of an incident. The matter was brought up at a meeting of the central conference of Chief Constables on 6 May 1943, when it was agreed that the Incident Officers' Service should be regarded as a civil defence service, but that except in London, it should be under the control of the Chief Constable. ... The conference agreed that responsibility for selecting and despatching the Incident Officer should rest with the Chief Constable, but that once this officer reached the scene he was to be responsible to the Controller in charge of the operations of the General Services. The Incident Officer it can be seen was a splinter – albeit a polished and specialised splinter – from the Wardens' Service[6]

In practice, this meant that control could be exercised by either the police or the Civil Defence service and the police had to train a large number of Civil Defence personnel in the task; in Liverpool alone 2,000 persons (wardens, police and special constables) received training as Incident Officers. They were equipped with blue covers to go over their steel helmet and blue flags and blue lights to mark their Incident Posts.

Today, some 50 years after the events described in this book, the role of the various services involved in a major incident have been clearly defined by the Home Office which has confirmed that each service or agency working at the scene of a disaster has its own role and functions. Nevertheless,

The police co-ordinate the activities of all those responding at and around the scene which must ... be treated as the scene of a crime and preserved accordingly. ... The police process casualty information and have responsibility for identifying and arranging the removal of the dead.[7]

The police are also made responsible for setting up a Casualty Bureau and for providing a central contact point for all enquiries.

Relations between the police and the civil defence services was always an equivocal one and a lot depended on the location and the calibre of the wardens and other civil defence personal. During the 'Phoney War' of 1939/40, the general public had very little time for these people who they felt were getting £3 a week (a good salary in those days) under false pretences, since there was no enemy action to justify their continued existence. Members of the ARP Service were accused of profiting from their involvement with civil defence and, in Blackburn, a number of wardens were dismissed for improper use of ARP property (using their issue gum boots for their normal work) and for the misuse of official telephones. Once the Blitz started the tune rapidly changed and the service as a whole performed extremely well and often with great courage.

Many policemen felt, with some justification, that the advantage the police had over the newer services was the former's history, tradition, discipline and high sense of public duty – something the newcomers had yet to acquire. Some civil defence personnel still clung to their peacetime concepts of demarcation of responsibilities and wasted time in useless bickering. Sergeant Grey, from Millwall, wrote of one such incident:

> One 'quiet' night, we paid a visit to a good surface shelter built into an old factory. As we entered the yard the warden ran to meet us with his part-time female assistant warden following him screaming. Everyone in sight was in a deep panic; the warden was incoherent. We entered the shelter and found that the central blast wall had collapsed onto the sleeping occupants. The whole building had collapsed, including the roof. The scene was one long smooth carpet of white bricks, strangely quiet, with projections and other indications protruding from it. Some of those who had been standing near the walls were still doing so. The piano was on top of the player and there, helping us as usual, was our street hawker of the cap and long overcoat. Help arrived from Limehouse police station and the Light and Heavy Rescue units who then argued over who should do what. The police knew it was a heavy rescue job and had to watch them standing by in silence while the police dug out the dead, laid them out and counted them.[8]

Barbara Nixon, herself a warden, also comments on this astonishingly petty behaviour:

There were jealousies arising from the fact that some service was much better looked after than another, members of one service did not know the members of another, and there could certainly have been more co-operation at incidents. Some times Heavy Rescue men would snub wardens who tried to help them, at others a warden would say that such and such a job was not his province; I met one Stretcher Party crew who even refused to go into a lightly-damaged building until Heavy Rescue arrived.[9]

In general and in most areas, relations between the members of the civil defence services and the police reflected the normal, peacetime relations which the force had with the general public in the district, especially the working class. In most rural areas and the quieter market towns, the police were an accepted part of the community, respected if not actively liked, and their relations with the local wardens was usually quite cordial. The latter were often small businessmen and shopkeepers, well known to the local police with whom they were accustomed to pass the time of day in peacetime. Ted Maidment, a constable in the East Riding Constabulary at the time and who eventually retired with the rank of superintendent, describes the relations between his force and the civil defence in the following terms:

The firemen were our colleagues in arms. The air raid wardens (men and women) together with members of the ambulance service, were with us – all for one and one for all.

But in Barbara Nixon's area of London, the police were treated with distrust and suspicion, largely because several of the locals had fallen foul of the law through some nefarious activity in which they had been engaged. However, many of the barriers came down as both found themselves in the same, uncomfortable boat as the pace of the war hotted up.

Our only company was occasional police and demolition workers. The police patrol was doubled in an attempt to stop looting, without much noticeable success. It was an eerie and a dismal patrol for them, and they welcomed our cups of tea, and

*in return would often, unofficially, light the fire for us as soon
as the dawn came up. It improved our relations with the police
considerably. Before, anyone who took a policeman into a Post
was usually told to choose some other friends, but a year later
we were playing them amicably at darts or cricket, despite
occasional asides as a batsman came in, that 'that was the guy
who ran in Bertie Simmonds.'* [10]

At its peak (June 1941) the General ARP Services (wardens, rescue
and first aid parties, report and control centres, messengers, etc.)
employed 127,000 full-time workers and 907,500 part-timers – a total
of 1,034,500). This compares with 64,800 regular police officers, plus
38,500 full-time auxiliaries and 157,000 part-time auxiliaries (total
260,300) so the police were heavily outnumbered by these newcomers.

Another new body with which the police were closely associated
was the Home Guard. When on 14 May, 1940, Anthony Eden, the new
Secretary of State for War, made an appeal on the six o'clock news for
'Local Defence Volunteers' to sign up for duties in connection with the
defence of the British Isles, this met with an immediate response.
Enrolment was carried out at police stations, many of which were
overwhelmed by the sheer number of volunteers; on the first day, these
were still queuing at Folkestone police station at midnight. By July,
1940, when the title was changed to the 'Home Guard' on Churchill's
suggestion, there were nearly one and a half million volunteers, 100,000
having enrolled in London alone. The upper age limit of 65 was only
loosely enforced and there was no medical examination. It was
intended that these volunteers should be vetted in case the LDV turned
out to be a Fifth Columnists' dream but it was clearly impossible – if
indeed desirable – for the police to make any real investigation into the
character and antecedents of this number of volunteers. All they could
do was to inform the authorities in confidence of any applicants they
had spotted who might be regarded as unreliable or undesirable, basing
this largely on their extensive local knowledge.

For some policemen stationed in out-of-the-way places, the surprise
announcement and the even more surprising response caused
considerable difficulty. R C Dyson, whose father was the village
constable in Glenfield, about three miles from Leicester, writes:

Within minutes of the broadcast men began to walk past our window to the door to enlist – old men, veterans of the First War, young men not yet called up – all came in a steady stream for the remainder of the day. My father had received no instructions and knew only what he had heard on the radio so he could do no more than record their names and addresses and tell them they would be contacted. I think that incident typified the spirit of the nation at the time – unconquerable.

The new body had no uniforms to start with, just an armband or 'brassard' with 'LDV' on it to distinguish them from ordinary citizens or armed Fifth Columnists. Lack of weapons led to a concurrent public appeal for any form of weapon which they might use, coupled with an amnesty for those who were in unlawful possession of firearms, in the form of war souvenirs, etc. The result was astonishing; a veritable tidal wave of assorted firearms and blunt instruments poured in, from assegais and blunderbusses to 300 guinea Purdy shotguns.

Within an hour of the broadcast we had a queue of people, ... lining the steps of the station stretching along into Lucan Place [Chelsea]. Intermingled amongst them was a good number of middleaged and elderly men, and a considerable sprinkling of elderly ladies, bearing an assortment of arms. Every widow of every Indian Mutiny survivor seemed to live in the police area and the whole scene seemed like an apparition from the distant past as these determined daughters of the pioneers of the 19th century British Empire resolutely advanced upon us with every sort of rifle, muzzle loader, elephant gun, shotgun, revolver, pistol, blunderbuss, fowling piece and even spears. I sorted the queue, separating those who wished to hand in weapons from the men who were volunteering to use them. All this took some time as no prior notice had been given of the appeal. ... As soon as Eden had made the announcement, the Commissioner had instructed Superintendents by teleprinter to organise the LDV on police boundaries and to find suitable civilians with military experience to run the units.[11]

Eric St Johnston, whose experience as the Sub-Divisional Inspector in Chelsea in 1940 is outlined above, was fortunate in finding amongst his volunteers the very man to command the Chelsea LDV; no less a person than General Gough, the celebrated commander of the 5th Army in the previous war.

In all, some 20,000 weapons were handed in for the Home Guard's use, while many of the rural volunteers already possessed their own shotguns. The authorities were not entirely enamoured with the idea of arming the 'lower classes' and the War Office left it to the local commanders to decide whether their men should keep their own rifles at home or not. It was reported that, in some cases, the commanders having wheedled their shotguns away from the local yeomanry, promptly locked the weapons up at the local police station[12].

The training of the Home Guard was a military matter rather than one for the police, but the police were involved in a number of combined civil defence/ home guard/police exercises, some of which were positively dangerous. From time to time a Home Guard unit would unilaterally decide that a particular police station was a target which must be surrounded and captured at dead of night as a training exercise. More than once an unwary constable pursuing his normal duties found himself faced with agitated bayonets and had some difficulty in getting himself released from captivity and able to continue his proper duties.

Not all confrontations were was as friendly, however, as the Home Guards were occasionally overcome by their newly-acquired powers. Many a policeman was irritated and exasperated by demands for him to identify himself, even though he was in full uniform and going about his normal duties. On one occasion a chief inspector's car was stopped at a Home Guard road check in Liverpool where the corporal in charge thrust his rifle in the officer's face and demanded his papers. The chief inspector produced his identity card and badge but was ordered to pull into the side of the road. Annoyed by the corporal's officiousness, the policeman asked another Home Guard to call someone in authority but was told, 'He's the corporal and what he says goes, mate'. Another police car approached and was similarly stopped and the constable driving this produced his identity card. When the chief inspector told the constable to inform Liverpool Police headquarters that he was being held at the road block, the Home Guard corporal pointed his rifle at him and shouted, 'Arrest this man. Come on, do your job.' By this time the chief inspector had had enough and grappled with the corporal, wrestling his rifle away from him, whereupon the corporal snatched a rifle from another Home Guard. The chief inspector knocked this out of his hands and the corporal struck the officer on the neck. The disarmed corporal was arrested and was subsequently fined for being drunk and disorderly. It was later found that the rifles were, fortunately, unloaded but it is sobering to think what might have happened had the inebriated and self-important corporal been armed with a more effective weapon[13].

This was not the only bothersome encounter in which the Home Guard were involved and it is recorded that a number of motorists were in fact shot by trigger-happy personnel. Courting couples were subjected to considerable harassment and it is on record that on the night of 2/3 June, 1940, four people were killed in separate incidents in which they either did not hear, or chose to ignore the challenges issued by personnel manning a Home Guard roadblock. In September 1940 it was announced that 'any Home Guard who shoots out of a personal grudge is liable to be suspended'(!). Meanwhile, no less a personage than the Chief Constable of Glasgow, Sir Percy Sillitoe, proceeding on urgent business with a police surgeon, was stopped and had a loaded rifle pushed into the pit of his stomach, his identification papers waived aside. He formed the opinion that, in the neighbourhood of Glasgow at least, criminals had taken the opportunity to enrol themselves, with what he saw as alarming possibilities.[14]

The unbridled enthusiasm of certain Home Guard personnel meant that the police had to arrest some who insisted on marching around the highways and byways, armed with weapons ranging from antique muzzle-loading rifles of Crimea War vintage, to elephant guns as used by big game hunters, challenging anyone who crossed their path. The fact that the 'suspect' came from the same village and was well-known to the Home Guard made no difference. Whilst these encounters were undoubtedly disconcerting, what was more worrying was the occasional discharge of a firearm due to excessive zeal or nervousness. Because of the growing concern about these bands of armed vigilantes roaming the countryside, apparently unaccountable to anyone or anything other than their own sometimes perverted sense of duty, the new Secretary of State for War, Sir Edward Grigg had to make a statement in the House of Commons that the main job of the Home Guard was to protect vulnerable railways and roads, to man official roadblocks and to keep a sharp lookout for enemy parachutists.

Before we leave the various civil bodies involved in the war effort and with whom the police collaborated during those very trying times, mention must be made of the various voluntary services who did such sterling work to back up the more official bodies. Two organisations which instantly spring to mind are the Women's Voluntary Service (now the WRVS) and the Salvation Army. The distinctive uniforms of both of these bodies could be seen at all crisis points – in air raid shelters, at the scenes of bombing devastation, in the rest centres and in places where evacuees were gathered for the journey to their new homes – in fact anywhere where there were people in need. Quietly, efficiently and with the minimum of fuss, they would be doling out tea and sympathy in equal measures, as well as providing a great deal of very practical assistance to the homeless and destitute in the form of Rest Centres and the distribution of much-needed clothing, bedding and other basic essentials for those who had lost everything they owned.

Many a policeman had reason to be thankful to these marvellous, voluntary organisations for the very welcome cups of tea, buns sandwiches and hot pies offered to them while they were helping to extricate the trapped victims of air raids or organising the evacuation of those who had been bombed out. The task of the police in organising casualty bureaux was greatly assisted by the work of these unpaid but ever-willing and unfailingly cheerful volunteers. Their stories have been told more fully elsewhere but no account of the work of the police in wartime would be complete without at least a mention of these tireless workers.

The reader will by now have gained, rightly, the impression that there was no civil defence task that the policeman did not get involved in to some extent. Like the warden he reported incidents to the Control Centre and got the other services into action. He guided people into the deep shelters and moved the occupants from shelters which were under threat from unexploded bombs or collapsing buildings. If an unexploded bomb fell he went to the nearby householders to warn them of the danger, evacuated them and diverted the traffic, all at no little risk to himself. Where there were trapped victims he set to work to rescue them pending the arrival of the specialist rescue parties on the scene. If there were casualties he rendered first aid, compiled lists of the dead and injured and took care of their personal property.

Outside London (where it was the job of the warden) he was expected to take charge of any incident, co-ordinate the work of the various services and provide some general direction for their activities. He helped to put out incendiary bombs and dealt with fires unless they were serious enough to require the services of the fire brigade (which was often very overstretched). Where a shop front had been smashed he found members of the Home Guard to protect the contents from looters or stood guard himself if there was nothing more urgent which required his attention. His continually varying work called always for personal initiative.

It was a very responsible and often dangerous job. It meant performing duty in the open air, under enemy attack and, as we shall see in a later chapter, some of the rescues carried out by the police rank with the more heroic episodes of that hazardous craft. During a heavy raid, when the calls on the rescue services were extremely heavy, police constables could be found working long hours among the debris in highly dangerous conditions. When the raid was over the police had to keep records of the casualties, notify the next of kin and deal with a hundred and one enquiries from anxious relatives and friends. They had to pass on the news, often bitter and grievous, to people who were already overwrought by their own experiences. There was no room for any lack of tact and kindness – and there was none.

Every one of these tasks arose directly out of the normal functions of the police as upholders of the law and guardians of public welfare. Although the comparison between a road accident and the explosion of a land mine may seem facile, there are in fact many points of resemblance between them. In fact, it became a common police saying that a war time incident was merely a large accident. There were greater risks and the task more complex but they learned to cope with these as they had learned to cope with other matters.

In the provinces in particular the police were the linch pins of civil defence and these services were built around the police. The new partners looked to the police for guidance and leadership and the wardens in particular became the junior partners of the police, especially where the chief constable was the chief warden. For administrative reasons the position was somewhat different in London where the police stood a little apart from the civil defence organisation, performing their traditional functions of traffic control, supervising the movement of the public and the maintenance of order. But the distinction was more theoretical than practical. On the ground the police in London worked shoulder to shoulder with the wardens, the rescue units and the first aid parties much the same as their provincial colleagues.

7. A Woman's Cause

When Tennyson wrote – 'A woman's cause is man's; they rise or sink together', he could have had no possible conception of how the women of Great Britain would take up the cause of their menfolk in the Second World War. As a women's magazine recorded in November, 1939, 'The last war was a soldier's war; this one is everybody's'[1] and this was proved by the numbers of women who rushed to fill jobs vacated by men called to the services, or took up often unfeminine work in factories and on the land. The police service was no exception.

Sir Robert Peel had no thought of including women in his new law-enforcement body when he formed the Metropolitan Police in 1829, and this situation remained unchanged for the best part of a century. The story of women in the police goes back to the period just before the First World War when calls were made, mainly by the Suffragette movement, for the introduction of some form of female policing system to aid women and children. On the outbreak of that war, there was a national call for special constables and two women were appointed at Sandgate (Kent) 'to keep a look out for suspicious persons and lights on the beach'[2].

A Women's Police Volunteers organisation was formed in London by a leading suffragette, Nina Boyle, and a wealthy philanthropist, Mrs Margaret Damer Dawson and the Commissioner of Police agreed that they could train and patrol London on a purely voluntary basis. Elsewhere various religious and similar groups united as the National Union of Women Workers (NUWW) in order to promote Voluntary Women's Patrols to work in the area of army camps and other places where it was felt that women and girls were exposed to moral danger. Grantham (Lincolnshire) was particularly affected as some 20,000 troops were camped out in Belton Park and the NUWW sent one of their number there to organise local volunteers but, hardly had she arrived, before two WPVs, both former suffragettes, arrived fully trained and in uniform to work in the area on a full-time basis. The Chief Constable's reaction was one of, 'Do what you like but keep out of the way'. The Provost Marshal was more accommodating but merely gave them very vague instructions. However, so successful was

171

the Grantham experiment that it was repeated shortly afterwards in Hull.

None of these women was sworn in as a constable and they merely used their common law powers as a citizen until, in 1916, the Police Act allowed for the employment of women on police duties. In fact, one of the WPVs in Grantham, Edith Smith, had been sworn in in 1915 but His Majesty's Inspector of Constabulary declared this to be illegal. However, the constabularies were notoriously independent in those days and his advice was ignored by the chief constable. In the same year the Women's Police Volunteers were renamed the Women's Police Service (WPS).

One or two forces took advantage of the Police Act to employ a few women and Lancashire employed a policewoman from as early as 1917 (although no uniforms were issued until the 1950s) but the Geddes Axe, which introduced swingeing economy measures in 1922, decimated even that small nucleus.

One of the original Grantham women, Mary Allan, who later went to Hull to organise the WPS there, was sent to Germany in 1922 as part of the forces of occupation, with a brief to organise vice control. She later stood (unsuccessfully) for Parliament, learned to fly and went on lecture tours around the world. She is described as being a very masculine woman who later became a Fascist and an ardent supporter of Hitler.

In 1929, one hundred years after the formation of the 'New Police', a Royal Commission recommended the employment of women police officers to take statements in sexual cases, etc. This initiative was reinforced in 1933 with the passing of the Children and Young Persons Act which called for the sort of action which could best be taken by females. Despite this, in 1939, the employment of women in the police was still at a rather equivocal stage and the views held in the various forces varied widely; only 44 of the 181 police forces had any women police and over 15% of these were unsworn. For example, in West Sussex there was just one policewoman in the whole force and she had to be transported to wherever she was needed, often from one side of the county to the other. The total number was still only around 220, of whom more than 100 were in the Metropolitan Police. By this time Mary Allan's WPS had virtually gone out of existence, police forces appointing their own women's section where a need was perceived.

The outbreak of war stimulated interest in women police in a number of ways and recruiting, which as we have seen, was very slow, quickened to some extent; by July, 1940, there were policewomen in 8 county and 33 city and borough forces, numbering 128 in all and the Metropolitan Police had 153. It was about this time that considerable agitation sprang up for the recruitment of more policewomen. The Archbishop of Canterbury was enlisted by the women's organisations to make personal representations, and the Home Office was moved to take a more definite line in a circular issued on 8 August, 1940. The response was not very prompt or encouraging. Some of HM Inspectors of Constabulary attributed this to lingering prejudices against the employment of women in the police, but others felt the problem was the limited number of suitable women who were available and the rates of pay which were offered. But later the same year, with the end of the Phoney War and the commencement of air raids, the Home Office made definite moves to encourage the employment of more women. By the middle of 1941 the Home Secretary was on record as saying that he wanted to see more women enroled in the police, either as regulars or as auxiliaries :

> *It is true that police duty is, for the most part, a man's job but such work as driving cars, typewriting and attending the telephone can be done by carefully selected women. There is no reason why canteen duties should not be taken over entirely by women.*

To those of us today who are used to women performing the full range of police duties, including riot control, the somewhat protective attitude expressed in this quotation seems quaintly dated and it is clear that the role of the policewoman was seen as being very much a supporting, rather than an active one.

This exhortation was not always heeded, however. Bradford decided not to increase its establishment of two police women, Brighton decided not to employ any, the chief constable saying that, when he was the chief constable of Huddersfield (pop. 123,000) he had had a police-woman but there had been insufficient work for her to do. Cardiff made a similar decision and the Chief Constable is reported as saying that :

> *Moral welfare work is outside police duties and, in my*

experience, a woman investigator should not be so vilely contaminated in the general interests of her sex. The less decent women saw of these aspects of life, the better it would be ...[3].

However, Kent at this time (1942) was advertising in the *Police Review* for not just a police women but for a woman *inspector,* although the post does not seem to have been filled until 1944. The county force had had no policewomen of its own, but had inherited a number from the borough forces which had been amalgamated with it and, in July 1943, just three months after the amalgamations, the new chief constable, Sir Percy Sillitoe, reported that, in his opinion, police-women were essential to the efficiency of the force. An inspector was required to take charge of a new section of 23 police women and the post was filled in May, 1944 by Denise de Vitre on transfer from Leicester City. De V. as she was known, had spent part of the war manning a mobile canteen in the smoking ruins of Coventry and in fact left Kent after just 10 months to become a staff officer to His Majesty's Inspectors of Constabulary and is now regarded as one of the great proponents of the women police.

Similarly, the Commissioner of the Metropolitan Police, Sir Philip Game, wrote appreciatively in his report for 1943 of the work done by the 167 members of this branch in the last few years. He stated he was of the opinion that the women police were in a unique position for dealing with the adolescent girl in need of care or protection and that they were doing valuable work with young offenders, especially in the West End of London.

In 1944 the Home Office suddenly dropped the velvet glove and told the chief constables and police authorities that any police force in an area where troops were stationed must appoint women police, or it would be done for them under the Defence Regulations. However, this may have been a somewhat empty threat since the Home Secretary was well aware of the dearth of suitable candidates. When asked in the House of Commons what the Home Office was doing to improve the situation, Mr Morrison replied, 'If my hon. Friend knows of any women suitable for this position, perhaps he would be good enough to bring their names to our attention'! This point of view was shared by the Commissioner of the Metropolitan Police who, in his report for

1943, referred to earlier, stated:

The inference is that the Ministry of Labour will have to give a lot more help to the present campaign for more Women Police if anything more than propaganda talk is to come of it.[4]

Such was the difficulty in recruiting suitable women, given the competition from the armed forces and other essential services, that most recruits to the regular force during this period in fact came from the Women's Auxiliary Police Corps.

However, by the end of the war, there were still only 416 regular policewomen employed in the whole country. The sterling work performed by these women police officers was recognised by HM Inspectors of Constabulary who, in their reports for 1945 and 1946 recorded that :

... the emphasis laid on the importance and value of the work of police women in the report last year was justified and it is now recognised that no force can be regarded as complete unless it has an appropriate number of police women.

The policewoman had arrived!

It is very clear, then, that the attitude towards police women and their duties was very different to that which applies today. Their original role was to keep young girls out of trouble and to divert them from an immoral mode of living. The 1933 Children & Young Persons Act gave them wider responsibilities, albeit very much of a social worker nature. The war widened their scope even more and the number of jobs which can be better done by women than by men is even greater in war than in peace. Children and young persons are especially vulnerable and liable to get into trouble and difficulties when their normal course of life is interrupted and many of these problems fall within the province of police women. They were invaluable during evacuations and in the reception of refugees; lost children, separated parties and expectant mothers all naturally turned to the policewoman (if there was one), especially when the sirens sounded. The firm kindliness and calm competence which characterises policewomen inspired confidence and averted any tendency to hysteria.

Another area in which policewomen excelled was the round-up of enemy aliens and various escort duties. In July 1940 the chief constable of the Cardiganshire Constabulary in Wales complimented his women police officers on their good work, especially in the control and searching of enemy aliens. This acceptance of women police was largely influenced by the fact that one of his women sergeants spoke German and was in great demand as an interpreter. One policewoman well remembers the many times she had to escort female refugees either to Holloway prison, if they were suspected of being engaged in espionage or otherwise 'unreliable', or to a reception centre in a large house if not. Joan Salhurst, the policewoman we met in the last chapter, particularly remembers that these women were mostly well-dressed and had fruit and chocolate – which they never shared!

'I didn't find the majority particularly friendly even though I could speak French, but doubtless they had their reasons' – one of which may have been their less than pleasant experience with the police in their own country.

Agnes Cook, a WAPC serving in Fife, Scotland during the war, also remembers refugees flying in to the Leuchars Air Force base from Scandinavia and having to escort any women amongst them to a holding centre, pending questioning and determination of their status.

Visits to air raid shelters was another task undertaken by police-women. Some shelters became the haunts of vagrants, deserters, criminals, prostitutes and all the riff-raff of the neighbourhood and children sometimes made a nuisance of themselves in and around the shelters, apparently out of parental control. In some of the larger shelters, such as the one at the Midland Railway Goods Depot and those in the various underground stations in London, women police were supplied on a regular basis to help keep order and give general assistance. This was not a popular duty as these shelters were stuffy and, packed with hundreds of bodies and with minimal toilet facilities, soon began to give off a most unpleasant odour.

During the air raids police women turned their hands to anything which might be of use, including comforting the bereaved and the homeless and even packing live chickens into a wardrobe for transport to safety! On one occasion, when a flying bomb hit a public baths, the police women had to find clothes for the unfortunate bathers. A more sombre duty was accompanying those who had the sad task of identifying loved ones who had lost their lives in the raids. But perhaps their main headache in many areas was the number of 'good-time girls' who flocked wherever there was a congregation of servicemen, especially the Americans. Mention was made in the last chapter of the 'assistance' given to Joan Salhurst, the Bristol policewoman, by a special constable and the type of duty described in that anecdote was fairly common to all police women in the war years. They were required to make regular patrols around the army camps to move on the 'camp followers' and to identify the under-age ones who might be regarded as being in need of care and protection. The younger policewomen were themselves not immune from the attentions of the self-confident and over-friendly GIs, some of whom found the idea of a 'lady cop' very novel and tried hard to date them. Even their officers and NCOs were not above playing tricks, such as ordering an 'eyes right' as their squad marched past a policewoman, hoping to see her blush with embarrassment.

Escort duty was a fairly regular task and Joan Salhurst describes how she had to escort a persistent absconder from Hyde Park police station in London back to Bristol without any assistance. Considerable reservations were expressed (and no doubt some bets laid!) as to whether the prisoner would ever reach her destination, given her propensity for escaping and the single-handed escort. Such was the girl's reputation that WPC Salhurst was accompanied by two London policemen and a driver from Hyde Park to Paddington station. On the train, the guard was told to lock the prisoner and escort in the compartment until they got to Bristol. The escort was quietly confident until the guard returned, asking if two military policemen and their two black GI prisoners could use the same compartment as he had nowhere else to put them. Despite her misgivings, the policewoman could not refuse and, to her surprise, her charge improved by the minute, finally revealing 'US Army' tattooed on her knees, to the delight of the American prisoners. The three prisoners got on famously and exchanged names and addresses and the train reached Temple Meads station without any trouble. In fact, the girl was in very good spirits, to the astonishment of the two Bristol policemen waiting to assist WPC Salhurst with the 'difficult' prisoner on the final leg of the journey.

One of Joan Salhurst's colleagues, Ella Johnson, a former WAPC who transferred to the regular force, tells how the first prisoner she had to escort was a young girl on remand who had to be taken to Cardiff prison from Bristol. As the trains were completely blacked out, she offered the girl a cigarette as they approached the Severn tunnel and used the glow of this to keep a check on her charge, since it was forbidden to place handcuffs on female prisoners. On arrival at Cardiff station, the escorting policewoman looked in vain for one of the rare taxis but suddenly the prisoner emitted a piercing whistle and a taxi duly pulled up. "Buckingham Palace", ordered the prisoner, climbing in the vehicle. The taxi driver raised his eyebrows, the escort shrugged her shoulders and away they went – to Cardiff gaol.

The same policewoman was called out one morning to question a 13 year old who had been discovered in the back of an army lorry with some American soldiers. After taking a short statement from her and then taking her underclothes to the forensic science laboratory for semen tests, she continued her normal duty. WPC Johnson was soon called to the telephone and told to examine her clothing as that taken from the girl had been covered in lice. She has often wondered since how the soldiers fared!

On another occasion, two prostitutes who were having treatment for VD before being sentenced for soliciting escaped through a toilet window with the aid of two black GIs. The soldiers took the girls to a sort of cave in a quarry opposite their barracks, provided them with food and clothing, and then queued up for their services. It was the unusual sight of a line of black soldiers outside the cave in the early morning which gave the game away. and provided another task for the Bristol policewomen.

Other duties in which the services of police women proved invaluable included the shadowing of IRA suspects and dealing with bag snatchers and pickpockets – often being used as decoys. Fears that the female sex would be unable to cope with the rougher side of life proved largely unfounded, as a report in *The Times* for 7 October, 1943 illustrates:

> *A woman police constable of Hyde Park Station was commended by ... the Marlborough Street Magistrate yesterday for arresting an American soldier and a civilian at the meeting ground in Hyde Park on Tuesday. After she had arrested the soldier and was taking him through the crowd, a building operative started an argument with the soldier and struck him. The soldier retaliated, and as the civilian was about to*

A Woman's Cause

continue the fight, the woman constable arrested him as well.

Similarly, *The Police and Constabulary World* in 1944 reported that a Glasgow City policewoman, taking part in the apprehension of four young van thieves, knocked one of them down and out when he had the temerity to resist arrest. She, too, was commended by the Sheriff although one suspects that, if the scene had occurred in more recent times, the policewoman would have been the subject of disciplinary or criminal proceedings for assault.

The range of tasks performed by these women is astonishing, especially when one realises how few of them there were. At their peak, there were only 480 policewomen in the whole country, around one third of whom were in London. Fortunately they received considerable assistance from a new body formed, like the Police War Reserves, for the duration of the war – the Women's Auxiliary Police Corps.

In February 1939, the National Council of Women of Great Britain had protested that they were not eligible to serve as special constables (although some individualistic chief constables flew in the face of Home Office advice and appointed a few women to their Special Constabulary). For its part, the Home Office, although dilatory about allowing women to serve in the Special Constabulary, was eager for women to replace men in the catering, clerical, telephone, wireless, driving, vehicle repair and maintenance tasks in police stations and force headquarters and, consequently, formed the Women's Auxiliary Police Corps in August, 1939. Entry was restricted to those between the ages of 18 and 55 and no duties were to be performed in peace-time, other than training. In October, 1941 the Home Office recommended the provision of uniform for whole-time members of the WAPC and, where deemed necessary, for those part-timers who were performing regular duties. It was felt desirable to maintain as nearly as possible a standard pattern, following that worn by the regular officers but distinguished from these by a WAPC badge. The fact that they were issued with a uniform similar to that worn by their regular colleagues (including in some areas, the curious hat which resembled a tropical pith helmet) did not endear them to the senior policewomen who felt that the WAPCs wore the uniform with less circumspection and, worse still, they carried shoulder-bags! These 'accessories' were felt to be an anachronism since, if they contained anything of value, they could be lost in a rough and tumble and, if they only contained a handkerchief or – heaven forbid – make-up, these should be put in a pocket. This attitude was perhaps a little unfair since even the regular officers were now expected to carry a gas mask and a steel helmet and, in the early days, even a haversack containing their anti- gas clothing. (The rapid donning of anti-gas trousers presented something of a problem and women officers were instructed that, in the event of a gas alert, they were to step inside the nearest doorway, pull on the trousers and then remove their skirt over the top of them. Decorum must be maintained at all costs!) However, even senior policewomen admitted that the haversacks were useful for carrying the odd book or packet of sandwiches, as were the steel helmets.

Not all police women were lucky enough to have uniform, at least in the early days. Agnes Cook from Fife was a long time without her WAPC uniform and remembers escorting a female prisoner to Perth prison in plain clothes, where the warder in charge started to question her closely until the driver of the police car told him that she was the escort, not the prisoner!

Policewomen had inevitably become involved in the competition for men and women for the armed forces and industry. The Ministry of Labour and National Service, keen as it was to get men with special skills for industry, recognised that the police could not be depleted beyond a certain point, and that if women auxiliaries could be made available to the police force, it might be possible for it to spare men whom they would otherwise have to retain.

It was decreed that these Auxiliaries would not be sworn in as constables (although, as the war progressed, a number of them were in fact sworn as temporary constables). In the light of the formation of this body, the employment of women special constables was actively discouraged and the majority of the existing female special constables transferred to this new body.

The pay for full-time members of the Corps was set at £2. per week to which 'proficiency pay' for qualified shorthand typists, and 'service pay' for those with more than one, two or three years service was later added. The WAPC differed from the male Police War Reserves in that it was not included among the 'Civil Defence Forces' within the meaning of the 1941 National Service Act and women were only rarely directed into the Corps, making it an almost entirely voluntary service.

These new recruits had something of a hard time of it. Not only were many of the men totally opposed to women in the police force in any capacity whatsoever, many of the proponents of a women's police section looked upon them with disfavour, anticipating that they would be employed as an alternative to 'proper' policewomen by those forces who wanted to resist taking women on permanently but might be under pressure to appoint some as the war went on (pressure which, as we have seen, was indeed applied later in the war).

Fortunately, several forces which employed their first female members under this scheme found the experience not so horrific as they had expected and were converted to the concept of women police. For example, the North Riding of Yorkshire had never previously felt the need to employ women but, in the light of this new opportunity, decided to take on no less than 40. They then went further and attested 12 of them, gave them a special intensive training course, similar to that provided for men but of shorter duration, including the Highways Acts and Code, and then put them on motor patrol duties, unaccompanied by a male partner. These new-style 'traffic cops' came from all works of life; one was a school teacher, others were clerks, shop assistants or farmers' daughters. A similar scheme was introduced in Stafford where WAPCs were attested and then put on motor patrol in the course of which they chased speeding drivers and escorted wide loads. The cars they drove were normal patrol cars, complete with bell and public address system.

The women turned out to be much more successful in performing police duties than had been expected and it is recorded that :

> *... the WAP Constables who were employed on motor patrol duties, although many were well below the physical standard now expected of policewomen, were not afraid of interrogating suspects and made many arrests, particularly of deserters of both sexes ...*[5].

And the *Police Chronicle and Constabulary World* reported on 21 January, 1944 what appears to be almost a re-enactment of some of the Great War scenes. A Liverpool City policeman had gone into a pub to quell a fight and found himself surrounded by a hostile crowd. A WAPC saw his plight, sent for assistance and, without waiting for its arrival, joined wholeheartedly in the fracas. She was later commended by the chairman of the local magistrates.

Most of the WAPCs were employed on 'inside' duties, as clerks, typists or telephonists where their assistance was invaluable. Even these jobs were not sinecures in wartime as the hours were long and the work often arduous. A former inspector in the now-defunct Walsall Borough force describes how, when a red alert was sounded, these girls came to the control room and stayed until the all-clear – often from 5 or 6 pm to 6 or 7 am the next day, and on numerous occasions during the day. As the control room was in the dungeon-like cells with a sealed door (in case of gas), after a night's duty the odour given off by the various perfumes used (possibly to hide other smells) could be quite overpowering. On one occasion, the chief constable visited the control room with his Chief Clerk and commented on this fact when the door was opened. 'It smells like a brothel in here, Hannifan', he said. Without a trace of sarcasm the Chief Clerk responded, 'I wouldn't know, never having been in one, Sir'.

On the whole, the response to this new body can scarcely be described as overwhelming; by July, 1940, a year after the formation of the Corps, there were 242 members serving full-time in 29 provincial forces and 649 employed part-time in 14 forces. These figures compare with the 128 regular police women employed in the provincial forces and 153 in London.

Some forces had more luck in recruiting auxiliaries than others. In Oxfordshire, a flotilla of Home Guard had been formed to patrol the Thames to combat any attempted seaplane landing. The members used their own river cruisers for the purpose and were assisted by a back-up team of some 30 women who acted as couriers and drove the cars used to ferry the crews to the boats. These women were all married and thus prevented from volunteering for full-time work but they were tremendously enthusiastic and even bought their own navy blue uniforms, blouses and caps. One can imaging their frustration therefore when the War Office ordered their disbandment on the grounds that they could be regarded as combatants, contrary to the Geneva Convention. When this group was offered to the Chief Constable he accepted with alacrity and they formed the basis of the county's WAPC. Anyone who could afford a cruiser on the Thames in those days had to be fairly affluent and what might be termed 'top drawer'. Their womenfolk came from the same social strata and the

Oxfordshire WAPC consequently consisted almost entirely of titled and land-owning ladies and celebrities such as Celia Johnson, the actress, and the daughter of the captain of the *Titanic*.

To begin with the Metropolitan Police had no female auxiliaries and did not begin recruiting until 1941 when they were needed to release more men for active service. The reluctance of the Metropolitan Police may be attributed to its comparatively strong policewomen's branch, a situation largely reflected across the border in Scotland where all policewomen were engaged on plain clothes duties. The creation of the WAPC saw the re-emergence of uniformed policewomen in Scotland for the first time since the mid-1920s. In Glasgow, for example, there were already 15 women police officers but the chief constable, Sir Percy Sillitoe, wasted no time in recruiting WAPC. To set an example, both his wife and his daughter were recruited, his wife being instantly raised to the (unofficial) rank of Assistant Commandant, described by his biographer as '... *a flagrant example of the nepotism of which Sillitoe was guilty on more than one occasion...*'[6].

In fact, ranks were not officially introduced until March 1943 when a Leading Auxiliary grade was introduced for women exercising minor supervisory duties or carrying special responsibilities, and the grade of Senior Auxiliary for those women supervising at least 50 women. The Leading Auxiliary wore sergeants' chevrons, while the Senior Auxiliary wore inspectors' 'pips'. These appointments were strictly controlled and, as a general rule, only one Senior Auxiliary was permitted in any force.

Over the years the number of attested WAPCs (1,093 out of 4,247) far exceeded the number of regular policewomen (348) in England and Wales. The Metropolitan Police long held out against employing WAPCs, the first move coming from the Receiver (the head of the civilian staff at Scotland Yard). He wanted more drivers and proposed to employ them on industrial rates of pay. The Home Office, however, remembering that a number of women were employed as drivers in the various Civil Defence services, thought the analogy should be followed and that these drivers should take the form of WAPCs and approved the establishment of 30. (There were none on the Commissioner's side and he said he did not want them). By the autumn of 1941 the Receiver had 23 uniformed drivers and wanted 80 more but it was not long before the mounting protests at the employment of these women on Civil Defence rates of pay led to their discharge from the WAPC and employment on industrial terms. By this time the Commissioner had been convinced of the value of female auxiliaries and decided to introduce a WAPC section for telephone duties and to staff clerical posts in the Divisional offices. In addition, the Metropolitan Police and one or two other forces employed female First Police Reserves. These were mainly former policewomen who had left the force on marriage (the existence of married policewomen was inconceivable in the pre-war years) and, unlike their male counterparts, were therefore not in receipt of a police pension. Originally the Home Office's view was that these women should be paid at the minimum of the policewomen's pay scale but in 1943 a more generous line was taken and it was recommended that married women who had previously served in the force should be paid at their pre-marriage rate, plus any increments to which they would have been entitled had they remained in the force.

By March 1942, there was a total of 2,800 full-time policewomen (regular and auxiliary) and a further 844 part-timers. The Metropolitan had 204 regular policewomen (of whom 22 were not attested) and 99 unattested WAPCs. In other forces there were 154 regular police-women, 188 attested WAPCs and 2,165 unattested auxiliaries working full-time, plus a further 844 part-timers. Although the WAPC was essentially formed as a voluntary body, like most of the civil defence services, in 1942 unmarried women between the ages of 19 and 30 were eligible for conscription under the National Service Act or were subject to the Control of Employment Order and, although most were channeled into the armed forces or to work in the factories, a few were directed into the police service. Resistance to women in the police service continued unabated in many places and the female members of the force all seem to remember the problems they experienced with some officers who just did not know what to do with women and felt extremely uncomfortable in their presence.

By the summer of 1945, with the war in Europe over and the battle against Japan in its final stages, the numbers had grown to a total of 4,118 but such a level could not be sustained for long since most of the WAPCs, who made up nearly 90% of this total, were anxious to return to their peacetime occupations.

In March, 1946, the Women's Auxiliary Police Corps was disbanded and members had the option of joining the regular force (if they met the physical and educational requirements), taking a job as a civilian employee in the force (if there were any vacancies) or returning to their former occupation.

Not all females employed by the police were necessarily police-women or WAPCs; most forces had for many years employed part-time 'matrons', called in whenever a female prisoner needed supervising and a few of the more daring chief constables had already begun to take on civilian employees to work in the police offices. One job seen by the Home Office as a suitable one for civilianisation was that of secretary to the chief constable. Accordingly, in late 1941, 25 hopefuls were tested for the post of secretary to the chief constable of the Luton Borough Police Force. All took a mass shorthand dictation test and typed this up, from which a shortlist was prepared. When 20 year old Mrs E Duffield was offered the job she was both delighted and terrified. She was told very clearly how confidential the work was and how it was essential that she be able to 'switch off' when she left the office, leaving all aspects of the job behind. After which the chief constable, George Scott (later knighted as chief constable of West Yorkshire), told her quite categorically that he did not want a female secretary and that no females had ever been employed by the force before! It was clearly up to her to prove that she could cope with the work, be unobtrusive and generally keep out of the chief constable's hair. The first few days were not easy, especially as she had to be shown the ropes by the constable who had been the chief's secretary up until then. This young man was an excellent stenographer and was not too keen on the idea of being replaced by a female but, with others, he had been accepted for the RAF. (In fact, this young man did not return to the force after the war but became a dentist). Apart from typing the usual letters and reports, the duties of the chief constable's secretary included taking reams of shorthand notes at disciplinary enquiries (no tape recorders or computers in those days, just a few dictaphones), the whole proceedings being taken down verbatim. In the event of an appeal, the whole sheaf of notes had to be transcribed and typed up.

As the war progressed, so the male members of the police force increasingly came to appreciate the work done by the gentle sex. In addition to the female members of the police and other sections of the civil defence service, organisations such as the WVS and the Salvation Army did wonders for morale and helped to foster the inimitable spirit of comradeship which comes out of shared adversity. But there is one section of the women of this country who remain 'unsung heroines' and whose exploits are often ignored, despite the formidable contribution they made to the war effort, particularly in support of the police: the police wives.

Mention has already been made of the restrictions placed on policemen in the pre-war years and it must be remembered that similar restrictions were imposed on any woman who dared to espouse a policeman. Before she could marry she had to produce two references and her family history and her antecedents were carefully scrutinised. Any hint of scandal or illegality would promptly render her unacceptable and her prospective husband had either to give her up or leave the force. For his part, in some forces the policeman had to show that he had at least £100 behind him before he could be given a house. Where policemen were permitted to buy their own houses (mainly in London or in provincial city and borough forces) they were often required to reside within one mile of their station.

Police Regulations banned the wife of a policeman from certain types of employment, such as running a public house, a place of entertainment or a shop but many forces added further restrictions. Until hostilities demanded that every possible pair of hands should be put to war work, in many forces the wife of a policeman was forbidden to take on or continue in any type of employment, nor was she even allowed to take on any form of voluntary work; her sole role was to support their husband and act as an unpaid auxiliary to him and to the service. For example, in some smaller stations and rural offices, the wife was expected to clean the office(s) and act as receptionist, telephonist, counsellor and friend to all and sundry, provide meals for prisoners (for which she would receive 1/6 [7$\frac{1}{2}$p] to cover the cost) and act as matron where female prisoners were concerned. She was expected to answer the telephone within 20 seconds, or questions were asked by the policeman's superiors and all of this was, of course, unpaid. In fact, the police service was getting the work of two people for the price of one. Much like the country parson's wife, the wife of a policeman was very much part of the community in a village or small town, and it must be remembered that virtually every village and hamlet had its local policeman who lived and worked there.

With the war, these wifely duties did not diminish and the long-suffering police wives found they had other tasks to contend with. More and more their husbands were kept away from home, dealing with one kind of incident or another; a crashed aircraft to be guarded, an unexploded bomb to be dealt with and, following an air raid, all manner of extra tasks to be coped with. One rural constable recalls that his wife often had to cycle out to find him when he was delayed in this manner, bringing him some sandwiches and a Thermos of tea. She also found it necessary to learn first aid, which she was increasingly called upon to apply. Another officer recalls that, in the height of the London Blitz, his wife always knew, by some curious sixth sense, just where she would find him at the scene of some 'incident' and would bring some refreshments to him as soon as things quietened down a little.

Not all new wives found their unaccustomed role easy to assume. One evening, Sergeant Ball, the officer in charge of a small station near Bristol, brought in a prisoner and locked him in the cell, pending his appearance before the magistrates the next day. He remarked to his wife that he would have to provide his charge with some breakfast in the morning and was astonished the following day to see his wife bearing a tray, complete with tray cloth, best cutlery, napkin, and a cooked breakfast, all intended for the prisoner. Sergeant Ball was highly amused, saying, 'If we go on like that, they'll be queuing up at the door to be arrested!'. He took the tray back to the kitchen and found a hunk of bread and a piece of cheese which, with a cup of water, formed the prisoner's more traditional breakfast.

The same sergeant shortly afterwards arrested on a vagrancy charge a man who had been pushing his two filthy, lice-ridden and under-nourished young daughters around in a wheelbarrow. Sgt. Ball's main motive was to get the children some proper care so he put the man in the cells and asked his wife to bathe the two girls. This she did and, feeling sorry for them, replaced their rags with some of her daughter's cast-offs, combed their hair and put ribbons in it. Next morning, ready to go to court, Sgt. Ball took one look at the tidy and well-scrubbed children and asked his wife, 'Now how can I take them before a magistrate and say that they are uncared for?' So, reluctantly, Mrs Ball had to rummage through the garbage for the old clothes and dress them in these again for their court appearance.

Wartime conditions added significantly to the work of the police wife. A sergeant in a Welsh force, learning that a German plane had been shot down some two miles from his station, set off to secure the wreck. Anticipating that some of the crew may have baled out, he sent a message to the local Home Guard before he left, asking them to send someone to his home as his wife would be alone and may need some help. For some reason or other, his request was not acted upon and, as a result, the sergeant's wife had to look after two German prisoners brought in by members of the public, one of whom was badly wounded. Having telephoned for assistance, she rendered first aid to the prisoners and then had to provide the customary British refreshment for the numerous policemen and soldiers who turned up, thereby exhausting the whole of her meagre ration of tea for the month. Fortunately the neighbours rallied round and provided a spoonful here and a spoonful there and so kept them going until the next ration was due. As for the wife, she was so exhausted by her sterling efforts she had to receive medical attention herself. No word of appreciation was ever received from the authorities!

In November, 1940, listeners to the 1 o'clock news heard Constable Ayers of the Kent County Constabulary (whom we met in Chapter 1) describe his experiences which included the following tribute to his wife:

> *My busiest but happiest day was when four planes were shot down within the boundaries of my four parishes..... My motorcycle careered from plane to plane at a very undignified speed and it was not long before my wife had four German prisoners in the parlour. By her triumphant attitude I knew that they were more scared than she was and their sullen behaviour did not affect her a bit. I almost believe they were glad when the military took them over. My wife is invaluable to me, telephoning reports to my headquarters and generally conducting my station whilst I am away. I should be lost without her.*

In May, 1941, when all available women were needed to help in the war effort, the Home Office asked chief constables not to place any obstacles in the way of a police wife seeking employment (other than those jobs proscribed by Police Regulations) unless she was really needed to attend to police business, such as answering the telephone in her husband's absence. Even as late as 1946 the Home Office had to press a county chief constable not to insist on the wives of four of his officers giving up their valuable work as teachers.

However, in most cases, the war forced chief constables to accept that times were changing and that the old values had to go, at least for the duration. In the Metropolitan police plans were made for the recruitment of a number of police wives to work in the police canteens. One who took up this work was the wife of the previously mentioned future chief constable of Oxfordshire, Eric St. Johnston.

It must be added that, in addition to carrying these multifarious duties, police wives had access to a great deal of confidential information and there is no record of any occasion when this confidence was breached. They seem to have acted like the proverbial clams when questioned by the press or the public. All in all, the contribution made by the so-called weaker sex to the police war effort is incalculable – yet it is often forgotten or ignored.

8. Raiders Overhead!

'The Battle of France is over; the Battle of Britain is about to begin.'
So declared Winston Churchill in the summer of 1940 following the fall of France. It was anticipated that the next phase in the conflict would be the invasion of Great Britain and, as a prelude to this, the German military machine concentrated on destroying the Royal Air Force by bombing to extinction its airfields in the south of England. Such was the strength of the RAF's riposte and its refusal to be destroyed that the term 'Battle of Britain' has now come to be applied to that period of the war, from June to September, 1940, during which the RAF engaged the might of the Luftwaffe in mortal combat.

For Sergeant Fred Harding of the Metropolitan Police the Phoney War came to an end one balmy summer evening in August, 1940. He was quietly shaving at the kitchen sink prior to going on night duty, when the enemy made a surprise attack on nearby Heston aerodrome. A bomb fell close to his house, the blast from which lifted him bodily and threw him ten feet into the hall where he stood, momentarily transfixed and speechless like a cartoon character, shaving soap still on one side of his face and holding the razor close to his cheek, staring vacantly into space. Luckily, he quickly recovered and was able to help in fighting the fires caused by this massive firebomb.

But this raid, like many others, failed to stop the RAF fighters from getting airborne and the Luftwaffe suffered heavy losses. In September, 1940, frustrated by his lack of success in destroying the RAF, the Führer instructed that the main thrust should be diverted from the airfields and concentrated on industrial cities and other military targets. Centres of population were also to be targeted in an effort to destroy the morale of the British people. This policy of concentrated bombing was known to the Germans as *Blitzkrieg,* abbreviated by the British to 'The Blitz' and the period was subsequently referred to by Churchill in another of his eminently quotable speeches as 'Their (the British People's) Finest Hour.'

Many books have been written about this chapter of Britain's history; about the amazing courage of the population under the most

191

terrifying of conditions, about the sterling work performed by the fire brigade, the wardens, the rescue services, the ambulance drivers and many others. There is no intention to merely repeat these feats here; what this chapter concentrates on is the role played by the police in the face of enemy attack – a role which has been sadly neglected up until now. One difficulty which researchers experience is the reluctance of many former policemen to talk of their experiences during the war. Time and again the subject of the interview will declare that he had tried to forget all about it; it was too horrific to remember. When one considers that these were men well used to seeing life (and death) in the raw, that they had removed the mutilated bodies of suicides from railway lines, had rendered first aid to horribly injured victims of road accidents and had built up a wall of detachment around their feelings, one begins to appreciate just how terrible the effects of this aerial bombardment were. If these experienced men were profoundly affected by the ordeal, one can only begin to guess at the effect all this had on the inexperienced civil defence workers and the ordinary man and woman in the street.

Blissfully unaware of the sudden change in the fortunes of war, Geoffrey Taylor, a Metropolitan Police constable stationed at Bow, was ordered, on that fine Saturday morning, the 7 September 1940, to go with a colleague on their 500cc Triumph Speed Twin motor cycles to Abridge airfield in Essex to escort a crated Spitfire to the docks. After waiting several hours and listening to various excuses put forward by the RAF, they were told that the plane would not be released and there were hints of 'a big "flap" across the Channel.' The police motorcyclists replenished their tanks from the Air Forces's supply of high octane aircraft fuel and returned to Bow, practically airborne! A few short hours later, the great aerial bombardment began and Geoffrey Taylor, by now off duty and enjoying a well-earned meal, went outside to see the astonishing and unprecedented sight of an armada of German aircraft being harried by Spitfires and Hurricanes. The reason for the RAF's reticence at Abridge now became apparent. By the time the 'All Clear' sounded around 7.30 pm, the darkening sky was aglow with the huge fires now burning out of control in the area of the docks and inner London. The respite was short-lived, however, and half an hour later, the siren sounded again and further raids began which lasted all night.

Next morning, Constable Taylor left his Greenwich home at 5.15 to cycle to Bow for the six o'clock shift, his eyes still gritty from lack of sleep. It seemed to him that the whole of London was burning and the only part of his five mile journey over which he could cycle normally was in the Blackwall Tunnel. Everywhere else the road was littered with bricks and masonry and fallen overhead wires. Once he reached Bow he and his colleagues were quickly briefed and sent off on their motorcycles to North Woolwich to escort bus loads of children, with a few parents and teachers, out to Epping Forest for safety. During the previous afternoon's bombing many residents had been made homeless and had some been accommodated in schools and halls in the area. A number of these reception centres had then been hit in the raid the following night, killing scores of the sheltering homeless.

As Laurence Thompson points out in his book[1], in spite of their elaborate pre-war plans, the authorities were ill-prepared for the Blitz. They had thousands of shrouds and papier-mâché coffins, a million burial forms and thousands of hospital beds. What they had not planned for was the obstinate unwounded living. Although a very precise estimate of the damage which high-explosives would do to bricks and mortar had been available since 1936, such was the fascination exercised by the myth of the knock-out blow that this had been disregarded. As a result, by the end of September 1940, thousands of Londoners were homeless, forced to live and sleep in rest centres which had been set up and equipped on the assumption that they would be needed for no more than an overnight stay. As we have seen, this massing of homeless people resulted in horrendous casualties on the occasions when these rest centres were themselves hit.

The accommodation of the homeless and those unable to get to their homes was yet another task which the police had to take in their stride. Wyn Wheatcroft, who was just fourteen at the time, was at Liverpool Street station, intending to get a train home to Epping:

> *... a policeman asked, 'Where are you going, Missy?' I told him I was going to Epping. 'Not tonight, you're not,' he replied. 'The line has been bombed at Leyton.'*
>
> *He told me to go to Maryland where a policeman would take me to a shelter. The shelter ... was filled with people as it was the night they were to bomb London with thousands of incendiary bombs. ... I got a real good hiding when I got home from my Mum as she had been worrying about me all night[2].*

Others, having lost their homes and possessions, turned to the one public service they knew would be able to help them:

> *... there was a little old lady sat on the police station steps all by herself, no one else around at all. She was sat there with this little parcel and I went over to her to see if she was alright. And she said, 'This is all I've got, love.' This is when it hit me. She'd just got this little parcel and she was sat on the police station steps just by herself. And she said, 'You go on love, ... The police'll be here soon and I shall be alright then.'*[3]

In anticipation of a disruption of communications, several forces, notably the Metropolitan Police, had largely decentralised responsibility, giving the local officers full discretion as regards the deployment of their personnel. Many opted for the system of keeping a substantial reserve at the police station or at a reserve centre so that, as soon as an incident occurred, sufficient police could be dispatched immediately to the scene. It was customary for a car to be kept in readiness and the first available men would pile in and set off for the scene in a matter of minutes. At the same time, officers on the beat would also make their way to any incident occurring in their neighbourhood. The same degree of preparation did not always apply in some other cities. One Coventry War Reserve, finding himself at the scene of a shelter which had received a direct hit, duly cycled to the nearest police box to report the incident and to receive his orders, all in accordance with his clear instructions. However, the line was dead and he had to cope on his own and on his own initiative. He bitterly described the official procedures as '... proper Army style "bull"; all theory and no good in practice.'

The duties specifically assigned to the police in the event of an air raid were the cordoning off of the affected area, directing ordinary traffic to keep the roads clear for essential traffic, earmarking suitable sites for emergency vehicles, crowd control and the prevention of looting. Under ideal circumstances there would be sufficient wardens, rescuers, foremen, ambulances and so on to deal with the incident, each in their own way. In practice this often was not the case. The police were frequently the first on the scene and, without losing any time, they got stuck in, using their bare hands to release trapped victims. Where a large block of flats or similar building had been struck it was impossible to say how many people might be buried under the rubble and it was a question of 'all hands to the pumps.' Another unexpected task was the urgent extinguishing of lights left burning during an air raid and exposed when bomb blast removed the windows and blackout curtains. This often consisted quite simply of smashing the light bulbs with a truncheon – no time to look for light switches with enemy air-craft overhead.

The London Blitz began with a heavy raid on the Docks area on Saturday, 7 September 1940 and continued almost unabated until the following May. The fires at midnight were so fierce that the whole of London was lit up. On the Sunday evening, Sergeant Grey of the Metropolitan Police, stationed at Millwall, the area on which this first attack was concentrated, was returning from a weekend spent with his family who had been evacuated to Brighton. At Victoria station :

> *I jumped on a bus but the conductor said, 'We ain't going nowhere, mate, except home. There's nobody about and we're getting out as fast as we can.' This statement proved to be only too true; the roads around Victoria were deserted and the smell of smoke and burning was everywhere. 'Stay on the platform with me mate,' the conductor relented. 'We're not stopping for anything.'*[4]

There followed the wildest and most hair-raising ride Sergeant Grey had ever experienced. The bus took to the side streets to avoid fires and bomb craters, driving along the pavement, over piles of debris, through clouds of smoke and dust until the bus was finally brought to a halt by a huge crater in the road.

The German bombers flew over London every night for 57 consecutive nights, an average of 200 bombers involved in each raid. In the midst of all this death and destruction, life went on. Sergeant Fred Harding's wife was about to give birth to their second child one cold December day but the cottage hospital was unable to contact him.

> *With other officers on that night I was fully occupied in dealing with clusters of incendiary bombs which were falling like rain. ... The whole range of civil defence – police, fire service, air raid wardens, the lot – fought a desperate battle to prevent major fires. At the end of that hectic night's work I reached home totally exhausted and collapsed into a cold and lonely bed. I failed to hear the pounding on the door by the kind doctor who had safely delivered baby Jeremy. In the afternoon*

195

when I visited the hospital Jeremy was 10 hours old and Nan in tears until I explained my absence[5].

Sergeant Grey of Millwall writes of how he patrolled the streets of Dockland immediately after a particularly heavy raid and

... watched as one house just quietly sat down on itself, all three floors of it, having been on the end of some previously damaged houses and unable to support itself any longer. Every house in the street had been damaged in some way, some were down, some still standing. I went into several of these houses, all of which were empty, the ceilings down, the walls cracked, the doors and windows missing, dinners still on the table, beds unslept in, valuable items such as radios, radiograms, pianos all abandoned. At that stage of the war little was known of the effects of a bomb on a row or workmen's dwellings. Some remnants of casualties still to be seen, awaiting collection by the Civilian War Dead Service. The whole place was eerie and deserted.[6]

Desperate for human company, Sergeant Grey went to a small park where he knew there were good concrete shelters and a warden but these had received a direct hit. The horror of the scene was enhanced by the sight of several chickens picking over the human remains. The police boxes were all empty and there was still no one about. An overwhelming feeling of desolation and abandonment overcame the traumatised policeman:

The war seemed to be all mine and I wanted to share it or give it away.

In his search for company, Sergeant Grey made his way to Poplar police station where, at last, he found human company. In fact, every corner was filled with policemen and civilian employees, dozing, sitting, chatting, resting. One was even quietly ensconced in a corner studying for his promotion examination; he was now eligible to sit and no war was going to stop him. The station canteen was packed like a pub on a Saturday night but there was no food. There was a complete lack of official instructions or direction.

The East End was not the only area affected, of course. A station sergeant (a now defunct rank) from a south London division went out after a raid to assess the damage and found a row of small, terraced houses had been completely destroyed. In the garden of one of these was an Anderson shelter with the entrance firmly secured. He knocked on the makeshift door, apprehensive of what he might find, but eventually the door opened a crack and a man's face appeared. 'What's up?' he asked. 'You've been bombed. Look at your house – it's gone!' 'Blimey,' said the occupant of the shelter, mournfully surveying the scene. 'Well, the bloody thing never was much good.' His whole family had slept soundly (and safely) throughout the raid.

One gets a good idea of what a policeman's duties were like during the London Blitz from the unpublished account written by Special Sergeant Frank Butler, of the City of London Police. On 10 May, 1941 he had arranged to perform police duty during the afternoon and, in response to a request from the warden at his place of work in Fleet Street, agreed to help out with the firewatching duties that night. There was no question of sleep that night as it proved to be one of the heaviest raids of the war and much of London was soon on fire. With the 'all-clear' around seven o'clock the next morning, a weary special, still in his police uniform, made his way towards his home.

> *I had to deviate and go through the Temple... It is no exagger-ation to say that nearly half [the City of] London was in ruins. Further afield the House of Commons was hit and the roof burnt out. I got as far as Ludgate Circus and a police sergeant stopped me. I was not in his division and had been on the go since three the previous afternoon but he insisted on me taking up a post in the Circus. He relented sufficiently to say that it would only be until he had more men available. Night duty men had gone off exhausted (what about me?) and the first relief had been unable to get to the City as yet. Not long afterwards another sergeant came along and moved me some-where else but he released me about nine.... I got to the junction of Cannon Street and Queen Victoria Street and a D Division sergeant saw me. There was no escape and indeed I did not try... I adjoined the premises of De Beers, the diamond corporation which was being used as a temporary police station... From De Beers I was moved ... opposite Mansion House Chamber, a long row of shops with offices above and wine vaults in the cellars. I saw the first one fill with smoke*

and then suddenly burst into flames... Fire appliances stood by but there was no water... The Police Commissioner (Sir Hugh Turnbull) came along, the only time he ever spoke to me. His principal remark that time was 'They'll just have to let it burn.' He was quite casual and unperturbed. Word was passed round that every available Special must report at seven the next morning. Soon after that I deserted. I had been on duty more than 24 hours and had no food or drink for the last 18. I was filthy and covered with dirt and dust. I walked as far as Shoreditch where ... I stopped a car and begged a lift, not very willingly given... I was disgusted that everywhere people laughed and pointed at me in derision.

The next morning I reported for duty at seven and was posted to the Cannon Street barrier ... [an] almost solid line of Specials who let no one pass... (the great fear was of hordes of looters, which there were not)...

The next morning I was summoned to the office of the Managing Director who was furious with me for being absent without leave the previous day.

A few days later Special Constable Butler noticed some incendiaries had dropped on the roof of the Bank of England. He rushed to the entrance and hammered on the door which

... was opened by a gorgeously attired flunkey. When I told him, he turned to a few overalled men standing by who were equipped with the usual paraphernalia and said calmly and politely, 'Gentlemen, there are incendiaries on the roof.' To me it was, 'Thank you, Sir,' and the door was closed.

As a postscript to this tale, Frank Butler telephoned the Daily Telegraph the next morning and the story appeared as a footnote to the Peterborough column and earned him a guinea.

The number of narrow escape stories are legion; in fact, it has been said that every Londoner who lived through the war years within 15 miles of Charing Cross has his own near-miss story to tell, and much the same applies to the inhabitants of many other cities. The police, who were required to be out and about even during the heaviest attack, were not immune from this phenomenon and the number of such stories could easily fill a further volume. One tale which does deserve mention perhaps, is that which concerns four London policemen patrolling in an official car during a heavy raid. So many incendiaries were falling that the driver was unable to see far because of the glare of these but he knew the road well and made good time on the way to an incident. Suddenly the car mounted at a steep angle and then fell back so violently that all the occupants were thrown about, some discovering that the steel helmet can prove an offensive as well as a defensive weapon. 'A bloody bomb hole,' one of them shouted. And so it was – a deep one with a steady flow of sewer water at the bottom. But the car was *on* it rather than *in* it? The reason was that the tram lines had somehow survived the explosion and the police car, after mounting the surrounding debris, had kept its wheels neatly on the bridge formed by the two bare rails until the car came to a rest. The astonished driver had to suffer many a jibe that he should waste no time applying for membership of the Tram Drivers' Union[7].

One policeman clambered onto the roof of a bus during a raid and busied himself knocking incendiary bombs off with his truncheon. Later, at the scene of another incident, he was puzzled as to why two young ambulance girls were sharing a joke, apparently at his expense, until a colleague pointed out to him that the seat of his trousers had been burnt away. In fact it was one of the fascinating sights of the war to see middle-aged women and young girls rushing about dropping dustbin lids, buckets, etc. over incendiary bombs as though it was the most natural thing in the world to do. On numerous occasions shop-girls, City gents and farm labourers could be found putting out small fires or helping to rescue trapped victims. The sight of young girls in their nightdresses and dressing gowns, shovelling away burning incendiary bombs was almost commonplace and many a house, shop or farm building was saved through the sterling work of the ordinary citizen.

It is true that London did not have to stand up to anything like the weight of bombing which was later endured by places like Hamburg or Dresden. In the former city it is officially estimated that at least 43,000 people were killed in three nights in 1943 whereas the whole of Britain only suffered a total of 60,000 fatalities from the results of air raids. But what London did endure was a continuous bombardment for 76 nights on end and it was the repetition of the raids, heavy though many of them were, rather than the sheer weight of bombs or the number of casualties which took its toll. It was the problems of lack of sleep, of trying to get to work the next morning with a minimum of public transport and with the roads blocked by debris which was the depressing factor. After working long hours with very little rest for several weeks, everyone felt the effects of severe fatigue, not least the policeman. One, Geoffrey Taylor, remembers sitting in a car in the garage at Bow police station, half asleep, and feeling the car being rocked from side to side by the bomb blasts but being too fatigued to seek a better form of shelter.

While London was a target of the highest importance from the beginning to the end of the war, and there is no question that it was the hardest hit city, measured both in the number of attacks (354) and the number of casualties (80,000 killed or seriously injured), heavy raids were directed at Coventry between November 1940 and May, 1941 and on Birmingham, Bristol, Sheffield, Merseyside, Manchester, Hull, Southampton, Portsmouth, Plymouth and Devonport during a similar period. These attacks, although extremely severe (especially that on Coventry), were of comparatively short duration and the number of casualties was accordingly lower than those in London. In fact, only in Birmingham and Liverpool did the number of casualties exceed 5,000 killed or seriously injured. Nevertheless, such was the ferocity of these attacks on comparatively small cities that one can readily understand the feelings of Constable John Uren GM, who returned home after a particularly heavy raid on Merseyside in May, 1941 with tears in his eyes and announced to his family that 'Liverpool's finished!' Fortunately, the Liver bird took on the mantle of the Phoenix and Liverpool rose again from the ashes. Perhaps this was partly due to the irrepressible humour of the Liverpudlians, one of whom, a lady, approached Special Sergeant Ben Kelly and asked him to lend her two-pence to phone her husband, working on the nightshift in the docks, The conversation he overheard went as follows:

'Is that you, Fred? ... Well, don't come home to the house – it ain't there. Go to mother's for breakfast. 'Bye for now.'

So badly hit was Coventry over a short but highly concentrated period, that it gave a new word to the English language : coventration, meaning to almost raze to the ground. The unexpected speed at which a raid could develop caught many people out and trapped them where they were. One Coventry special constable trying to get to the Central Police Station to report for duty was turned back by a senior officer who told him it would be hopeless to try to get any further and opined, very correctly as it turned out, that there would be plenty of work for the special to do in his own area before long. Another Coventry constable describes how, once the raid had begun, he and the other reserve officers were lined up in the corridor ready to attend any reported incidents. The first report was of a direct hit on a shelter and he and three colleagues were directed to attend.

> *When we stepped out of the station, even after 15 minutes, we could see it was going to be a heavy raid.... The air was filled with the crash of guns, the whine of bombs and the terrific flash and bang as they exploded... Before we reached Warwick Road we must have dropped flat a dozen times and thought our end was near. However, the report turned out to be false and we began our journey back to the station. We put out several incendiaries and... we had our first experience of the explosive type. As we rushed in to extinguish one on [Greyfriars] Green, it exploded and blazing metal flew in all directions. A young AFS messenger and PC Timms were badly burned on the face and eyes[8].*

One of the most memorable aspects of the raids on Coventry was the destruction of the magnificent and ancient cathedral. The first warning that the cathedral was in danger came in the form of a shout from the battlements which was relayed to the police station. The station sergeant, Walter Groom, described the incident:

> *... Special Constable Marshall came in. 'Sergeant,' he says, 'the cathedral's on fire' ... I was at the desk so I made my air raid message pad out, picked up the direct line to the fire station which was one of the old 'candlestick and snuffer' telephones ... The fire station answered straight away.*
>
> *'Yes, police?'*
>
> *Fire at the cathedral.'*
>
> *'Right', and then down went the phone. Off went Marshall – I told him, 'It's been reported, let them know.' A quarter of an hour later he was back again. 'Sergeant, can you say when they're going to send the fire brigade up to the cathedral? The fire's spreading in the roof.' So I rang the fire station again and spoke to the officer in charge there. 'All our appliances are out,' he said, and of course that meant the cathedral was doomed.[9]*

The cathedral authorities, realising this fact, lost no time in removing some of the more valuable and historic items from the building, including the altar cross and candlesticks, the colours of the Royal Warwickshire Regiment, the altar service books and the books of the Epistles and the Gospels, all of which were conveyed to the comparative safety of the police station where Sergeant Groom saw them arrive.

> *A solemn little procession came into the police station. It was [led by] the Reverend Howard, Provost, bearing the flag of the Warwickshire Regiment and there was another flag being borne in, the Union Jack. In followed Supt. Brennan, Inspector Pendleton and one or two more with pieces of silver which they had rescued from the Cathedral. The party went through the charge office and down to the CID office in the sub-basement of the Council House. Now, I've trooped the colour on the Horse Guards' parade when I was in the Army, but never were colours carried more reverently than they were on that occasion...*[10].

After the most eventful week in Coventry's history the dreary, persistent Midlands rain fell, adding to the misery of the patrolling police, the wardens, the rescue units and everybody else who put their nose out of doors – assuming they still had a door! Water filled the many bomb craters and washed away some of the more gruesome reminders of these unforgettable seven days.

During the raids on Bristol in January 1941, WAPC Constable Ella Johnson arrived at the Bridewell police headquarters and, on entering the main entrance hall, saw all around, sprawled all over the floor, what appeared to be a large number of bodies. On closer inspection she discovered they were in fact seamen who had been sent in to help the fire service and were awaiting transport back to their shore establishment. After working all night they were so exhausted that they simply put their heads on their haversacks and dropped off instantly.

Often, of course, it was the working man's penchant for black humour which took him (and her) through the worst times. A typical example was the Sheffield policeman who crawled out from beneath the ruins of a house where he had been helping to rescue trapped survivors. He was covered with mud, grease, plaster, brick dust, etc, prompting a nearby warden to comment, 'Gosh, you are in a mess!' 'Yes,' replied the policeman with studied nonchalance. 'That's the worst of navy blue; it shows every mark.'

Other buildings were damaged, sometimes with bizarre consequences. In Bristol, a mine apparently intended for the Avonmouth docks, struck and destroyed a section of the massive wall around Horfield Jail and the astonished residents of the neighbourhood were treated to the rare sight of a number of prisoners, under the watchful eye of just one warder and one policeman, happily repairing their own prison wall, apparently content to do their bit for King and Country, or perhaps just grateful that the missile had spared the main residential block in which they had been housed.

When it became Manchester's turn to suffer the might of the Luftwaffe, a number of the bombers overshot and deposited their load on nearby Oldham. Some of these fell on a cemetery, disturbing a number of the graves and, until the Council could spare workmen for the 'non-essential' task of reburying the corpses and repairing the damage, the police had to include the cemetery in their patrols to prevent looting. This presented no problem during the day but at night, in the blackout and with even the use of a torch forbidden, walking around a cemetery full of open graves with an occasional eerie hoot of an owl was a nerve-wracking business, both for the police and for any intending grave robbers.

Belfast's turn to experience the fury of the Nazis came in 1941 and, such was the intensity of the damage and fires that additional fire fighters were called in from Glasgow and Liverpool as well as 13 brigades from Dublin, Dun Laoghaire, Dundalk and Drogheda in the neutral Irish Republic.

Portsmouth, being a naval port, was also badly hit and suffered a great many fires. On the whole, the hard-pressed city police coped admirably although one or two showed an unwarranted degree of officiousness. Two Royal Navy signalmen off a destroyer tell how they were sent, with a stirrup pump, a bucket and a small axe, to help in fighting the fires caused by the second night's air raid.

> *When we arrived the King's Road seemed to be ablaze from end to end. As we walked along the road a policeman dismounted from his bicycle. 'Are you a fire-fighting party?' 'Yes!' 'Then get on with it!' I explained that with our modest equipment we*

*needed to find a small fire. He rode off in disgust... We spotted
a house with smoke coming from the eaves. After a lot of
banging a very pale lady answered and ... we persuaded her to
come on to the pavement to see the smoke coming from her
house. She reluctantly allowed us into the house. Peter filled
the bath with cold water and I climbed into the roof space ...
Peter started pumping and I was able to direct a small stream
of water at the bomb. In a short while the glow disappeared...
and I called to Peter to stop pumping and started to lower
myself through the hatch. About three rungs down the ladder
both my legs were firmly grasped. Our policeman friend had
decided to take charge. 'Get back up there and finish the job,'
he said. 'It is finished and I'm coming down,' I said... As soon
as I reached the floor the policeman grabbed the hose end and
ascended the ladder to finish the job. He was a big man and
quite unable to get through the hatch. He ordered me to get into
the roof and follow his instructions. I refused to do so. Peter
was equally unco-operative, so he placed us under arrest. We
were taken to Portsmouth police station, questioned and placed
in a cell. Peter was telling me his opinion (worth listening to
since he was a solicitor in civilian life)... when we heard the
familiar voice of our captain demanding our immediate release
and addressing the sort of remarks we would like to have made
to our custodians.*[11]

The devices known as landmines or parachute mines were
particularly feared because of the immense damage their blast could do,
although to have one's home wrecked by one of these devices carried
with it a certain kudos, so that every medium-sized bomb came, in
retrospect, to be described as a land mine. The American, Ralph
Ingersoll described the effect of one of these devices in his book:

*I can best illustrate it to you by describing the effect of a land
mine that fell almost in the centre of a street crossing. The four
houses on the four corners, each five stories high, were
demolished, flattened to the ground, obliterated, without being
touched by the mine. The four blocks surrounding the four
demolished houses were rendered uninhabitable. The twelve
blocks surrounding the four blocks that were rendered
uninhabitable, surrounding the four houses that were*

demolished, all witnessed the explosion with broken glass.[12]

Constable Tom Jones of the Liverpool Police was one of the first to encounter one of these devices, fortunately unexploded and, when he was put in charge of a new recruit, he advised his young charge that, should he hear the flapping of a parachute he should try to determine the direction it was taking and then run like hell in the opposite direction. This advice had an amusing sequel some time later when Tom, standing in a doorway late at night, heard the sound of running footsteps coming down the middle of the road. Assuming the runner to be up to no good he let him approach and then stepped out and switched on his torch. He just caught a glimpse of a flying constable before the torch was knocked out of his hand and he was abruptly transported into the gutter by the impact of this high speed human body. As they both got their breath back, Tom Jones discovered his assailant to be the young constable and the cause of his panic a barrage balloon which was being released into the sky, making the usual flapping noise as its tail fins began to fill with air. Perhaps wisely the young man had not stopped to determine the cause of the flapping noise he had heard but had acted promptly on the advice he had been given.

Genuine land mines also provided some black humour, as when two special constables in Coventry, sent to inspect an unexploded parachute mine lying in the street, took 'shelter' behind it when another bomb was heard falling. Often the sight of a parachute was mistakenly thought to be a German airman who had bailed out of his damaged aircraft, sometimes with tragic consequences. A female warden and two Polish airmen, seeing a parachute coming down in Coventry, thought it was an airman and ran to meet it. Their bodies were later found apparently unharmed but the blast had destroyed their lungs.

In April 1942 the Nazis tried a new tack and, as a reprisal against the RAF raids on Lubeck and Rostock, directed their attention to the cathedral cities of Bath, Bristol, Exeter, Canterbury, Norwich, York, Southampton, etc. These raids, which lasted until July 1942, became known as the Baedeker raids after the well-known pre-war tourist guides which featured such historic cities. Then, towards the end of 1942 it became the turn of the Kent and Sussex coastal towns. These were subjected to 'tip-and-run' raids in which a light bomber would swoop in across the Channel at low altitude to avoid the radar and anti-aircraft guns, dropping their load on the first urban area they encountered. The same areas, especially Dover and Folkestone, were also subjected to shelling from the French coast, a situation which continued until the Canadian troops succeeded in taking the guns in late 1944. In fact, outside London, Dover suffered more enemy attacks (125) than any other town or city, while Folkestone was third (behind Great Yarmouth) with 83, thus fully justifying the appellation 'Hell Fire Corner' for this small part of Kent.

Even rural areas did not always escape scot-free, especially in the beleaguered southeast; in fact, the first bombs to fall on mainland Britain fell near Canterbury in May, 1940. Later, German bombers which had not released their full load over their specified target tended to drop the remaining bombs anywhere on the way back to the Channel coast. So it was that Constable Tom Longhurst, off duty and wearing his best suit, learned that a bomb had fallen in his village of Teynham, destroying a row of farm labourers' cottages and killing two of the occupants. There was little civil defence back-up in such rural areas and, having attended the scene on his trusty bike, Constable Longhurst set about helping to release the trapped cottagers, to the lasting detriment of his best suit. In all, the tiny village of Teynham, near Faversham in Kent, suffered around 50 HE bombs, 2 land mines, numerous incendiaries, two doodlebugs, and one V2 rocket. There were 5 crashed British aircraft and one German one. The nearby church at Lynsted was hit three times, while in a nearby village one bomb fortuitously revealed the whereabouts of a long-forgotten, medieval well.

There were further air raids on London between late 1943 and early 1944 – the 'Little Blitz' – and other limited attacks elsewhere, such as the tip-and-run raids described above. But the comparative calm which followed the Blitz and the Baedeker raids was shattered when the Nazis launched their latest terror weapon on the long-suffering British; the V1 or Doodlebug. These pilotless aircraft – little more than a one-tonne bomb with an rocket engine attached – had an approach speed of between 500 and 600 kph. They were launched randomly in the general direction of London and 2,341 came to earth in the Metropolitan Police District, killing 5,367 civilians and seriously injuring three times that number, but as there was no control over them many exploded in Kent and Sussex, well short of their target. Essex, too, did not escape and Constable Leslie Clarke was fetched from his village station by the army to help search the area around the crater made by one of the first of these devices for the pilot of this supposed crashed aircraft. It was sometime before they realised that what they had got was in fact Hitler's latest secret weapon.

In August, 1944, Constable Tom Longhurst was making a 'conference point' with his sergeant in the village of Bapchild, near Sittingbourne (Kent) when they saw a V1, pursued by a Spitfire, heading westwards towards the Medway Towns. Shortly afterwards they heard an explosion and rejoiced that the fighter had succeeded in destroying the flying bomb. Tom Longhurst then continued to Sittingbourne police station to fill his 'Indian' motorcycle with petrol where, on arrival, he was handed a first aid kit and told to go along the A2 road towards Gillingham, where there had been 'an incident'. Passing several vehicles loaded with troops (and some sailors who had obviously hitched a lift) he arrived at the railway bridge over this busy trunk road at Rainham and saw that the flying bomb had come down on the bridge, just in front of a packed train which had been unable to stop in time and had run into the ruined bridge. Eight passengers in the train had been killed and 33 seriously injured but, fortunately, there had not been any of the packed road vehicles under the bridge at the time or the toll would have been much higher.

On Christmas Eve 1944, a number of flying bombs were released over the North Sea, aimed at the north of England. Only one is known to have found a target and this fell on a quiet suburban road in Oldham (Lancashire), in which 27 people lost their lives, many of them children. Constable Macdonald of the City force, a veteran of the First World War, said that the sight of all the death and damage overlaid with Christmas decorations, the simple toys and the little food luxuries which had been saved from the meagre rations, all of which had to be sorted out on Christmas Day, was the most upsetting thing he had ever had to do.

This new weapon was superseded by the Germans' latest weapon, the V2 high altitude rocket. Fortunately the advance of the Allied armies in 1944 and 1945 curtailed the use of these fearful weapons before they had chance to do too much damage to the morale of the already weary and war-torn citizens of the capital.

All these various weapons, as well as causing a huge number of civilian casualties, wrecked or made uninhabitable an enormous number of buildings, including those belonging to the police or individual policemen. With the ever-present danger of looters, damaged property had to be guarded by the police until it had been made secure or the contents removed. If, as a result of enemy action, conditions at home occasionally left something to be desired, those policemen who were sent to relieve their colleagues in the more seriously damaged areas were often in an even sorrier plight. When a detachment from the Worcester City Police was sent to Coventry to assist the local force, together with units from the Herefordshire and Worcestershire forces, they thought their luck was in when they discovered they were to be accommodated in the General Wolfe Hotel. With visions of good food and hot and cold running chambermaids they were quite looking forward to their visit but the reality turned out to be quite different. There was no water, no gas, no electricity; outside, the sewers had been breached resulting in an unholy stench. The beds were powdered with dust and all around were craters and collapsed buildings.

In all, some 60,000 British civilians were killed through enemy action during the war – the population of a good-sized town. Many more were seriously injured while the number of minor casualties is incalculable. In peacetime the police are closely concerned with any sudden death, principally as representatives of HM Coroner, and this involvement does not lessen in time of war. Quite the contrary, in fact, since the number of cases is naturally very much greater.

Although largely immune to the effects of death and disaster through close contact with it in its myriad forms, the policeman was not always able to view the death of a particular person or group of people with complete detachment. Early in the war, perhaps before its full effects had become almost commonplace, Constable Bert Ayers had to attend the scene of an incident in which a German aircraft had crashed on some Kent farm outhouses, killing a girl of 9 and injuring her parents. The pilot was Hauptmann Hassel von Wedel, the Luftwaffe's official historian and one of Goering's right-hand men. At 47 he was probably one of the oldest pilots brought down in this country and was merely supposed to observe the German aerial activity from offshore but a Hurricane got him. He was apologetic but the constable was so filled with disgust at the 'murder' of this young child that :

> *I picked up its mutilated body and held it out to him, speechless. The German was very upset and had to be led away*[13].

208

Constable Arthur Marshall, who was in charge of the city mortuary on the night of the Sheffield Blitz, would empathise with this attitude;

> *There was only one thing that ever used to upset me and that was seeing kids killed. That was the only thing that upset me in the mortuary was seeing the bodies of kids. One little lad, a three-year-old, he crawled under the wash basin and got suffocated with dust. And he was just sat there and, oh, it did, it really did, if got through to the core[14].*

Arthur Marshall goes on to describe his harrowing task that dreadful night:

> *Most of the people employed to do the job were not used to seeing the sort of sights we saw. They were usually undertakers who had only dealt with clean, laid-out bodies and were absolutely useless. I was hardened to it after a while, but when a family came to identify someone, however you tried to hide behind the shell, it was hard.*

When a bomb fell on York Street Mill, Belfast, the whole of one side of the mill collapsed onto the small mill houses nearby, destroying a total of 63 houses. 35 people lost their lives but the death toll would have been considerably higher but for the efforts of two members of the Royal Ulster Constabulary. Together they pulled 60 people out of the remains of their homes, many of them still alive, and so averted a much greater disaster. One of the officers was awarded the George Medal for his actions.

In Chelsea, in August, 1944, a flying bomb dropped onto a block of flats occupied by the Women's Auxiliary Air Force (WAAF). Sergeant Fred Harding was one of the first on the scene as it was close to his own home where he had been in bed for the night. With a few other local residents he made his perilous way to the top floor where he knew the women's dormitory was situated.

> *The sight that met us is hard to describe. There seemed to be dozens of hospital type iron beds, all displaced, upside down or on their sides. Bed linen and female clothing was everywhere ... the background dominated by the pitiful sight of the women. Some were trapped and dead, some were trapped and*

screaming. A few were moving about like zombies... The irony of that incident is that all those women were supposed to be sleeping in the undamaged brick air raid shelters across the road, They had ignored the order and, regretfully, had suffered accordingly[15].

A macabre sight greeted the same sergeant when he entered a sturdy concrete air raid shelter during a heavy raid on London. Inside he found four men sitting upright around a piece of blanket on the ground, each holding some playing cards. They were all dead, although none bore any visible signs of injury.

A few days after the harbour area of Folkestone was destroyed by a parachute mine, Constable Richard Crane was called by the occupier of a small terraced house nearby who complained that he was unable to get into his lavatory at the bottom of the garden. On investigating, Constable Crane found that the roof had been smashed in and, although the door would not open more than a couple of inches, he managed to put his hand through and gradually remove some of the debris. Eventually he was able to open the door sufficiently to see that the cause of the damage to the roof was the torso of a heavily built man with telephone wires wrapped around it which had been blown some 75 to 100 yards through the air by the force of the land mine's explosion.

In Belfast, Special Constable Herbert Woolsey was intrigued when he saw a large parachute coming down with what appeared to be a man on the end. Two dock workers ran past him, shouting that they were going to get him and the constable was horrified when the parachutist turned out to be a land mine and the two dockers were blown to bits before his eyes. He thought his turn had come the following day when a German plane came over the docks at low altitude with a man leaning out of the cockpit, pointing what he assumed to be a gun in his direction.

'I simply froze. It was next day I learned it was a plane taking photographs after the raid.'[16]

When a land mine exploded in North London a postman was trapped in his public house, his foot being caught under a piano which was in turn held down by a great weight of debris. All kinds of tools had been applied to release him but without success and a fire which had broken out in a neighbouring bakery threatened to engulf the public house and burn the unfortunate man alive. With no fire appliance available to deal with the fire the only solution appeared to be to cut the potman's foot off at the ankle but there was no doctor at hand. After a quick consultation a constable went to him and offered to perform the operation with a hand saw, By this time the poor man was so frantic all he could mutter was, 'Don't leave me. Don't leave me.' Fortunately, this caused the constable to hesitate and, in the nick of time, a fire engine arrived and the fire fighters quickly set to work. The flames were subdued just before they reached the place where the potman was lying. After a further five hours the potman was finally released, with only minor injuries and a relieved policeman was able to contemplate how near he had become to being an amateur surgeon.

Not all casualties which the police had to deal with occurred on dry land. When the dockers went to unload one ship which docked at Belfast they found about 50 bodies in the hold, all in various stages of decomposition. They, not unnaturally, refused to unload it and the police were sent for. It transpired that the ship had been bombed off Freetown and her hold had been sealed up. The buck of responsibility was passed from one organisation to another; the Admiralty had notified the next of kin that the men had been lost at sea and they wanted nothing further to do with it. The shipyard owners naturally refused any responsibility and it was left to the Coroner to authorise burial, the cost being borne by Belfast Corporation.

As if the carnage resulting from enemy action was not enough, in some areas there were a number of casualties, many of which were fatal, as a result of people walking along the white line in the centre of the road to avoid obstructions on the footpath.

Other casualties were the result of accidents, such as that which occurred at the Royal Gun Powder Factory in Waltham Abbey, Essex, probably due to the influx of inexperienced workers. One explosion rocked the town in January, 1940 but a far worse blast occurred three months later in which five died and fifteen were injured when a mixing house erupted. The explosion was reported to have been heard as far away as Brighton, on the south coast. Considerable damage was caused to Waltham Abbey town centre with lesser damage up to four miles away. The police station in Sun Street was damaged and police from that station were called out to help in the search for human remains outside the factory's perimeter fence, the search inside being conducted by the War Department Police, since the civil police were excluded from entering the factory on security grounds, despite the fact that they had policed it up until the war.

Another major incident which was not the result of enemy action caused the deaths of 173 people, mainly women and children. During an air raid, some anti-aircraft shells of a new type caused people to rush to the entrance of the Bethnal Green tube station in order to shelter on the platforms. A woman carrying a baby and a bundle tripped and fell. Others fell over her and more and more people fell as the weight of those trying to get in pressed against them. Such was the crush of humanity in the entrance that the police had to approach the station along the rail tunnel from Liverpool Street station in order to try to tackle this human wedge from the other side. It was several hours before the tangle of humanity could be cleared and the full extent of the tragedy was revealed.

It must not be thought that the only casualties the police had to deal with were civilians. For instance, in 1940, Constable Bob Stewart (Kent) recovered the body of a French sailor from the sea off Broadstairs. By an uncanny presage of what the fates had in store for him, this unfortunate matelot had the words *Pas de Chance!* (Tough Luck!) tattooed on his arm.

Normal mortuaries were unable to cope with the enormous number of casualties and other arrangements had to be made. A typical example occurred in Belfast where the heavy raid on Easter Tuesday in 1941 resulted in so many casualties that the authorities were caught completely unprepared. The injured were treated by the hospitals efficiently and promptly under the most trying conditions but the number of fatalities was another matter altogether. The city mortuary was very quickly overwhelmed and bodies had to be taken to St George's market hall and the Falls Road Baths. Initially, the bodies in the Baths were laid out in coffins around the pool but the city quickly ran out of coffins and the Baths became so full that the bodies had to be placed in the swimming pool itself. Where they could be identified the bodies were tagged but others had to await the arrival of distraught relatives before they could be given a name. This was often a difficult or impossible task. Some bodies were hardly recognisable as human beings at all. One large and oddly shaped shroud was brought in and bore the label, 'Believed to be a mother and her five children'. After three days decomposition began to set in and the smell in the Baths became unbearable so the bodies were removed to Mays Field where they were laid out on the grass where they could still be identified. A volunteer sat all day playing a hose over the bodies in order to slow down the process of decomposition. In the end well over a hundred unidentified bodies were buried the following weekend.

Here, as elsewhere, some bodies were never found. A few would come to light during the final demolition possible a year later. Various parts and limbs might be collected and taken to the mortuary where volunteers would try their best to piece together the corpse. Here again, the stench was probably the most unbearable part of the whole process.

> *Then the question of identifying people came up. There was a viewing room and you used to have to go and put these coffins on a trolley with a blanket over it and call people in. Of course they'd been cleaned up as much as we could so they could identify them. People say, 'It sounds horrible; how could you do it?' They think you're callous and hard-hearted but you have to detach yourself completely from it, that's the only thing to do. ... You put all human feelings to one side. You've a job to do that has to be done. It took three months before that air raid mortuary was finally cleared and I took a load of old clothes and that down to the incinerator. That was a horrific time[17].*

Sergeant Fred Harding, whom we met earlier, was to have the effects of the war brought home to him very forcibly shortly afterwards when he had to deal with a 'normal' death; a man who had dropped dead in the street from a heart attack. The body and the officer were taken to a nearby hospital where a doctor certified life extinct and they then continued to the local mortuary.

> *By the time we reached there it was almost midnight. An air raid alert was on and blackout prevailed. I rang the bell of the mortuary keeper's flat. A window opened and a woman called out, 'He's ill in bed. You'll have to get on with it yourself.' and with that she threw over the keys. I opened the door and switched on the light. All around the wall on tiers of shelves were uncovered bodies, each with a tag tied to the big toe. These were the aftermath of recent air attacks awaiting disposal. Normally all bodies are shrouded but I guess that demand had temporarily exceeded supply. Be that as it may, I was there with yet another body. The two ambulance men*

carried it in and rolled it from the stretcher onto the post mortem table in the centre of the floor. Whilst I was going through the dead man's pockets to establish his identity and to take custody of personal possessions, I noticed the ambulance men pick up their stretcher and go outside. I thought they would return and give me a hand but no, I then heard the ambulance drive away. And there I was amid this terrible array of naked dead. It was a macabre scene! It was very cold in there but I felt colder. It was a weird sensation, a sense of fear, but fear of what? Perhaps the very stillness and the poor light had something to do with it but I just had to get out of there. I grabbed the bits and pieces of personal property and rushed outside and found comfort in looking up into the starlit sky[18].

An essential part of the police involvement with victims of disasters, both then and now, is the efficient maintaining of records of those missing, dead, injured or evacuated. During the war a Civilian War Death Form was introduced, to be completed by the person who actually found the body. This showed the precise place where the body was found and, where possible, the time and date of death. This latter piece of information, although seemingly irrelevant at first sight, could prove vital in the case of an inheritance dispute. Unfortunately, the sort of person who had to complete these forms – the heavy rescue units, wardens, first aiders, stretcher bearers – were often not of an administrative bent and no doubt wanted to get on with what they saw as their primary task: the extrication of victims from the ruins of their homes. Consequently often no enquiries were made on the ground and just a name or a place was entered on the form before it was passed to the Casualty Centre at the police station.

When I went on duty ... the Superintendent called me in. He had a pile of these forms, incomplete. And he'd got a list of all the men who were on duty... And we went through them, sat down there from six o'clock till one o'clock in the morning, worked straight through. And we'd get one marked out to Sergeant Smith or whoever it was. 'The information I want from him is – I want to know the address of this person, the age of this person, where the body was found, was any property found on the body...?'. All things like that, sufficient to fill it in.

214

Raiders Overhead!

They were all sent out and it took us four or five days to get it in anything like order[19].

In the Metropolitan Police, each police station was responsible for obtaining details of casualties from the mortuaries and hospitals in its area and for passing these to Scotland Yard where they were collated and passed on (usually by teleprinter) to Divisional Offices where they were duplicated and passed to stations. An essential feature of this system was speed and, inevitably, inaccuracies crept in. Another failing of the system was that as the lists piled up at stations the labour of searching through them to find names steadily increased (there were no computers to help in those days!). It was therefore decided to set up a central Casualty Bureau at Scotland Yard which would maintain a complete record of all London casualties and issue verified printed alphabetical lists at intervals, with occasional nominal indexes to facilitate searches. In all, this Bureau dealt with nearly 30,000 killed and over 50,000 seriously injured casualties.

The next of kin of those killed or seriously injured were informed by the police in the area in which they lived and a great deal of communications traffic passed from station to station and from force to force since the relatives of a victim often lived in a completely different area from that raided.

The police casualty bureaux were also inundated with calls from the military concerning servicemen who had not returned from home leave and requesting verification of reports of damage made by service personnel seeking compassionate leave. One constable ruefully recalls that, when his house was badly damaged, he was given one day to find alternative accommodation for himself and his family yet, only the day before, he had been sent to arrest a serviceman who had overstayed the seven days' leave granted to him in similar circumstances.

The sad task of informing relatives of the loss of a loved one was not confined to the victims of air raids. One of the most difficult jobs the police had to perform was to tell the relatives of a serviceman that he had been reported missing or killed in action. The police received these details by telephone from the military authorities and then, with a heavy heart, would have to knock on unsuspecting doors to convey the bad tidings.

Where casualties were concerned, the hardest hit were, of course, the

215

civil defence service, the fire brigade and the police, all of whom had to be out and about despite falling bombs and flying shrapnel. Being so closely involved in civil defence matters, it comes as no surprise to learn that many police officers lost their lives through enemy action. In London alone, 208 police officers were killed in air raids and hundreds injured, 54 of the fatalities occurring in the first eight weeks of air raids. Some of these were on duty while others were at home, resting between shifts but it is not possible to make a distinction because no hard and fast line can be drawn. During air raids it was commonplace for officers, technically 'off-duty' to turn out to lend a hand thus, as it were, putting themselves on duty. A number of lives – it is impossible to say how many – were lost in this manner.

In all, throughout the country, 278 members of the police service were killed as a result of enemy action while on duty with their own forces :

Regular police officers	119
First Police Reserves	9
Full-time special constables	3
Police War Reserves	75
Part-time Special Constables	67
Policewomen	1
Police Auxiliaries	2
Police civilian employees	2

The fire service was even harder hit, with over 800 dead and around 7,000 injured, although it has to be said that there were more than twice as many fire-fighters as there were policemen[20].

In Belfast, Sergeant Sam Hays was in charge of new recruits to the Royal Ulster Constabulary and took them to various police stations when the sirens sounded for them to act as a back-up for the more experienced officers. On 5 May, 1941, he went with a party of about 40 to Glenravel Street Police Station where they were all quartered in a reputedly bomb-proof ground floor room. Sam Hays's colleague suggested that there were too many men in one room for safety and it was agreed that Sam would take a party of about 20 outside where they busied themselves extinguishing incendiary bombs. Suddenly he heard a most awful roar like and express train and, looking up, saw a land mine swinging on its parachute.

*I shouted to get down and covered my head with my hands...
After the crash there was dead silence for about a moment, ... I
got up as they [the other lads] did and went over to the
barracks to see the so called bomb-proof room where the lads
were, smashed into huge slabs of reinforced concrete and the
bodies of six of our recruits under the rubble.... I went at
daylight to see them as they lay [in the mortuary] in their
uniform, still, silent and composed looking, killed presumably
by blast since there was no mutilation on them. Strangely
enough, apart from shock, there were no other wounded... The
six killed were the finest fellows I had ever seen, all over six feet
tall in the vigour of their youth[21].*

The American author, Ralph Ingersoll, had a first-hand experience of
the death of a policeman on duty :

*We swung off to one side to avoid it [a wrecked car] and the
pencil beam of our headlight picked out a figure lying on the
edge of the curb. We got out and went over to it. It was a dead
policeman. A red-headed policeman. He had been young and
good-looking. There was no one else around. It was very
quiet. ... We had flashlights and stood looking down at the dead
policeman, not knowing what to do next. Presently there were
footsteps ... First one and then several policemen came from
another street. They looked at the dead policeman but did not
move him ... While we were looking an ambulance or a truck
rolled up behind us, some men got out, went over to where the
warden was standing over the casualty. They lifted the dead
policeman on to the stretcher, carried him back into the
darkness. And no one said anything[22].*

In Liverpool, Constable John Uren, later to be awarded the George
Medal for gallantry, was walking with a colleague back to the Bridewell (the main lock-up) when they met up with two other policemen,
also making their way back to the station. At a fork in the road the two
couples split up (possibly to avoid their being charged with 'idling and
gossiping', a common disciplinary offence in those days); John Uren
and his partner reached the Bridewell shortly afterwards, their
colleagues never did, being killed by a bomb. On another occasion, the

same officer, with another colleague, was walking along the street when a German bomb blew the two of them along the length of the street, only for another bomb to promptly blow them back again. Constable Uren picked himself up, his uniform tattered and torn and with a number of cuts and abrasions but thankful that, unlike the other policeman, he was still alive.

Even some comparatively quiet towns had their share of police casualties, as the Brighton Borough Cemetery in Bear Road bears witness. There the graves of four constables, all killed in separate incidents, are to be found close by those of 14 German Luftwaffe airmen. Although it was naturally the lower police ranks who were most at risk, not all senior officers escaped unscathed and the deputy chief constable of Hull City Police was killed by flying glass. In Edinburgh, Assistant Chief Constable R C Thompson was shot and killed by an RAF sergeant while being driven to the ARP headquarters. The airman was subsequently convicted of culpable homicide while under the influence of intoxicating liquor.

Nor were all police casualties the result of enemy action. One young RUC recruit, on guard duty at the RUC depot, sat down on the steps of the dormitory when his loaded shotgun slipped down between his legs. He pulled it up and, in doing so, caught both hammers on the edge of the steps, detonating the cartridges which discharged their contents into his groin, this ending his young life.

Fortunately, not all police casualties were as serious as these; some were, in fact almost amusing. Special Constable Frank Butler remembers colliding with a warden in the blackout and, because the warden was somewhat shorter that he, the rim of his steel helmet passed under the officer's and gave him a nasty gash under the eye. Fortunately, no serious damage was done and, apart from a 'shiner' and a headache, the constable was unscathed. Steel helmets were often a cause of concern; another officer remembers cycling fast during an air raid and throwing himself off the bike into the gutter when he heard the whistle of a bomb. Strangely enough there was no explosion and he remounted and cycled off, only to fling himself to the ground a few seconds later when he heard another whistle. It was quite a time before he realised that the whistling was merely the wind blowing past the rim of his helmet!

The great weight of high explosives and incendiary devices which the enemy threw at this country caused many thousands of casualties but the toll would undoubtedly have been much higher, had all these contraptions exploded. In fact, a large number of bombs, especially the high explosive type, failed to detonate on impact and had to be first located and then made safe. The cool bravery of the Army, Navy and RAF bomb disposal units has been recognised by the award of numerous medals, including the George Cross – the highest possible award under these circumstances. The sheer courage of these men and the dangers they faced are clearly described by Sergeant Fred Harding in an article in a New Zealand magazine (he having retired to that country after his retirement from the police):

> *A UXB had dropped between two detached dwelling houses in a suburban street. It was a 500 pounder. When I arrived there were seven Sappers who had dug out all round the bomb. It looked about the size of a 60 gallon hot water cylinder lying on its side in the centre of a small crater. The leading Sapper said to me, 'She's ticking over Sarge – a real live cow. I hope there's no one in these houses?' This was calmly and seriously said by a dedicated man whose thoughts were for the safety of others. He was seemingly regardless of the risk to himself and his mates. I replied, 'Give me a few minutes while I check with the local Warden.' Finding the warden took me longer than I expected. I was 50 yards away, returning with an 'OK' answer when the bomb exploded. Instinctively I flattened out. I was wearing a steel helmet and was shielded from the blast by the intervening houses. ... A huge piece of brick chimney landed with a heavy thump just six feet from my head ... my thoughts raced back to the scene which I had left only a few minutes previously. Mentally repeating 'The men! The men''' I ran the remaining distance. The seven men had been blown to pieces and the two houses had disappeared. I was sickened, not so much by the ghastly mess around me, I was hardened to that, but by the tragedy of war and the waste of life.*[23]

The resemblance to a hot water cylinder fooled a number of people, especially where the mine had come down on or near ruined houses. This occurred in Liverpool, where an unexploded land mine which had come to rest in the bedroom of a seriously damaged house, was passed over by two wardens doing a hurried search by torchlight. When identified, Constable Tom Jones was sent to help quarantine the area and post the usual UXB notices. The next morning, on his way home after being relieved, he decided to have a peek at this monster and noted that it bore the date 11.11.40; it had taken just ten days to deliver it. Seeing the evil device brooding malevolently in a corner of the room, he crept downstairs very, very quietly indeed. On leaving the house he was astonished to see an elderly man nonchalantly cycling past the very house. On being hailed by the startled policeman, the man explained that he had to get to work and, as the cordon was in his way, he had simply lifted the ropes and ducked beneath them and resumed his usual route. On being told the reason for the cordon, the cyclist departed at a speed which would not have disgraced a motor-cyclist in the TT races.

Ignorance was another problem, especially among the untrained civilians. R Bennett was a fifteen year old lad when the war started and had a young man's enthusiasm for the excitement which had suddenly come into his life. One night, he and his father saw a parachute hanging from the parapet of a bridge carrying the South Circular Road over a railway line. Their first thought was that a parachutist had landed but, on going up to the bridge, they found a large, cylindrical canister to which the parachute was attached. This, they decided, was a container of arms, radios, etc. for the use of Fifth Columnists or saboteurs and they resolved to open it to see just what it contained.

> *All our speculation was suddenly brought to an end by the arrival on the scene of a local retired naval officer and eccentric. Although he had some undefined connections with the ARP, he was brandishing a sword and shouting foul imprecations about the rumoured Nazi hordes and what he intended to do with them. In the middle of all this the local bobby appeared as if by magic and managed to calm things down. He, it seemed, was fairly well 'clued up' about things that were dropped by German raids and informed us that the thing was a land mine and we should make ourselves scarce while he contacted his station to find out what he should do about it.*[24]

In south London a man called into the police station to report having seen a lady leaning against a wall nearby in a somewhat curious attitude. He thought she might be ill. A policeman was sent to investigate and quickly returned to report that the 'lady' was in fact an unexploded land mine with its parachute forming what had looked like a dress. Every building within a half-mile radius, including the police station, was evacuated – a sensible precaution since the mine exploded while it was being moved by the bomb disposal unit, causing widespread damage.

Another case of mistaken identity occurred in the same area of London. A hostile aircraft had been hit by anti-aircraft fire and a report was received at the police station that one of its engines had been seen to fall. A search was made and a large object was found deeply imbedded in the earth. A constable was posted to keep curious onlookers away pending the arrival of an RAF working party. It was a nice sunny day and the kind occupants of a nearby house provided the officer with a deck chair, a newspaper and some refreshments. He was perfectly content until the RAF party arrived and, after extensive digging, told him that they had discovered that the 'engine' was in fact a 1,000 kg bomb. The constable promptly decided to maintain his vigil at a slightly greater (and safer) distance.

Some police officers were less circumspect and displayed a dangerous degree of curiosity. Les Clarke, who patrolled a beat on the Essex border with London, had occasion to report an unexploded bomb which had fallen in his area. He called back at the scene a couple of days later to find the bomb disposal squad still busy at work and, curiosity getting the better of him, asked if he could have a look at the bomb. The obliging soldiers lowered him some 15 feet down the shaft created by the missile, at the bottom of which he saw a soldier busy scraping the mud off what looked like a six-foot water butt. In response to his enquiry, the soldier told him that this was indeed the bomb and added that it was in a highly dangerous condition. Constable Clarke, his curiosity more than satisfied, lost no time in clambering out of the hole, full of admiration for the cool bravery of the members of the bomb disposal squads.

This particular constable seems to have been blessed with more than the normal ration of curiosity as, some time later, he was under instructions to patrol a road through a wood where an unexploded bomb was believed to have fallen, his job being to keep everybody away. Shortly after his arrival he decided it would be helpful if he could locate the bomb so as to be in a position to guide the bomb disposal squad when it arrived. Leaving his bicycle propped against a fence, he entered the wood and quickly came across what was obviously a land mine, lying at an angle with the nose just touching the ground. The parachute attached to the device was caught up in the trees thus preventing the detonator from making contact with the ground.

> *There was a beautiful silk parachute and cords but I hadn't got my knife with me (just as well!) so I couldn't take a sample.*

One couple who lived in the Great West Road in London telephoned the local police station to say,

'A bomb has just come straight through the house. It hasn't exploded – it's disappeared.'

When Sergeant Fred Harding went to investigate the elderly lady occupant told him,

'We were in bed upstairs – we don't use the shelter. We had a bit of a tiff earlier on and weren't speaking so there was a space in the bed between us. Suddenly there was this awful crash and we seemed to be blown out of bed... The room was wrecked and there was a mess everywhere. Whatever it was came straight through the roof, through the ceiling and through the middle of the bed... It's gone right through the floors and into the cellar. It didn't explode.'

It was not until three days later that the bomb disposal squad arrived (a case of too few men and too many incidents) and dug out the 12 inch anti-aircraft shell which had actually passed between the couple lying in their double bed. Thanks to a domestic squabble, their lives were spared.

Sergeant Bill Henley was in the Mark Cross (Sussex) police station when a member of the public rushed in to say, 'Smithy's got a bomb under his house. I've heard it hissing.' Thanking the messenger, Sergeant Henley confided to his family that this was one he would not rush to attend. But attend he did and found that a bomb had gone off outside the front of three cottages, pushing the whole row back three feet. The front windows were still intact but all the windows at the backs of the houses were shattered. The occupant of the first house had been in the act of putting a kettle on the stove when the bomb went off. A mirror over the stove fell and hit him in the back of the neck. Muttering imprecations, he had rushed outside and fallen straight into the crater which had miraculously appeared in front of his door and became the only (minor) casualty of the incident. The hissing noise which had been reported was traced to gas escaping from a fractured main.

Inactive incendiaries were less of a problem (although still dangerous) and it was not unknown for people, including the police, to use the contents of these bombs to boil a kettle for the ubiquitous and indispensable cup of tea. When a large number of incendiary bombs fell on a Kent farm but failed to explode, the whole village turned out to dispose of them. Constable Les Taylor took two large loads away in a wheelbarrow and tipped them down a disused well but this proved such hard work that he changed tactics and merely kicked them into a small crater and kicked earth over them. By the end of the week, every house in the village had a polished incendiary bomb on the mantlepiece as a memento of the night.

The disposal of bombs and other missiles was usually the job of the army but the Royal Navy was called in where land or sea mines were involved and a considerable number of the latter were washed up around the coast and had to be destroyed or made safe. Constable Les Taylor was on duty in October 1939 when some large canisters were washed up on the marshes in the Swale Estuary (Kent). It was decided that these were aerial survey equipment but a closer investigation revealed that they were in fact German naval magnetic mines. The Royal Navy was called and disarmed these devices and, since the naval vehicles could not cross the marshes, the mines were loaded onto a farm trailer and towed away by a local farmer on his tractor. The Navy team and police were trudging alongside when there was a sudden explosion. Everyone threw themselves onto the wet, muddy ground and into a slimy water-filled ditch, convinced that their time had come. In fact, one of the trailer's tyres had burst!

Where a missile was found in a built up area, it was the normal practice to make it safe by removing the detonator and then to transport it to a remote area where it could be exploded in safety. One such bomb was loaded onto an army lorry in Walsall and a patrol car was detailed to escort it to the common, about three miles distant. One of the bomb squad nonchalantly sat astride the bomb throughout the journey, having been told by the officer in charge that it was now safe. On arrival at the common, the army officer confided to the driver of the police car that it had not been defused but he had said that it was so that the chief constable would not raise any query concerning it being transported in a live state across the borough. Had it gone off en route, there would have been no policeman or soldier alive to tell the tale and a large part of the town would have disappeared.

The mania for war souvenirs was another matter which occupied the attention of the police. One land mine which had landed in Waltham Abbey was made safe by the military by removing the fuse and it was then left until they had more time to deal with it properly. By the time they returned a few days later there was nothing left but a mere shell and it seems likely that even the casing would have found its way to a local scrap merchant had the local entrepreneurs had a little more time.

During the intense air raids of 1940/41 the sheer number of unexploded bombs was more than the hard-pressed bomb disposal service could deal with. By December, 1940, the few available Squads had over 3,000 unexploded missiles on their books awaiting investigation and disposal, all of which caused work to be held up, traffic diverted and houses evacuated. It was the police who, with perhaps something approaching the same disregard for their own safety as that demonstrated by the bomb disposal units, had to find the bomb, estimate its size, and report the details to the appropriate authority. It was imperative that genuine reports should be sifted from false or mistaken ones and so some police officers and wardens were specially trained as Bomb Reconnaissance Officers, whose work would be supplementary to the many informal and often dangerous reconnaissances made by beat officers. The need for this training may be gauged from the incident in which a Leicestershire policeman called the Royal Engineers experts to a suspicious hole in the ground which he had carefully cordoned off. The bomb disposal team leader took one look at the suspect hole and pronounced, 'Looks like a dog has been scratching to me.' And packed up his gear and went away.

Once trained, the Bomb Reconnaissance officers were issued with a 30 foot long, jointed rod, rather like that used for clearing blocked drains. The aim was to insert this rod into any suspicious cavity to determine the depth of the hole, thus enabling the Bomb Disposal teams to estimate the degree of risk and the size of the bomb. Some times the object was too deep to be reached with these rods and the entry hole was up to three feet in diameter, indicating a particularly large and especially dangerous arrival. On returning to the police station, an entry would be made by the reconnaissance officer in the Incident Book, reading 'A clean cut shaft', and 'Explosive evidence absent' and a report sent to the appropriate Bomb Disposal Unit. Despite the obvious dangers, many people became somewhat blasé as time went on and it was not unusual for policemen to pop a small missile, such as a cannon shell, an incendiary bomb – even butterfly bombs – in their saddlebag and cycle back to their station where a small sandpit was provided.

Due to the instability of the various unexploded missiles, reconnaissance work was perilous in the extreme. Sergeant Horace Petts of the Canterbury City force was called upon to investigate a suspected unexploded bomb in some allotments which were surrounded by a high fence to prevent theft. The gate to the allotments being locked, Sergeant Petts went off to find a keyholder and, when he eventually returned with the key, the bomb exploded just as he was inserting the key in the padlock. For the rest of his life, Sergeant Petts would be thankful that the gate had been locked, thus delaying him. Otherwise he would have been peering down the hole at the very moment it went off.

Some older and perhaps wiser heads were reluctant to get too involved in this dangerous work. Constable Edgar Storer, a patrol car driver, was on duty in Walsall after a particularly heavy raid when a warden came to the police station to report a suspected unexploded bomb. The duty inspector commandeered the patrol car and, accompanied by the warden and with Edgar Storer driving, went to the area near the canal where the warden believed the bomb to be, about 100 yards from the roadway. They all descended from the car and with the warden leading, went to look for the bomb. Constable Storer was following the warden when he realised the no-longer-young inspector was lagging behind so he dropped back to see if he was alright. 'Look Storer,' said his superior, 'If that **** wants to get blown up, let him. I'm going no further. That's a job for the bomb squad.' Shortly afterwards the warden returned having found no trace of any bomb and the incident was put down to another false alarm.

A similar reaction was displayed by another inspector, this time in Coventry:

> *The first-aid worker ... recalls how, while a small group were tunnelling into the debris of a bombed house, another bomb was heard whistling to earth. 'We all lay down, all but one police inspector who took to his heels down the road. Someone said he was trying to catch it.'* [25]

The bomb reconnaissance work became even more dangerous when the enemy introduced the devilishly ingenious and highly dangerous 'butterfly' anti-personnel bomb in March, 1942. On one occasion, Constable (later Superintendent) Ted Maidment of the East Riding force was sent to a remote farm where the farmer had reported finding a strange object in one of his fields. On examining the object, the officer found that it resembled a miner's lamp, but without the glass. He put the thing in his patrol car and, back at the station, the inspector put it on the mantlepiece, like some bizarre ornament. When the Bomb Disposal Unit arrived, the officer in charge immediately sent everyone outside while he made it safe. The device was an early example of the butterfly bomb.

Dropped in great numbers over Great Grimsby to begin with, and soon in many other places, these sneaky devices could lie undetected on roofs, on waste ground, in growing crops and woodlands and, unless found and destroyed, could present a hidden danger for all sorts of people, not to mention animals. These bombs were often dropped in rural areas, where they were intended to disrupt the production of food by injuring farm workers or making them too nervous to venture out into the fields. In the towns, their use was to inflict as much damage as possible on the civil defence and firefighting teams and to hamper their activities. It fell to the police to warn the public when these devices had been dropped and to organise search parties in conjunction with the wardens, Home Guard and fire service. Once they were discovered sandbags were placed around them – very carefully as they operated through vibration. Quite often the military would destroy them by rifle fire or by running a tank or Bren gun carrier over them since, being essentially an anti-personnel weapon, the explosive charge was small.

As an indication of the extent of the unexploded bomb problem, in Hull there were 73 air raids resulting in over 1,000 killed and 100,000 made homeless. There were 79 suspected unexploded bombs investigated by police Bomb Reconnaissance Officers and a further 267 by untrained policemen.

The police were empowered to take any necessary steps for the protection of life and property in the vicinity of an unexploded bomb, including the highway, and were entitled to enter onto any land, to restrict its use or demolish buildings thereon in the pursuance of this duty. One of their principal tasks was the cordoning off of any area in which an unexploded bomb was believed to lie, even in rural areas.

Constable Les Taylor had such a device land on his country beat in Kent and had to close the road to prevent anyone approaching the danger area. As no equipment was supplied he had to improvise and the discovery of a length of telephone wire behind a hedge was regarded by him as being extremely fortuitous. Stretching the wire across the road he then returned home to make up some handwritten notices, using the customary flour and water paste to stick these to pieces of card (he was paid an allowance of 2/- (10p) a week 'paste allowance' for use in connection with his Diseases of Animals duties). These signs were duly hung on the telephone wire, making a very clear barrier which was perfectly visible in daylight and, since no one was allowed out at night, this was felt to be sufficient. Unfortunately, during the evening it rained, dissolving the paste and the signs disintegrated into a mess of *papier mâché*. Equally unfortunately, during the night the Lord Harris, the local 'squire' drove along the road (he was exempt from the curfew) and, failing to see the near-invisible wire in the dim light cast by his hooded headlights, came close to being decapitated. By chance the rain dripping off the wire reflected the light from the headlamps and he saw the danger just in time. Constable Taylor prefers not to reveal what the noble Lord said to him the next day!

In the early days, before they had received much in the way of instruction, the police had little knowledge on which to proceed and it was no light matter to turn people out of their homes on the evidence of a hole in the ground and very little else. And it was not only homes. When Sergeant Grey got to his station at Millwall one afternoon he found it deserted like the *Mary Celeste*. On making enquiries in the area he was told that there was an unexploded bomb on some wasteland behind the station and everyone had been evacuated. However, the policemen soon began to creep back, despite the danger of the bomb, since the closure of the police station had a curious psychological effect; the policemen felt strangely homeless and unattached.

The policeman's penchant for a glass of ale was often his undoing; occasionally it saved his life. Sergeant Grey had attended the resting place of a large unexploded bomb and left one of his constables to guard the area which had been evacuated. As the sergeant was riding away on his bicycle it happened;

> *A great weight pressed me down, it became dark and a great*
> *cloud of dust and debris rose skywards. I jumped from my bike*
> *and ran to the scene, fearing the worst but there was the*

constable, 'as clean as a new pin'.

The fortunate constable admitted to the sergeant that he had popped into the Snug of a partially destroyed pub in order to 'console the landlord' and they both thus survived.

Throughout the war, on the Home Front as well as in the various theatres of war, there were innumerable instances of bravery, of courage which exceeded that which one might reasonably expect. Gallantry knew no boundaries and, like the other civil defence services, the police were well represented in this respect. Many received awards for their bravery and devotion to duty; others went unheralded, except by their peers and the persons who benefitted from their actions. Looking at the voluminous police reports written at the time, one is struck by the great variety of situations encountered and, at the same time, by their fundamental similarity. The task was essentially always the same – lives were in danger and had to be saved, but the methods employed, the dangers and obstacles encountered were seldom identical. Whatever the danger, whatever the complexity of the task, it is clear from eye-witness reports that the police seldom accepted that nothing could be done as long as there was a possibility that people's lives were still in jeopardy.

The most common scenario was probably that which involved a collapsed building in which the occupants were imprisoned by fallen masonry and furniture. A house which has just been partially destroyed is not as a rule a healthy place in which to wander, still less to start burrowing in. Any vibration or disturbance may bring down more of the unstable walls and precarious roofs and floors. If the raid was still in progress – as it so often was – there was plenty of vibration if nothing worse. But some form of tunnelling was frequently the only hope for those poor souls unable to extricate themselves. The situation was often aggravated by the presence of gas leaks and actual or potential fires, by the presence of foul-smelling and unhealthy sewage and of water gushing from fractured mains.

People became trapped not only in ground floor rooms or basements but also in multi-storey buildings such as one particular West End hotel which received a direct hit. An anonymous police officer, hearing cries from a room high up in the building, made his way up the rickety staircase until he found his way forward barred by a gap 12 feet across, 45 feet above the ground. Returning to the ground once more he found a scaffold board and, climbing the staircase once more, managed to place this across the gap, resting on two highly unsafe walls. Making his way Houdini-like across this narrow board he found four people. With more than a little difficulty he managed to convince them that their only salvation lay across this make-shift bridge and, one by one, led them to safety.

In fact, more than one tale is told of athletic policemen performing seemingly impossible feats to rescue those trapped in high places,

> *Closer examination disclosed a man leaning out of the window of a wrecked room thirty feet above the street. The remains of the house itself looked ready to collapse for it was worse damaged than at first appeared. Meanwhile, a rescue party had come up with a ladder which they placed against the swaying wall but it was too short by at least a dozen feet to reach the upper window. It seemed both foolhardy and useless to try to reach the man at the window by the short ladder but evidently the young policeman did not think so for, putting it as close to the wall as possible ... PC Mann began very carefully to climb, one rung at a time, holding himself as flat against the ladder as he could. ... he reached the top rung and, flattening himself against the wall, crooked one leg round the broken frame of a window... Balanced precariously on the top rung of the nearly vertical ladder and flattened against the front of the house he ... called to the frightened man to get out of the window backwards and let one foot down until it rested on the policeman's upstretched hand. ... PC Man talked to him calmly and soon persuaded him to get over the window sill and lower himself as far as possible ... [and] ... took the whole weight of the other man on one hand. ... the policeman managed to place the other fellow's feet on his shoulders and carefully work his way down the ladder, a feat of balancing that would have been remarkable without the added difficulty of performing it during a heavy air raid when bombs were shaking the very earth and threatening to bring the damaged building down on top of them.*[26]

The courageous PC Mann did not remain with the Metropolitan Police much longer as he was one of those young officers released to join the RAF for aircrew duties. Sadly, while undergoing training in Canada, he was killed in a road accident thus bringing yet another brave but short life to a premature end.

The highest award for exceptional courage whilst serving in the United Kingdom, is the George Cross, instituted by King George VI in September 1940 and available to civilians and servicemen alike. Most of these decorations were awarded to servicemen, in particular the heroic bomb disposal crews, but it was also awarded to members of the Home Guard, such as Section Commander George Inwood of Birmingham (whose award was posthumous), to members of the fire service, like Station Officer Mosdale of the Birmingham City Fire Brigade, and to Special Constable Brandon Moss of Coventry – the only such award to a member of the police service,

In November, 1940, Brandon Moss was 30 years old, a fitter in the Armstrong-Siddeley factory and had been a member of the Special Constabulary since the outbreak of war. On the night of the devastating raid on Coventry he was on duty and patrolling the streets when the raid started. A bomb fell close to where he was lying face down in the road, destroying several buildings. Another house was badly damaged and, knowing that there were three people inside, he decided to make this his priority. He had no tools or other equipment, bombs and incendiaries were raining down on the city but, with his bare hands, Special Constable Moss began to tunnel into the ruins of the house where he eventually found the occupants, suffering no more than cuts and abrasions. He then turned his attention to the alleyway between the ruins of two houses where three other men had been sheltering. Although the chance of saving them was remote, he determined to have a try and, after several hours heavy digging, came across their bodies. He then turned his attention to another house where he found two more people entombed, one of whom was still alive. Working alone and without respite the whole night, he saved four lives while bombs were falling close by. He never once thought of his own safety and his only concern was to do everything in his power to save others.

The three George Crosses referred to above, like most decorations for bravery given to members of the civil defence services, were awarded in respect of rescuing people from bombed buildings and it was usually this type of scenario which resulted in the next highest gallantry award – the George Medal – being pinned on the tunics of numerous other courageous workers. Here, the police were well represented with 82 George Medals being awarded to Metropolitan Police officers alone (among whom was Constable George Mann of Camberwell whose athletic feats were described earlier) and many other officers received a formal Commendation from HM The King. Even a small force like the Bootle Borough Police, with a total strength of 99 officers, could boast four George Medals, five British Empire Medals as well as numerous Commendations.

It would be impossible to describe all the various rescues which were officially recognised, and it would indeed be invidious to do so since many brave acts have gone unrecorded and unremarked. But the tale of Constable Sam Radford, GM is related as just one illustration of the sort of task involved and the dangers faced. Sam, a dour Yorkshireman, was 28 and had been serving in the Sheffield police for some years at the time of the heavy raid on that city in November 1940. The night immediately following the raid he learned that a young man, Jimmy Greenwood, was believed trapped in the cellar of his home in Fell Street. The house was a ruin – a mere pile of rubble but, discarding his tunic and helmet, Sam set about creating an excavation through the rubble. After digging down some feet, Sam found his way blocked by criss-crossed beams and boards. Any further progress would be extremely dangerous, aggravated by the strong smell of gas from ruptured gas mains and the smell of burning. But using his back to shore up behind him and rearranging the beams to provide enough room to force his body through towards the cellar, Sam slowly continued his painful progress, sometimes feet first, sometimes headfirst. At one stage he came across a door and spent some time clearing the aperture, only to find himself in a wardrobe. At one point his burrow collapsed behind him, sealing off his return route but fortunately opening up another escape route for him. After two hours there was still no sign of the ARP services for this was just one of a number of 'incidents' in the city that day. About this time Sam decided to take a short breather and squatted uncomfortably in a soot-encrusted cavern to assess the situation. Perturbed by the silence, the helpers outside called out,

'Ah tha alreet Sam?', which elicited the answer,

'Shurrup, I'm nearly there. Get everyone to stand still and not make any noise.'

Sam then began calling to the unseen victim, not knowing whether he was dead or alive but hoping for some response. In due course his efforts were rewarded and a weak voice replied from the depths of the cellar. Encouraged by this Sam dug with renewed vigour and, after a total of four hours, espied his quarry through a latticework of beams. Eighteen-year-old Jimmy Greenwood, black as the ace of spades but basically uninjured, remarked, '*Oh, it's thee is it Sam?*'.

But seeing the trapped lad was one thing; getting him out was another matter entirely.

> *In the process of edging himself into Greenwood's cavity, Sam found himself lodged beneath this beam and attached timbers. By spiralling his body around and arching his back he found he could create further space. Several thrusts and he managed each time to make the tunnel a little larger until there was sufficient room for young Greenwood to wriggle through the tunnel created by Sam's body. Under Sam's instructions and often being pushed from behind, Jimmy made his way to the surface with their escape route collapsing behind them as they progressed until, with the help of the waiting group of helpers, they were pulled from the wreckage. ... Sam had at some stage in the ascent lost his lamp but not his wit for his first comments were to the effect that he could '... murder a bloody pint!'. By some sort of miracle, a half-full bottle of ale found its way through the crowd to Sam who committed the 'murder' on the spot.*[27]

Some, like Constable John Uren (Liverpool), suffered for their bravery. To enable a trapped firewatcher to be released he supported a heavy beam on his broad shoulders (in a scene reminiscent of the song *Big John*). When the other rescuers had dragged the injured man from his living tomb Constable Uren was unable to move and the others had to pull him away and jump clear as the beam and all the rubble it was supporting came raining down. His bravery was rewarded with the George Medal and an injury to his spine which troubled him for the rest of his life and was a contributory factor to his early demise in 1966 when he was just 60.

Although most medals and commendations were awarded for acts of bravery in which officers had risked their lives, much useful work was accomplished in the way of organisation and control. When the world is being turned upside down, when people are frightened and in distress, what they need most is someone to turn to, someone to tell them, quietly and authoratively, just what they should do and where they should go. What they need are leaders and it is here that many policemen excel and have a natural gift, honed by experience. Policemen thus found themselves frequently organising rescue parties or fire fighters, directing essential traffic and telling people where to go for shelter and aid. There are instances of policemen who gained something of a local reputation by turning up at every incident, whether on or off duty, giving whatever help they could.

Despite the fact that they are trained and accustomed to working as independent individuals, there are sufficient cases recorded to illustrate that policemen could, when the need arose, work equally efficiently as part of a highly-competent team. One example occurred in February, 1941 when an exceptionally large bomb fell in a North London suburb. A police party arrived and found forty houses had been completely destroyed and more than 300 others severely damaged. People were milling around, injured, hysterical and near to panic while calls for help could be heard coming from almost every house. There had been no warning and, perhaps because of this, no ARP services had arrived. A formidable task, involving exertion and risk-taking as well as qualities of leadership, organisation and control faced the police team. The inspector promptly took charge, calling for assistance from the fire service, rescue parties, ambulances, etc. and directed the work of the police and their voluntary helpers before joining in with the actual rescue operations himself. The work went on for hours before all those trapped could be extricated. The death toll was over 80 with several hundred injured, including at least two of the police rescuers.

When talking of deeds of gallantry there is a danger of thinking that these were men cast in some heroic mould, who were afraid of nothing. In fact, time and again one comes across comments like,

> *...there were moments when I felt desperately scared. I felt sometimes that it was only my uniform which stopped me from hiding in some sheltered spot and burying my head in the sand. It was not the thought of being killed, a risk that was always with us; it was thoughts of being maimed or helplessly injured.*[28]

Not all gallantry awards were in respect of rescues from bombed buildings. In 1940, Constable Cyril Brown of the Dover Borough Police was attached to the Fire Brigade and was awarded the George Medal for his efforts in fighting a fire aboard a ship loaded with high explosives in the harbour, while an air raid was in progress. In nearby Folkestone, Constable Cyril Williams heard an explosion and, on arrival at the scene near the sea front, found that a workman had ventured into the grounds of a building which had been mined as an anti-invasion measure. He could see the injured man lying on the ground some distance away and, despite the danger from the remaining mines, went to the injured man and brought him to safety. He too, received the George Medal.

Some officers were involved in more than one rescue. Typical of these was Constable William Thomas Spain of Folkestone Borough Police who received the George Medal for tunnelling to an injured and pinned-down woman in August, 1940 and remaining with her and comforting her until the rescue squad arrived. At one point he started to treat the woman's injured hand until she said, 'Oh, don't worry about that. It's plum jam. I must have stuck my hand in the bowl when the bomb fell.' It must be appreciated that this was no young 'macho' officer but a fifty-one year old with 27 years in the police and who had served in the army in the Great War.

Shortly after this incident, Constable Spain had just left a police box and had not gone more than a few yards when he saw a German aircraft in the moonlight.

> It was only 400 to 500 feet up and I saw it bank,' said the officer. 'Almost immediately there was a terrific flash and an explosion. Something seemed to give me a fearful blow in the chest and I was knocked out for a few moments. When I came round I found myself standing at the entrance to a public house. I heard voices inside and on entering found three people trapped at the foot of the stairs. I rescued a little girl and brought her out. I carried her away from the scene of devastation and was on my way to the Police Station when I collapsed. Fortunately I met two other officers and they assisted me' The police box was razed to the ground.[29]

This incident damaged Bill Spain's eyes to the extent that he later lost the sight in one and had impaired vision in the other for the rest of his life. A few months later the Mayor of Folkestone, Alderman George Gurr, and his wife the Mayoress, were killed when a bomb fell on the adjoining house. PC Spain also attended this incident and was instrumental in rescuing the Mayor's son-in-law who had been in the same house. He also rescued an elderly crippled woman after she was heard calling for help from the ruins of her home.

Constable Spain's exploits are described above in some detail, not because this was a unique tale of heroism and devotion to duty, but because his actions were repeated in countless places by countless police officers, the activities of some being recognised in tangible form, those of many others merely being regarded by the officers themselves as 'all in the line of duty.' Certainly there is little doubt that the relations between the police and the public in at least the first few years of the war were as cordial as they have ever been, before or since. For once the police were not regarded as 'the enemy' but were seen as truly the natural protectors of life and property.

9. A Rapacious and Licentious Soldiery

Whilst the Blitz introduced a completely new phenomenon to policing, one of the other consequences of the war did not so much present new problems as greatly exaggerate what might be regarded as 'normal' policing matters. This was the general mobilization of most able-bodied men and women into the Armed Forces and the unparalleled arrival of enormous numbers of foreign troops in this country. These did not generally bring new problems but the sheer weight of their numbers and their 'live today for tomorrow we die' philosophy greatly intensified the work of the police.

The police were called upon to assist the military authorities in many ways. We have already seen how they were closely involved in such matters as billeting, the impressment of horses and vehicles, the control of traffic and so on, and they usually formed the main link between the military and civilian authorities. At the beginning of the war they held copies of the pamphlet the War Office had issued on the Territorial Army, they displayed the official posters concerning the obligation to report for military service, they issued railway warrants to the relatives of soldiers dangerously ill in France and verified the circumstances of requests made by soldiers for compassionate leave. When the Local Defence Volunteers were formed, they were charged with organising their recruitment (without notice and without any preparation).

In the first six months of the war most of those who had been called up for military service were dispatched to France as soon as they had completed their initial or, in the case of reservists, refresher training. Consequently, they were not on British soil long enough for them to give the police any great difficulties. However, following the withdrawal of the British Expeditionary Force from Dunkirk, the greater part of the British forces were concentrated once more on these islands. When the remnants of the BEF returned from France in the summer of 1940, the authorities had to find accommodation for unexpectedly large numbers of military personnel. Once again the police service was called upon to assist and George Whitcomb was one of the many police officers who had to find shelter for the weary troops who were arriving in various parts of the United Kingdom – in Bradford in his case. The proprietors of the various boarding houses and small hotels in that Yorkshire town were very sympathetic but found all sorts of very cogent reasons why they could not possibly put up the troops who were due to arrive the next day. By lunchtime Constable Whitcomb had not been offered a single bed and he decided to change tactics. During the afternoon he went back to each of these establishments and told the owner that six soldiers would to be compulsorily billeted on her the next day. Throwing up their hands in horror, they reluctantly agreed that they could take one or two but no more. So well did this ploy work that the list was rapidly completed and the next day, a large number of battle-weary soldiers were able to sleep in a proper bed for the first time for weeks.

Some of the troops performing duty in the United Kingdom in those early days were very raw and virtually untrained. Many were city lads and unused to the ways of the countryside in which increasing numbers found themselves. Les 'Buck' Taylor, an archetypal 'country copper', was astonished one day when visiting a searchlight unit to find the sentry wearing his gas mask when no warning of gas had been given. On being questioned, the sentry claimed to have smelt a strange odour which he had assumed was gas; in fact, the perfume came from a nearby field of coriander. 'Buck' Taylor later stopped visiting this particular camp because the town-bred sentries were so nervous; being out of their native element they were inclined to take fright at the sound of a grunting hedgehog or a coughing ewe and were likely to shoot first and ask questions later.

The fact of being in uniform sometimes gave some of the less-disciplined troops a feeling of being untouchable. Constable Taylor has less than happy memories of units of the Guards Armoured Division being stationed on his Kentish rural beat. The Coldstreamers and Grenadiers were inclined to fight each other on the slightest pro-vocation and were also responsible for a great deal of unnecessary, if not criminal, damage. It was not unusual for them to use a Churchill tank to go to buy their cigarettes from the village shop, tearing up the road surface and knocking down trees and items of street furniture on the way. The use of tanks and other heavy equipment on unsuitable roads and terrain occasionally had tragic results as Constable Les Clarke from the Essex force witnessed. A number of tanks had drawn up onto the village green and the crews bedded down beside them for the night. Unbeknown to them, the weight of these great machines had cracked a gas main laid under the grass and a couple of the soldiers sadly lost their lives from the toxic fumes.

Although the encounters the police had with individual soldiers, sailors and airmen were often of a confrontational kind, there were numerous occasions when policemen were able to assist them. One typical example occurred during the time reinforcements were being rushed to the British Expeditionary Force in France prior to Dunkirk. A convoy of army lorries bound for a Hertfordshire holding unit made an over-night stop in London. One driver asked his officer for permission to visit his family in Bethnal Green which was granted on condition that the vehicle was immobilised and that the soldier was back, ready to move off, first thing in the morning. All went well until, on his return journey, an air raid alert sounded and, in the confusion, the soldier got on the wrong train and ended up in Leytonstone. He tried to get a taxi to take him to where the convoy was waiting but none were willing to turn out and so he called at the police station to see what they could suggest. The duty inspector was sympathetic but was unable to offer any help. Constable Bill Cavey, a patrol car driver who was never loth to bend a few rules, offered to give the distraught soldier a lift but the inspector understandably said he could not authorise such an unofficial trip. However, he did make it clear that, if he were not asked, he would not be in a position to forbid the course of action proposed. On the basis of a nod being as good as a wink to a blind horse, Bill Cavey left the station and the soldier soon found himself ensconced in the rear seat of the patrol car being rapidly conveyed the few miles to his destination. With dawn just breaking, having driven with scant regard for speed limits, they arrived at the place where the convoy was waiting, the drivers of which had just received the order 'Start engines'. Pausing only to slip a pound note in the policeman's hand (a lot of money in those days) the soldier leapt into the cab of his lorry and joined the convoy on its journey westwards. Over the years Bill Cavey has often wondered what eventually became of that grateful young soldier and whether he survived the war.

Later, when the great armada was being formed for the invasion of Europe, not a few military personnel slipped away to pay a visit to their families to see how they were coping and to get a few home comforts before they were shipped across the Channel. The police were usually asked to go to the homes of these 'absent without leave' troops to see if they were there and to return them to their units. On countless occasions there would be a knock at the door of a small terraced house or cottage and a policeman would walk in to find the subject of his visit tucking in to his last home-cooked meal (possibly made with army rations!) and with his washing drying in front of the fire. There was seldom any trouble, the miscreant having been expecting the visit from the police. Together, they would take the short walk to the police station from where the serviceman would be collected by the Military Police or even permitted to make his own way back to camp.

Some were not quite so innocent. Constable George Whitcomb visited a Bradford 'doss house' on his beat one night and discovered a young airman completely hidden under a rather large blonde in a make-shift bed on the floor. When told to get dressed the blushing young man sheepishly donned the uniform of a Group Captain complete with two rows of medal ribbons – and he had only been in the service a couple of months! He had a great deal of explaining to do when the military police took him back to his station.

Police canteens in London and elsewhere, often staffed by volunteers, were thrown open to servicemen in need of a meal and many a stranded squaddie was bedded down in a cell for the night.

If the aid given by the police to the military authorities tended to be one way, this was perhaps due more to the reluctance of the civic authorities to admit defeat and 'call in the military' than to any reluctance on the part of the military.

> *What puzzles one here is the narrow spectrum of authority delegated to the Army. But this is in line with the patently ad hoc way the forces were brought in to help, differing strikingly from town to town. No special role was allocated in advance, sometimes no role at all afterwards, despite dire needs. Sometimes one branch took over more or less on their own, as with the RAF in the case of emergency evacuation in Southampton, or some of the transport problems in Plymouth and elsewhere. There was no clear-cut plan; and there was plenty of jealousy*[1].

On the other hand, when Coventry was Blitzed in November, 1940, the chief constable, as ARP Controller, decided at 3 am to appeal to the authorities for troops for 'control and repair of damage'. Six hundred troops were ordered to attend and, less than eight hours later, the first three hundred were there assisting the police in maintaining law and order, mainly by setting up a series of cordons around the city to divert all through traffic and to prevent the entry of unauthorised traffic. Meanwhile, a detachment of Royal Engineers was busy helping the fire service fight fires and demolishing dangerous buildings. Eventually a total of 1,800 troops were present in the city, aiding the civil power.

On a more mundane note, as the village constable responsible for the Boxgrove area which included Tangmere fighter station at the end of the war, Dennis Vorley was on good terms with the RAF personnel as well as with the local farmers. On his first Christmas in the area, he was delighted to receive as gifts from the latter half a sack of potatoes, a brace of rabbits, a pheasant, some pigs' fry as well as a goose from the Duke of Richmond and Gordon, the local 'squire'. The only problem was that his small electric cooker was totally inadequate for the goose and so he approached his RAF friends who were only too pleased to help. On Christmas Day he received a message to call over to collect the bird and to bring with him some jars for the goose grease. At a time when there was still very strict rationing, this little windfall was, as may easily be imagined, very welcome.

Military secrecy was occasionally a problem for the police. The local police were unaware that the RAF had set up a light beacon on the North Downs in Kent which gave out a Morse signal to aircraft until a sentry on the Isle of Sheppey, some 20 miles distant, saw it and reported it to his commander. The officer contacted the Admiralty who professed no knowledge. The nearest RAF airfield at Detling was also contacted and they too, claimed not to know of the beacon. The police were asked to investigate and the local 'Bobby' cycled out to where the light was believed to be coming from and found the area closely guarded by RAF personnel. They refused to let the policeman in or to give any information about the establishment so he used his initiative and waited until an RAF truck arrived with the rations. He stopped the vehicle and questioned the driver who freely admitted that he came from the RAF station at Manston and the police were thus able to direct the military enquiries to the correct source.

As the war progressed the number of British troops was augmented by arrivals from the Dominions and Colonies overseas. Indians, Australians, New Zealanders, South Africans and (especially)

Canadians poured into Britain to reinforce the woefully inadequate British Army, Navy and Air Force. These arrivals from the declining British Empire joined the small but significant remnants of the armies of continental Europe: the Poles, Czechs, Dutch and Free French. The inhabitants of the United Kingdom, accustomed by now to seeing the khaki and blue uniforms of the British troops, began to notice a multitude of small shoulder flashes proudly indicating the country of origin of the wearer and the sight of antipodean slouch hats and Sikh turbans ceased to be remarked upon.

The British found the customs of some of these Allied troops a trifle bizarre and the police occasionally found them to be a cause for concern. The inhabitants of the small Kentish village of Eastling were intrigued by the members of the 6th New Zealand Field Army, a unit made up almost entirely of Maoris. The local constable had to find billets for two whole companies but the locals were none too keen. However, he persevered and these strange men, from so far away, found themselves living with country families, many of whom had never even been to London and to whom New Zealand was as remote as the moon. They seemed to be heavy drinkers to a man and had the habit of slipping out at night to do a spot of poaching with their .303 rifles which did not endear them to the gamekeepers and land-owners but, when the time came for them to leave the area, many of the villagers were in tears. Apart from their drinking and poaching habits, the local constable, Leslie 'Buck' Taylor had to contend with their vexatious practice of 'borrowing' the locals' bicycles in order to get back to their camp and then dumping them in a ditch outside the camp gates. It was never possible to catch the culprits and so Constable Taylor had to employ a little diplomacy and ask them if they would kindly take better care of these machines. Ever obliging, the Kiwis took to leaving them neatly where they could easily be found which was regarded as a reasonable compromise.

Their practice of stealing boxes of fruit left by the farmers outside their orchard gates for collection was not appreciated and, by way of recompense, the constable made arrangements for these soldiers to lift one farmer's entire potato crop and honour was felt to be satisfied.

One of the largest contingents of troops from the Dominions was the half million or so from Canada. These varied from streetwise men from the cities of Toronto, Ottawa, Quebec and Vancouver, to prairie dwellers and, the butt of all the Canadians' jokes, the 'Newfies' from

Newfoundland. Many of those who joined the Canadian forces in 1939 were the long-term unemployed, for whom the prospect of a regular if modest wage, army rations, a good pair of boots and a warm khaki suit was quite appealing.

The 1st Canadian Division arrived in England towards the end of 1939 and was accommodated in the British Army's Victorian barracks in Aldershot. The members of this Division were almost wholly untrained on their arrival in England and the men were largely unaccustomed to discipline. The accommodation was regarded as spartan by Canadian standards and the British civilians, accustomed for centuries to what Edmund Burke described two centuries before as 'the rapacious and licentious soldiery', did not welcome these rough troops with open arms. The 2nd Division, which arrived later, was quite a different kettle of fish but had to live down the reputation which its fellow-countrymen had gained.

To be fair to the bewildered men of the 1st Division, English society was, to use a more modern term, much more permissive than that to which they were accustomed. In particular, it was more permissive as regards intoxicating liquor and the concept of the British pub was totally alien to these men who were more used to the seedy and dismal 'beverage rooms' of Ontario.

> *To the unsophisticated young Canadian soldier, a place where men, and even women, could meet ... to drink freely what they chose and enjoy themselves, a place known as the 'poor man's club' was a novel experience. Much could be written about the impact of the British pub on the Canadian serviceman, and vice versa. ... People in Hampshire and Surrey towns in 1940 complained that, in the evenings, the streets were full of drunken and profane Canadians, noisily making their way back to the barracks which they found so disagreeable[2].*

The move of the Canadians to Northampton in the spring of 1940 was a turning point in their relationships with their British hosts. The people of Northamptonshire were less accustomed to the presence of soldiers than those of Aldershot and the disastrous news of Dunkirk had a bearing on the attitude displayed to troops in general. Nevertheless, an overnight miracle had not been worked; a month later, the Canadian Force's stay in the Oxford area was not so agreeable as that in Northamptonshire. The proof of this is contained in a letter written by Peter Howard (a leading light in the Moral Rearmament movement), a copy of which was sent to Mike Pearson, the official secretary at Canada House:

> *The best story from Oxford is the conduct of the Canadians who are there in force. They are becoming really disliked by the population as well as by the British soldiers and military police. ... they are a little extreme in their pleasures. There were hundreds of them around the streets last evening, and without exaggeration half of them were drunk. They were ... breaking a certain amount of glass etc and grabbing hold of the women. They were driving their military vans fast and recklessly and I was told they have had several accidents[3].*

This account is supported by the fact that on 29 June two officers from the Canadian Provost Company were interviewed by the Chief Constable of the Oxford City Police who asked that the company arrange for patrols to be on duty in the evenings (had the Provost been more experienced this might have been done earlier). As a result, 12 military policemen under the command of a sergeant were sent out that night and arrested five men who were placed in the city police cells to await escorts back to their units.

One may well wonder why there was such a difference in attitude between the Canadian troops in Oxford and those in Northampton. The answer would seem to lie in the fact that, in Northamptonshire they were billeted with families in the towns and villages and made immediate contact with the locals. In Oxford they were camped under canvas in the surrounding countryside and Oxford was just the nearest town, the place where they sought amusement – and booze. They had no chance to meet the people as friends. Whilst this cannot excuse the behaviour of a significant element within the Canadian forces, it does help to explain it. In fact, it was the considered opinion of General McNaughton, the officer commanding the Canadian Forces in the UK, that the behaviour of his men was no better and no worse than that of the British. He maintained that, whilst it was true that certain public houses had been placed out of bounds at the request of the licensee, this was so that the regulars would not be crowded out, rather than because of any misbehaviour. Although this was the substance of his report to his government in Ottawa it did not prevent him from sending a strong letter to all the Canadian units a fortnight later, drawing attention to the complaints of drunkenness, disorderly behaviour, damage to property, scruffiness, misuse of official transport, dangerous driving and loss of equipment.

The difficulties the Canadians (and later the GIs) had with their civilian hosts paled into significance beside the trouble which arose between them and the British servicemen. Lest this be thought to be a criticism of the former, it is worth recalling Kipling's words regarding the fights which the British regular army had with any other unit:

> *There was a row in Silver Street that's near to Dublin Quay*
> *Between an Irish regiment an' English cavalree ...*

This particular dispute ended in tragedy when someone drew his sword:

> *T'was Hogan took the point an' dropped; we saw the red blood run.*
> *An' so we all was murderers that started out in fun.*

Rivalry in the armed forces is rampant and officially encouraged. Each regiment, every ship of the line, believes that it is infinitely superior to any other and will fight anyone who disputes this. It is not surprising that these somewhat xenophobic and insular men, trained to use the most extreme forms of violence against their country's enemies, should occasionally use violence against those who ought to have been their friends and comrades in arms. And when the other party is better paid (the Canadians got approximately 26p a day against the British private's 10p) and appears to be having better luck with the girls, jealousy will play a significant part.

There is no doubt that the biggest problem which the Canadians caused the British police was through drink. Cases of drunkenness were widespread, largely through the soldiers' lack of experience with intoxicating liquor and the concept of the British pub. They had a reputation for getting 'fighting drunk' and the police tended to leave them to their own devices or let their own Provost company take care of them unless they really got out of hand. For the late Inspector Bill Henley of the East Sussex Constabulary, the Cape Breton Highlanders stationed outside Crowborough were a constant thorn in the flesh. On one occasion his son remembers him standing outside a pub as one of the Highlanders staggered out and fell in a heap in the road.

'He's drunk, Dad.' said the young man. 'You'll have to arrest him.'

The inspector paused for a while, during which time the Canadian staggered to his feet, swayed across the road and into a wall on the other side, collapsing once again at the foot of the wall.

'No he's not, son,' said the inspector. 'He can walk.'

Upon which he continued his perambulations without any loss of dignity and without the bother of yet another drunken soldier vomiting in the cells. He knew the man would be taken care of, since the Canadians were in the habit of putting their paralytically drunk comrades in the telephone kiosk outside the pub, where they would eventually be picked up by the truck which made the rounds of the pubs for this purpose.

On another occasion a serious brawl broke out in a public house involving Canadian troops which Police War Reserve Constable Izzard attended. He was a very big man and one soldier, keen to show that he was not afraid of this large representative of the law, called out, 'If you come any closer copper, I'll smash this glass in your face.'

Constable Izzard took stock of the situation and, eyeing the half-full glass in the man's hand, said, 'Well, I should drink up first, son. Beer's in short supply; it'd be a pity to waste it.'

This pragmatic and calm approach instantly defused the situation and the soldier sheepishly put down his glass, to the good-natured laughter of the audience, all thoughts of fighting now forgotten.

That the Canadians bore the locals no malice and the police no grudge may be seen by the fact that, each Christmas, they gave hampers to the police to be distributed to the 12 poorest families in the Crowborough district. It was left to the police to decide who these were, an unenviable task at a time when any extra rations were eagerly sought-after.

It is fair to say, in fact, that with one or two notable exceptions such as the riot in Aldershot in July 1945, relations between the British populace and the Canadians improved to the extent that congratulatory letters were sent to the General Officer commanding these troops and even the ill-used British police and magistrates had some kind words to say about them.

'As this is probably the last Annual Licensing Meeting before the departure of our Canadian friends, I think a word of commendation is due to them and the troops generally. ... the Justices feel that the average standard of behaviour ... has been very good, especially in the streets at night... I should like the Superintendent to bring this expression to the notice of the officer commanding Witley Camp. Some share of the credit is due to the Licensees and to the police and we hope Godalming will preserve its good name in the matter.' Superintendent R Webb endorsed entirely the remarks with regard to the behaviour of the troops, to which the Chairman replied, 'Great credit is due to you personally.'[4]

Superintendent Webb himself wrote to Brigadier T J Rutherford, commanding E group of the Canadian Reinforcement Units, expressing appreciation of the 'excellent conduct' of the Canadians during the local VE Day celebrations. Not one complaint had been received. These congratulatory remarks tend to show that the locals had not forgotten that Witley camp had been the scene of an extremely nasty riot in 1919 and a Canadian soldier had killed a local man in a brawl in 1940.

It must not be thought from these accounts that relations with the Canadians were unrelievedly sour. Following the raids on Coventry, large numbers of young children and babies, mainly from residential homes, were evacuated from the city. One destination was Birmingham where a woman, visiting the Canadian Military Hospital at Marston Green, was amused to find :

... approximately sixty proud faces turned in my direction as I entered this long ward. I see them now, with their peaceful, mellow, smiling quietness, each of the Canadian wounded lying against his pillows with two babes, one in each arm, sleeping peacefully[5].

If there were difficulties with the Canadians, these paled into insignificance once the United States came into the war in December, 1941, and US troops began arriving in Britain. Whilst certain sections of the population welcomed these new arrivals with open arms (mainly young girls and ladies of easy virtue), the general antipathy towards the

Americans was succinctly expressed in the phrase 'Overpaid, over-sexed and over here'.

All this was still in the future, however, when Pfc Milburn H Henke stepped ashore in Northern Ireland in January, 1942, officially the first of many United States troops to do so. 'Officially' because, in point of fact, he was more like the 501st, since a whole contingent of GIs had already disembarked before PFC Henke was greeted by the various dignitaries formed up on the quay to welcome him and his comrades. A case of what the Americans would have describe as SNAFU – Situation Normal: All F***** Up!

As the Americans began to arrive in their thousands, and spread throughout the United Kingdom, a new phenomenon made its presence felt; the 'colour problem.' This phrase was unknown in this country prior to the arrival of the GIs but, in a matter of months, the Home Office was advising Chief Constables

> *It appears that ... difficulties may be caused by the presence among the population of coloured troops.*

Segregation was strictly enforced in the United States and this extended no less to the US Armed Forces. White GIs refused to drink in the same establishment as their black comrades, shunned any woman who danced with them. The problems this could cause the British police was promptly recognised and the Home Office letter went on to say :

> *It is not the policy of His Majesty's Government that any discrimination as regards the treatment of coloured troops should be made by the British authorities. The Secretary of State, therefore, would be glad if you would be good enough to take steps to ensure that the police do not make any approach to the proprietors of public houses, restaurants, cinemas or other places of entertainment with a view to discriminating against coloured troops. If the American Service authorities decide to put certain places out of bounds for their coloured troops, such prohibition can be effected only by means of an Order issued by the appropriate American army and naval authorities. The police should not make themselves in any way responsible for the enforcement of such orders.*

In fact the coloured troops themselves caused very few problems and the Home Office received reports from Chief Constables to the effect that on the whole the coloured troops in this country had behaved well. What did cause problems was the fact that most Britons accepted both black and white at face value, with no obvious discrimination, something the white troops found incredible and totally unacceptable. As Brendan Bracken, the Minister of Information, wryly commented, 'The Americans have exported to us a local problem which is not of our own making.'

Apart from the colour problem, the main effect of the American 'invasion' so far as the police were concerned was the sheer number and concentration of these troops. Areas such as East Anglia and the East Midlands were particularly affected, with airfields springing up everywhere almost overnight. A typical example was Polebrook near Oundle in Northamptonshire where one of the eight airfields occupied by the 1st Bombardment Wing was established. Prior to 1942 Oundle had a population of just 1,400, swollen during term time by half as much again due to the presence of 600 pupils from the public school in the village. Up until then the war had seemed fairly remote to the residents of this peaceful inland village but suddenly it was surrounded by a ring of USAAC bases from which B17 Flying Fortresses set out daily on their daylight missions. In particular, Polebrook, just two miles away, was to have a profound effect on the life of Oundle. The first occupants of this base arrived in July 1942 and the station was occupied continuously by hundreds of US airmen until 1945.

Norman Longmate describes how these new inhabitants of rural Britain formed a high opinion of the village policeman, one of whom

> ... toured the 'badlands' of the American airbases in Suffolk on his trusty bicycle. 'This quiet, soft-spoken, pink-cheeked man more than anyone else represented England to us. If you wanted to buy a bicycle, just ask Mr Moody.' PC Moody, for his part, accepted with the traditional constable's calm the sudden addition to his responsibilities of a 'roaring pioneer community of 700 young, hard-working and hard-playing soldiers.' When the construction gangs' work was done he referred with proprietorial pride to 'our little old aerodrome.'[6]

Constable Moody's feelings towards his new 'parishioners' is not recorded, but it is clear that many policemen regarded them as indisciplined, noisy and lacking in morals. Constable Bert Ayers remembers them as being very well-equipped and proud of this but, as he was wont to remind them, they had had an extra two years to prepare for the conflict. He describes them as 'very laid-back' and recalls an occasion when he was required to escort one of their convoys at a strict speed and spacing but was quite unable to get the drivers to move as they were busy playing craps. As a result, the convoy started late and had to proceed at an unprecedented speed with little regard for spacing once it did get going, in order to make up time. Their lack of British reserve sometimes shocked the locals and a member of the Royal Ulster Constabulary remembers disapprovingly that 'Americans who crashed were easily picked out, kissing the ground, running around drawing attention to themselves.' The other side of the coin is shown in the recollection of a US combat engineer who tells of encountering a crowd and saw that 'a London bobby was beating the hell out of a man down on the sidewalk with his nightstick.' Even in the violent Nineties, it is hard to visualise this scene unless it involved a violent and/or armed criminal or someone involved in a tumultuous demonstration. Whilst it would be naive to deny that British policemen ever use excessive force, it would be extremely unusual for one to do so in front of a crowd, even in wartime, unless he was very sure that he would subsequently be able to justify his actions. Fortunately the image most American troops took back with them to the States coincided more with that of a coloured GI from Wyoming who remembers '... the green countryside, the friendly people, the polite Bobbies ...' For their part, the British mostly remember a crowd of noisy, dynamic, generous and generally likeable young men who were a great draw for the young women. One London War Reserve constable was the proud possessor of an old-fashioned horse drawn cab which he continued to use on his days off. This mode of transport was very popular with the Americans who were taken on tours of the sights of London in it and presumably made the fortunate constable a comparatively wealthy man. In Hammersmith, 24 regular policemen offered their services as guides to the US troops in their spare time. In view of the provisions of Police Regulations, it is assumed that this was a voluntary and entirely free service, although the good-hearted officers undoubtedly received some recompense in kind as the Americans had access to foodstuffs and luxuries which the British had not seen for two years.

One police officer who has very clear memories of the American troops is Ella Johnson who was a policewoman in Bristol during the war years. Her recall is understandable when one appreciates that she was a plain clothes liaison officer attached to the US Army Judge Advocate's Department. As such she was responsible for organising courts martial and escorting the witnesses to the US Army camp where the case was to be heard. Where a female witness wanted to use the toilet a strict ritual had to be observed.

> *I informed the officer in charge, who called the guard, who then shouldered his rifle and marched us to the toilets allocated to us. He waited outside and then marched us back to the waiting room again. All very embarrassing, to say the least.*[7]

Ella's colleague, Joan Salhurst also had vivid memories of the Americans in Bristol:

> *There were a lot of Americans on my division, both coloured and white but segregated. ... They were a big attraction to the local girls and I had to make regular patrols to move them on. Also to identify the younger ones in order to notify their parents. The GIs found a 'lady cop' very unusual and were always wanting to date me. I got very annoyed with one sentry who would persist in calling me 'Red.' When I remonstrated with him, he just said, 'OK, Ginger.' So that was that! Another of their embarrassing tricks was for the officer to give an 'Eyes right!' (or left) as they passed me and salute me.*[8]

If the GIs got a little out of hand, the American Military Police (known as 'Snowdrops' on account of their white helmets) would stand no nonsense. When Constable John Uren GM was called to the local cinema in Liverpool he found a group of drunken and noisy American servicemen occupying the front seats. He asked them politely to leave but got no response and so he called upon the MPs for assistance. The Snowdrops arrived and said, 'Come on, buddies, out you go.' which was met with further abuse so they just walked along the row behind, hit each man on the head and then dragged the senseless bodies outside to where the 'paddy wagon' was waiting.

Not all servicemen with whom the police came in contact were simply out on the town, enjoying themselves. A considerable number of Allied airmen crashed or made forced landings in the British countryside and provided yet another headache for the police. Although crashed aircraft were primarily the responsibility of the Royal Air Force (or the USAAC in the case of American aircraft), the police were usually among the first on the scene and had the task of keeping unauthorised persons and sightseers away from the site of the crash. What Angus Calder describes as 'a rustic comedy' might ensue as the village policeman cycled furiously across the fields to anticipate the local children[9], while the local Home Guard would endeavour to send a couple of men to take over. That there was good reason for this is illustrated by the incident which occurred at Waltham Abbey in 1940 when the pilot of one of three Hawker Hurricanes staging an impromptu air show by practising their aerial combat techniques, misjudged his height and struck a tree top, crashing into a field. The pilot was killed but the aircraft was not completely destroyed and, by the time the police and ARP personnel had arrived, small boys were to be seen running off in all directions clutching prized pieces of the machine which had been scattered over the field. Only those at the front of the crowd realised the full extent of the tragedy and the tragic loss of yet another nineteen year old pilot. Most of the parts taken as souvenirs were recovered, the biggest fear being that, amongst these, there could be something of danger to the public as was the case when an American aircraft in difficulties jettisoned all its weaponry which was found and collected by a group of youths. The thought of young, inexperienced fingers on the triggers of these deadly machine guns was enough to make the calmest policeman break into a cold sweat.

Many policemen spent several cold, weary hours searching for aircraft reported to have come down in their area. It was often a case of driving along country lanes, stopping and shouting for a few minutes and then moving on to repeat the process a little further on. This frequently proved successful and Sergeant Sam Rounce of the Lincolnshire force was more than a little embarrassed when one crew he discovered sitting disconsolately on a farm fence, embraced him and his colleague with great passion when he drew up in his little Standard 8. Because of the large number of airfields in rural Lincolnshire, Sergeant Rounce found more and more of his time being taken up with this onerous but necessary task. In the summer he found it helpful to take his schoolboy son with him on such missions, the youngster being periodically sent to climb a suitable tree to see if he could see anything of the downed aircraft.

The extent of this task may be gauged from the fact that, on just one rural beat in Kent, there were 10 crashes or forced landings of British aircraft. On one occasion, the village constable arrived on the scene just as a Blackburn 'Skua' aircraft was making a forced landing and was astonished to see the engine fall out as the plane rolled to a standstill.

Important though the guarding of crashed aircraft was, some other duties were deemed more pressing. Due to an outbreak of Foot and Mouth Disease, Constable Tom Longhurst was on duty outside a farm gate to prevent unauthorised movement to or from the farm when he saw a Spitfire and a German bomber collide in mid-air, the wreckage coming down close by. He contacted his headquarters to get permission to attend (it was a miserable, drizzly day and he would have welcomed some relief) but was told to stay where he was as other officers would be sent to the scene. As it happens he had reason to be thankful for this unwelcome order as the bombs in the German plane suddenly exploded some hours later, killing two firemen and slightly injuring his colleague, Police War Reserve Sid Kemp.

Apart from guarding the wreckage of crashed aircraft, the first persons on the scene – so often the police – would endeavour to extricate any of the crew still in it, whether alive or dead. When an American 'Marauder' aircraft crashed in Sussex through icing problems, Sergeant Bill Henley was passing nearby in his car with his wife beside him. He immediately stopped and rushed over to the plane where he managed to get six of the crew out of the burning wreckage, with ammunition going off all around and the ever-present danger of the highly-sensitive bombs exploding. His wife could only sit in the car and watch with her heart in her mouth. Unfortunately all six crew members were found to be dead and, when the US authorities were informed, they instructed that the bodies should not be removed from the scene until they had been covered with brand-new shrouds. To the strictly rationed British this seemed a dreadful waste of good material!

Eventually the regular military personnel would assume responsibility but even these were a source of problems for the police. Richard Crane remembers one plane making a forced landing near Folkestone hospital. The young RAF men sent to guard it were fine during the day but, as night fell, the rural noises unsettled them to the extent that one guard thought he heard something moving and called out a challenge. Getting no response he called on the others who quickly caught the atmosphere of tension and nervousness and, before long, one was sure he had seen something suspicious and fired a shot. The others, believing they were being attacked, followed suit (it is not clear what they thought they were shooting at) and the police were summoned to attend. Not without considerable trepidation, the police officers approached the scene calling out and shining their torches on their uniforms to identify themselves. After a few fraught minutes the panicking guards were calmed down and order was once more restored.

Sadly, all too often the pilot or crew did not survive the crash and the policeman would have the distressing task of taking the remains to the mortuary. As one recalls, the smell of burnt flesh and clothing, mixed with the pungent odour of aviation spirit from a crashed Spitfire, has remained with him to this day. On another occasion two Flying Fortresses collided in mid-air, killing both crews whilst the wreckage fell to earth in Essex. After a couple of hours the policemen guarding the remains of the aircraft were told to leave the area as quickly as possible, as both aircraft still contained a full load of ready-primed and highly sensitive bombs.

Constable 'Buck' Taylor was close to the scene when a 'Stirling' bomber crashed at Arnold's Oak in Kent. The rear turret had broken off on impact and so he entered the fuselage through the gaping hole which it left but there was no one in the aircraft. Ammunition was exploding the whole time and he had the fright of his life when the plane's rubber dinghy suddenly inflated itself beside him. On leaving the aircraft he searched the area and found the body of the New Zealander pilot who had baled out too late. He carried the body to a nearby barn to await collection by the RAF and, in due course a van arrived with an RAF orderly and a girl driver, The latter was very smart, with her bright lipstick and red nail varnish and Buck Taylor had reservations about letting her see the body. However, the RAF orderly decided to undress the body before rigor mortis set in and asked the girl to help. Without hesitation she pulled the body up by the head, indifferent to the fact that the back of the head had been stoved in, and held the body while the two men undressed it. Just one more example of how war led the most unlikely people to tackle jobs they would recoil from in normal times.

Others were more fortunate and the same officer remembers that one lucky British pilot who had baled out was picked up by the local publican who took him straight back to his hostelry where the celebrations lasted well into the night. It is most unlikely that the cheerful pilot was in a fit state to fly again the next day!

Another British pilot baled out one night and, on reaching the ground, his parachute got caught up in a tree and he was left dangling over a cemetery where he remained for several hours. With the coming of daylight he was spotted by a patrolling policeman who hurried to his aid, apologising for not having come to the rescue earlier.

'That's all right,' replied the pilot nonchalantly, 'I'd rather be here than in the cemetery!'

Another Battle of Britain pilot was seen to bale out over Kent and, when found in an orchard by Constable Tom Longhurst, was leaning against an apple tree with a bullet in his thigh, calmly combing his hair. Small wonder the RAF gained the soubriquet of 'Brylcreem Boys'! An American airman who was found hanging from a tree by his parachute was cut down by the crew of a nearby searchlight and the NCO in charge was rather peeved when the local constable asked him if he had checked the airman's identity!

One unusual landing involved two pilots from the Belgian Air Force who had escaped from Nazi-occupied Belgium in a small biplane trainer. After many adventures they had managed to get the aircraft more-or-less airworthy and amassed sufficient fuel to cross the Channel. There was no opportunity to test the machine and finally, in July 1941, they took off, with their fingers crossed and pointed the nose of the plane towards England. Coming down through the cloud cover some hours later, they were dismayed to see the words HOLLAND painted on a garage roof and surmised that their navigation had gone awry and that they had flown round in a huge circle. With their fuel tank empty, it seemed they would have no option but to land in another Nazi-occupied country. With heavy hearts they put the plane down on a farm and set off to surrender to the German forces, unaware that the sign they had seen referred in fact to Holland Motors of Holland-on-Sea, Essex.

Out on patrol, Sergeant Percy Brown of the Essex Constabulary saw the plane come down and was making his way towards the scene of the landing when he came across two men making obvious signs that they wished to surrender. Assuming them to be Germans, he took them to Thorpe police station where he questioned them and realised their true nationality. After a special constable had been sent back to the plane with one of them in order to recover their documents and being satisfied as their story, the two intrepid airmen were handed over to the authorities. In due course they joined the RAF in which they served with distinction while the little trainer was returned to Belgium after the war and can now be seen in the Musée de l'Armée in Brussels.

Not all those who came down on British soil were members of the Allied forces, however, and the main contact which the police had with the nation's enemies was often the crew of a German aircraft which had been shot down by an Allied fighter or by anti-aircraft fire. The plight of one of the first of these during the Battle of Britain when the might of the Luftwaffe was thrown against these islands is described in a newspaper article:

> *Considerably elated with their new-found success, the Bofors crew watched the crippled fighter with fascinating interest as it skimmed the sea towards Folkestone Warren. ... Barbed wire throttled all but one of the many well-worn paths which descended to the foreshore and, down this path, the soldiers rushed headlong. ... Vogt [the pilot] ignominiously slid into the sea. On reaching the shore he stood up. They were all around him now. With solemn faces the soldiers led their prisoner back up the winding path. But before reaching the cliff top they were confronted by Inspector Bill Floyd and PC Cyril Williams. Vogt flinched and drew back when Williams elbowed his way through the soldiers.*
>
> *'You Nazi bastard!' Williams shouted. 'Shooting women and children.'*
>
> *... at Folkestone police station ... Williams had time to reflect upon his vehement accusation on the cliff path. He offered an explanation.*
>
> *'War is a terrible thing,' Vogt replied. ... 'You must remember that your own flyers are equally involved with outrage and shame.' Williams returned the black and silver Iron Cross insignia to his young prisoner and placed other items in a cloth bag and said simply, 'I suppose you are right.'*

256

If only he had had a crystal ball he would have foreseen,
perhaps, that within two years he himself was to be awarded
the George Medal for gallantry[10].

For most people, the opportunity to capture one of the enemy was
something not to be missed. A G Street the author and broadcaster was
also a keen Home Guard and joined in the search for a German who
had baled out.

I was dead keen to hunt that fellow, felt the same exhilaration
as I did when the hounds were running, and would have shot
him on the instant if need be. But, somehow, when he was
caught I had no further quarrel with him[11].

Dennis Vorley, then a constable with the West Sussex force,
attended the scene of a crash-landed Me 110 – the first undamaged
example to fall into British hands. The crew were being held captive
by some farmworkers brandishing pitchforks and, on the arrival of the
police, the navigator handed over his pistol to Constable Vorley as a
token of surrender. The pilot, however, conscious that he had allowed
this state-of-the-art machine to fall into enemy hands, fired his pistol at
the plane in an effort to destroy it but was unsuccessful, much to the
relief of the Air Ministry.

About this time, instructions were issued to the police that, should
the crew have left a crashed enemy aircraft, they should not approach
nearer than 250 yards for at least 15 minutes in case the wreck had
been booby-trapped or fitted with a self-destruct device. After this
time, the police were advised to take one of the crew with them and, if
the crew members displayed any reluctance, to wait a further 15
minutes. The crash was to be reported to the RAF and the crew kept in
custody and handed over to the RAF or taken to the police station,
whichever was the nearer. Sergeant Bill Henley captured the pilot of
an Me 109 which had been shot down in East Sussex and was
somewhat non-plussed when the tall, blond, true-Aryan airman
demanded to be taken immediately to Nazi-occupied Britain!

Most captures were far from dramatic as Mick Fitzgerald describes
in Ben Wicks book:

The pilot parachuted down and went towards an orchard. The
local policeman lived nearby. He was a very tall man, six feet

seven. He was on his bike and asked us where the pilot had dropped down. I pointed to where I had last seen him and he said, 'Let's go and have a look and see where he is.' We went over some fields and into the orchard and looked through the trees and we saw him standing by a tree with his parachute caught up in the tree. The policeman said, 'Come on, lad.' He put his hands in the air. He was a nice lad, blond. The policeman took a Very pistol from him and took him to his home and phoned the military[12].

The transport of these prisoners in the days before the police were really mechanised often presented problems and many a German airman rode to captivity on the tonneau cover of an MG two-seater patrol car or the pillion of a police motorcycle. Some enemy airmen showed great initiative where their transport was concerned, as an article in the Kentish Express of 22 January, 1943 disclosed. A senior fire service officer attended the scene of a crashed German aircraft, leaving his car in the road. The pilot, who had remained undetected in the dark, climbed in and hid under a rug on the back seat and was unwittingly driven to Ashford where the fire officer stopped to make his report at the fire station. The German seized his opportunity and, moving into the driver's seat, drove off at high speed on the wrong side of the road towards Maidstone. On the way the car ran out of petrol and the airman took to the woods where he was later captured by Constables Ashby and Hack who were part of a search party mounted to look for him.

Questions of jurisdiction also arose as when an Me 109 made a forced landing in a cornfield just outside Margate (Kent). The pilot was uninjured and the first officer on the scene, Constable Bob Stewart of the Kent force, was quickly joined by the Chief Constable of the Margate Borough force. After discussion the two officers agreed that the scene of the landing was outside the borough and therefore came within the jurisdiction of the county force. The pilot was consequently taken into custody by the Kent constable, despite the other police officer's more senior rank.

On other occasions, officers pulled rank in surprising ways. Detective Constable Shoobridge of the Surrey force was dealing with a prisoner when there was a loud 'thump' and he was given a revolver and told to take the station car and investigate. Just at that moment the uniform sergeant arrived back at the station, looking forward to knocking off duty, but he was ordered to accompany the young detective. At the scene a woman with a hurricane lamp told the policemen that a German plane had crashed nearby. The detective went straight to the scene while the sergeant elected to take a roundabout route (to avoid getting there too quickly?). Once at the scene, DC Shoobridge found an airman on the bank of a pond with a broken thigh who told him that there were three others somewhere. With the aid of half-a-dozen bystanders, he began to search the woods and two bodies were discovered in the pond. By this time the sergeant had arrived and it was decided to get the bodies out of the pond by tying a rope round their parachutes. On the order 'Heave!', they all pulled on the rope and the sergeant, who was nearest the pond, slipped on the muddy bank and slid into the water on his posterior. A very dignified old-timer, he was very put out by his ignominious ducking and he spent some time restoring his waxed moustache to its proper rigidity before ordering the detective to run him home to change his uniform, 'Otherwise I shall catch my death of cold.' And so the younger officer had to drop everything and take the sergeant home before returning to the scene to complete the retrieval of the bodies and arrange the removal of the injured man to hospital. This episode demonstrates an interesting question of priorities at a time when a wet bottom was the least of one's worries and it no doubt served as an object lesson to the younger officer who eventually retired with the rank of chief superintendent.

On some occasions all was not what it seemed. Following a report of enemy parachutists in the Thanet area of Kent, the police quickly captured two and sent them by army truck to the nearest army unit. Constable John Taylor was instructed to continue the search and shortly came upon another two, only to be confronted by a revolver pointed at him by one of them. To his horror, this man pulled the trigger and there was a deathly 'click'.

'All right,' said the man in perfect English, 'You're dead.'

He then explained that, as bad weather had grounded the RAF aircrews, they had been sent out on an escape and survival exercise and were supposed to make their way back to camp undetected. Possibly to add to the realism, the police and other organisations had not been informed. Once the initial shock had worn off and he realised that he had not been in real danger, Constable Taylor was, to put it mildly, a little cross.

Like their Allied counterparts, a good many German aircrew failed to survive the crash. In the early part of the war there was not a little confusion as to who should deal with the bodies of such casualties. John Taylor, the constable whose beat included Manston aerodrome in Kent, had such an experience when a Dornier was brought down in open fields near the airfield. The crew of five were all killed and, although a guard was mounted on the wreckage, neither the army not the Air Force would accept responsibility for the bodies. It was mid-summer and extremely hot and the bodies lay there all day. In the end the Coroner instructed that Constable Taylor should deal with the matter as a normal 'sudden death' and later held an inquest into the circumstances, complete with jury.

When three German airmen were seen to bale out of a stricken Luftwaffe aircraft over London, the police immediately went on the hunt for them. Two were captured shortly afterwards and an officer was sent to look for the third, being warned to be careful as the airmen were believed to be armed with guns and knives. He very soon returned with the news that he had got the third one. Seeing no prisoner, the station sergeant asked, 'Where is he? Mind he doesn't get away.'

'It's all right, Sarge,' said the constable confidently. 'The mortuary door's locked,' and went on to explain that the third airman's 'chute had failed to open.

On one cold, wet December evening in 1940, a Junkers Ju88A was shot down by anti-aircraft fire and crashed in a ball of flame in the Loughton district of London. The first units on the scene were from the Loughton fire brigade, quickly followed by other services, including the police represented by Sergeant Styles and War Reserve Constable Albert Newton in the station Wolseley. The area was brightly illuminated by the burning aircraft, although lashed with rain and extremely muddy. Various parts of the plane were visible to the two policemen as they stood guarding the perimeter (which few outsiders had any intention of penetrating). It was not until one of them picked up a glove – only to find a part of the previous wearer's hand still inside it – that they decided that the idle collection of debris was best avoided in the light given by the flames. As daylight dawned the whole of the blackened and blasted area became visible and it was possible to see that the surrounding trees bore a previously unnoticed gory harvest of human and aircraft parts. It was many days before a mixture of RAF personnel and civilian undertakers were able to collect the remains for burial. In the event only enough parts were found to account for three crew members, all of which were buried at Chingford in a single coffin. It was only after the war that it was established that there had been four crew members, all of whom had perished in the inferno. Neither Sergeant Styles nor PWR Newton were able to enjoy their food for several days afterwards.

Those German airmen who survived joined their army, navy and air force colleagues in the various prisoner of war camps scattered about the country. The employment of these men on various types of work, notably in agriculture, involved the police to some extent but not, apparently, as much as might have been expected and certainly not as much as would have been had there not been adequate precautions which were generally respected by the military and other authorities. As a first step, some 3,000 Italian prisoners of war were brought over from the Middle East to work on the land. They were divided into groups of around 500 and housed in camps with a military guard. Each morning they were escorted to the various farms where they were to be employed and returned, again under escort, each night. As time went by, selected prisoners were allowed to live on the farms where they worked and, later still, small parties were housed in local hostels. While working on the farms they wore a distinctive uniform but were not under guard. The police were somewhat dubious about the plan to allow the prisoners to live out and when the hostel plan was decided on, they were informed by Home Office Circular of 22 February, 1942, that they would not be responsible for this arrangement. On the other hand, the farmers were well-pleased with the Italian workers and reported that they had done much to make their harvest a success.

As might be expected, this sort of arrangement raised all kinds of questions about the relations of the prisoners of war with the general public. Regulations had already been made regarding the conduct of the public towards prisoners in the camps[13] and it was a condition of their employment on the farms that there was to be no fraternisation. When complaints began to come in regarding fraternisation on the part of the public (mainly young women who had been somewhat deprived of male company) and letters began to appear in the Press about mis-behaviour on the part of the prisoners, the possibility of extending the non-fraternisation Order to the farms was considered but it was decided that this was not a practical proposition. Certainly the growing tendency for some young women to fraternise in the fullest possible way with these good-looking young men was a cause for concern and one wartime policeman noted that they were very popular with the local prostitutes and were prized even above the GIs as lovers. Possibly because of this reputation there were a few scuffles with local lads which resulted in some of their privileges being curtailed.

The natural propensity of the Italians to break into song and to laugh uproariously was a source of astonishment to the more phlegmatic English countryman. Not all were in favour of these ebullient young men being allowed out in their towns and villages and a letter to the Cambridge Daily News questioned whether it was 'seemly' for them to be allowed to lounge along the roads, blocking up the footpath and appraising the looks of any British girl who happened to be passing.

In August 1944 there were two important developments. First, in accordance with the declaration of co-belligerency made by the Italian Government, Italian prisoners of war were to be invited to participate in the common war effort by joining labour battalions. They were to be issued with a chocolate brown uniform, would carry identity cards and would be permitted to exercise outside the camps within a two-mile radius. A second Circular announced that selected Italians, working in agriculture, would be permitted to drive the lorries taking parties to and from the camps. The latter circular also revealed that some 16,000 German prisoners of war were to be brought over and would occupy the camps vacated by the Italians. These would also be employed on agricultural and forestry work, working in groups under armed escort. The difference between the two nationalities may be judged by the fact that one batch of Germans, due to take over a former Italian camp near Skipton (Yorkshire), refused to move in until the camp had been cleaned up. Such was their militancy that the local police had to be placed on stand-by in case of a full-scale mutiny.

As time went on, more and more German prisoners of war arrived and conditions were gradually relaxed, except for prisoners from the German U-Boat service and the Luftwaffe. By May, 1945, there were 160,000 Germans being held in this country, 40,000 of whom were employed on the land. In fact, these prisoners were very much in demand from the hard-pressed farmers who were being required to produce more and more with fewer and fewer labourers.

Although as a general rule, prisoners of war were held in moderately comfortable camps or hostels, at one time a number of them were held on ships moored in the middle of the Thames Estuary below Gravesend in a manner reminiscent of the prison hulks of the late eighteenth century. These prisoners were guarded by policemen, one of whom was Police War Reserve Norman Buchanan, the peacetime hairdresser. A non-swimmer, he was always terrified when getting from the launch to the rope ladder leading to the deck of the prison ship, loaded as he was with a rifle and other heavy equipent.

On some of these ships there were limited entertainment facilities, such as a piano and Norman Buchanan, an accomplished musician and part-time dance band leader, would amuse himself and the prisoners by playing and leading the singing of 'Lily Marlene' and other well-known songs. He never felt that the prisoners were a threat as many seemed to be completely traumatised by their experiences and some were in a pitiable state. Looking back, the picture of a British policeman in full uniform, playing a piano to try to cheer up some German prisoners seems somewhat bizarre.

The repatriation of these prisoners of war was a long drawn-out affair and Dennis Vorley, who returned to the West Sussex force after five years in the RAF as a pilot, was very pleased when one was allocated to him to help with the large garden attached to his country police house. Working solely in return for meals and cigarettes (the prisoners were not allowed money), the former enemy rendered very welcome assistance.

When one considers the many escape stories involving Allied personnel from prison camps in Germany and other parts of occupied Europe, it is interesting to note that escapes by Axis prisoners were virtually non-existent. Part of the reason may lie in the fact that many were shipped to Canada while those who remained in the British Isles were possibly deterred by the difficulty in finding a means of crossing the Channel to get back to continental Europe and thus to their own people.

Certainly, so far as the police were concerned, Axis prisoners of war in this country gave rise to very few problems once they had been captured and disarmed.

10. Wartime Crimes

The average pre-war policeman, who was well-versed in the provisions of the Larceny Acts, the Malicious Damage Act, the Offences Against the Person Act and various other nineteenth-century statutes, not to mention some obscure local bye-laws, suddenly found himself burdened with a whole range of new offences against the criminal law which had been introduced as a result of the war. Principal amongst these were the various offences created under the Defence Regulations and the legislation which introduced the rationing of a wide variety of items – food, clothing, petrol – to name but a few. On the other hand, whilst the police were being burdened with additional laws and regulations, some existing traffic regulations were being relaxed, such as the movement of RAF articulated lorries through the Blackwall Tunnel, and the conveyance of dangerous loads (including bombs) by road.

Among the crimes which the war suddenly created or made more prevalent, perhaps the most important and possibly the most widespread was that of looting. A repellent word, it conjures up images of human ghouls moving surreptitiously among the dead and dying in the hope of picking up some unguarded valuables or even removing rings and other jewellery from the corpses. Since looting is essentially a straightforward case of theft, aggravated by the circumstances of the war, it is perhaps this ghoulish image which makes this crime seem so grave. Under Defence Regulation 38A, the death penalty was applied to acts of larceny and malicious damage in war-damaged areas – although in fact no-one was ever actually executed for it.

Before trying to estimate the amount of looting which took place, it is necessary to determine just what the word means. Is it looting when a small boy sees a packet of cigarettes lying in the street and takes it home to father? Is it looting when a shop which has been damaged by blast three months earlier is broken into? The taking of property from premises immediately after they have been opened up by a bomb is clearly looting, but the breaking into a shop which is less secure because of damage sustained some time previously is more doubtful.

From the point of view of criminal statistics looting does exist as a separate offence but it is not always easy to be sure that offences prosecuted as ordinary stealing were not in fact looting. Because of the seriousness of the offence and the existence of the death penalty it is probable that many borderline cases were reduced to theft but the official criminal statistics show that the following number of cases were dealt with under the Defence Regulations :

1939	1940	1941	1942	1943	1944	1945
Nil	426	508	415	255	561	93

It is impossible to be sure just how many offences actually took place; indeed, statistics would only show the number of cases reported, the proverbial tip of a probable iceberg. All one can say now is that, out of all the larcenies, burglaries and other breaking offences, a certain number incorporated at least some of the characteristics of looting. In 1941 a judge referred to what he described as a 'perfect outburst of looting' in Sheffield following the air raids the previous December, while the Annual Report of the Commissioner for the Metropolitan Police for 1940 quoted 4,584 cases of looting, 45% of which were committed by young persons under 18 years of age. A study of the reported cases of looting reveals the sad and strange fact that many of the items looted were of little or no value – a curtain, a lady's vest, a crumb brush, a pair of shoes, shoelaces, a torch. In fact, the vast majority of items stolen were of low value – around £5. What is fairly clear is that there was little or no organised looting but there were hundreds of cases of opportunist thieves taking advantage of the situation created by enemy action to steal the property of another. Even so, there was probably proportionally less looting from bomb-damaged property than there has been in more recent years from shops whose windows have been deliberately shattered in the course of a civil disturbance.

Like any form of theft, looting covers offences of widely varying degrees of seriousness, from the theft of an unwanted pint of milk to the semi-organised stripping of bomb-damaged houses and commercial premises. In the event, most incidents involved personal and household possessions of relatively low value. One family, returning to their shattered home the morning after an air raid, found only a three-piece suite, the dining room table and three chairs, a radiogram and a cabinet: nothing else. Everything which was portable, unbroken and usable had been taken. This was by no means an uncommon experience, although in some cases neighbours no doubt thought it better to make use of goods left in the open rather than let them deteriorate. But many offenders were thieves pure and simple, some even breaking into properties in which goods removed from bombed houses had been stored. As one survivor recalls:

A pilferer had been before us, stealing the best of what we had so painstakingly saved from destruction. What was left was dirty, torn or cracked, with burn or scorch marks.'

Another remembers that,

We begged a lift back to the ruins of our house ... looters had already preceded us, and sightseers were cutting the parachute from the land mine into small pieces for souvenirs. My mother found her handbag but otherwise we retrieved nothing[1].

One attraction for looters was the large number of prepayment gas and electricity meters, many of which were found to have been rifled when they were eventually removed from the ruins of a house: in Coventry alone 800 electricity meters were found to have been broken into following the Blitz on that city in December, 1940.

Although it is clear that looting in one form or another was extremely widespread, a number of people who should have known better vociferously doubted its existence. When Portsmouth was subjected to heavy air raids, the army objected strongly to being given the task of guarding against looters. Some of the officers later opined that there was '... no sign of anyone *thinking* about looting' and they expressed their frustration at not being given some more useful task. In Coventry there had been considerable resentment of the fact that, while women and girls were out fighting the fires created by incendiary bombs, the troops in the area were under orders to remain under cover. There were reports that, despite this, some soldiers had crept out of the shelters and were seen helping themselves to the contents of bombed shops and, when other troops were drafted in later to help with the clearing up, a number were found breaking into the gas meters of the bombed properties. Sightseers poured into the city after the raid to gawp at the devastation and to see what they could 'salvage' for their own ends. One sixteen year old boy, who had travelled all the way from London in a car with two men, was charged with stealing over £60 worth of property – a sizeable sum at that time.

Had the army officers who complained about the futility of anti-looting patrols been in a position to hear some of the accounts which victims gave of their experiences, they might have revised their opinion:

> *We all saved and got the children their Christmas presents and the looters came in the night and took everything. It was heart-breaking because we could not afford any more. Their fingers should have dropped off, but they done it to most houses, not only mine....*

> *We lost our home and all our belongings. The hundredweight of coal got in for the winter was looted along with some unbroken movable objects and clothing[2].*

Another contemporary view of the scale of looting was expressed by Michael Stapleton in Alan Kendall's book[3]:

> *... I think a lot of people would be surprised at how much casual looting went on. I don't mean that people waited for their opportunity to see that they could grab something and hung about with this expectation, but I do remember that in Chapel Street market there was a direct hit on a double-fronted grocery store ... next door to a branch of the butchers' shop chain that I worked for. Of course, we found that we could slip out into the yard where all the dustbins were kept and the brine barrel, and step over what was left of the wall into their old store room. ... It was perfectly easy to extract three or four pounds of butter and several pounds of sugar and scrape the dust and charcoal off them and use them, and we did so. We didn't feel any particular shame about it. When a shop was a write off after a direct hit from a bomb, what did it matter? It might be salvaged or it might not.*

The same author also quotes the tale of another victim who thought that the fumbling hand she felt as she was lying amid the ruins of the Café de Paris in London was that of a rescuer. But she found to her stupefaction that it was a looter removing the rings from her fingers. What she found particularly shocking was the speed the looter had arrived on the scene⁴.

Given the widespread incidence of looting, a survey carried out by the Mass Observation organisation during the war is very revealing of the general public's attitude to this crime. 52% expressed very strong disapproval of looters and described them as 'Scum', adding that they should all be shot. 35% were more philosophical and less condemnatory of the offence, making remarks such as, 'Well, you can't call a woman a looter for taking a few lumps of coal.' or 'It's a great temptation.'

Others comments included, 'They're not like ordinary thieves who steal on purpose.' and 'It's difficult to know what is looting.'

In October, 1940, the chief constable of Croydon complained about 'Canadian soldiers interfering with property left exposed by the smashing of windows consequent on the raids', which would appear to be a euphemism for looting.

Late one night, Constable John Thompson was checking property near to the RAF station at Manston (Kent) when he came across a soldier with an army lorry, busy removing the furniture from an evacuated house. The offender was arrested and handed over to the military authorities who, at his court martial, sentenced him to 6 months in the 'glasshouse.' John Thompson was also involved in the arrest of another two soldiers for looting some time later. Possibly because the increasing prevalence of this crime, these two were each sentenced to five years imprisonment. A NAAFI worker from Eastbourne commented:

> *There was so much looting done as well. Many a time after a raid, we would get some of the soldiers bringing different articles in that had been looted and tried to sell them to our NAAFI.*⁵

If the theft of personal property from damaged houses was not bad enough, some evil people would even steal from the dead and injured. The Rector of St Peter's, Walworth in South London was also an ARP volunteer and was involved in caring for injured people who had been brought to the local hospital noted that :

> *... nothing helped their recovery more than the knowledge that*

their personal treasures were safe. The usual practice of those who took shelter was to put all their cash, savings certificates, items of personal jewellery, and personal papers such as birth and marriage certificates, in their handbags which they left under the chair on which they were sitting, or by their side if they were in bed. As soon as it was daylight, I used to take two of my wardens and tunnel through mountains of rubble to find these handbags. We dared not leave them, even for a few hours, or they would be gone. As soon as we recovered dead bodies, I had to put them in an empty room, under the guard of two wardens, until a stretcher party could remove them to a mortuary. Otherwise their clothing would be rifled, there in the midst of the darkness and dust and falling bombs. I often said in those days that it was a good thing that I was not armed with a pistol or a gun: I would probably have shot those whom I suspected of this kind of activity.[6]

Whilst most incidents of looting were opportunist, there seems little doubt that there was a measure of organisation in some of the bigger cities. It was claimed that, in London, gangs of looters employed 'spotters' to identify likely properties for looting. The owners of shops and factories would return to their shattered premises to find them completely stripped of all valuables and stock. One man, charged with stealing two lighters and a pipe from a bombed tobacconists shop complained, 'I'm unlucky. They're all doing it.' – a complaint not without some justification.

What is particularly disturbing is the character of some of the offenders. With raids in progress, virtually the only people officially on the streets were members of the civil defence services and, possibly, the military. These had 'first pickings' and certain members of the civil defence organisation were not slow in taking advantage of this fact. The Commissioner of the Metropolitan Police, in his report for 1940, stated that the worst feature of the reported cases of looting was the number of cases in which members of the various public services had abused positions of trust. It is an indisputable fact that a great deal of the looting was carried out by wardens, rescue services, stretcher bearers, the fire service – and, it has to be admitted, even the police.

... there was widespread pocketing of valuables from bombed

270

houses by demolition squads and even by auxiliary firemen or rescue workers. A blind eye was turned: it was often regarded as a reward for their gruesome task. 'Our sergeant says loot as much as you like as long as you're not found out,' said one auxiliary fireman to Mass Observation. A girl in the AFS was said to bring home something every night, but often it was nothing more valuable than a tin of pineapple[7].

Norman Longmate[8] tells how another AFS man, on his way back from vainly attempting to put out a fire at a large department store in Coventry, passed a wine shop, the front of which had been shattered by blast. He helped himself to a bottle, broke the neck and drank some of the contents before he realized that he had committed a hanging offence! He very quickly returned the bottle to the shop.

Frank Whipple, who was a War Reserve Constable in the docks area of London, confirms the involvement of civil defence personnel in looting:

There was a terrible lot of looting. You'd find bent wardens, heavy rescue men, even police doing it. People were like vultures, going into bombed-out houses and shops, and they'd even take rings and valuables off dead bodies. We would have to accompany them to the mortuary to stop that happening[9].

In the Metropolitan Police during the Blitz, men were often sent from one station to help out at another which was trying to cope with the multifarious problems arising from this form of concentrated enemy action. One constable, sent from Wanstead to Leytonstone, was patrolling what the police would describe as a good class residential area when he heard a noise from the rear of a substantial, unoccupied dwelling. On making his way to the rear of the house he came upon two local constables, in plain clothes, with a pile of furniture which they had obviously 'liberated' from the house. He told them to put this back and to clear off, which they did. Later, he made a 'conference point' with his sergeant and reported, 'All correct' in the time-honoured manner. But he was worried by the incident and eventually told the sergeant what he had seen. The matter was promptly taken to the highest level and the two offending constables were appropriately dealt with. As for the reporting officer, he was not commended for his action; on the contrary, he was fined a week's pay for not reporting the matter immediately.

Barbara Nixon was a warden in London throughout the Blitz and writes about one of her colleagues who :

> ... *was an inveterate hanger-on of bomb damage, and would rush off to incidents that were no concern of ours. It was not until he had left to go into the army that I found out why. He would certainly not have taken anything from a private dwelling, but about a business firm he had not the same scruples*[10].

Even given this propensity for wardens to engage in what might be deemed minor forms of looting, their attitude towards some of their other colleagues was quite strongly antipathetic:

> *We did not have a great respect for the demolition workers. The 'top men' were skilled, and risked their necks on the perilously insecure roof tops to collect the lead in the interests of national economy. But even their efforts were nullified. One evening just after 'knocking off' time a lorry drew up, loaded the six-foot high pile of lead from the road and drove off. Some of this lead, and some of the furniture from our square, was found by the police five months later at an auction sale in Norfolk, along with a great deal of other stolen property*[11].

Where any of these civil defence workers were caught looting they were brought before the courts (by the police) and were usually severely dealt with. Two ARP workers who stole £12 were sentenced to 12 months imprisonment and a number of other cases of heavy sentences being passed were reported in the Police Review in 1940. On occasions the police turned a blind eye to some incidents and even helped where they felt it to be justified, as a very young Scots lass discovered:

> *We were taking wood from round [the] football pitch when two policemen appeared. Dad said, 'Just carry on,' but we were shaking. Policemen came and helped gather the wood and board up where our windows had been*[12].

In an effort to combat the problems of items going missing at the scene of an incident, the police in Chelsea introduced a 'one-way' anti-looting box. Placed under the control of a constable, ARP workers who found articles of value could deposit them in this box, which had a capacity of some 6 or 7 cubic feet, from which items could only be removed by an authorised person using the key which was held at the police station. Once the incident had been cleared, the box would be taken to the police station where the contents were removed and recorded as found property in the normal manner.

Although the authorities had anticipated a measure of looting, they were more concerned with the likelihood of sabotage, whether by enemy agents, Fifth Columnists or Nazi fellow-travellers. In fact there were few Nazi sympathizers among the British people although one must make a distinction between Nazi sympathizers and those who for one reason or another would have collaborated, as some French did, in the event of a defeat. Extensive measure were taken to combat this possibility which, in the event, really never came to anything. It is hard to believe that the Germans, who were reputed to have a talent for this sort of thing, did not make more of an attempt. Whether the police and military presence, coupled with the various other precautions defeated him, the fact remains that sabotage attempts were so few as to be almost negligible. A woman in the Isle of Wight was sentenced to death for cutting military phone wires, though the conviction was quashed on appeal and she was sentenced to 14 years imprisonment for other charges. An avowed Fascist was sentenced to seven years' imprisonment in July, 1940, for causing damage to a number of telephone kiosks, with the admitted intention of preventing members of the civil defence services from using them[13].

Closely allied to the crime of sabotage is that of treasonable activity if not actual treason and a number of prosecutions took place, especially in 1940 when the invasion scare was at its height. For example, an Admiralty clerk was given three months imprisonment for possessing a list of aerodromes which might have been of use to the enemy and a member of the IRA received a similar sentence plus a £100 fine for having in his possession a military map. Others were prosecuting for promoting the New British Broadcasting Corporation, many of whom were totally unaware that it was operated by the enemy.

Another serious matter in war time was sedition or incitement to disaffection. A Stafford café proprietor, who had previously been convicted of receiving stolen petrol from soldiers, was heard to say, in the presence of two RAF airmen, 'The poor buggers in Dunkirk have been cut up. Look at the guns at the aerodrome here, they're all obsolete ... when Hitler comes ... he will blow us all to Hell. We don't stand a cat in Hell's chance. I know where all the guards at the camp are and ... could walk in there any time. You [the RAF men] might as well take your uniforms off for all the good they are going to be. The plane's they have here are only for instruction.'

He was reported by the airmen and prosecuted by the police. Pleading poverty, he was fined just £6.5.0. (£6.25p). Several activists of the Peace Pledge Union were charged with 'endeavouring to cause disaffection among persons in His Majesty's service' in June, 1940.

The crime of sedition was extended by the Defence Regulations to encompass the spreading of alarm and despondency. In June 1940, the *Police Review* reported that the police in Coventry, Chester, and Worcester (among other places) were reporting cases of the spreading of 'baseless rumours'. These were generally dealt with under the provisions of the Defence Regulations for the spreading of statements relating to war matters likely to cause alarm, although the journal pointed out that, had these not been in existence, there would have been the possibility of prosecuting the offenders with 'causing a public mischief'[14]. This new offence was restricted to the spreading of baseless rumours while the dissemination of alarmist but true stories was dealt with under the regulation covering 'the giving of information likely to be useful to the enemy.' Examples quoted in the *Police Review* article included :

(1)   A teacher who told his pupils that the Germans would land in Ireland and blockade the United Kingdom and that the children would be reduced to eating cats and dogs. If they were fortunate they might get the odd rat or some snail soup.

(2)   A meter reader who told the occupant of one house he visited that 'The Nazis are not after the likes of us and we would be as well off under the Nazis as we are now and the government has interests in Germany and has no intention of winning the war.'

The spreading of false rumours was considered to be more serious where the rumour-monger held a position which might suggest to his listeners that he was privy to confidential information. Thus a GPO telephone operator was fined £25 for telling a woman that 20 German parachutists had been dropped at Hawkhurst in Kent and that none had been captured. The comparatively heavy fine reflected the fact that, as an official telephone operator, he might be presumed to have access to official information. Another tale concerns a part-time special constable in Carlisle who was said to have performed splendid service in that capacity since the outbreak of the war. His daughter had married a German 18 months previously and had returned to the United Kingdom just before war was declared. Her husband was believed to be an officer in the Wehrmacht. The special constable told people in his club that he knew for a fact that four parachutists had landed in Scotland the previous week, two of whom had been caught while the other two remained at liberty. He knew this to be a fact as he had the number of the car used, and pointed to his official pocket book in his breast pocket. In fact, the landing of three parachutists had been reported and the police had been asked to keep a sharp lookout for them – something the special constable knew from his connection with the police. He also made other statements, including a claim that, of the planes delivered to France from the United States, 200 – 300 had fallen into German hands in the past week and that the reinforcements sent to the BEF in France had only one rifle between 30 men. In view of the special constable's access to privileged information he was fined £50 and costs.

On the whole the public claimed to be opposed to all forms of rumour spreading but, in fact, the average person's delight in gossip was not going to cease simply because there was a war on; far from it, since the war provided so many additional subjects to talk about, whether true or false, whether witnessed or merely hearsay. It is a sad fact of life that many took advantage of the official exhortations to report rumour mongers to settle old scores for vengeful or simply malevolent reasons. Harbourers of long-standing grudges, haters of Irishmen, the politically biased, officious minor functionaries and many others seized the opportunity with alacrity. Regrettably, it would seem that, all too often, such reports were taken at face value by the police and proceedings were instituted with very little supporting evidence. Many of the cases concerned individuals who prophesied that the Germans would soon invade Great Britain (not an unlikely scenario in 1940/41), often coupling such forecasts with the opinion that life under the Nazis would not be unpleasant.

Other cases reported included a vicar who told a soldier in a canteen that, 'Now France has capitulated, we might as well lay down our arms.'

When the soldier said he was prepared to fight to the last, the vicar responded, 'I don't see any sense in that because they would bomb us until they had finished us off. We would have no government, Churchill would be shot and Mosley would be a dictator.'

A few weeks earlier he had been heard to say, 'The best side's won and we may as well pack up.' As he appeared to be trying to influence soldiers, he was sentenced to three months imprisonment.

One of the more ridiculous prosecutions arose out of an incident in a London pub. A French soldier, slightly the worse for drink, cried patriotically, *'Vive la France!'* to which another replied, *'Vive l'Angleterre!'* An Englishman, not to be outdone, cried. *'And to Hell with Hitler!'* (or so he claimed) but a woman immediately left the bar and returned with a policeman and, pointing at the Englishman, accused him of saying *'Heil Hitler!'* The Englishman was able to convince the officer of his innocence but did so in such a manner and using such language that he was promptly charged with using insulting words and behaviour. He was later fined five shillings (25p). Some individuals were prosecuted for insulting behaviour without even saying a word; persons selling Fascist, communist and pacifist literature were liable to be arrested if they provoked others to abuse them!

The Mass Observation organisation noted that many of the prosecutions for 'spreading alarm and despondency' were directed against foolish people who were 'shouting their mouths off rather than seriously attempting to affect the war effort'. This category could presumably include the lance corporal who created a great deal of alarm in the Taunton area by announcing that parachutists had landed and that he had commandeered a van to go round and warn the villages. In fact, the van was one used by his friend and the two of them were merely out for a joy-ride. The story was a complete invention on the soldier's part and resulted in him getting one month's hard labour.

Although not strictly a war time offence, desertion and absence without leave became much more prevalent, largely due to the enormous increase in the number of military personnel, many of whom had no desire to serve in His Majesty's Forces. It has been estimated that some 80,000 men had gone AWOL from the army alone by the end of 1944 while, at its peak in 1941, about one per cent of the army was absent without leave. Although many were merely taking some unauthorised leave of absence to visit their families, there was a hard core of vicious men who, because of their outlaw status (no identity card, no ration book, etc.), resorted to a life of crime and violence. By the end of the war it was estimated that there were some 20,000 unpardoned deserters at large. Many deserters were prepared to go to any lengths to avoid being apprehended and returned to their units, probably via the military prison, and so presented a serious policing problem.

One such case involved Signalman Thomas William Dennison, a 21 year old Glaswegian of the Royal Corps of Signals who, in February 1943, was in military custody at Prestatyn on charges of larceny and being an absentee. One morning he managed to escape from his confinement by removing the bars from the guard-room window and, although chased by an army sergeant, grabbed a bicycle and made good his escape. Dennison was well-known to the police and Constable 111 Williams, 28, of the Caernarvonshire Constabulary was off duty and in plain clothes one evening when he saw him on the other side of the street. The constable crossed the road and, having satisfied himself that he was indeed the wanted man, told him he was being arrested and subjected him to a cursory search. On the way to the police station Dennison suddenly jumped into the road and, pulling a revolver out of his battledress blouse, pointed it at the officer. The constable closed with him and,

> *... pushed the revolver up with my left hand and managed to get a slight hold on the muzzle of the revolver but, as he was in the act of drawing back, I lost my hold on the gun. He ran back a distance of about three yards and fired a shot at me which passed on my right side level with my thigh... and when a distance of about eight yards away, he fired another shot at me sideways as he was running. At that time I was running after him and I felt the bullet passing just under my left hand that was extended across my chest to my right side, level with my chest.*

Despite his efforts, the constable lost his prisoner and so went to the police station to report the incident. A full-scale search was immediately mounted, employing both regular and special constables, which lasted all night. Over the next few days various reports were received concerning Dennison's whereabouts, none of which resulted in his arrest but, two days after the shooting incident, information was received that the wanted man had been seen on the foreshore between Conway and Penmaenmawr. A party of six constables, including Constable Williams, all under the orders of Sergeant Roberts, went to the scene where they managed to surround Dennison. On seeing the policemen, Dennison ran backwards into the sea, waving his revolver. One of the officers, Constable 99 Jones, a 38 year old man with 15 years service, removed his jacket and helmet and, taking a stone in each hand, bravely pursued the armed man into the sea. Dennison retreated until he was up to his chest in the water, still holding the revolver. As the constable got nearer to him he held the revolver to his own head but then pulled it away. When the constable was a few feet away from him he dropped the revolver into the sea and was promptly arrested. The .38 Smith & Wesson revolver, which had apparently been stolen from the effects of an officer at the army camp, was later recovered from the sea and found to be loaded with six rounds. More ammunition was found on Dennison's person, together with a quantity of stolen property.

Dennison appeared at Caernarvon Assizes the following June when he was sentenced to 22 months hard labour. Both Constable Williams and Constable Jones were awarded the King's Police and Fire Services Medal for Bravery.

Not all deserters were so reluctant to surrender. Detective Inspector Len Winter, who was stationed in the West Riding of Yorkshire, tells of one Canadian deserter who moved in with one of the daughters of a family of poor farmers who scraped a living in the area. The house was a 'tip' and utterly filthy and the girl concerned had a reputation for being a bit 'fast'. The deserter was caught stealing goods from a parked car and, instead of putting up any resistance, thanked the officer for getting him out of the situation in which he had landed. Even the glasshouse would be an improvement on the living conditions and quality of life at the farm!

Other peculiarly war-time offences included the assumption of false identities and the use of radios. Although in normal times a citizen may tell a wide variety of untruths without fear of prosecution, it now became an offence to make a false statement on any matter which could be held to affect the interests of the State. A Birmingham man who was unable to get work because his name was O'Shea changed it to Rigby without making the formal declaration required by law, for which offence he was sentenced to 21 days hard labour by the magistrates. If it was an offence to pretend not to be an alien, it was equally an offence to pretend to be of foreign extraction since exemption from military service could be obtained in this way[15]. This prohibition on the use of false names was obviously a problem for those who were planning an illicit liaison in a hotel or boarding house. Use of the traditional pseudonym 'Mr and Mrs Smith' was now inadvisable and secret lovers had to choose between breaking the law or risking their secret coming out. One photographer's model who used a false name while spending the night with a serviceman was sentenced to two months imprisonment and a woman who visited a ship at Dundee using a permit made out in the name of the master's wife got a month inside.

In retrospect it is difficult to see the reasoning behind the decision to ban car radios in case they were converted into transmitters. The police enforced this regulation rigorously and prosecutions were even instituted against people taking their domestic battery-operated radios in for repair. Even radios in caravans were prohibited, although the government later realised the absurdity of this and allowed their use in residential mobile homes provided no wheels were attached. Radios could be carried on a bicycle or in a pram without offending the law and sets which operated on mains electricity were exempt, on the basis that they could not be used in the vehicle.

The shortage of batteries made the life of the many cyclists very difficult. The police continued to report those who failed to display the obligatory white light to the front and red light to the rear although the magistrates tended to take a lenient view. One Suffolk girl explained to the court that she had been unable to obtain a battery for her lamp but had to get home to her parents who would otherwise worry. She was fined eightpence, which she paid with a shilling piece, saucily telling the clerk to 'Keep the change!' The Police Review for 10 May 1940 reported that four women had been fined in Walsall for pushing perambulators on the highway without red rear lights!

Shortages are, of course, only to be expected in an island nation at war and the logical solution for these is some form of rationing. Staple requirements such as food were subjected to strict rationing from the beginning of 1940 (although surprisingly bread was not rationed until after the war was over!), as was clothing and luxuries such as sweets and confectionery. Many other goods, although not rationed were extremely scarce or impossible to obtain. By the following Christmas shops were displaying notices showing what they were unable to supply, a list which included onions, oranges, carrots, lemons, eggs, chocolate, tinned milk and bananas. When a lorry arrived in Chelmsford market on 20 December, with 12 cases of citrus fruits, the police had to intervene to control the hordes of women who were besieging the unfortunate driver. Beer and spirits became scarce as did stockings, torch batteries and many other mundane items. Where a shop managed to get a stock of these rare items queues rapidly formed, causing the chief constable of Derby to threaten shopkeepers with prosecution for obstructing the footpath. There was also a school of thought which regarded queues as unfair to those who were too busy to join them but the practice persisted and became a feature of the war which was continued into peacetime lifestyles.

One common method of supplementing the meagre meat ration was the formation of pig clubs. Under an initiative fully supported by the Ministry of Food, a group of individuals would club together to buy piglets which they would then fatten on scraps until they were big enough to be butchered, when at least one of the carcases would be divided amongst the members. There were a number of police pig clubs, one of which kept its pigs in Hyde Park. A G Street, the writer and broadcaster on country matters remembers this particular pig club:

> *The policemen bought some materials from bombed houses, and with these in their off duty hours built a pigsty. I could tell at a glance that policemen had built that sty. Whatever else might happen to its inmates none would ever escape for it was built solid, like a gaol.... Since the forming of this pig-club the pigs have been bought by policemen, fed by policemen, and most of their food collected from police barracks (sic) by policemen. The allure of these pigs is so great that all this work is eagerly done by policemen during their off-duty hours. ... when you catch, as I did, a London policeman out of uniform and wearing an apron of bagging while he mixes up the pigs' food, well, he doesn't look like a London policeman at all. Instead he looks just what he once was, an English*

280

countryman, and this particular policeman talked to his pigs in broad Devon[16].

When one of the smartest sergeants in the whole division, dressed in the most disreputable civvies, tried to wheel a load of swill across Hyde Park Corner to his beloved swine, a newcomer to the division stopped him and told him he was pushing a barrow to the danger of the public.

'You ignorant ****,' replied the sergeant. 'Can't you see who you're talking to?'

The abashed rookie, anxious to redeem himself, promptly stopped all traffic coming into Hyde Park Corner from every direction while the priceless barrowload of swill made its way to the sty.

Other policemen kept rabbits and there were well over 200 in lock-up garages at Bow, while others cultivated extensive allotments in response to the exhortations to 'Dig for Victory'.

With clothing rationed, policemen had to surrender 18 of their annual allocation of 66 coupons for their uniform (9 for the tunic and trousers, 3 for their greatcoat and 6 for a pair of boots). Policewomen had to give up an additional 6 coupons for their stockings which were provided as part of their uniform, a concession which caused considerable resentment amongst other female workers. Why couldn't the NFS girls enjoy a similar concession? The authorities argued in response that, unlike their fire service colleagues, policewomen could not wear trousers and, furthermore, their stockings had to be black which was not a colour they would normally choose.

Representations were made in an attempt to get an additional concession in the way of an enhanced meat ration for police officers. Soldiers were entitled to 60 ounces each week while heavy manual workers got 40 oz, compared with the normal civilian ration of 20 oz and it was argued that the police should at least get 40 oz but this was not accepted, nor were claims for an enhanced cheese ration. In fact, there were many complaints in 1941 about the food wasted by the military and the preferential treatment given to them, a situation which became even more acute with the arrival of the Americans two years later, whose profligacy with foodstuffs was regarded as downright scandalous by the impoverished British.

A letter to *The Times* from Lord Cranworth drew attention to the iniquities of the system:

> *A policeman works 12 hard hours a day. His ration is 9 oz of beef steak a week. His daughter does some 7 hours clerical work a day but because she wear His Majesty's uniform, she gets 42 oz a week.*

The police did, however, benefit from the concessions granted to the canteens set up at many police stations. Run by local volunteers who were thrilled at having an opportunity to help with the war effort, these were a boon to the many 'grass bachelors' whose wives and families had been evacuated away from target areas.

Petrol too, as we have seen, was rationed and strictly controlled. Late one night Constable Bill Little of the Birmingham City force was on duty at the police station when an official from the Board of Trade came in and told the constable that he was on his way to an important meeting and had run out of petrol. He had petrol coupons but was unable to find a garage open to supply him. The constable, with his knowledge of the local businessmen, was able to contact a garage proprietor who agreed to turn out and supply the government official with the petrol he needed. The latter returned shortly afterwards, his car now refuelled, and handed to the policeman a bottle of whisky in return for his kindness and trouble. Unfortunately, by this time the duty inspector was also in the police station and, hearing the offer being made, said, 'I'm sorry Sir, but we aren't allowed to accept gratuities although I do appreciate your generosity. I'll see you to your car and you can be on your way.'

The disappointed constable thought no more of the matter until a few days later, he was enjoying an off-duty pint in his 'local' when the licensee said to him, 'By the way Bill, where does your guv'nor get his whisky from? He came in here and sold me a bottle the other day.'

Occasionaly a dubious transaction had a fortuitous outcome, as was the case in which a constable bought (illegally) some petrol coupons from his local greengrocer. When he went to buy the petrol the garage queried the provenance of these coupons as the details had been circulated to all garages as having been stolen. Hurrying back to the greengrocer, the constable learned that they had been purchased from a man in Covent Garden market. The next day the constable went with the greengrocer to Covent Garden where the latter pointed out the supplier who was promptly arrested.

Where there are shortages there are always some individuals who are willing and able to exploit the situation. Goods which were generally unobtainable or subject to rationing could usually be obtained on the Black Market and, although illegal and possibly immoral, few ordinary citizens were adverse to taking advantage of the opportunities presented to them, at a price. A surprising number of people were willing to admit that they had bought goods on the black market.

Although there appears to have been a small amount of large-scale organised black marketeering, operated by major crime syndicates, most professional black market activities involved the one-man concern, the 'spiv'. Often a deserter from the services or a draft dodger, living on his wits, this type of petty criminal was more often a receiver than an active thief, a retailer rather than a wholesaler or supplier. Apart from goods obtained by straight-forward breaking and entering, many of the black market items were secreted out of service canteens and cook-houses, especially the American ones which seemed to have an inexhaustible supply of scarce goodies. In 1942 a Colchester Court Martial dismissed four RASC officers for 'irregularities', including receiving coal and paraffin, improperly drawing allowances, stealing food and permitting repairs to be carried out by army mechanics on private cars.

The black market, as such, was not really a police matter and the Ministry of Food and the Board of Trade employed a whole army of inspectors in an endeavour to combat this unlawful trading. Ration books were closely guarded, not always successfully. One large consignment was stored in an old house with a cellar, the door of which was secured with two huge padlocks. Two night watchmen were installed in an office, in touch with the local police and under strict instructions not to open the door to anyone. This seemingly impregnable store was, however, successfully raided by some enterprising thieves who broke in through an outside lavatory, pulling up the floor-boards and gaining access to the cellar. While the watchmen were ringing through to report everything in order, the crooks were loading thousands of ration books, worth £500,000 on the black market, onto their lorry. In order not to destroy public confidence in the rationing system, this theft, which was on a par with the Great Train Robbery, received no publicity.

What did concern the police was the means by which these 'spivs' gained possession of the goods they were offering for sale, which was frequently through shopbreaking and theft from warehouses, coupled with an enormous amount of comparatively petty pilfering. Bill Cavey, who was working as a CID Aide in the East End of London, was approached one day by a man who said he was worried that there was some 'tricky business' going on at his place of employment and he didn't want to get involved. He worked for a firm which bought and recycled all the packing cases from a large wholesale grocers and other, similar concerns, storing these in a row of railway arches rented for the purpose. The employee said a case of currants had been delivered to the store that day and he believed this had been stolen. The constable decided to investigate and, as the premises were difficult to observe unobtrusively, he collected his bicycle and, within sight of the arches, pretended to be mending a puncture. His patience was rewarded when a man came from the arches carrying a package under his arm. This suspect was stopped and searched and found to be carrying a large tin of Spam. With this evidence, the policeman went to the foreman and told him that he believed that he was in possession of stolen property. 'Oh?,' said the foreman. 'Where?' and showed the astounded policeman six large arches, stacked floor to ceiling with packing cases. Although ostensibly empty, it was entirely conceivable that at least some of these still contained goods and so Bill Cavey summoned some assistance from his station. After several hours hard work by a team of officers, a total of £4,000 worth of groceries were discovered mixed in amongst all the empties. It transpired that the firm's drivers, with the collusion of some employees from the wholesale grocers, were bringing back the odd full case mixed in with the empty ones, the contents of which were quickly sold to ready customers on the black market.

One East Anglian police inspector got to hear that an army cook was leaving certain choice items of food – a piece of ham, a few tins of fruit – amongst the swill to be collected by a local pig farmer. He kept observation on the camp gates and, when the farmer drove out, he made him tip his whole load out onto the roadway. Imagine his chagrin when, after sorting through this odoriferous heap, he found nothing untoward; he had unfortunately chosen the very day the crooked cook was off sick with food poisoning!

Jock Jones, who served with the CID in Leicester, dealt with many break-ins connected with the black market:

> *We had a well known hosiery factory broken into one week-end. Thousands of pounds worth of stockings were stolen and they found their way onto the London black market. They forced the lock on a Friday night, got a van inside and then put a fresh lock on, so the offence wasn't discovered till Monday morning. By that time the stuff was all down in London, on the market. Very valuable commodity, ladies' stockings[17].*

The docks and railways were prime sources of black market goods and the LMS lost more than £500,000 worth of goods in 1941. Peter Gannon, who worked for the Port of London Authority Police, described how :

> *... the lorry would arrive in the docks for, say, 100 sides of beef. The checker would ask him if he wanted some extras. If he was that way inclined, he'd take 110 and sign for 100 and then, on the way to Smithfield, drop the extras off at a butcher's shop[18].*

It has already been demonstrated how the police themselves were not always lily-white and, in the matter of the black market, they were perhaps no better and no worse than the majority of the population. One morning a Ministry of Food inspector came to Walsall police station and asked for a detective officer to accompany him to a certain butcher's shop where it was believed the regulations were being evaded. Edgar Storer was in the Walsall Police CID at the time and duly reported this request to his inspector and, as he knew that the butcher concerned supplied the latter as well as several other police officers, he was not surprised when the detective inspector told the man from the Ministry that there was no-one available at the time but that he would provide an officer as soon as possible. When a detective came in about 20 minutes later the detective inspector took him to one side and had a quiet word with him, after which he went scurrying out of the office. The DI apologised to the government official but said that the detective had had to go out on a serious criminal matter. Other detectives came back to the office from time to time and each time there was an excuse as to why they were not available to assist him. Eventually an officer was detailed to go with the patient official to the butcher's where nothing untoward was found, thanks to the efforts of the first detective. However, the official apparently realised that he had been 'fitted up' and returned a couple of weeks later with a detective from Birmingham. They went straight to the butcher's where he quickly found the illicit meat he had been looking for. The butcher was heavily fined and a number of Walsall police officers had to make do with the basic meat ration from then on.

Even where the police were not involved, there often existed an efficient early warning system:

> *Every now and then you would suddenly be told to keep quiet or people would grimace at you. Once my mother was in a dairy when somebody came charging in and grimaced at the manager who disappeared into the back and despatched a few riders, who jumped on their bicycles and were all over the town in no time at all. Then you would have found the most regulated ration system and anyone wanting anything off the ration would have been very firmly put in his place until the Inspector left from his visit a couple of days later[19].*

There are innumerable stories of policemen turning a blind eye to minor black market activities, especially in the country. It is claimed that, in one village in Devon, a shoulder of pork was regularly put aside to ensure the local bobby's complaisance. A contributor to Sadie Ward's book[20] recalls a similar ritual in another part of the same county:

> *I remember that we had some Devonshire cream delivered inside our front door, bang opposite the police station the very weekend after we arrived as evacuees. My father remonstrated with the dairy that Devonshire cream was on the taboo list for the war and what would happen if the police found out about it? The dairyman said that trouble would be unlikely since, if my father liked to watch him, he would see him dropping a container at the police station before crossing the road to deliver it to us.*

In fact, although most black market transactions took place in the towns and cities, the source of a lot of the goods was the country, especially where foodstuffs were concerned. Farmers were particularly well-placed. Although any dealing outside Ministry channels was illegal, there was a guaranteed demand and plenty of ways of meeting it. A cow might mysteriously injure itself and have to be slaughtered, the tally of sheep or pigs might be somewhat incomplete or foxes could cause havoc amongst the poultry. Large farmers would farm out their sheep to other, smaller farmers so that their movements were obscure and difficult to track down. One Kentish farmer took over a disused village slaughter house and, although there was no hard evidence of any illegal slaughtering going on there, the local bobby had some very shrewd suspicions. There was no doubt about the slaughter-house set up by a Hampshire farmer. This had a concrete floor and a tarpaulin roof, the whole being camouflaged as a rick of baled straw. The illegal activities were detected by a special constable who heard voices coming from what appeared to be an innocent straw stack and the sound of bones being sawn. Inside he found the carcases of a cow, two calves and three pigs. The farmer claimed that the animals were all lame but the magistrates were not inclined to believe this excuse and committed the farmer and his two sons to Winchester Assizes.

The Ministry of Food insisted that all the cherries grown in Kent – the Garden of England – had to be sold through proper channels at a price set by the government. However, the local police were well aware that a lot disappeared northwards on lorries which arrived at the orchards, the drivers of which happily paid an inflated price in cash for their load.

Although many commodities were in short supply during the war, crime was not one of them and, as we shall see in the next chapter, there was no moratorium on the sort of crimes and offences which traditionally occupied the police in more peaceful years.

11. With Felonious Intent

The new offences discussed in the previous chapter in no way diminished or supplanted those peacetime crimes and offences which had occupied the police since its inception more than a century previously, although the gravity of some (such as theft by looting) was increased by the circumstance of war while other offences took on a new dimension. In 1939 there had been just over 300,000 indictable offences known to the police in England and Wales and there was a marked drop in the first months of the war. But by 1943 the total had risen to 373,000 and continued to rise until it reached 478,000 in 1945. Most convictions in 1943 were for theft of one form or another, including burglary and housebreaking. Offences against the person had risen but little and only 29 persons were convicted of murder – a negligible figure when looked at against the casualties of war, both at home and in the various theatres of war. Convictions for homicide generally (murder and manslaughter) averaged around 99 per annum, with a peak of 122 in 1945, possibly as a result of servicemen returning from overseas.

It is interesting to note that Sir Philip Game, the Commissioner of the Metropolitan Police in his report for 1943, confirmed that the great bulk of crime in Britain consisted of 'burglary, house and shop break-ings and stealing of all kinds'. But he claimed that there had been little increase in crime in London since the beginning of the war and one must therefore assume that the overall increase referred to above took place almost entirely in the provinces.

In the early part of the war, many hypotheses were advanced as to the reason for the perceived crime trends. Where increases had been recorded, these were put down to the blackout, the presence of evacuees swelling the normal criminal population, the lack of parental supervision and the fact that many schools were operating part time by 1941. Where there had been decreases, these were attributed to full employment on war work and the additional police supervision provided by the enrolment of Police War Reserves. It was suggested that improvidence, rather than want or viciousness, was the principal causal factor in the increase in war-time crime. Certainly the police

289

appear to have been better able to combat crime in those more law abiding days. Leonard Winter, who was a detective inspector in Harrogate, recalls that the CID in his force was expected to have a detection rate of at least a 90%, otherwise all leave was suspended. It must be said, however, that this does not square with the national 'clear up' rates for the war years which were rarely more than 75%. In the Metropolitan Police District, the clear up rates averaged around 30% between 1941 and 1945[1].

So far as non-indictable offences were concerned there was a significant drop throughout the war years as compared with 1939, when there was a total of nearly 600,000 prosecutions. Of these, 360,000 were traffic offences and, with the diminution of private motoring, this number had dropped to a mere 92,000 by 1944 when the total number of prosecutions for non-indictable offences amounted to 291,000 – less than half the 1939 figure. However, these figures were augmented by prosecutions for offences against the Defence Regulations, notably lighting offences, so that the grand total in fact remained very similar throughout the war at around 700,000.

Murder was a comparatively uncommon crime in those more innocent days with an average of 128 reported cases resulting in an average of 25 convictions in each of the war years. Many of these were domestic matters or of the *crime passionnel* type. A typical example was the Exeter case in which the body of a NAAFI canteen manager was found in a hotel bedroom with six bullets in his body. The victim had been conducting an affair with a civil servant's wife who had finally left the marital home for her lover. The civil servant went to the hotel to appeal to his rival in love to 'give him a break.' But the philanderer merely laughed and said, 'You can have your wife back when I've finished with her.' Upon which the by now very uncivil servant pulled out a revolver which he had obtained by (falsely) claiming to be a Home Guard instructor and shot the other dead. Since *crime passionnel* has never been recognised in English law (in fact, contrary to general belief, it is not an excuse in French law but the presence of overwhelming passion or emotion may be regarded as an extenuating circumstance when deciding the penalty), the civil servant was duly sentenced to death. However, the jury made a strong recommendation for mercy. In another case in which a returning serviceman found his wife with her lover and shot her it was conceded by the prosecution that 'if a man finds his wife with a lover and in his fury and red anger kills one of them on the spot, the charge may be reduced to manslaughter.' In this particular case the judge accepted this argument and found the defendant guilty of manslaughter rather than murder, sentencing him to 15 months jail. In yet another case, similar to those which have just been described, the jury returned a verdict of manslaughter, but the trial judge (Charles) objected strongly to this verdict and argued that it would create a dangerous precedent if a husband, who returned and killed the wife who had been unfaithful while he was away in the forces, was then effectively exonerated by the court. He reinforced this viewpoint by sentencing the killer to five years on the grounds that '*If manslaughter it be ... it is a bad case of manslaughter.*'

Another murder in which love, passion and jealousy played a part was that which occurred at Portslade, near Brighton in March 1943. The assailant was a 25 year old Canadian soldier and the victim a married Englishwoman whose husband was a prisoner of war in Germany. The Canadian discovered that the object of his affections had another Canadian lover and he shot her dead with a Bren gun which he had stolen from the Home Guard, wounding his rival at the same time. He was found guilty of murder and was duly hanged for his crime.

In Yorkshire, a farmer was returning home late one night when he was shot in the back. He carried on home, however, and died in bed the next day. The bullet was a homemade one and it was believed that the assailant was the father of a young girl the farmer had 'wronged.' A search of the suspect's home revealed a mould for making bullets but this was of the wrong calibre and no charges were ever laid and the case remained officially unsolved.

These are but a few examples of the many cases in which the alienation of affections played a significant part. Another common cause was (and still is, come to that), abuse or ill-treatment. The victims were usually the weaker members of the public – women and children – and evacuees were particularly prone to this sort of maltreatment. Occasionally the worm turned, as occurred in Derbyshire when a 15 year old evacuee from Manchester was charged with the murder of the 58 year old farmer with whom he had been billeted. A known drunkard, the farmer had no other help on his 170 acre farm but the boy who was overworked and verbally abused. Eventually the boy took a swing at his tormentor with a hoe which caught him on the side of the head. The pathologist gave evidence at Derby Assizes to the effect that the blow had not been sufficient to kill the man but that he had probably fallen awkwardly, striking his head on the ground. The jury found the boy Not Guilty, a verdict which drew unprecedented applause from the public gallery, which in turn provoked a rebuke from the judge. It is questionable whether the public would have applauded such violence in peacetime and one may, perhaps, detect here a slight swing in public attitudes. With the benefit of hindsight and with a better knowledge of the unhappy experiences of many evacuees, one is mildly surprised that there were not more cases of this nature.

In other homicide cases, it was the ready availability of arms and munitions which facilitated the crime. One can but wonder what was in the mind of the 19 year old Rochdale man who obtained a large quantity of ammunition and hand grenades and stored them in his father's cellar. These were placed in a box with a wire connected to the pin of one of the grenades, so arranged that the opening of the box would cause the pin to be extracted. When the police called at the premises to search it in response to 'information received', an explosion occurred, killing a detective inspector and a detective sergeant and injuring several other police officers. The offender was sentenced to 7 years penal servitude for manslaughter.

Mention has already been made of the problems arising from the presence of large numbers of foreign troops in this country and it will come as no great surprise to learn that they were responsible for a number of serious offences, including murder. When Sergeant Avis of the Bognor Regis police went to investigate a reported burglary in the town, the offender, a Canadian soldier, shot him dead. The murderer was subsequently hanged for the crime. In all, six Canadian soldiers were found guilty of murder by the British courts during the war years and were hanged. There were also a few cases of murder in which the supreme penalty was not exacted and several cases of manslaughter. In all these cases the Canadian authorities assumed responsibility for ensuring that the accused was properly defended and had every chance and, in most cases, the Canadian government made unsuccessful representations for clemency.

Of course, the Canadians were not the only ones to be involved in serious crime. In December, 1944, just outside Norwich, Sir Eric Teichman, a distinguished traveller, diplomat and expert on Chinese affairs, had just finished lunch when he heard the sound of shots coming from the direction of a wood on his land. On investigating he came across two American servicemen armed with stolen carbines, apparently intent on a little poaching. Sir Eric challenged them, whereupon one of the GIs cooly aimed his weapon at the land-owner and shot him dead. A joint investigation by the Norfolk Constabulary and the US Army authorities resulted in two men being arrested, one of whom, George E Smith Jr., was charged with the murder of Sir Eric. He was tried by court martial the following January when he was shown to have been a constant thorn in the side of the authorities, having been court martialled eight times previously. Smith remained cool, even cocky, throughout the trial and, despite a plea of insanity, was convicted of the murder and sentenced to death.

Earlier that same year, two American soldiers appeared before a court martial at Ashford (Kent), charged with the rape and murder of a local 15 year old girl. The court was told that both men had been drinking heavily on the night of 22 August and, when they left the public house about 10.15 pm, they met the girl and went with her into a field. One of the Americans told the court that he had held the girl down while the other had sex with her. He thought she had fainted and claimed that she was still alive when they left her in the field where her body was found the next morning. The court martial disbelieved this tale and found both men guilty of all the charges; they were sentenced to death by hanging.

Sometimes crimes were not all they seemed to be. Four soldiers from the 6th Royal Tank Regiment discovered the body of one of their comrades in an air raid shelter at Eastling (Kent) and were promptly placed under military close arrest on suspicion of having been involved. Detective Constable Bob Stewart attended from Sittingbourne police station and found that the body had a thin belt tied tightly around his neck. The knuckles on the corpse were badly scraped and it looked as though he had put up a spirited fight before being overpowered by his assailant. The full machinery of a murder investigation was set in motion and the body was subjected to a thorough post mortem examination by the eminent Home Office pathologist, Sir Bernard Spilsbury. It was he who decided that the pathological evidence pointed clearly to this being in fact a case of suicide, the soldier having tied the belt around his own neck and garroted himself. As for the abrasions to the knuckles, close examination revealed that these were the result of the hands having been nibbled by rodents after death. Although this was an unusual and somewhat macabre example, suicides were not uncommon among servicemen, usually by shooting.

Living in violent times, the prevalence of assaults and woundings was perhaps to be expected. Most offences of this nature arose out of inter-service, inter-regiment or international rivalry. The army fought with the RAF and the Royal Navy, the soldiers fought amongst themselves and an enormous number of brawls involved British and Allied troops, especially the Americans, of whom many Britons were intensely jealous. One American airman remembers that the first casualty of the war on his base was at the hands of the British, in the shape of a soldier who arrived back from North Africa to find a GI in his bed with his wife. The British soldier threw the American out of a second-storey window and the fall killed him, an impulsive act for which the Tommy served a prison sentence.

In a Britain unused to problems of race and colour, the populace was totally unprepared for the vicious and violent attacks made by white GIs on their black comrades and such attacks were sadly all too common. A woman living in Weymouth remembers two horrifying incidents within a week. One night, staying with friends after attending a dance at a US Army camp, she heard 'the most awful screaming.' The next day it was discovered that a black soldier had been castrated by his white comrades for dancing with a white girl. As this was a predominantly southern unit with a 'Southern Gentleman' in charge, the offenders were merely transferred to different units and the matter never came to the attention of the civilian police. A few days later, climbing down from the pier for a swim, the same woman found herself treading on a dead black man with a knife in his back. He had apparently been guilty of a similar 'crime'[2].

In the years immediately preceding the war there had been a worrying spate of gang fights in London and some other large cities, in which rival gangs fought each other for control of the gambling and vice rackets. These did not cease with the outbreak of the war; on the contrary, rationing and general shortages made black market dealings extremely lucrative and provided a further impetus to this sort of non-military violence. The use of guns was, however, quite rare, the knife and the razor being the preferred weapons. But this was not always the case where American or Canadian deserters were concerned, many of whom made very free use of firearms when carrying out robberies. Unused to this phenomenon, the British judges and magistrates were at first unsure how to tackle the growing problem of armed robbery but, before long, they demonstrated that they were prepared to jail a man for the mere possession of a firearm. It is no coincidence that, after 1945 when the British troops began to return home and the North Americans left for their homeland, the incidence of robberies and assaults involving the use of firearms decreased significantly.

The crime which is nowadays commonly referred to as mugging is no new phenomenon; indeed, it is deeply rooted in our history and was practised by highwaymen and footpads centuries ago. All that has changed is the name – a euphemism for robbery with violence. With the introduction of the blackout in 1939 there arose a spate of robberies on the public highway. One London gang used to wait at main line railway stations, acting as if they were a group of revellers making their way home. On meeting a likely target some would good-naturedly throw their arms around him, pinning his arms to his sides while another took his wallet. If the victim resisted he would be beaten senseless and left in the road where he ran the very real risk of being run over by a car being driven by the light of its inadequate, hooded lights.

The relatively wealthy Americans were the preferred subjects for this sort of attack and, in many cases, it was their weakness for the female of the species which led to their downfall. It was quite common for a prostitute, or a girl pretending to be of easy virtue, to lure a lusting and unsuspecting GI into a dark alley, where her accomplices set upon the unfortunate man, violently separating him from his wallet and the coveted cash and no doubt effectively damping his ardour. When two English soldiers were found guilty of assaulting and robbing a US soldier of £10 in Leicester, they were sentenced to one month's imprisonment and nine strokes of the birch. They offered what was becoming a standard defence in such cases – they had been offended by the American's blatant display of wealth and the unwelcome attentions he was paying to a young lady[3]. In another case, three English civilians were jailed for systematically robbing at least seven US soldiers. Their method was to wait outside the railway station at night, pretending to offer a taxi service. When hired by GIs they would drive them to a lonely spot and rob them[4].

In other cases, unbridled lust resulted in cases of rape and sexual assault. Once again, the influx from North America was held largely to blame, perhaps understandably since, being separated from their wives and girl friends across the Atlantic, many of these young men were unable to restrain their sexual impulses, especially if there was any suggestion of complaisance on the part of the eventual victim.

The well-known propensity for the Americans to indulge in illicit sex occasionally led to unwarranted charges being levied against them. In May, 1944, a court martial sentenced a Negro GI to death for raping a woman in a village near Bath. According to the victim, the offender had knocked on her door late at night to ask the way to Bristol. On going outside in her nightdress and coat to point out the way, she was pushed over a wall into a field and raped. The GIs story was that he had had intercourse with her twice before in the same field and had paid her £1 each time for her 'services.' On this occasion, however, she wanted £2 and, when he refused to pay, claimed he had raped her. Fortunately for the American, the *Daily Mirror* took up his case and amassed 30,000 signatures on a petition for clemency. In the end, General Eisenhower set aside the conviction on the grounds of insufficient evidence, a decision which, from a study of the facts half a century later, seems to have been more than justified. Despite the animosity directed at the Americans from many quarters, this was one occasion where a GI owed his life to British public opinion[5].

One Kent woman complained to the police that she had been raped by a negro GI and enquiries led to a strong suspect. It was decided to put him up for identification and the victim was duly asked to attend an identity parade at the camp. After carefully examining the row of dusky faces she confessed her inability to pick out her assailant as '... they all look the same in the dark!' Another 14 year old girl returned home late one night and, in response to her parents' irate enquiries as to where she had been, claimed she had been raped on the cliff top at Ramsgate. She was duly interrogated by the local detective sergeant who, scenting that something was not quite right, asked, 'Have you been raped before?'

'Oh yes,' came the reply. 'Often!'

Some sexually-motivated men content themselves with merely exposing their genitals to unsuspecting females. One such menace was in the habit of stalking Albert Street, Llanelli during the blackout, wearing nothing more than his shoes. Special Constable Cross determined to put an end to this man's adventures and so, one night when Albert Street was on his beat, he lay in wait. Several long weary hours later he was rewarded with the sound of footsteps and a dim, nude figure appeared in the gloom. On the spur of the moment Special Constable Cross adopted a singular but effective method of dealing with the offender: using his sturdily-made police issue torch he hit the startled nudist hard where it would hurt most and then ran! A large dent in the torch and a complete cessation of the 'flasher's' appearances bore testimony to the efficacy of this novel crime prevention initiative. Shortly afterwards Mr Cross was conscripted into the services but his battered yet still effective torch gave sterling service with his family (who knew nothing of the incident) for the rest of the war.

Although there was in fact little increase in most types of crime, the black-out and the general atmosphere of anxiety gave rise to a largely unwarranted fear of crime. The trepidation experienced by many women when travelling alone in blacked-out trains was almost always unfounded. The wife of an RAF pilot, in her early twenties, travelling at night from Ipswich to Stroud was cared for the whole way by servicemen, each of whom handed her on to another group or individual. Five Hussars crowded onto one seat so that she could stretch out and sleep on the other. Unfortunately this happy state of affairs came to an end when she arrived at Stroud at 6.30 am and lay down in the waiting room to await daylight.

> *A local bobby sat with me for protection, I thought, but he ran his hand up and down my thigh so obviously I was wrong.'*

Another young train passenger was more fortunate when, at 2 am her train came to a halt at Warrington instead of carrying on to her destination in Manchester. Having made her way to Weaste she took an all-night tram to a station where there was a taxi full of young airmen who were going her way. The taxi driver was prepared to take her as well 'at her own risk' and she was not encouraged by a cry from the airmen of 'Oh good, a girl!' but she was reassured when she learned that the cocker spaniel belonging to one of the airmen had had four pups on the train and they were unable to keep the bitch contented because they couldn't manage to hold her and her pups on their own. The relieved woman found herself placed in charge of both bitch and pups and had her fare paid by the grateful airmen[6].

So far as organised crime was concerned, by the time the war was but a matter of months old, three distinct trends could be distinguished. Firstly, thieves were becoming more mobile, they were turning their attention to the opportunities which arose in the process of social change and, finally, they were increasingly exploiting the criminal possibilities of business and vice versa. The role of rationing and the black market as catalysts in all three was decisive[7]. Whereas before the war around half the major thefts occurred in private houses, this decreased after 1940 to less than a quarter, the emphasis now being on warehouses and the theft of goods vehicles. The reason for this is clearly the fact that consumables are much easier to dispose of in a time of shortages than works of art, jewellery, etc. There was also a change in the size of the gangs involved; whilst most pre-war crimes were committed by individuals or groups of two or three, it now became common for gangs of up to six 'cunning, ruthless and well-informed criminals' to be involved, many of whom were able to put military training to unlawful advantage.

The blackout was, of course, a boon to the burglar and by 1941 there had been a 26% increase in the number of persons convicted for breaking and entering. Bill Cavey, of the Metropolitan Police was naturally suspicious when he saw two men carrying large and obviously weighty suitcases and went to question them but, on seeing him, they made off at great speed. After a chase he caught up with one of them and, on opening his suitcase, found it contained rolls of material. The suspect was closely questioned, as a result of which a house in the area was raided and found to contain a large quantity of woollen material stolen from a nearby factory. The factory owners were delighted to get most of the stolen property back, especially as fabrics were in short supply, and offered to have a suit made up for the constable, out of whichever bolt of cloth he preferred. The officer had had his eye on a very nice grey worsted suiting but, when he asked if he could have that, he was told that, unfortunately, the CID had already taken that particular roll and he had to choose an alternative.

Many of those involved in breaking offences were amateurs and not a few of these were servicemen, made daring by their new status.

> *They caught the two silly lads who broke into the canteen – only 20 and 21. I was talking to a thoughtful young sergeant, and he said, 'The Scotties here have a bad name for wanton damage and mischief, but civilians have really no idea the trouble the 20/21s are to the Army. In towns and cities (like Glasgow, say), the lads have just run wild since leaving school, with fathers away, mothers working – tempted often by big wages, and wasting as they earn – the blackout and a mob spirit. Then they come into the Army, know restraint for the first time, and break out in little mad sprees, difficult to control, hard to pin down on anyone – or even on a group.*[8]

Len Winter was a detective sergeant at Skipton around the time of Dunkirk and noted a considerable increase in cases of housebreaking when troops began to be based in the area. There had been reports that a 'Gentleman Farmer' type had been seen near the scene of several of these burglaries and, when he saw a man who answered this description in a local pub, he talked him into 'accompanying him to the police station.' The suspect had an educated accent and a very definite air of authority, so much so that the local police superintendent addressed him politely as 'Sir' when he questioned him. However, once he was in the station, the suspect freely admitted that he had been responsible for a lot of the burglaries, proving that one should not look for stereotypes.

In Harrogate, the hotels were full of elderly, genteel ladies, who were regarded as easy prey by some. One ostensibly respectable man who claimed to be a doctor, used to befriend the old ladies and then, during lunch, would slip up to their rooms and steal their possessions. He was arrested and put up for identification, which presented problems for the police as he was 84 and, unusually for those days, sported a beard. He was eventually convicted and given nine months imprisonment, the judge adding, 'I don't suppose you will ever come out alive.' But he did, and went back to his old tricks before he was caught and sent down once more, this time dying in prison.

Another wealthy lady reported that a woman she had recently employed as housekeeper had run off with some of her jewellery. This woman was quickly traced and said she had sold the jewellery to two Leeds pawnbrokers. The first of these, a rather scruffy and seedy individual, readily admitted having taken the jewellery but the second, a much more up-market jeweller and pawnbroker, denied all knowledge. The detective making the enquiries returned to the loser who was waiting outside in a car with the superintendent. The woman got out of the car and had no difficulty in immediately pointing out her rings which were prominently displayed in the window, which rather undermined the pawnbroker's claims to be totally innocent and he was duly convicted of receiving.

It is a curious fact that there seems to have been an exceptional number of burglaries and related crimes committed by the guardians of law and order themselves. Encouraged no doubt by the blackout and by the large number of unoccupied furnished houses in many coastal areas, it is sad to relate that, in places, the crime reached almost epidemic proportions. It is all credit to the force that offences by police officers were investigated and prosecuted by their peers with the same, or greater, rigour as those involving others.

A particularly serious case arose in war-torn Folkestone, from which town the vast majority of the population had been evacuated, although the offences apparently had been taking place since 1935. Richard Crane was a constable in the Folkestone Borough force at the time and recorded his involvement in this case in his book:

> *A constable of similar age to me ... was discharged from the Borough Force soon after the war started for what I believe were domestic reasons. He remained within the district and, with his brother, ran a business removing Folkestone residents to other parts of the country... One summer evening ... I received instructions to await transport and go with another constable to Capel-le-Ferne, a village between Folkestone and Dover and keep watch at a bungalow for the return of the owner. He was the constable who had been discharged from the force... We had hardly settled down inside when there was a tapping at the window and ... we saw ... it was the local constable of the County police. We learned to our surprise he had been keeping surveillance at another bungalow in the village, also owned by our former comrade. At the County man's request, I accompanied him across the village to this second property and on the way he told me that a ... man had gone into the building. He thought it was the ex-policeman we had all been waiting for and had promptly gone to the bungalow and asked to speak to him. The wife ... had come to the door and told the village Bobby that her husband had gone across the fields. The local copper had then panicked and rushed over to where we were. I was a bit annoyed with our CID for not putting us completely in the picture. I went to the door of the bungalow and ... the door was opened by my ex-colleague's wife. She knew me and, in friendly tones, I asked to see her husband, using his Christian name... After a short period her husband came to the door. We exchanged greetings, after which he asked ... 'What do you want, Dick?' He was told I had been keeping observation on his other property and it was filled with stolen property and I would have to arrest him... I*

was sorry I had to take him in as one suspected of theft. He then imparted some astonishing news, alleging that 13 other members of the force had been involved in one way or another... At the Quarter Sessions, after [he] had received a prison sentence, his wife is said to have asked loudly, 'What about the others?' It transpired that the others had been concerned in shopbreaking: many of the shops were closed due to evacuation by the firms but goods had been left in them. Subsequently, other members of the force were interrogated by two senior Scotland Yard detectives and some were obliged to resign, while others avoided this degradation and remained in service with the police.[9]

As a result of this scandal, the chief constable of Folkestone resigned and was replaced by R C M Jenkins, a strict but fair disciplinarian, who went on to become the deputy chief constable of Kent after the war. The *Police Review* for 16 January 1943 takes up the story:

A sergeant and five constables have resigned from Folkestone Police as an alternative to dismissal as a result of the inquiry held by Mr R C M Jenkins, the new Chief Constable, assisted by two Scotland Yard officers into allegations made by a woman.

Last October Eric David Morgan, aged 28, a haulage contractor and a former Folkestone policeman, was sentenced to nine months hard labour for 32 cases of theft involving goods worth £1,592. His wife alleged that 13 other policemen had done the same thing while on night duty and had borrowed her husband's car to take the stuff away. Mr Jenkins stated: '... I was able to secure the assistance of Det. Insp. Hawkyeard and a sergeant ... The Scotland Yard attitude was that after so much delay (the first of these offences is alleged to have occurred on July 31st 1935) it was most unlikely that sufficient evidence to justify criminal proceedings would be forthcoming, and that the efforts should be towards clearing the Force of the persons concerned. If criminal proceedings were instituted and they failed .. it might then be difficult to deal with the person in a disciplinary manner. ... It was only after close and continued questioning that any admissions were obtained. Ultimately the

> *five constables ... made statements in which they admitted committing felonious acts while on night duty.... Sergeant Griffiths was alleged to have been concerned in certain cases ... but ... he strenuously denied the allegations. ... however I found ... that he was unfit to remain in the force and I called for his resignation... He resigned forthwith. ... Morgan had made certain allegations concerning five other men who are still serving in this force and after four days of exhaustive enquiry I was satisfied that there was no evidence whatever against any of these officers'.*

This affair brought the whole of the borough force into disrepute, especially as there was a possibility that some of those involved in this wholesale wave of burglaries and theft were still serving. The authorised establishment of the entire force was only 73 and Richard Crane talks bitterly of the gossip and innuendo which followed every member of the force for a long time after the case was closed, even where they were totally innocent. This case undoubtedly encouraged the Home Office to pursue the proposal to amalgamate all the borough forces in Kent into the County force the following year.

Although this was one of the most spectacular cases of serious malpractice by the police during the war, it was by no means unique. In 1943 four Glasgow constables were convicted of the theft of sugar and syrup from a dockside shed and were sentenced to 60 days imprisonment, while the following year two Coventry constables were each sentenced to four years penal servitude for shopbreaking and theft. There were undoubtedly other cases involving serving police officers which did not make the national press and it must be assumed that these cases represent just the tip of what could be quite a large iceberg. The police force has always had its black sheep and probably always will; as the police service comprises a cross-section of the population, it has to be expected that there will be the occasional maverick and it does seem that the police during the war years were affected by the same diminution of moral standards as that which afflicted the nation as a whole – a subject we shall be returning to a little later on. It also seems quite clear that there was more than a little corruption in the police force at this time – a situation which came to a head 15 to 20 years later with a series of corruption scandals which resulted in the passing of the 1964 Police Act. 'Bribery' or 'sweeteners' could take the form of the odd game bird left on the back doorstep of a rural constable or, at the other end of the scale, considerable sums of money passed to a few senior detectives, especially in the big cities where crime was very much organised. Provincial policemen always had reservations about their colleagues in the Metropolitan Police, whether justified or not. One man, suspected of stealing from hotel rooms, told Detective Inspector Len Winter of the West Riding force that he was working for a crime syndicate in Hatton Garden who sent him on stealing sprees 'up North.' Anything he stole was immediately passed on to a bookie at the racecourse for transporting to London so that he would not have anything incriminating on him if he were caught. This information was duly passed to the Metropolitan Police for them to make further enquiries and, in due course, the reply came back that the allegations were all a fabrication. The Yorkshire detective had found the prisoner's story very convincing and still wonders whether this was indeed the case, or whether somebody's palm had been greased. As he says, we shall never know.

Corruption was obviously not confined to the police. The war increased the opportunities for what we now refer to as white collar crime and the two occupations most susceptible to this form of criminality (as judged from the number of prosecutions) seem to have been the managerial side of the building industry and the civil service (including local government). So far as the government employees were concerned, the unlawful activities seem to have been concentrated in three main areas: the sectors responsible for coping with the social problems arising out of war damage; those in charge of food distribution; and the people whose job it was to place contracts with outside firms. The various types of government grant given to help those whose property had been damaged by enemy action was an area wide open to abuse, both by the claimants and by those who controlled the issue of the grants, as was the food distribution system and many officials (and their contacts) made small fortunes. Unscrupulous building contractors joined forces with corrupt local government officials to obtain favourable treatment in the award of contracts for construction and repair work. The contractors made huge profits, a proportion of which found its way into the pockets of their accomplices in the town hall.

Fraud is not a specific war-time offence but the peculiar conditions which applied at that time were quickly seized upon by unscrupulous individuals. For example, the *Kentish Express* issued a warning in its issue of 22 January 1943 that an unauthorised person dressed in soldier's uniform was collecting from house to house and in the street, ostensibly for the Ashford Penny-a-Week fund. The Commissioner of the Metropolitan Police, in an article written for an American journal and reported in full in the *Police Review* for 8 December 1944, referred to a *'subtle class of crime,'* a broad definition of which he gave as

> *the exploitation of the community for private gain and would include such crimes as blackmail, fraud, forgery, share-pushing, embezzlement and the confidence trick. ... These crimes cannot be prevented by the vigilance of the uniformed police officer in the streets ... they can only be dealt with and discouraged by subsequent detection.*

The introduction of specific wartime measures gave rise to other forms of fraud such as a spate of bogus gas mask inspectors, ARP workers and firemen. The law came down particularly hard on those who masqueraded as servicemen or wore other uniforms for improper purposes, although often these were merely men who were trying to impress a lady. The *Police Review* in 1941 referred to 'human ghouls ready to profit from the suffering of their fellow men and women' by looting and pretending to be bomb victims. A considerable number of women were charged with spinning heart-rending stories about bombed-out homes and lost relatives. Since this despicable business was likely to deprive genuine claimants from receiving assistance, the *Police Review's* contributor went on to suggest that the appropriate penalty for such villainy would be flogging for a first offence and shooting for a second! The shortage of batteries for torches (essential items in every household during the blackout) resulted in 'spivs' selling dud batteries to an unsuspecting public. There was a spate of advertisements for 'luminous' paint and buttons which, in almost every case, were totally ineffective. Moreover, the war did little to stem the common practice of fraudulent clocking-in at factory gates, although strenuous efforts were made to tighten up procedures.

A favourite target for con-men and other fraudsmen was, of course, the American serviceman who was seen as rich and gullible and whose lack of familiarity with the complicated British monetary system and coinage provided an added opportunity for sharp practice. A woman who was a teenager in Beeston (Nottinghamshire) during the war recalls being very angry when she saw a waitress serve an American with a 3d cup of coffee and then give him only five shillings (25p) change from his £1 note. The GI was quite unaware that he had been rooked. Another example of sharp practice was the use of a separate tariff in some cafés for the GIs. One café proprietor told an English airman that the rate was '2d a cup of tea for you and 3d for a meat pie. For the Yanks it's 4d a cup of tea and 6d each the pies.' The outraged airman told the Americans how they were being overcharged and they expressed their displeasure by wrecking the café which never reopened. It is said that the proprietor called the police but they took no action, presumably regarding the damage inflicted as his just deserts.

A developed fondness for Scotch whisky cost a number of GIs dear. When an honest publican asked the proper price of £1 for a bottle, an indignant American refused it as he wanted 'the real stuff' which he knew from experience cost £5. Other Americans were sold bottles of an amber coloured liquid which had never seen the inside of a distillery, paying £5 for a pint of cold tea if they were lucky, or some lethal moonshine liquor if they were not. There were numerous cases of servicemen being temporarily blinded by some of the toxic whisky substitutes sold to them.

Getting more canny, it became a practice to ask to taste the liquor before buying it but even this was not foolproof. Some American servicemen were mystified when the bottle of excellent quality whisky which they had bought in good faith, curiously ran dry after the first glass. Closer inspection revealed that the bottle had been filled to the neck with cold tea, a wax seal applied and just the neck topped up with the genuine article.

If their fondness for hard liquor did not get the GIs into trouble, their apparently insatiable appetites for female company often did the trick. A typical case involved a female of easy virtue who met a GI one night in a pub and, after he had bought her a number of drinks, offered to repay him 'in kind.' She took her escort to a secluded air raid shelter where she invited him to remove his trousers while she also undressed. However, as soon as he had dropped his pants, she grabbed them and ran off, complete with well-filled wallet. Unable to pursue her for obvious reasons, the unfortunate GI could only shout for help and, when the police arrived, they quickly found his trousers, minus the wallet. Unfortunately for her, the woman was rash enough to return to the same pub a few nights later when the GI was there with some friends. They grabbed hold of her and threw her unceremoniously into a static water tank where she might have drowned but the for timely arrival of the police, who had been called to the disturbance, and who rescued a wet and chastened female from a watery grave.

If the traditional British public house was a great draw for our over-seas comrades, the curious British licensing hours – a relic of the previous war – were a constant source of perplexity. Even before the war, the tight restrictions and short 'permitted hours' were a stimulus to ingenuity and various ploys were used to circumvent or avoid these constraints. The greater freedom granted registered clubs was one way those who so wished could obtain a drink after the pubs had closed and another '30s phenomenon which extended into the early war years was the bottle party. Since even members of a club could not obtain alcoholic beverages after 11.30 pm, the club owners devised a system whereby, in theory, the members would purchase drink during licensing hours and then consume it later. The system involved members tele-phoning their orders during permitted hours to a club official who passed on their requirements to a licensed victualler who, in turn, reserved and marked the ordered drink in the name of the customer. When the drinks were asked for, a boy messenger was sent to collect them from the supplier. This ingenious process was completely within the law and was used by a number of respectable clubs. However, there were many more clubs and completely unlicensed establishments which were conducted with complete disregard for the licensing Acts. Approved customers paid an entrance fee and a bottle of their chosen liquor was put aside for them against payment of the very high price charged. Since this practice was illegal, a great deal of police time was devoted to stamping out these unlawful drinking dens, especially in the West End of London. The outbreak of war did nothing to reduce this problem; on the contrary, the need for relaxation led, if anything, to a proliferation of this sort of artifice, fuelled by the high wages earned on some forms of war work. Whether due to the pressure of other work or merely through laziness, it is clear that the police in some areas did little to curb these breaches of the licensing acts. Eric St. Johnston describes how, as the newly-appointed sub-divisional inspector for Chelsea, he walked into eight clubs in plain clothes, had a drink and walked out again, proving they were nothing more than unlicensed public houses, a situation he lost little time in rectifying[10]. The Defence Regulations strengthened the hand of the police in this matter and, in August 1940, the Home Secretary announced that he had made orders under Regulation 42C for the closure of six bottle parties, going under the exotic names of Boogey-Woogey, El Morocco, Hi-de-Hi, etc.

The secret of the illegal bottle parties was their mobility. Normally, before any action was taken against such activities, observation had to be kept on the premises for several nights to counter any claim that it was merely a private party but these organised events moved from house to house, from flat to flat. One London policewoman who had done a lot of club work noticed an unusual amount of activity at a certain house and thought she recognised some of people so she hailed a taxi and, in the time-honoured tradition cried, 'Follow that car!'   S h e eventually arrived at some empty premises where a party was in full swing, the guests having been sent initially to the first address from where they had been redirected to another in order to put unwanted visitors (especially the police) off the scent. The observant police-woman managed to get a message back to her station and a successful raid quickly followed.

Alcohol abuse had been a problem for a number of years, especially among members of a certain strata of the population, and this was aggravated by the feelings of despondency aroused by the Depression. Cases of drunkenness, in the form of being drunk and incapable or drunk and disorderly, had been a police problem virtually since the formation of the modern police force, a century earlier. With the onset of the war, the Temperance Council of the Christian Churches appealed in *The Times* for the exercise of restraint in drink during the war and called for the reimposition of the restrictions which had been applied in 1914 (and only partially lifted in the inter-war years). In fact, reported cases of drunkenness varied widely, many areas experiencing a considerable drop in this type of offence in 1939/40. In Glasgow, it was reported that there had been an increase in the number of persons arrested for being drunk and incapable in 1940 but this was followed by a substantial decrease in 1941. The chief constable, Sir Percy Sillitoe, ventured that the shortage of supplies and the high price were deciding factors in this situation which he regarded as 'decidedly satisfactory', especially as the city was not distinguished for its sobriety – rather the reverse.

Where cases of drunkenness did occur, these tended to involve servicemen from the Antipodes or North America where even more restrictive licensing laws were, or had recently been, in force. The chief constable of Croydon complained in October 1940 about the number of incidents of drunkenness and disorder involving Canadian troops. However, with the passage of time, cases involving the Canadians decreased considerably and they came to regard the pub as a place where they could enjoy themselves and not just somewhere to get drunk. There is statistical support for this decline of drunkenness among the Canadians; in September 1942 the Canadian Military Head-quarters prepared a general 'Report on Discipline of the Canadian Army Overseas' which revealed that:

> *The most prevalent offence is absence without leave ... The next most prevalent class of offence is ... conduct or neglect to the prejudice of good order and military discipline... The third most prevalent offence is that of drunkenness which accounts for a remarkably small percentage of the whole.*[11]

Subsequent reports submitted in March 1943 and June 1943 confirmed this point and added that *'Drunkenness does not appear to be a very serious factor.'*

Drunks are always treated warily by the police as they seldom behave rationally and one is never too sure what they are going to do next, much in the same way as those suffering from a mental illness. Bill Henley, who served as a sergeant and, later, as an inspector in the East Sussex force, was called one day to a house where a man had apparently had a 'brainstorm' and had barricaded himself in an upstairs room, armed with an axe. Anyone trying to mount the stairs was met with a hail of glass shards, taken from the shattered skylight over the door. It was decided that the best plan would be to get the fire brigade to play a strong jet of water on the man so as to pin him to the wall while the policemen went in to subdue him and avoid anyone getting injured. This plan worked perfectly and the demented man was carried downstairs by two constables, one on either side. He was still struggling and began pumping his legs, shouting that he was riding a bike. 'Well, freewheel a bit, would you?', said one of the struggling policemen, 'We're going downhill now.' And the prisoner duly obliged!

Pilfering and petty theft have always been a problem but it seems clear that during the war there was a veritable epidemic of this sort of crime, possibly fostered by shortages and the existence of a black market on which goods could easily be disposed of. Whether this was entirely due to these general shortages, to an overall lowering of moral standards, or to some other cause, is not a question for us to delve into here. Suffice it to note that it existed and added to the already onerous workload borne by the police. Stealing from places of work was especially rife and the fact that such thefts could put the lives of servicemen in jeopardy appears to have made little difference. Dockyards seem to have been particularly prone to pilfering, sometimes on a wholesale scale. The police in such areas made full use of any 'stop and search' powers they possessed, occasionally with considerable success. Cases were reported of dockworkers carrying home bottles of spirits in the sleeves of their overcoats, other had stuffed ties, handkerchiefs, fabrics, paint, tools and foodstuffs in their pockets and tool bags. Many of the thieves were small-scale pilferers but there was a minor hard core consisting of true professionals. One Birkenhead docker was convicted after the police raided his home and discovered 250 items of stolen property, ranging from a cooking stove to cans of oil, clocks and even dog collars. Another docker was convicted of stealing 24,000 cigarettes, seven bottles of gin and 24 bottles of peroxide – the latter being a very rare commodity in wartime England and much in demand by would-be blondes.

It has been said that any movable object in a dockyard risked being stolen, the loss of which would often never be noticed by the losers. The chief constable of Birkenhead summed up the situation by stating that

> *'...much of the thieving is...carefully thought out and varied and ingenious methods of concealment lead me to believe that a great number of offences will remain undiscovered'.*[12]

One Belfast shipyard 'matey' is reputed to have asked a workmate to come and see his new house. As he was leaving, the proud owner said to his mate, 'Well, Billy, what do you think of the house?'

Billy replied, 'It's great, Joe. When are you going to launch it?'.

The police did their best to control this pilfering, of course, but where every shift included a rush hour during which some 50,000 men, women and children, including some of the highest service ranks, experts of all kinds, foreign seamen, scroungers, dodgers, crooks and bookies runners passed through the dockyard gates, they could only touch the tip of the iceberg. The shortage of regular policemen meant that the job of supervising this flow of humanity was left to reservists, many of whom were no longer young and none too robust. Such a man was on duty at the Dee Street gate to Belfast harbour one day when the Assistant Chief Constable of the Royal Ulster Constabulary, in plain clothes, drove through. The constable made no effort to stop him so the ACC returned later with the Head Constable in charge of the police detachment at the docks to ask why he had not been stopped and checked on his arrival. The policeman on the gate replied, 'Ah, sure Sir, I know you are one of the big men in Shorts.' (Short Bros. was a major aircraft manufacturing firm, making the Sunderland flying boats). The ACC replied wryly, 'I wish I were. Tell him who I am, Head.' The man's supervisor lost no time in giving the chastened constable a short object lesson in the recognition of his own senior officers. The dockyards were not the only source of pilfered goods, of course. In 1942 the entire staff of five at the LMS Cremer Street goods depot in Shoreditch were charged with stealing sought-after goods from the depot, while other cases were detected at Fords, Ever Ready, London Transport, Romford Council, the Post Office, Berger Paints and even the Metropolitan Police canteens. Wireless sets and radio components, batteries, paint, foodstuffs, all found a ready market in wartime Britain, with no questions asked. And, for once, low pay and poor working conditions could not be blamed since many of the firms involved enjoyed good conditions and relatively high pay.

The response by the police was to launch raids on those industrial concerns considered by the management to be seriously at risk, that is to say, when the level of pilfering exceeded the company's tolerance level. Where it proved impossible or impracticable to carry out searches of staff when they knocked off, the police were compelled to embark on more laborious enquiries, lasting several months or even years. One investigation into thefts at a North London haulage contractor took nearly two years before the half-dozen culprits were identified and sufficient evidence had been amassed to arrest them. Between them these men had been systematically robbing the firm of around £40 each week.

It must not be thought that pilfering was confined to the lower paid shopfloor workers; managers, directors and other senior staff were also involved. At the depot set up in Shoreditch to supply meat to the Metropolitan Police canteens, the chief butcher was held mainly responsible for a spate of thefts, while the assistant manager had also been helping himself. At the Express Dairy, stolen goods were found on a security officer while a railway detective was found guilty of stealing £10 from the LMS. Obviously the amount of police resources which could be devoted to this sort of operation in war-torn Britain were limited and many of those who were caught felt that they had been merely unlucky, since 'everybody's doing it.'

Sometimes pilfering was regarded as justified where it was done for the best of intentions. A hospital worker in Sheffield offered to get the ambulance drivers something to eat after they had been on duty for many hours during the Blitz on that city. She made her way to the hospital kitchens which she found deserted but, rummaging around, she discovered a cold leg of lamb, some bread and butter and took these, together with some knives, down to the Lodge where the ambulance drivers were based. Using these purloined victuals she was able to provide the weary crews with a cup of tea and a sandwich. Some time later a couple of CID men arrived at the hospital lodge and were also offered a sandwich.

'By the way,' said one of the detectives, 'have you seen any strangers around here?'

'Why?' asked the hospital worker.

'Well,' came the response, 'they've had thieves up in the kitchen and they've lost some meat, some butter and some bread.'

The somewhat embarrassed worker had to tell the even more embarrassed policemen that they had just partaken of the stolen foodstuffs. As this misdemeanour was committed with the best of intentions the guilty party was let off with a severe reprimand by the hospital management.

Those who were not in a position to purloin the property of their employer supplemented their income (or made their living) by other means. The confidential reports submitted by chief constables to the Home Office in 1939 referred to an increase in pick-pocketing and a continuance in the theft of bicycles, despite an overall decrease in crime generally. As the war progressed so this problem of cycle theft (and the stealing of bicycle accessories) appears to have grown, largely due to servicemen taking them to return to their camps. Although often not of great value in themselves, these represented the only means of transport for many working men and women and their loss more than a mere inconvenience. Prams, too, attracted the attention of thieves. In one case in Norwich a woman left her three year old child in its pram outside a chain store while she popped in to make a quick purchase. On her return a few minutes later, both pram and infant were gone, the latter being found by the police soon afterwards in an air raid shelter. A statement issued by the Norwich City Police read:

> *Recently numerous perambulator thefts have been caused because of the difficulty of obtaining new 'prams' and the increased value of second-hand ones. The Norwich Police are keeping a special watch for perambulator thieves.*

Letters to *The Times* in 1940 referred to the number of beggars in London and elsewhere which appeared to be a source of disquiet. Many of these letters came from the clergy, sadly not always it seems inspired by Christian charity.

Crime in the rural areas was always low or non-existent (at least according to the local Bobby). If a country copper reported too many thefts his superiors would soon decide that he was not doing his job and he would very soon find himself trying doorhandles in some urban agglomeration. To avoid this dreaded possibility, the rural officer would get up to all sorts of tricks to keep his crime figures low. Constable Bert Ayers remembers there being a spate of chicken stealing on his patch during the war (chickens made a tasty and luxurious supplement to the niggardly meat ration). He managed to get these written off as 'natural causes' with the aid of a fox's paw, which he happened to carry on his person. Whenever a local farmer complained of chicken stealing the constable would ask him if he planned to go into Ashford market that week because, if he was, it was quite possible that he would bump into the divisional superintendent and mention the matter, so a crime report had to be made out. If the farmer was not planning to visit the market, the matter would be quietly shelved. So successful was the ploy that this officer was greatly embarrassed when a thief admitted 24 cases of poultry stealing on his beat, none of which had been officially reported to police headquarters! Another colleague recalls that, in 20 years, there was only one case of housebreaking on his rural beat.

Much of the chicken stealing could be put down to troops stationed in the area, trying to supplement their cookhouse rations. Sergeant Bill Henley used to tell how the Canadians were very adept at catching and dispatching poultry but were not always too bright. They were in the habit of plucking the bird on the way back to camp, leaving a trail of feathers like a paper chase. This tale is supported by the definitive Canadian work on the subject[13] which suggested that the Canadians did not regard chicken stealing as a particularly serious offence. One soldier is reported to have written home:

> *The English soldiers lived on hard tack, but that wouldn't do for Canadians, especially when farmers go to bed so early and cannot take their orchards and chickens with them ... so I and my mates lived like kings.*

No less a personage than the Canadian High Commissioner had this fact brought home to him somewhat forcibly one night when he dined with Lord and Lady Moyne at their West Sussex home. According to the High Commissioner, Mr Massey :

> *At dinner we ate two chickens which had been purloined by Canadian soldiers from the Moynes' poultry house, traced to their billet by a trail of white feathers, followed by the two girls and returned by the officer's order plucked, cleaned and dressed, to be eaten in part by a Canadian.*[14]

Another eminent person to witness the chicken stealing exploits of the Canadian troops was Captain John Hughes Hallett, the chief naval planner at Combined Operations Headquarters who hit upon the idea of getting himself attached to a Canadian unit, disguised as a private soldier, in order to find out what the grass roots view of the combined operations was. Describing the daily routine of the Queen's Own Cameron Highlanders of Canada to which he was attached, Hughes Hallett reported that:

> *... about 9 pm we had an unofficial meal which the Canadians called "lunch" and which normally consisted of one or two chickens stolen from a local farm and boiled in milk. After that we went to bed and slept the sleep of the just.*[15]

Poachers also managed to do very well out of the war and the odd rabbit was always a very acceptable addition to the family meat ration. *Country Life* magazine noted, in 1941, that as rabbits were regarded as a pest, no one was too bothered about the source of these animals. The village trapper charged 1/8 for a decent sized rabbit, with a refund of 2d if the skin was returned for him to resell. Inevitably, some people, including servicemen and avaricious townsfolk, began to look beyond the wild rabbit and grazing animals presented a tempting target. When one soldier was sentenced to 18 months imprisonment for this sort of offence, the judge made it clear that he was getting off lightly as the maximum sentence was 14 years penal servitude. Not surprisingly, the problem reached its peak around Christmastide when as many as 20 geese or 50 chickens would disappear from a single farm.

One Yorkshire farmer reported that he had had some sheep stolen and a van seen in the vicinity of the crime was traced to Pontefract. Detective Inspector Len Winter went with the farmer to a field owned by a Pontefract butcher where the farmer quickly identified his sheep from among the rest of the flock in the field. The butcher was very sceptical, pointing out that the farmer had identified the best animals, all of which were of very superior quality. At the subsequent court hearing much was made of this fact, it being alleged that the farmer had not in fact identified his own sheep but had merely indicated the best of the flock. Nevertheless, the offenders were convicted and given nine months imprisonment, it being stressed that a few years previously they could have been hung for this offence.

Officially sanctioned crime prevention was still in its infancy and potential victims had to make their own arrangements. Constable Bill Cavey recalls that the owner of a small Italian café in London's East End had a unique and effective system. On being told that his café had been broken into the owner was not unduly bothered. Very little food was kept on the premises and he knew that the burglars would not get away with much cash since he kept it all in 2/- and half-crown pieces. In all he had two tea chests full of coins, weighing the best part of a ton.

Young women, feeling themselves somewhat vulnerable, learned how to take care of themselves should they become the target of unwelcome attentions. One Sheffield nurse claimed that she never had any trouble with servicemen. If she heard anyone's footsteps she used to call out and explained :

> *Sergeant Rhodes showed us how to go on. He used to say, "Smack 'em. Anybody comes near you, doesn't matter, hit 'em." If anybody comes near, then you put your knee up, get him down. "Don't stand no nonsense," Sergeant Rhodes used*

to say, "Don't wait." I never had any trouble, only once and this is a laugh. I'm going up Spital Hill, and a pair of arms came right round me from behind and threw me into a doorway. He didn't do me any harm, he pulled me into a doorway but I didn't give him a chance. I swung round and hit him, straight into his chest. And then my hand slid down and I held his lapels. And I said to him, "What do you think you're doing?" And he said, "Good God, girl, there's a raid on. What are you doing out?" I said, "What are you doing?" He said, "I'm a Mobile – an Ambulance man." I said, "And I'm the nursing sister up the street." So he said, "You've just hit me." I said, "You're lucky. If you hadn't been as tall as you are, I'd have killed you."

One phenomenon noted by most observers in this period was the increase in juvenile crime and delinquency. As early as November 1939, the *Police Review* was reporting an increase in juvenile crime, especially shoplifting and blamed this on evacuation, coupled with the opportunities provided by the blackout and lack of distractions through the closing of places of entertainment. The emergence of gangs of hooligans was commented upon, including those formed from the 17,000 London evacuees in Northampton. This disturbing form of criminality did not decrease as time went on and prompted further comment in 1941 when a general increase in juvenile crime was reported, amounting to 55% of all crime in some areas. The Commissioner of the Metropolitan Police, in his report for 1940, noted that 45% of the 4,584 cases of looting in his area were committed by persons under the age of 21. Where a group of youngsters was brought before the juvenile court in Lowestoft in 1942, the emotive word 'looting' was avoided and they were charged with theft. But the chairman of the magistrates was having none of that;

It appears that there is a gang of these youngsters going about looting from bombed houses. It is a very serious thing and the magistrates feel that it is time a stop was put to it. So we are going to do a thing we have never done before since juvenile courts were instituted in Lowestoft. We are going to order four strokes of the birch for six of the boys (aged nine to twelve).

Despite this salutary lesson looting in the town continued and four months later two girls, aged ten and eleven, were found guilty of looting watch straps, darning silk and penholders from local shops.

Other forces reported a similar escalation in juvenile crime, an overall 41% increase being recorded. The offences committed by juveniles (defined as being those under 17 years of age) covered the whole gamut of misdemeanours, virtually all of which showed an increase during the war years. Outstanding amongst the crimes which showed a marked tendency to increase were theft, receiving and malicious damage (vandalism). It is ironic that, at a time when Hitler was doing his best to destroy as much British property as possible, our own young people were lending a hand to smash things up. In fact, it is now recognized that vandalism fosters further vandalism, that one broken window will quickly lead to the total destruction of the glazing, that one scrawled word will soon incite a veritable epidemic of graffiti. Damage to telephone kiosks was widespread, shelters were stripped of everything removable – wires, tools, bulbs, fittings – and even the mesh over the static water tanks cut and removed, rendering them even more dangerous to children. In the university towns of Oxford and Cambridge, the undergraduates appear to have refrained from the traditional pranks to a large extent and, in fact, the Cambridge University dispatch riders proved their worth during the Baedeker raids on Norwich and were described as the eyes and ears of the Regional Commissioner. Derelict houses offered endless opportunities for adventure games and no barriers, notices or police patrols could keep youngsters out of them. It is certainly true that there was more juvenile crime in the urban areas than in the countryside, despite the invasion of the latter by evacuees.

Shortages of desirable goods affected schoolchildren as much as their parents, although the craving may have been more for sweets and chocolate rather than drink and tobacco. Once group of boarders from the Bryanston School in Blandford (Dorset) thought they had found a way of supplementing their sweet ration when they heard that certain boxes of supplies held at a bomb dump at Tarrant Rushton airfield contained chocolate. The boxes concerned were, in fact, containers of supplies destined to be dropped to resistance fighters abroad, some of which did indeed contain foodstuffs, cigarettes and chocolate. Although the dump was patrolled by the RAF Police, a few adventurous boys cycled there on more than one night and succeeded in gaining entry to the airfield where they rifled the containers – not an easy task as they gave no indication of their contents, merely a code number. Constable George Woodsford of the Dorset Police was given the task of searching the boys' tuck boxes in which some incriminating bars of chocolate were found. There is some evidence that a number of hand grenades were also stolen and used for 'fishing' in the river which ran through the school grounds. A few boys were expelled but on the whole the miscreants were leniently dealt with by the court.

Gambling was widespread amongst youngsters under 14 in the air raid shelters and local toughs constantly fleeced their less 'wide' peers. Barbara Nixon[16] writes of seeing a child of less than two, still in nappies, dicing for halfpennies with girls of eight or nine and boys of 12. If they were stopped by responsible adults, they merely moved their activities into the toilet, which was unhygienic into the bargain. The same writer quotes a story about one gang of enterprising youngsters:

> *In one of the shelters ... all the equipment disappeared three times. It was puzzling as the shelter was locked all day and all night except when the [play] centre was in use... But clearly there must be some alternative means of entry. One afternoon, I and two wardens determined not to give up until we found it. We looked everywhere and got filthy ... After two and a half hours we found it. In the furthest cubicle of the lavatory bay there was a twelve inch gap between the wall and the ceiling. In the ordinary way it was too dark there for it to be noticed but if you crawled through that you dropped down into a completely disused and separate bay which, for some inexplicable reason, had been bricked off and forgotten. It had an emergency exit into an alleyway which could barely be seen from the outside. Here we found an amazing assortment of goods; very few of the toys but 50 cases each containing 500 metal boxes stolen from the firm next door, a gas stove, a billiard table lamp, sets of 'housey-housey,' blankets, saucepans, a chopper, and iron bars. Unfortunately we were seen climbing out and though we were certain that a lad called Snorty was one of the gang leaders we could not prove it as the hideout was never used again.*

The causality of this delinquency was attributed to various factors;

the lack of parental (especially paternal) control, reduced schooling, coupled with a general lowering of moral standards. Of these, the lack of the discipline associated with regular schooling and an excess of free time is the cause favoured by most contemporary commentators and subsequent writers. Schools in many places were closed with the out-break of war and the pupils and staff evacuated *en bloc* to safer areas. In most of these areas they remained closed as part of a deliberate policy, to make the premises available for other uses and to 'encourage' parents to evacuate their offspring. That this policy was at best a partial success may be gauged from the fact that, in London there were still some 80,000 schoolchildren at the end of 1940 and 68,000 in Manchester the following Spring. These children were left to run wild all day, especially as their parents were usually either in the services or engaged on war work. Not until the trickle back from so-called safe areas had become a steady stream did the education authorities have to take steps to provide some form of education. With few teachers remaining in these areas, the few reopened schools had to take pupils on a half-day basis; perhaps infants in the mornings and juniors in the afternoon. Lack of education, boredom and opportunities all combined to a degree of lawlessness among those of school age.

In those areas to which the children had been evacuated, the schools system was overloaded to the point of collapse and truancy was rife. Some writers were of the opinion that there was a reluctance on the part of the police in the areas receiving evacuees to prosecute the newcomers but, whilst this may have been so in some areas, in others the evacuees were subjected to very close scrutiny and any who over-stepped the mark were quickly brought before the courts. The Chief Constable of Northampton announced that he was taking drastic action to curb the criminal propensities of the 17,000 evacuees in his area and, in a single week in the autumn of 1939, 22 intractable and defiant youngsters were taken before the courts, mainly for shoplifting and receiving[17]. The police in the university towns of Oxford and Cambridge appear to have followed a similar policy and 30% of all juveniles prosecuted in Oxford in 1941 were evacuees, while in Cambridge, the number of juveniles prosecuted in 1940 increased by 50% over the previous year.

It is interesting to note that some observers seem able to blame the economic circumstances for increases in crime, whatever these circum-stances might be. Thus, before the war when unemployment was rife, it was this deprivation which resulted in crime, yet when the war brought full employment and high wages, it was this fact which was blamed. Asked to explain the correlation between high wages and crime, the proponents of this philosophy tended to fall back on well-worn clichés such as that propounded by the Medical Officer of Leeds prison :

> *...too much money without responsibility...leads in some cases ...to a lack of appreciation of property rights and values with regard to first one's own property and then to that of others.*[18]

In fact, the greatest increase in juvenile crime was occurring amongst those of school age who did not have access to these excessively high wages.   It must also be kept in mind that the vast majority of the offences were of a trivial nature, even if they were technically indictable, and arose out of a propensity for mischief and adventure rather than anything more serious. Even the Lord Chief Justice, Lord Caldecote, who was certainly no wishy-washy liberal, warned in 1942 of the danger of treating young offenders as the outcasts of society since they were more the victims of society than offenders against society. Certainly some juveniles were involved in serious crime but these were atypical and were concentrated on the larger cities such as London, Leeds, Liverpool and Manchester. But even smallish market towns had their gangs like the one rounded up in Maidstone responsible for the systematic and organised theft of cycles.   The stolen machines were taken to a garden shed where, in a matter of minutes, they were stripped, rebuilt using parts from other bikes, given a lick of paint and sold.

And bicycles were not the only means of transport which attracted the attention of thieves and 'borrowers,' even though, in this case, it was not necessarily young persons who were involved.   One peacetime crime which grew to unprecedented proportions during the war was the unlawful taking of vehicles without the owners' consent. Under the Larceny Acts it was necessary to prove that the thief had the intention 'permanently to deprive the owner' of any stolen property but, where a vehicle was merely taken for a 'joy-ride' or as a means of getting home, with a view to abandoning it later, there was obviously no such intention. Any prosecution for its theft was therefore doomed to failure and all the offender could be charged with was the theft of a small amount of petrol. Consequently, the 1930 Road Traffic Act introduced a new offence of 'taking a motor vehicle without the owner's consent' to cover this lacuna in the law.

The siting of military camps and airfields some distance outside the centres of population, and often in quite remote areas, meant that the temptation to take a vehicle or a bicycle to get back to camp was a very strong one for many servicemen. These unlawful 'borrowings' sometimes had unusual consequences as one young Herefordshire girl, whose parents ran a golf club, recalled. One evening in February, 1944 the family were peacefully listening to the wireless when the door of the living room was suddenly flung open and three strange men in khaki walked in, arguing and shouting at each other, one of them obviously being in great pain. It turned out that the intruders were American servicemen whose truck had run off the road nearby and was now lying upside down at the bottom of a ten-foot drop. The concerned family dressed the injured man's wounds as best they could but he refused to allow them to call a doctor and insisted on accompanying his friends on the three-mile hike back to their base. The reason became clear the next day when the police called to enquire about a missing American truck, apparently stolen the previous night[19].

The courts, too, were under stress, both from enemy attacks and from the pressure of work coupled with a shortage of staff. To save fuel some courts were closed down and amalgamated with another court while others moved into temporary accommodation. At Waltham Abbey the Petty Sessions (Magistrates' Court) was moved to a 1914 shed behind the police station, used as a recreation room, where the situation soon began to border on a farce, with the magistrates, court officials, police, press and witnesses all crammed into a single room. When a case was being heard, all witnesses waiting to give evidence had to leave the room and wait in the station yard, regardless of the weather which, in the winter of 1939/40 was extremely severe. Reason eventually prevailed and the court was allowed to move back into its normal accommodation in the County Court – provided no fuel was used to heat it!

A story in the London *Evening Standard* on 21 September, 1940 describes how the courts coped with the air raids which were then beginning to become more than just a nuisance:

> *Obedient to the siren, Marlborough Street went underground. Magistrate and clerk gathered up their papers and disappeared. I followed others out of the other door and down a flight of steps and found myself in the cells. The large and jolly gaoler jingled his keys and had his little joke. The skilly,*

he told us, as we arranged ourselves on the prisoners' plain plank beds, was on the hob and would be served at any moment.

Presently word came that the court was being resumed in another part of the cellarage. We wormed our way through devious passages and found the law's majesty in a sort of cave. Stout wooden struts strengthening the ceiling caused the proceedings to be presented in vertical slices, like pieces of cake. In one slice we saw the magistrate seated at the head of a kind of kitchen table, with the clerk nearby in another slice. The prisoner, a curly-haired and swarthy person with a foreign accent [was] pleading that he had no idea what went on in his own house in Soho.

Odd echoes of London night-raid life trickled down to our legal cellar in the stories which we were told there – a Canadian soldier emerging into the blackout from a deserted shop, carrying six bottles; a young woman in a public shelter with a pile of fur coats, silk stockings and other dress goods beside her.

A proposal made in June, 1940 to set up special War Zone courts, presided over by a stipendiary magistrate, to deal with cases of looting, etc. met with a very mixed reception. Some saw it as a halfway house to martial law –

'A bit like Hitler ... I suppose there will be a lot of innocent people condemned.' :

'You have to have something like that in a war – it's not like ordinary times." :

'I don't think there should be just one man ... if the man's an enemy of mine he'll have me ... shot for no reason at all.' :

'It's hardly fair, one man without a jury. He could turn it into a racket and get paid.' : 'It's the beginning of Fascism.' :

'We have to use the methods of the enemy in order to beat him;

in fact, driving out Satan with Satan. No, it seems to me it is
Fascism pure and simple – well, impure and very subtle.'

Overall there were 42% in favour of the proposal and 34% against it and the idea was quietly dropped.

The existing courts were subjected to a great deal of criticism for lack of sensitivity to the war time conditions. A visitor to the Fulham Court found it closed despite a notice stating that the court would sit from 10 am to 2 pm. He made enquiries and was told the court had adjourned until 3.15 pm. When the visitor returned at 3.15 pm he was told the court had finished for the day. This sort of cavalier attitude did much to make the general public feel that the courts were not taking the war seriously. On a more august level, in October 1940 not a little criticism was levelled at the Worcester Assizes which opened with all the traditional pomp and ceremony, including military trumpeters and police 'javelin bearers.'

So far as the Commonwealth forces were concerned, these were subject to the powers and jurisdiction of the British civil courts under the provisions of the Visiting Forces (British Commonwealth) Acts and the Army Act. These provided that :

> *A person subject to military law ... may be tried by any competent civil court for any offence for which he would be triable if he were not subject to military law.*

This worked well since the British and most Commonwealth legal and judicial systems were virtually identical and the Commonwealth troops had an inherited respect for British justice. So far as the Canadians were concerned, there was also the precedent of the First World War when, at the beginning, the Canadian were simply the troops of a self-governing colony and no-one thought of questioning their subjection to the jurisdiction of the British courts. As a result of this arrangement, many Canadian servicemen appeared before the British civil courts and, since their American cousins were dealt with by courts martial (the proceedings of which were seldom reported), it often seemed that the Commonwealth troops were always in trouble. Where Commonwealth servicemen were arrested by the police for an offence which could properly be called military, such as drunkenness, they were normally handed over to the military to be dealt with. But where the offence was a purely civil one, such as burglary, theft, rape or murder, the offender would be held in a civil remand prison until dealt with by a civil court. The offender could be sentenced to a period in a civil prison or handed over to the military for his sentence to be served in a detention barracks. Where the offence was murder, the offender could be hanged and, in fact, six Canadians were hanged by order of the British courts. But, on the whole, the British courts were exceptionally lenient towards Commonwealth troops where the offence was a comparatively trivial one. The magistrates appeared to take the view that here was a young man, who has come thousands of miles to help us in our time of trouble and severity would therefore be unwarranted. In fact, the leniency shown by the courts was such that, when two Canadians were found guilty of robbery with violence in the autumn of 1940, the court merely bound them over to keep the peace. In time senior Commonwealth officers became alarmed and made various attempts to discourage the British courts from showing misplaced kindness to delinquent troops and the matter was raised with the Home Secretary, Herbert Morrison by the Canadian High Commissioner.

Not all servicemen who committed crimes against the English criminal law were necessarily dealt with by the British courts. Under the provisions of the United States of America (Visiting Forces) Act, the American authorities retained the right to try by court martial any of their servicemen who broke the law in this country. It was argued that the American soldier was conscripted and sent overseas against, or at least without, his will. The American public would look with jealousy on the treatment he received while outside his native country and particularly any sentence imposed on him by a foreign court. It was also feared that, if American soldiers were tried in a British court and subsequently detained in a British prison, the court would be inclined to show undue leniency and that the United States Government would be obliged to assume responsibility for his defence[20].

In practice the system worked well; one of the first cases involving an American serviceman in East Anglia involved a US private who was court martialled for driving an army vehicle at a reckless and dangerous speed in Cambridge. He was found guilty of the involuntary manslaughter of a four year old boy and was sentenced to six months hard labour. However, it came to be the accepted rule that, where only American citizens were involved, an American court martial would deal with the matter, but where a British civilian was the victim the offender was often handed over for trial in a British court. The British policeman as always, tried to avoid arresting GIs causing trouble, giving the average Bobby a reputation for leniency and good-nature which, coupled with the fact that he was completely unarmed, was a constant source of amazement to the GIs and helped to foster the esteem in which the British law-enforcers were held.

This was a time of harsh penal regimes, including penal servitude, preventive detention and corrective training as well as the old-style Borstal, although it has to be admitted that, for some, conditions 'inside' were preferable to those they were accustomed to on the outside. Corporal punishment was also inflicted in 'suitable' cases and had numerous proponents among the police. The chief constable of Leicester advocated its use on those delinquents who had become so hardened that the 'benefits' of the probation system were lost on them; the chief constable of Bacup made a correlation between success in life and corporal punishment generously inflicted in youth, especially parental spanking. Critics of this form of punishment included the chief constable of Plymouth who believed it was no remedy for juvenile crime and several other commentators pointed out that hardened young toughs were the persons best equipped to withstand this form of punishment. The advocates appeared to have gained the upper hand, however, since although there were only 50 birchings carried out on boys under 14 in 1939, in 1940 this number had risen to 283 and to over 500 by 1941[21]. However, the number fell dramatically after the Hereford birching scandal of 1943 and only 31 birchings were administered in 1944, the punishment being finally abolished in 1948.

Servicemen convicted of civilian crimes were usually sent to civilian prisons while deserters and other offenders against military law would serve time in a detention barracks or 'glasshouse.'

> *I visited the detention barracks where men come to serve their sentences from 14 days to two years ... The bulk of the work is military training ... I have never seen such polished metal, such carefully folded blankets and laid-out shaving tackle. The place was scrupulously clean. About 85% are sentenced for overstaying leave or otherwise deserting; some thieves are there, and a good many former Borstal boys ... the dormitories are warmed and, in the matter of sleeping, they are better off than many soldiers outside (Similarly, some Borstal boys in peacetime are better looked after in Borstal than in the homes*

they come from). No smoking is allowed and no beer.[22]

When the Canadians first arrived in Britain, any soldier sentenced to military detention was housed in the British military glasshouses but, after Dunkirk, overcrowding led to great difficulty in accommodating other than British troops and the solution was to create discrete Canadian Army detention barracks to house the 400 'incorrigible bad characters.' A new temporary glasshouse was therefore built at Witley, Surrey and moved in April, 1942 to a permanent location at Headley Down, Hampshire, the number of inmates having risen to 650.

Numbers in the Canadian glasshouse continued to grow and, in 1945, permission was sought to take over Reading Gaol (famed by Oscar Wilde) as additional detention barracks. Permission was given by the Home Secretary on 9 April which proved very timely since a month later, the inmates at Headley Down celebrated VE Day with a riot and mass break-out. The police were immediately called out and, with a large contingent of Canadian troops, surrounded the barracks to subdue the rioters, most of whom were quickly moved to Reading. In all, 60 prisoners escaped, all but seven of whom were almost immediately recaptured (contrary to sensational and inaccurate reports in the press).

12 : Morals, Manners and Mores

The war gave rise to a profound change in moral attitudes, possibly resulting from the perceived uncertainty of any future. This found expression in public behaviour, with fights and brawls becoming much more commonplace, in a noticeably relaxed attitude towards the property of others, and in what occasionally amounted to a flagrant disregard for normal standards of behaviour, especially in sexual matters. Discipline appeared to have ceased to exist and even public officials accepted and adopted what, at best might be called rule-bending and, at worst, unequivocal corruption. When a number of garage owners were prosecuted for selling petrol outside the rationing system, their illicit customers were revealed to include a knight, a former mayor, a distinguished soldier, a schoolteacher, a hotel proprietor and *several police constables.*

All of these facets of the changing social attitudes closely affected the police and the policing of the country, perhaps none more so than the frequent and violent breaches of public order. The signs were there well before the outbreak of the war with the violence which accompanied the marches of the British Fascist Movement through the East End of London and similar demonstrations elsewhere. The entry of Italy into the war on the side of the Germans in June, 1940 provoked considerable anti-Italian feeling and there were numerous attacks on Italian shops, restaurants and ice cream parlours, much of which ceased with the internment of the owners.

In the early stages of the war, there was considerable concern about public morale and the possibility of panic and public disorders in the event of air raids or invasion – a fear which fortunately proved unfounded. Official documents made it clear that, in the event of an invasion and where communication with the outside world was lost, the military commander would assume control. A notice issued in East Anglia specified that, in the event of an attack, it would be the duty of the local Military Commander, aided by the civil authorities, to hold the town until relieved, completely regardless of the cost to civil and military life and property.

The police were trained in the use of firearms, mainly for use when protecting vulnerable key points but also for use against their fellow citizens, should the need arise. Police War Reserve Constable Frank Whipple was one of those trained to use a rifle:

> *I remember saying to the inspector, 'Who are we going to use these on, the invader?', and he said, 'You'll use them on Londoners if you have to. If they get out of control when the invasion and the bombings come you'll have to use them on them'. I remember being quite shocked at the time.*[1]

One conscientious objector, seeking exemption from military service, told a tribunal that he had contemplated joining the police but had abandoned the idea on learning that police duties might include the use of force.

The Metropolitan Police sent a series of letters to the War Office, urging it to provide the police with military back-up, able to get to any part of the capital within one hour of being called upon. There were already several thousand troops stationed in London whose principal task was 'aid to the civil power'. They were used to protect vulnerable points such as docks, factories, airfields and the transport infrastructure. There was always a piquet outside the Bank of England and Broadcasting House to prevent sabotage which had a secondary role of supporting the police in the event of serious civil disorder.

Such was the fear of riots and wholesale looting that the police, especially in London, occasionally broke up peaceful demonstrations with an unnecessary degree of violence. When a deputation marched on the ARP headquarters in Tilbury to demand decent sanitation, bunks with proper tickets and official bunk allocation in the shelters, they were met by mounted police who charged the 40-50 strong deputation, wielding their batons to devastating effect. Although the story was passed to the *Daily Express*, it was not published on the grounds of the damage it could cause to morale. The reason for this heavy-handed reaction appeared to lie in the fact that Tilbury lay in the communist stronghold of Stepney and any complaints were immediately seen as communist-inspired and therefore subversive. The police and other officials were not the only ones fearful of subversion; the general public also deeply resented the anti-war propaganda put out by the British Union, the Communist Party and the Peace Pledge Union and their activities often resulted in scuffles and the breaking of windows. There were numerous other incidents of overbearing behaviour on the part of individual policemen such as that involving a small party of young men and women who were returning home after visiting a dance hall in Welling. An air raid was in progress but, as there was no shelter handy and they were all more than a little merry, they continued on their way, singing and dancing as they went. Suddenly a policeman appeared and told them to be quiet as they were causing a public nuisance.

> *It seemed funny considering the noise all around us, but we did go home quietly chatting. We were frightened but we had to have our social life. It wasn't much fun in the Anderson shelter or under the table.*[2]

Air raid shelters were a constant source of irritation, both as regards the facilities provided and their use. The practice of taking prams, bedding and other household items into the shelters frequently caused complaints and disputes, some of which ended in fights and scuffles. The police and shelter wardens experienced considerable problems in maintaining order and a reasonable standard of discipline amongst the overnight users of public shelters and there were numerous prosecutions for being drunk and disorderly in them. Despite the fears expressed by the authorities at the beginning of the war that troops would be needed to keep order and prevent panic, the police generally managed quite well. At the railway goods depot under the Tilbury Arches off the Commercial Road in East London, a single policeman was enough to control the long queue which formed each evening:

> *Indians with huge bundles on their backs; fat, blowsy women shouting to grubby children in the gutter; a thick-lipped Negro with a tart; youths in tight-waisted jackets of blue and green check with padded shoulders, split, down-at-heel shoes, wide flannel trousers. As the evening siren sounded, the policeman stepped aside and there was a rush, not of panic, but of eagerness to secure a favoured place ... The discipline was impressive, the sanitation ... was not.*[3]

The police also had the task of controlling the crowds seeking a place in one of the deep shelters, such as that under the Dickins and

Jones store in Regent Street, and organising those seeking admittance into orderly queues. The idea of using the Underground stations as shelters was born shortly after the first raids of the London Blitz when thousands of Eastenders took refuge there and refused to leave. As the stations had been earmarked for the accommodation of the injured and to transport troops, police and London Transport officials tried to prevent people bedding down on the platforms but their efforts were all in vain. They were overwhelmed by ticket-holding crowds who refused to leave the platform and, within a matter of days, 150,000 people were crowding into the Underground platforms each night and quickly becoming accustomed to this strange troglodytic existence.

The regulations requiring certain classes of people to register at the Labour Exchanges was far from universally popular and, at several of these offices, it was necessary to post a regular police presence during office hours to prevent disorders. At one Labour Exchange it was the practice of the policeman detailed for this duty to poke his head round the door at 9 am to announce his arrival and to do the same at 5pm when he knocked off. In between these times he would pace up and down outside, keeping an eye on the queues and generally looking out for trouble. This casual arrangement continued without problem until one day the clerk at the Labour Exchange rang the police station to say there was a fight outside and he was unable to find the policeman. Other policemen attended and, when everything was quiet once more, made enquiries about the missing policeman. No one in the Labour Exchange could remember with any certainty when they had last seen him and so a constable was dispatched to the man's lodgings to see if he was there. At the lodgings the missing policeman's landlady was astonished by the enquiry and told the constable that his colleague had left to join the Foreign Legion a week earlier. He had apparently neglected to inform either his employers or his colleagues of his intentions!

The police in some areas were well accustomed to disorders and none more so than the Royal Ulster Constabulary. The influx of a number of Irish Americans into an already volatile Ulster did nothing to alleviate these problems. Requests to the American Military Police for assistance did not always have the required effect :

> *It seemed this particular night a group of one faction was coming back home from a visit to another town and due to arrive some time around midnight. By ten o'clock the area*

was filling with people and the Chief already expecting trouble. ... After he explained the situation I said I would be behind him and his men. I failed to mention that I had already fully decided I would be far behind.... I notified all my men to stay close and be ready to depart at a second's notice.... The crowd got bigger and more boisterous and the local constables took it in their stride.... Finally the train arrived and the local group got off, formed a marching line and with a full band going full blast, started off down the street, the milling crowd swarming beside them on both sides shouting, catcalling, and so forth, till during a short intermission someone was heard to shout in a loud, strong voice, 'Down with the bloody King!' followed with an equally loud and strong 'Down with the bloody Pope!', with which fists and clubs started flying. I quickly gathered my men together and we watched for a few minutes and then quietly got into our vehicles and departed. Somehow I couldn't see myself travelling all those miles to indulge in a local brawl and I admired the local police for never ever mentioning our deserting them.[4]

The same American, while serving as the Acting Provost Marshal for Northern Ireland, was to face an even more serious situation when, this time, it was he who found himself without any back-up from the local police. A GI had been accused of cheating at cards and was now surrounded by an angry mob which was proposing to string him up – no idle threat it seemed since several of the men had ropes in their hands.

We looked over the scene for a minute or two, then my First Sergeant drove the jeep through the crowd to the GI. I got out and forced him into the jeep and told the sergeant to take off. I never realised I would be in any danger but found myself in turn surrounded with words flying to the effect that I would be as good a rope candidate as the man I had rushed off. I drew my .45 and advised, after making sure a round was in the chamber, that if I had to go there were going to be a few go with me. Fortunately, my sergeant looked back and he had the man we rescued get out and again drove the jeep into the crowd and I jumped in and we took off.

On this occasion, it seems that the local police were, in the narrator's words, *'most conspicuous by their absence.'*

As mentioned previously, most of the disorders were between service men, often after the pubs had turned out. During the early part of 1944, most of southern England was overcrowded with servicemen of numerous nationalities, all waiting impatiently for the invasion of Europe, an event for which they had been training and preparing for many a long day. The pubs and dance halls were all crowded and, typical of these was a ballroom in Poole, Dorset, which, being close to the harbour, was a favourite haunt of the Royal Navy and the US Navy. The competition for the local girls as dancing partners was intense and often ended in a fight. The Royal Marine Shore Patrols did their best to keep some semblance of order but they were often grossly outnumbered. On one occasion the patrol arrived at the dance hall where a fight had broken out and most of the girls had fled in terror. The whole hall was a seething mass of fighting seamen, the British versus the Americans, and the Royal Marines, sensing that there was little hope of their stopping the disorder, decided to 'nail their colours to the mast' and discreetly join in on the side of their Royal Navy colleagues who, since they were in the majority, were gradually getting the better of their opponents from across the Atlantic. The US Military Police had arrived and started to evacuate their walking wounded when the local police constable, alerted by the manager of the dance hall, appeared on the scene and took complete control of the situation. As the Royal Navy personnel made good their escape via the fire exits, the Marine patrol was left to face the policeman's wrath. The Marine sergeant having been floored during the fight, the constable singled out Marine H who, being no more than 19 at the time, was flattered by being addressed as 'senior soldier.' With his bicycle clips still on his ankles, the constable could have been a figure of fun but his massive frame and air of quiet authority sufficed to remind the servicemen that they were still only boys and Marine H was later to be grate ul for the lesson in discipline he received from the British Bobby, especially when soon afterwards he found himself involved in a much bigger scrap, this time alongside the Americans and against the common enemy on the Normandy beaches.

At another brawl between British and American sailors, this time in Woolwich, the police had to intervene to stop our allies being beaten to death by a little old lady who was wielding her umbrella to devastating effect in support of the Royal Navy. On yet another occasion, when one inoffensive GI was badly beaten up in an unprovoked assault by two British sailors in Bristol, his buddy, a tough character from New York, went into town the next night and returned with nine Royal Navy caps which, he said, should even the score.

When some GIs, stationed at Great Ashfield in East Anglia, innocent ly went to a village dance to see what they could pick up in the way of girls, they were met by a large contingent of the Black Watch who were also stationed nearby and the resulting brawl only ended when a fleet of ambulances arrived to convey the badly beaten Americans to the medical centre. Even where the Americans organised their own dances they were not exempt from trouble, as a unit in Littlehampton (Sussex) discovered. When the organisers prevented a party of British commandos from entering the hall, the latter retaliated by overturning some of the Americans' trucks, slashed tyres and put sand in the fuel tanks. This vandalism provoked retaliation and reprisals from both sides which, like so many disputes in 1944, ended with the protagonists finding themselves bound for the invasion of Europe.

There were also numerous battles between British troops and the Canadians. Some 'pretty bad fights' were reported between men of 110 Squadron, RCAF and the Royal Tank Corps and between the Welsh Guards and the Saskatoon Light Infantry. A 'small fracas' occurred at a dance hall in Croydon between the Scots Guards and the Canadian Seaforth Highlander which was apparently started by the British troops. Camberley, in Surrey, the home of the British Army Staff College had more than its share of disorders. At Christmas, 1941 there was trouble between the Black Watch and the No.1 Canadian Armoured Corps Reinforcement Unit and it was reported that the Scottish troops were told by their adjutant not to come back with black eyes but to 'let the Canadians have it.' The men went further than their officers apparently intended and took bayonets with them when they went to meet the Canadians who came in trucks into town. The anticipated fight began and the Black Watch drew their bayonets, causing the Canadians to flee the town. The fight was continued some days later when men from both sides got drunk and fighting took place all over the town with broken bottles being used by the Scots. In the same series of incidents two Royal Canadian Dragoons were knifed and one is said to have died from his injuries, although there is no corroboration of this story. Hostility towards the British military personnel was not a monopoly of the male Canadians. After the Canadian Womens' Army Corps arrived in Britain in 1942, a Canadian soldier wrote home about the CWAC laundry personnel, *'I think they are about the tuffest bunch of girls I ever seen the first thing they done was get drunk and start to clean up on the ... ATS ... but the English girls are well able to look after themselves.*[5]

Once again, there is no official record of this incident but there seems little doubt it happened. The period of low morale in the winter of 1941/42 was probably the worst moment in the Canadian soldier's relationship with the British army and, from that time, there was a gradual improvement with reports of actual street fighting becoming less frequent. Much space could be given to describing what the Canadians' commander referred to as 'our worrisome disciplinary problems.' Mention has already been made of the Canadians' introduction to the British pub and its consequences in the form of chronic drunkenness. This was not an entirely new phenomenon as the fathers of these troops had been involved in a great many disorders during the First World War and it was the memories of this which affected the attitude of some British people towards the Canadians. In particular, the bad riots at Witley Camp at the end of the 1914-18 war, in which a Canadian killed a civilian in a brawl, were still remembered by many of the locals. In fact, one is constantly drawn to make a comparison between the Second World War and its predecessor. In the 1914-18 war the final months of the Canadians' stay in England was marred by turbulence because of the slowness in repatriation, and there were 13 instances of riots or disturbances involving Canadian troops between November 1918 and June 1919. The worst of these occurred at Kinmel Park, near Rhyl in North Wales in March 1919 in the course of which five soldiers were killed and some 25 wounded. In another riot at Epsom an elderly police sergeant was fatally injured and seven other policemen seriously injured and, although the Canadians had a number of influential defenders among the press and judiciary, the events of 1919 did Canada's name no good in Britain and this was still in people's minds 20 years later. But, in fact, there was no repetition of the happenings of 1919 in 1945-46. There was, it is true, one disgraceful episode: the Aldershot riots of 4 and 5 July 1945 when shops were looted and a great deal of damage done.

One aspect which did not involve the Canadians, who were almost exclusively white, was the racial discrimination which marred the relationships between the British people and the American troops. In an effort to reduce the spate of conflicts between white and black Americans, certain areas were designated 'Blacks Wednesdays, Whites Thursdays' to keep the two races apart. This compromise was introduced in Newton Abbot in Devon and in the cathedral city of Hereford amongst other places. To the British, unused to racial disharmony, the attitude of the majority of the white Americans to their black compatriots was utterly perplexing and represented an entirely new problem for the police, although the consequences were merely another form of disorder which they had to quell. Sometimes these interracial conflicts reached alarming levels of violence such as when parties of a dozen or more GIs armed themselves with razors and knives and went 'nigger hunting.' To these ostensibly civilised men the black was little better than an animal, to be beaten up or even killed at their pleasure. As one white GI explained to an Englishwoman who remonstrated with him about this attitude, 'Ma'am, we shoot niggers where we come from.'

In Leicester, the US military police, despairing of ever being able to subdue or prevent large scale brawls, merely cordoned off both ends of the street and let the two groups fight it out. Any passing GI could, after being frisked for weapons, step over the ropes and join in the affray. In Wrexham, British commandos joined in a fight on the side of the blacks against the hated Yanks and only left when the 'Snow-drops' arrived on the scene. With guns being readily available shooting incidents were comparatively commonplace and, in a village near Preston (Lancashire) a machine gun was used. In Devon in December, 1944, a pub which had been serving blacks was subjected to a fusillade of rifle fire, in the course of which the licensee's wife was killed. A full-scale battle broke out in Launceton when a group of black GIs fetched rifles and avowed to teach the whites a lesson. Their response to the police to disperse was a verbal barrage of obscenities and they eventually opened fire on the American MPs, wounding two of them. Arising out of this incident 14 black soldiers were court martialled for mutiny and attempted murder, the details being widely reported in the British press, although the final verdict was never published.

But it was not only the armed forces who were involved in incidents of disorder. A Sheffield mine worker who was employed part-time as an ambulance driver recalls that the ambulances had to drive up a steep incline on leaving the school yard where they were based, causing their headlights to shine into the bedroom windows of the houses opposite. This upset the occupants who reacted violently:

> *Believe me, we had quite a few riots, and I mean riots, with the neighbours on the Arbourthorne estate. They come and they smashed windows, they were going to smash ambulances, going to smash headlights. There was no end of fights. We had to call the police out and everything.*

The police, who had more than their hands full of other matters, could have well done without these disputes. Air raids also brought out the usual crowd of sightseers and morbidly curious onlookers who often impeded rescue operations. Their presence also caused resentment on the part of those who had been bombed out or injured and the police often had to intervene when this resentment boiled over into physical action. It was not only the casually curious who presented problems. One Metropolitan constable remembers an occasion when a bomb fell on a row of thatched cottages, causing some injuries and considerable confusion. While attempting to restore order, the constable found his efforts being somewhat negated by the local MP who arrived on the scene, 'full of his own importance and generally getting in everybody's way.'

Eventually, his patience exhausted, the officer told the member of parliament to clear off and, when he objected, threatened to arrest him for obstruction. The MP decided discretion was the better part of valour and went, thus saving the constable from the dubious distinction of arresting his Member of Parliament.

Special Sergeant Butler of the City of London force was on duty the day after the Bank underground station was hit by a bomb, causing something like 230 fatalities:

> *I was on duty next day, Sunday, and crowds came to see the damage, not that they could get very near. No account of it appeared in the papers but news of major incidents soon got around. I was at the barrier and a young reporter, notebook in hand, plied me with questions which I refused to answer. Later I wondered if he really was a reporter.*

Fifty years later on, the image one has of Britain during the war is of a nation of plucky people, thumbing their noses at the aggressor and all doing their bit to defeat the common foe. It therefore comes as something of a surprise to learn that, in certain trades, there seems to have been little or no reluctance to lay down tools and go on strike for some real or imagined grievance. In 1940, thanks to Dunkirk, only 941,000 man days were lost through industrial disputes against 1,354,000 in 1939. But this happy state of affairs did not last long and, in 1941 over a million man days were lost and, in 1942, the total exceeded the pre-war figure! This was despite the fact that average basic weekly wage had risen by 1943 to some 35% above those earned in 1938, although it has to be admitted that the cost of living had also risen sharply. Nevertheless, because of the ready availability of overtime, actual earnings had increased by around 75%.[6] Average weekly earnings rose from some £4.10.0 in 1940 to £6.4.4 in 1944, after which they fell back slightly due to a contraction in the war industries. In the engineering and shipbuilding sectors they peaked at around £7.0.0. a week in 1944.

Although strikes were declared illegal under Order 1305, there were only 71 prosecutions in Scotland and 38 in England and Wales, involving 6,300 individuals. Offenders were fined but it became impossible to enforce these penalties since the numbers involved were so great that the jails would have been flooded. Whilst strikes are not in themselves a police matter, every industrial dispute has the potential to turn nasty and the police are invariably required to supervise the picketing arrangements to ensure that the King's Peace is maintained. War time conditions did not obviate this requirement and strike duty became yet another chore to be added to the list of policing responsibilities.

The breakdown in accepted, prewar moral standards was to be seen in all aspects of life, in particular in the attitude towards the property of others. The 'borrowing' of things extended to all manner of items, especially items of service uniform and equipment. Where servicemen or servicewomen found they were short of something, from a cap to coal, from a book to blanco, from knives to knickers, from webbing to waterproofs capes, the common practice was to 'liberate' the property of another unfortunate who, in turn, had to appropriate someone else's or pay the quartermaster and risk being put on a charge for failing to take care of the property of His Majesty. The same attitude quickly

337

extended to civilian life. A clerk in Bury St Edmunds made an entry in his diary:

> *A lot of kleptomania about and things keep vanishing from the Shirehall. Lost my best fountain pen last week – shouldn't have left it on my desk, I suppose. The Solicitor lost his gloves today.*

Standards also dropped in the home, as Nella Last, an educated middle-class housewife noticed:

> *... I thought of other little changes, both in myself and friends. Of our slaphappy way of 'doing the bits that showed most', making beds soon after rising without the turning and airing we once thought so needful: now, in my rush out on two mornings a week, they are lucky to be straightened. I saw pillow slips and towels, even underclothes, scrutinised to see if they were quite soiled or would they do another day, or week?.*[7]

The courts were kept busy with petitions for divorce and cases of bigamy occurred more and more frequently. But even more noticeable was the relaxation of the moral standards concerned with sexual behaviour. Young girls were particularly susceptible to this phenomenon and, by 1943, there was growing concern about their 'delinquency'. The military bases which had sprung up all over the country, especially the American ones, formed a magnet for girls intent on getting their share of the soldiers' pay through crime or prostitution, or who were simply looking for some excitement. At a conference on juvenile delinquency it was reported that some young girls were 'throwing themselves' at the American, Canadian and other troops.

'The men need as much protection from these girls as the girls from the men' claimed one speaker.

The *Bath Weekly Chronicle and Herald* of 27 March, 1943 carried a letter from the town's probation officer which claimed,

> *There are girls in Bath whose only ideas in life are men, lipstick, and showing as much of their bodies as they can... War time conditions ... were having [an] appalling effect ... on some girls in all parts of the country ... Too much money and many soldiers with money to fling about were ... factors*

leading to their downfall.

The police in Bath and elsewhere devoted a great deal of time and energy on these girls, many of whom were obviously in great moral danger and in need of care and protection. One 15 year old ran away from home four times in three weeks to 'consort' with American soldiers and the court was presented with a detailed account of her activities over Christmas, 1943. On the Christmas Eve she went to a camp party and spent the night in a railway cloakroom. She wandered around the town until 7 pm on Christmas Day when she dined with a GI, leaving him at 10 pm to spend the night in a barn. She then met another US soldier and went with him to London where she met yet another GI with whom she went to the pictures. She returned to Bath and put on a new dress given to her by an American, went to a dance, went on to a camp with a soldier, went to another pub with a soldier who was later intimate with her, and so on ... At the time of her court appearance the girl was pregnant and did not know which of at least six members of the Allied armed forces was the father. She was sent to an approved school[8].

Another girl was reported to have been 'found with American soldiers at midnight and to have slept on park benches', while another, aged 15, was said to have preferred the company of coloured American soldiers to white ones and to have more knowledge of sexual matters than some women of 40. The efficacy of remand homes or approved schools to which such girls were usually sent may be open to question but at least they had the effect of removing them from the streets and at least partially alleviating the problems faced by the police, especially the over-worked female members of the force.

Appreciating that the GIs were going to be a big attraction for young girls, especially those of easy morals, the police authorities found the comparatively rare policewomen a great boon. Regular patrols were made to move on the groups of young girls who congregated outside the quarters of these men and to take details of those who appeared to be under age in order to notify their parents or to arrange for them to be subjected to a care and protection order. It was not only the Americans who benefitted from the favours bestowed by young girls who found the relaxation of morals to their liking. A lady farmer in Monckton (Kent) told Constable John Thompson that a

12 year old girl in her care was being visited late at night by a man. In view of the girls' tender years the constable reported the matter to his sergeant and the pair of them kept the farmhouse under observation. Sure enough, late into the night, a dim hurricane lamp was seen being taken into the farmhouse. Giving the visitor a little time to get settled, the two policemen crept into the farmhouse and mounted the ancient staircase which creaked more than somewhat under the weight of the 16 stone sergeant and his companion. On entering the girl's room she was found to be in bed, quite naked but equally quite alone. However, a search of the room revealed a naked man in the wardrobe who could really think of no good excuse for being there. He was duly charged with 'unlawful carnal knowledge' of the girl.

Older ladies too, indulged in activities which they would probably never have thought of in peacetime, often to the disapproval of their neighbours. The sergeant in charge of a small Welsh village near Monmouth was asked by the head teacher of the village school to find out who had written, in large white letters in the middle of the road, the words 'DANCING CLASSES HELD HERE', with an arrow pointing towards the door of the school house. The head teacher was puzzled as to the significance of this but most of the villagers knew that, in the teacher's absence, his wife (who was much younger and quite attractive) was in the habit of entertaining some Indian soldiers who were stationed nearby and dancing with them to records. It appeared that a couple of the local lads had been spying on her and decided to have a bit of fun at their old teacher's expense. The sergeant made some cursory enquiries but, needless to say, the culprits were never identified although everyone in the village had a pretty shrewd idea who they were.

In their quest for sexual gratification some couples appear to have abandoned all sense of shame and decency. A special constable, walking with a friend in broad daylight in the middle of Reading,

> *... became aware of ... an erotic sound and lo and behold by the side of the Law Courts were a Yank and a girl. The girl was very young ... her knickers were around her ankles and his trousers were open and by the time we had finished gasping this couple had completed the act. What staggered me was that he was smoking a fat cigar whilst this was going on.*[9]

Not all couplings were quite so blatant but the blackout fostered a spirit of daring among young couples, some of whom openly boasted of having intercourse in shop doorways in busy streets, screened by another couple awaiting their turn.

Although enemy action meant that both sexes had to sleep in close proximity to each other in, for instance, the shelters and Tube stations, in most cases a degree of decorum was maintained. When one couple was bombed-out they had to share a bed with the wife's sister, but the wife circumspectly occupied the middle of the bed to maintain propriety.

The war did nothing to hinder the activities of the prostitutes in London and other big cities and ports. In a letter to his wife in September, 1940, General Raymond E Lee, the US Military Attaché in London, wrote:

> If there was ever a time when one should wear life like a loose garment, this is it. I particularly admire the little tarts who wander about the streets of Mayfair every afternoon and evening in their finery. When everyone else is hurrying for the air raid shelters, they are quite indifferent and continue to stroll undisturbed.

Before the war there were three main types of prostitute: the better class 'call girl' who relied on introductions and arrangements, the prostitute who solicited in pubs, clubs or the streets but used her own flat or house for the culmination of the transaction, and those who both solicited and provided their services outdoors. Prostitution was not an offence, *per se;* only the act of soliciting for the purposes of prostitution or the keeping of a disorderly house were against the law and so, in the normal course of events, the first category of prostitute did not come to the attention of the police. As long as she was the sole user of the premises a call girl was within the law but, if she shared with a friend or allowed others to use the flat or house, she could be open to a charge of brothel keeping.

Certain parts of London and other cities were recognised as being the haunt of street walkers and, such was the extent of the problem, the police could do little more than try to keep it under control. Those they arrested for soliciting would spend the rest of the night in the cells, appear before the magistrates the next morning, be fined a modest sum, and then go straight back on the streets to recoup the fine as quickly as possible. Arrest and the payment of fines were an occupational hazard and usually regarded as preferable to paying income tax. It was not unusual for a prostitute to have between 60 and 100 convictions for soliciting.

The relationship between the police and prostitutes was somewhat ambiguous and it appears to have been accepted that regular street-walkers would be arrested on a rota basis while prostitutes' folklore had it that it was inadvisable to plead 'Not guilty' since the police 'would mark you down otherwise.' Obviously the police did not prosecute every case of soliciting, brothel keeping or living off immoral earnings but used considerable discretion. It was often suggested that junior policemen relied on making a large number of arrests in order to be marked out for promotion and were therefore quick to bring in prostitutes and other easy game. Whilst a reputation for 'collar-feeling' may have done a policeman no harm, it would be doing his superiors less than justice to suggest that they were only interested in numbers and that the 'quality' of the prisoner was immaterial. In fact, the arrest of a much wanted burglar did much more for the reputation of a police officer than any number of prostitutes, beggars and drunks, most of whom are regarded as scarcely worth the effort required in getting them to court, especially if the cells have to be deloused after they have used them.

The arrival of large numbers of Allied troops in Great Britain was a great boon to those practising the oldest profession, the numbers of whom were rapidly augmented by others anxious to make what seemed to them to be an easy living. These newcomers included a number of young girls – 14 or 15 years of age – and the wives of servicemen posted overseas. The vice squads in the various police forces found their work increasing daily as more and more 'good-time girls' arrived to claim their share of the pickings. The availability of property due to evacuation and enemy action was responsible for a significant increase in the number of brothels, many of which were exceptionally busy. Police kept observations on one such property in Paddington and noted that 47 couples visited it in the course of a single night and that the male in 30 of these was an American serviceman, sometimes accom-panied by very young women. But the record was probably held by the Brighton brothel to which the 14 regular girls brought 154 service-men in the course of one night, no doubt exercising the by now customary 'ten minute rule' to ensure that not too much time was devoted to any one client. It was not unusual for the police keeping covert observation on premises in vice cases to be solicited themselves and they sometimes had great difficulty in ensuring that their cover was not blown. A sharp increase in the number of prosecutions for brothel-keeping around 1942 suggests that there was a deliberate policy to close these down, although there is no official documentation to support this contention.

The American servicemen were understandably popular with the ladies of the night and it became virtually impossible for them to walk along certain blacked-out streets in London without being accosted by streetwalkers every few paces. So persistent were these women that they became known as the 'Piccadilly Commandos', while their sisters who sold their favours in the open air were referred to as the 'Hyde Park Rangers'. Touts pretending to be newsvendors would stand on street corners on the lookout for likely customers for their girls. The US Provost Marshal issued a guide in August 1943 on *How to Stay Out of Trouble* which warned against 'females of questionable character' but, for many GIs, these were just the type they were looking for. Such was the growth of the profession that, by the end of the war, space on the pavements in the recognised soliciting areas was at a premium and newcomers got very short shrift from the regular street-walkers.

Public houses were traditionally a favourite haunt of prostitutes and it was an offence for a licensee to harbour them. The police had to make regular visits to all licensed premises to ensure that the Licensing Acts were being respected and that there was no gaming or prostitution going on. This was not always an easy task as an inspector in the naval port of Chatham discovered in 1943 for, as he entered one particular pub, the haunt of several prostitutes, one of them recognised him and said in a loud voice, 'He's a ******* copper. Someone wants to crown him', whereupon two Australian sailors began to jostle him, offered to fight him and used obscene language. The licensee was standing behind the bar but made no attempt to interfere and, on one occasion, was grinning. The police inspector persisted, however, and the licensee was later fined £10[10].

The police themselves were obviously not above a little rule-bending and, in some case, downright corruption. Sometimes, as we saw in the previous chapter, quite large numbers of policemen were involved in dubious or even criminal practices and this could extend right across the ranks. For example, during the war a certain wholesaler in Billingsgate fishmarket came to an arrangement with the City policemen on traffic duty to allow vans with deliveries for him to pass with the minimum of delay and with precedence over those of other wholesalers. The policemen were naturally rewarded for their efforts. Over the years this had grown to be such an established practice that only certain constables were given this plum duty and only certain sergeants were in the know. One inspector, and a chief inspector were also party to this arrangement and shared in the spoils, which must have been considerable to pay off so many officers. The other fish wholesalers had a pretty good idea of what was going on but, given the extent of the corruption, were able to do little about it until one day one of them found himself sitting next to the Commissioner of the City of London Police. He seized this opportunity with both hands and made sure that the commisioner was fully acquainted with what was going on in the City. As a result, the chief inspector was retired on ill-health grounds on a reduced pension, the inspector was reduced to sergeant while the two sergeants were busted down to constable and transferred to another division. The constables were all docked several increments of pay and transferred. Whilst these may seem fairly light punishments, it must be remembered that a policeman's pension was based on his average pay for the last year or so of his service and that all these men therefore suffered a reduced pension for the rest of their life. Moreover, had this not been at the end of the war when manpower was at an all-time low, the punishments would almost certainly have been much heavier.

Such was the burden placed on the police that it is not surprising that there were occasional suggestions that they were cutting corners in order to obtain convictions, an allegation which has been repeated regularly in more recent times. In 1942, the Recorder of Liverpool gave these accusations greater credence in a case involving a 17 year old labourer charged with theft who claimed to have been beaten for three hours in order to extract a confession. The learned Recorder stated,

> ... it is no use telling me that ... beating up of arrested men in Bridewells does not go on ... I am certain this sort of thing does happen to extract admissions and something has to be done about it.

He added that he had received many complaints about beatings and that he had had the advantage of hearing the evidence of police officers who had left the force with good records[11].

These claims were vigorously denied by the Liverpool City Police and members of the judiciary entered the controversy with Mr Justice Oliver commending the City Police on their –

> *...scrupulous fairness ... I am glad to think that the police, who are so often attacked in a public and irresponsible way ... have done absolutely the proper thing'.*[12]

A sub-committee set up by the Liverpool Watch Committee to look into the allegations reported that it was satisfied that adequate protection was provided for prisoners in the city's police stations. The Recorder persisted with his allegations, however, and dismissed the findings of the sub-committee as a whitewash. But the weight of other news brought the matter to an abrupt close, at least as far as the press was concerned, without any satisfactory result. Had the matter arisen in peacetime it is probable that the argument would have persisted until the press and the public were satisfied one way or the other. What is not in question, however, is the fact that the average Scouse is proud of his physical prowess and there is little doubt that the Liverpool force was equally 'firm' in dealing with offenders. Indeed, it is extremely likely that the police in many, if not all, parts of the country could be brutal in their dealings with known criminals or those known to belong to criminal families. This is illustrated by a case which occurred in Reading in which a youth was walking home with his girl friend one summer evening in 1941 when two policemen stopped them and asked for their identity cards. They were unable to produce these and, after questioning, the girl was permitted to carry on but the boy was taken to the police station. There he was closely questioned about a jewel robbery and, when he denied any involvement, was repeatedly struck in the face and kicked by a number of officers. Medical evidence revealed that his nose had been broken and so the denials made by the police officers were given short shrift. The boy's father took out a civil action against the police, in the course of which the judge drew attention to the injury and the police denials. He further commented that the boy was on probation at the time and that his family were well known to the police who *'were just as liable as anyone else to resentment or to bear grudges.'* The judge found against the police officers who were ordered to pay damages of £90.

There is plenty of anecdotal evidence, supported by court records, to show incontestably that, on occasions, the police did not shrink from using violence against certain suspects and prisoners. What is not clear is how extensive these abuses were since it is notoriously difficult to get to the bottom of such allegations. Some prisoners undoubtedly made (and still make today) spurious complaints in the hope of getting away with the offence with which they were charged.

For the same reasons it is difficult to say whether this form of abuse became more widespread during the war years or whether the cases mentioned were merely a continuation of the status quo, something which had been going on for decades. The allegations made from time to time in the post-war years suggest that the position remained unchanged for some 20 years, at least until the 1964 Police Act brought in certain measures which were intended to prevent this kind of abuse of authority.

But it was not until the introduction of the 1984 Police & Criminal Evidence Act (PACE) with its comprehensive rules and procedures that any meaningful curbs were placed on the possibility of ill-treatment of persons in custody. Even so, it would be unwise to suggest that no cases of ill-treatment now arise but at least it is much more difficult to harm a prisoner or suspect without the fact becoming evident and the appropriate action being taken against the police officer or officers concerned.

The Victorian Statutes, many of which were still in force during the war, were comparatively simple and capable of fairly liberal interpretation – a situation which caused no great judicial difficulties, since the courts, especially the so-called police courts presided over by a local justice of the peace, were generally strongly biased towards the evidence given by 'their' police. It was not until the police evidence began increasingly to be questioned that the police felt themselves constrained to bend the evidence to counter cleverly constructed defences. Paradoxically, the less the police were readily believed, the more they tended to have recourse to short cuts, to the fictitious 'Ways and Means Act' – a situation which, rather than decreasing, has shown clear evidence of growing in prevalence right up until very recent times.

There is, however, little evidence that the war had any effect on the credibility of the police; it was perhaps more the corruption scandals of the 1950s which began the growing loss of confidence in the police by the general public.

13. All Our Troubles & Adversities

It is difficult in these modern days, when police, firemen and ambulance drivers receive stress counselling after they have attended a particularly nasty accident, to appreciate that their forebears suffered physical and mental stresses far greater than most of us can imagine, without the benefit of any psychological or other aid. Not only were they exposed to horrific scenes of carnage and destruction, they were (at least during the Blitz) on the point of exhaustion through lack of sleep and long hours without any break or refreshment. Many were no longer young, especially the senior officers, the First Police Reserves and, as time went by, some of those officers who would normally have been in line for retirement on pension but whose services had been compulsorily retained under the Police and Firemen (War Service) Act, 1939. In the Metropolitan Police, the average age in 1945 was 45 as against 35 in prewar times. The strain of wartime policing manifested itself in an increasing incidence of sickness, escalating as the war progressed so that, by 1945, the number of days lost through sickness had almost doubled. Whereas the average number of days which each policeman had taken off through sickness in 1938 had been 9.8, by 1945 this had increased to over 23 – around four weeks lost each year per man. Although London undoubtedly suffered worst from enemy action and the stress to which members of the Metropolitan Police were subjected was unquestionably the greatest, other forces throughout the country recorded similar, alarming rises in rates of sickness.

These figures should not be seen as evidence of mere malingering; in Birkenhead, three sergeants and eight constables (representing 11% and 25% respectively of the strength of those ranks) had to be retired in 1945 on medical grounds. Their chief constable wrote that:

> ... this large number may be due in some measure to the average age of the force being so high and to many of the men having completed at least 26 years patrol duty; or it may be an indication that 30 years of patrol duty are too exacting for the average man ... A middle-aged police force has been growing old. Some were already old by police standards at the out-break of the war and many have already been pensioned

*on the grounds of ill-health. Blackout, bombing and war
strain have taken serious toll of the health of the remainder,
many of whom are waiting to claim a pension as soon as they
are permitted to do so.*[1]

The senior ranks came under particularly severe pressure as their
responsibilities increased. Many chief constables died in harness,
resigned or retired to make way for younger men, sometimes
voluntarily, sometimes as a result of pressure applied by the Home
Office. At least one, Captain J A Davison, MC, the Chief Constable of
Kent, committed suicide. To quote the official history of the force,

> *In his personal conduct he was absolutely fearless. He would
> stand in exposed positions at any time of the day or night
> during bombing and shelling incidents in utter disregard of his
> own safety. He was completely tireless, and managed to infect
> the whole force with something of his restless energy and zeal.
> Undoubtedly he drew too much on his latent reserves of
> strength and his tragic death...ended a period of outstanding
> energy and example.*[2]

Constable Bill Cavey of the Metropolitan Police remembers one of
his colleagues was a fearless and skilful driver with nerves of iron:

> *He never turned a hair in the most dangerous situation,
> whether this arose from enemy action or confronting armed
> and violent criminals. Suddenly, however, he completely lost
> his nerve and became agrophobic and eventually had to be
> invalided out of the force.*

Special Constable Frank Butler of the City of London Police was
another who confessed to suffering from shock:

> *The sirens went at 7.10 pm. I soon had to help to deal with a
> scatter of incendiaries and, about an hour later, was caught in
> the blast of a high explosive bomb which hit an insurance
> company's premises in King William Street ... I was told to 'Go
> home, you'll be suffering from shock by the morning.' I got as
> far as Moorgate station where a Police Inspector told me to
> take over from the regular constable on the Underground
> platform... somewhere about three in the morning I had orders*

to clear the people into a train that had been sent to fetch them. This was the night when the wholesale warehouses of the Wood Street and Fore Street district were destroyed and I saw flames meeting across the width of Fore Street as I made my way to Moorgate. ... I did indeed suffer from shock for a few days and faced the next few duties with a sad lack of confidence, which I did not disclose to anyone.[3]

Another Special Constable, 'Tibby' Clarke, who was in normal life a famous Ealing Studios scriptwriter commented:

Most of us who went through it [the Blitz] have ever since been a little wary of it as a subject lest we be labelled bomb bores. We in S Division were luckier than many London police, but we still had our fill of its cruelty and horror, its sickening destructiveness, its white dusty filth and its peculiar stink of fresh decay ... Just these few words and it begins to depress me again.[4]

Sergeant H F Grey, who served in the East End throughout the Blitz tells a similar tale:

After a serious incident we just kept on working until you suddenly sell out and come to and that's it. You can do no more.[5]

His family having been evacuated to the country Sergeant Grey was left alone and goes on to say how much he missed his family during the rough times. What he sorely felt was the lack of even a couple of days off to visit them. Many of his colleagues were in the same boat and occupied their limited spare time in the necessary household chores, often made more onerous by the dust and mess from bombings. Sergeant George Williams described his normal day in a letter to his wife in 1944, at the height of the flying bomb attacks:

I got up at 2.30 pm, went and got my rations, came back and cooked my breakfast, had same and washed up. I then had a bath and put on my clean undies. I next got busy with my whites and then my coloureds and finished up with three pairs of socks including the ones that I had been wearing. I got that job finished about 7 pm and whilst they were doing their stuff on the line I got busy mending my braces once again. That finish I decided to wash over the front room floor as I had plenty of nice soda water. It certainly looks the better for it but it will not be so easy to find my way to my shelter bed now as I had worn quite a pretty footpath through the white-wash and now, of course, it all looks the same. Next I gave the garden the benefit of all the water in the various baths and bowls I had used for the washing and the floor (a bit thick by this time) and got finished at 8.45 pm. Just time to shave and come up here [the police station] for dinner.

Many of those who saw at first hand the horrendous effects of modern warfare managed to put it out of their minds – or so they thought. Constable Arthur Marshall had the terrible and morale-sapping task of being in charge of the public mortuary at the time of the Sheffield Blitz. Nearly fifty years later he was asked by Joyce Holliday to tell her of his experiences for her play, 'It's a bit lively out-side!' (extracts from which have been quoted elsewhere in this book). The first night of this play proved a harrowing experience for him:

Nearly all policemen who were on duty in air raids had to attend to some really nasty results of the bombing. I too was one of those and I thought I had put them out of my mind completely. One used the professional method of not getting personally involved. The first night of the play at the Crucible Theatre proved to me how unrealistic that was. I was given two tickets for the opening performance and, being a widower, I took the Curate from our church with me. ... I was totally unprepared for what was to follow. It was a weird experience hearing your own words coming out of the mouths of actors but the play then continued with a particularly poignant scene in which I had been involved and it seemed as if a small door in my memory opened and that scene seemed as real to me as it had been on the night it happened. I just could not help myself as tears ran down my cheeks and I was grateful for the comforting arm of my friend round my shoulder and the offer of his handkerchief. I thought I had consigned it to oblivion after over forty years. But I was wrong!

Some of the new, auxiliary policemen (and, quite possibly, some of their regular colleagues) found the strain of enemy action more than they could bear. The *Police Review* for 17 January, 1941, reported that Police War Reserve Constable Edward Spencer was sentenced to 2 months imprisonment for failing to continue his employment as a police officer. Unable to face the rigours of the night Blitzkrieg he simply ran away. When he was seen in a room at Greenwich police station and was asked why he was not on duty he replied, 'The gunfire was too heavy and there was too much risk.' He immediately handed in his resignation and was found two months later in Somerset, where he was handed the summons. His subsequent appeal against his sentence was allowed and he was bound over for two years instead of being imprisoned. He later joined the RAF.

The police, like their emergency service and ARP colleagues simply had to carry on as long as they could and their attitude was reflected by the public at large, particularly during the Blitz. The American writer, Ralph Ingersoll, was anxious to determine what scientific evidence there was of the effect of bombing on the emotional balance of the population of London. Having heard that Anna Freud, the daughter of the great Sigmund Freud and a psychoanalyst herself, had set up a clinic for the study of bomb shock, he went to visit her:

> She said, 'You have never seen anything like these people. You wouldn't believe it unless you lived here. They are so calm, and they take it all so well.' She said that the psychiatrists of London had met the week before to talk about the very subject I was asking her about. She said the retreat from Dunkirk had produced many cases of shell shock amongst the soldiers and sailors who took part in it. But that none of the psychiatrists who discussed it together had a single case of true shell shock to report among the civilians of London. There were no nervous break-downs that could be directly attributed to the bombing.[6]

Whilst this may be true, it must not be assumed that the people of London and other blitzed cities were impervious to the effects of the war, especially over a period of time. Mary Bloomfield was the wife of a Coventry policeman and worked in the City Council offices:

> I was just an ordinary housewife. I worked from nine to five-

*thirty and until twelve-thirty on Saturday, so you did every-
thing else – washing, ironing, washing your hair, whatever
cooking you could do in advance, every thing like that. I
would never have dreamt of doing the washing on a Sunday
before the war. I was cleaning my floor one Sunday afternoon
and I suddenly thought, 'I don't know how long it is since I
was in town.' So I went. It was deserted. Everyone was doing
what I was doing, straightening up their homes so that they
could go to work on Monday morning. I was brave during the
war. I never complained to my husband. I never whimpered. I
did what had to be done – spent hours on my own in the
shelter and lived by routine, just like other women. That's
what kept us going – routine. But it was misery for 99 women
out of 100. We lost our husbands or sons or parents. We
suffered from grief. But everything that happened to us we
accepted. We were very different people ... and we were never
the same again.*[7]

It would be foolish to suggest that, during the heavy raids, people
were not frightened but most managed to hide their fears from others.
Morale in the shelters in Coventry during the Blitz on that city was
described as 'excellent' and the occupants of one passed the night singing patriotic songs until :

*...the soldiers from the smokescreen unit...came in.... One of
them was crying and very frightened; he was swearing and
hysterical and one could feel the hysteria catching on. My
father shook him and told him to pull himself together as he
would upset the women and children and eventually his pals
took him off.*[8]

Another man whose nerve gave way at Coventry's Central Police
Station was dealt with even more firmly by the imperturbable Sergeant
Groom whose bearing throughout the traumatic hours of the Blitz on
that city was an object lesson in self-control and professionalism:

*... a little man came into the charge office. 'Sergeant,' he says,
'your men and the wardens are digging out some people
who've been trapped and they want some cigarettes and some
tea.' ... Twenty Players and a box of Swan matches were*

handed over to the little warden... He'd been gone about five or ten minutes I suppose when suddenly he dashed into the office. He was like a gibbering lunatic. He said, 'They've all been killed, they've all been killed,' and he threw the cigarettes and matches down on the desk. Now as far as I was concerned this sort of conduct in the police station didn't meet with my approval. You could burn down the Cathedral, you could ruin all the buildings round it, but the police station should be a little oasis of calm and quiet... I said, 'What did you say?' and he was shouting and screaming his head off. I picked him up by his coat and shook him and smacked his face and said, 'Behave yourself. Don't carry on like this. What's happened?' and he said, 'I've just been in Dun Cow Yard and a bomb fell in front of me and it killed all the people who'd been rescued. One of your officers has been killed and some of the others have been killed.' So I sent out one of my officers ... and he confirmed the tragic story.[9]

If morale was at an all-time low in Coventry on the morning after the raid, by the following day it was strikingly different. A good night's sleep had done wonders for the exhausted populace and, equally important for morale, was the evidence all around that the authorities, including the police, were already beginning to regain control of the situation. The journalist Hilde Marchant was highly impressed with the Coventry police 'who that day provided the big shoulder for the public to rest on.' The improvement in morale was further fostered by the visit of H M The King , although the Mayoress was not quite so enthusiastic, reportedly saying,

'Oh dear, doesn't he understand that we're in too much of a mess and have so much to do without him coming?' – a point of view which was probably shared by most of the already overworked police who would now have the additional responsibility of ensuring the King's safety. Not that he was in much danger as his visit was enthusiastically received. One customer at a mobile canteen, a little old lady of around 70 who had nothing left but what she stood up in, summed up the feelings of the citizens of Coventry by crying,

'God bless you, lad. You've got more pluck than that Hitler bloke!'

At least one prominent citizen declined the honour of being

presented to the King. Councillor Pearl Hyde told the Chief Constable, Captain S A Hector,

'I'm too busy. Secondly, I'm too dirty and, thirdly, I'm wearing a pair of your trousers.'

In the event, the Chief Constable – one of the few to admit to anxiety about the morale of the citizens – was enthusiastic about the visit and reported to the Home Office,

> *The visit of H M The King to the city on the 16th ... completely set aside any doubt I had as to the attitude of the inhabitants. The visit ... completely sealed the steadiness of the citizens.*

It was to be expected that the war would have an effect on the population as a whole, although the anticipated riots and panic did not materialize. How did the British public react to being the target of determined air attacks? The broad outlines seem fairly clear. When an area suffered a heavy raid for the first time, morale took a severe battering but, after the initial shock, most people adapted remarkably quickly. A distinction is sometimes made between *active* and *passive* morale, active morale being expressed in heroic gestures, the promoting of patriotic slogans and so on. This was confined to relatively few, the majority showing a high level of passive morale by a willingness to soldier on in the face of what sometimes seemed overwhelming adversity. It was perhaps examples of high active morale shown by individual policemen (amongst others) which helped to foster the passive morale of the remainder. One Mass Observation diarist wrote:

> *I think bus conductors can easily be bracketed with policemen as being the most consistently cheerful and helpful of public servants.*

To enable the Government to keep its finger on the pulse of the nation, chief constables were required to submit fortnightly reports to the Home Office, covering a number of aspects of morale including;

(i)   the conduct of the public during air raids

(ii)   the reaction to evacuation, rationing, blackout, restrictions on places of entertainment, etc.

(iii) the effect of enemy propaganda

(iv)   the attitude to censorship and publicity in general

(v)   the reaction to subversive and pacifist propaganda

(vi)   the industrial conditions, particularly signs of unrest and strikes

These reports were introduced in 1939 and continued to be submitted until February 1942, by which time they had become so stereotyped and routine that they were abolished and replaced by a monthly report, plus immediate reports on items of particular interest. This revised scheme continued for the duration of the war.

The early reports showed that there was no panic and a marked reluctance to seek shelter when the air raid sirens sounded. There was also a general acceptance of wartime conditions such as rationing, food shortages, the blackout. It is evident from these reports that morale paradoxically rose after the fall of France in 1940. This may be attributed to (a) the now accepted gravity of the situation, (b) the fact that the British were no longer reliant of any foreign country (other than our dominions and colonies), (c) the new leadership (Churchill) and, (d) a new feeling of decisiveness. For once the Government and the people were united in one great, common purpose: victory. There was general indignation regarding the bombing of London, especially when Buckingham Palace was hit but morale generally remained high.

There have been suggestions that, at least in some towns, the civic centre and police headquarters were moved to safer but comparatively inaccessible places and that, as a result, the higher police and other supervisory authorities were physically out of touch and, being busy with direct administrative problems, readily accepted the officially sanctioned versions of events but there is ample testimony to the remarkable *sang froid* and phlegm demonstrated by the British in the summer of 1940. Mollie Panter-Downes, wrote in *New Yorker* after the fall of Belgium and the first news of Dunkirk that 'the calmness of the average non-military citizen was magnificent'. One of the Mass Observation's correspondents reported on a public meeting held in his area in August, 1940, at which there was :

> *... good humour, friendliness and curiosity combined with an almost passionate interest in the speaker [Duff Cooper, the Minister for Information] as a celebrity. The meeting began with a civic procession, led by mounted and foot police. Procession met with a good deal of good-humoured jeering,*

'Here come the Wardens – keep a straight face!' and 'The charge of the Light Brigade' (mounted police). Even the police entered into the spirit of the thing – a significant indication of the mass-feeling being generated.

The report continues :

The police still hold back the crowd ... The mounted policeman moves the crowd in the middle of the road and makes funny remarks to ladies who have to pass near his horse; 'He won't hurt you, lady. In fact, he likes ladies.' He keeps the crowd in very good humour.

It has to be appreciated that this upsurge in morale was clearly fostered by an ignorance of all but the broadcast military facts. Any news item deemed to be detrimental to morale was quickly smothered. The high point of morale in the summer of 1940 was quickly followed by a degree of disillusionment resulting from the 'Phoney War' but this, in turn, was soon replaced by the Blitz. In the period September to November 1940 morale was greatly improved by the visible and efficient way the police and the other civil defence services performed their tasks, both in the lulls and during air raids[10]. George Lewis was a constable in the Worcester City Police and was one of those sent on Mutual Aid to Coventry shortly after that city was blitzed in November, 1940. They were accommodated in the General Wolfe Hotel and were still helping with the clearing up when Christmas approached and things gradually began to assume an air of near normality:

Sprigs of greenery and coloured paper chains and lanterns began to appear in those public houses that were open and conversation turned to things seasonal. Shortly before Christmas Eve an impromptu concert was held in the General Wolfe Hotel and, when 'Time' was called, both customers and policemen stood as one as the pianist struck the opening chords of the National Anthem. It was a most moving experience – we were comrades in arms – and I can still taste the salt on my lips as the tears coursed down my cheeks.

It was around this time that one chief constable reported that use of the expression 'Britain can take it' was widely disliked. He said that, although it was true that the people could take whatever was thrown at them if they had to, they had no desire to do so if it could be avoided and greater attention should be given to relieving them of the necessity. However, as one Clydebank woman said, as she swept up the glass and debris from her path the morning after a raid, 'Well, there's one thing about these raids; they do make you forget about the war.'

As the war progressed, the morale of the nation plummeted until by early 1942 it was at its lowest ebb. The country had effectively stood alone for over two years and the news for Britain could not have been bleaker. The Japanese had invaded Singapore, the Wehrmacht's tanks were closing in on Stalingrad, the Allied armies were in retreat across Libya and even more ships were being lost in the Atlantic to U-boats. The Americans had recently joined in the fray but the effect of their intervention was yet to be felt. Even the troops were suffering the same malaise and the winter of 1941-42 has been described as a particularly bad period for the morale of the Canadian soldiers in this country and a time when misbehaviour was particularly high[11].

The nervous and physical strain borne by the populace was manifested in other, more sinister statistics. Less care was taken of babies and young children, more infants than usual suffocated in their cots or choked over their food. More fatal accidents occurred to young children in their homes and elsewhere, especially in the static water tanks placed in the street for use in fighting fires and, although there was much less traffic on the roads, more children died from road accidents than before the war. Mothers who would normally have been at home looking after their offspring were now engaged on war work and, with fathers away in the services, discipline was conspicuous by its absence. The neighbourhood community had disintegrated and the older children were taking on the role of parents[12].

With the opening of the 'Second Front' on D Day, 1944, morale took an immediate upswing. At last it was clear that the fortunes of war were favouring the Allies, at least in Europe. The Blitzkrieg had ceased and air raids were now more sporadic and light. Even the introduction of the V1 or flying bomb did little to curb the spirit of the nation. Sergeant Grey describes how he witnessed Sir Hartley Shawcross prosecuting a case in No 3 Court at the Old Bailey. He was addressing the Bench when the familiar sound of a 'doodlebug' was heard. Counsel continued his address and the court continued its business. Then the motor of the bomb cut out and an awful silence fell as every-one looked at each other, everyone immobile – waiting. Then came the bang as the device came to earth and struck Cloak Lane police station just across the road from the Old Bailey. There was a slight pause and then Sir Hartley continued his speech as though nothing had happened. The course of English justice was interrupted but temporarily[13].

On the whole, the morale of the British public was remarkably high throughout the war and that of the police similarly high. Nearly every correspondant has remarked that the police felt they were doing a good job and that they were appreciated and respected by the general public, something which was not always the case before the war.

One effect of the war was a fundamental change in behaviour towards others, a hardening of attitudes, even by those who would normally regard themselves as essentially civilised and educated. The official Civil Defence historian, Terence O'Brien, wrote that :

> *The temper of the British people does not become warlike until a war has actually started.'* [14]

- and this appears to be borne out by contemporary reports. The writer and broadcaster, A G Street, regarded by all as a bucolic, avuncular type of man, admitted being keen to hunt down a German airman who had baled out and experienced the same feeling during the manhunt as he got from riding to hounds in more peaceful times[15].

Nella Last, a peace-loving middle-class housewife from Barrow-in-Furness tells how, in October 1940, a group of rough youths banged into her and her husband as they made their way through the blackout, whirling them round and pushing and shoving:

> *I was amazed at the fury I felt. I kicked one lout very hard on his shins, and grasped the ear of another who pushed his silly face close to mine, and said severely as I shook his head, 'Young man, where's your manners?' My husband said I spoke like a schoolmarm... I felt a mad desire to roll up my sleeves and fight someone. I did not feel flurried or upset – or even angry – but a 'Come on, then' feeling. Most amazing in a peaceable – and gentle – woman of fifty-one!'* [16]

There are grounds for believing that the public's perception of the police changed dramatically as a result of the war. Police historians such as T A Critchley have since stated that the reputation and morale of the British police was never higher than it was during the Second World War. Certainly the shared vicissitudes brought the police closer to the people it served and there is no doubt that certain sections of the public had hitherto viewed the police in a less than friendly light. Mention has already been made about the changes which occurred in the attitude of wardens towards the police in the East End of London, being mainly drawn from the lower working class strata of society which traditionally saw the police as their natural enemies. Most contemporary policemen regarded the inhabitants of the East End as rough and tough but some were of the view that 'they didn't let you down.' Most of the trouble in the area is alleged to have come from visiting seamen. It seems to be accepted that policemen selected to work places like Limehouse tended to be those who had a reputation for toughness and who would be prepared to use their fists first and ask questions later. The local superintendent was regularly heard to tell his men that he didn't want reports – he wanted bodies (ie, prisoners).

The view that the locals rallied round their policemen in this time of shared problems is supported by Constable Arthur Marshall. Referring to the George Medal awarded to his colleague, Sam Radford, Arthur Marshall is sure that the gallantry shown by this officer would have gone unremarked and unrewarded were it not for the actions of a few of the locals, some of whom he had previously arrested, who went to the station and made statements commending his actions.

> *You see, with all the rogues, thieves and vagabonds on the other side of the fence, when the war came, that didn't matter.*

The middle classes, for their part, still tended to look down on the police as Sergeant Grey of the Metropolitan Police found when he was bombed out of his home. As a temporary measure, a flat was found for him at Blackheath in the virtually unscathed southern suburbs of the capital. Here his neighbours included a retired Captain and a Royal Navy Commander and others of that social standing and Sergeant Grey soon found that he was not very welcome because of his East End antecedents. His short stay in the area was not a very happy one[17].

Obviously, attitudes towards the police depended very much on the area; the East End of London and similar areas in other big cities had always had a confrontational relationship with the police, whereas small towns and, especially, country areas enjoyed a generally amicable relationship with their local policeman. Constable Bert Ayers took over the Bilsington beat on the Romney Marsh in Kent in 1939 and, since his predecessors were not particularly popular and inclined to be lazy (according to him), he had an uphill battle to establish himself in the area, a battle not helped by the fact that he was born in London and was therefore a 'foreigner'. However, once he made it clear that he was willing to admit his lack of knowledge of country ways and was prepared to learn, he was quickly accepted and the glasses of cider came with increasing regularity. During the very bad winter of 1940/41 he earned the respect of his 'parishioners' by struggling through the snow to deliver bread to outlying and cut-off farms. However, he insists that he was no pushover and that he enforced the law rigorously, for example by insisting that the farmers carried out their sheep-dipping properly – something his predecessors had apparently neglected to do.

A sceptical reader might believe that this view of rural life is tinged with the glow of nostalgia; this may be so but, if it is, it is a view which is shared by many of those who served in the countryside. The rural man was usually closely involved in community affairs – helping with the village fête, for example – and he was usually respected if not actually liked in all cases. Much of this attitude may be due to the lack of pressure on them to submit offence reports or take prisoners. This was firmly brought home to a young constable who had just been posted to a small East Sussex market town. When he brought in a sheaf of reports against the drivers of cars found parked in a 'No Waiting' area, the inspector asked him if he had spoken to the drivers. The constable admitted that he had not.

'Have you told them you are reporting them?', asked the inspector.

'No, Sir,' was the reply.

'Don't you think you should?' pursued the inspector.

When the constable questioned why he should adopt this course of action, he was told,

'If you don't you are going to make a lot of enemies and I know that a lot of these people are in a position to be very helpful to you in the future. If you tell them not to park there, they won't be offended and if they persist in doing so you have every right to prosecute them, but a friendly warning in the first instance could pay dividends.'

So ended the constable's first lesson in the art of rural policing.

At the other end of the country, Ted Maidment, who served with the East Riding Constabulary during the war (and retired in due course as a superintendent) supports this view of rural policing:

> *Ninety per cent of the public thought we were great. On reflection this could probably be due to the fact that, in the main, we were serving a rural area. I am inclined to think that the only real friends the police have are among the Country Folk.*

In the south-east of the country, where many of the inhabitants had been evacuated, even many moderate-sized towns found themselves with a population not much greater than the average village. Because of this, those that remained got to know their policemen better – got to know them as people rather than mere figures of authority. Like the rural areas, there was little crime and so the emphasis was on the service side of policing, rather than the repressive side which may have been the case pre-war. Public morale in these areas was high, largely due to the fact that most of those remaining were engaged on essential work and had sent their families away to quieter areas, which meant that this worry was removed from their minds. The morale of the police was similarly high, the overworked officers happy in the knowledge that they were doing a good and useful job, appreciated by the public they served. Mrs Jess Williams, the widow of Sergeant George Williams of K Division of the Metropolitan police reflects Winston Churchill's view of the police and remembers how she liked the force -

> *... we seemed one happy family, we had our social side and it was lovely. All the men were gentlemen and afraid of naught and the public respected them.*

The average British Bobby was also highly thought of by the US troops in this country, not being like his counterpart across the Atlantic, and even some unpopular policemen surprised the locals by their unprecedented behaviour, such as being seen dancing in the streets on VE night. At Ramsgate (Kent), a massive fire was lit on the sands on VJ night, watched by at least 22,000 people. 22 incendiary bombs, intended for ARP practice, were included in the blaze. One policeman was carried shoulder-high through the streets by a jubilant crowd, which later got rather out of hand and tipped beach huts onto the blaze.

Although it is now suggested that relations between the police and the public were at an all-time high during the war, this did not prevent the Commissioner of the Metropolitan Police calling upon the people of London in 1944 to co-operate more in the prevention of crime. Much is said and written these days about the good old days when one could leave one's door unlocked and a pie on the windowsill without fear of thieves and it is interesting to see that, half a century ago, the Commissioner's Report was giving 'bits of advice', so simple and obvious that he was almost ashamed to mention them -

> *That is just the trouble. All that is needed to prevent serious loss of personal property even under existing wartime conditions of life in the Metropolis is the exercise of a little commonsense, care and forethought. To lock one's door and window fastenings, to leave as little of value as possible in the house or flat when there is no one there to look after it, ... to keep secure hold of handbags – these are simple precautions but a vast amount of trouble, anxiety and loss would be avoided by their habitual observance and the work of the police would be greatly assisted.*[18]

Police accommodation was often very poor by modern standards, both for personal use and for official purposes. Eric St Johnston describes the situation which pertained in Oxfordshire when he took up his appointment as chief constable there in 1940.

> *At Headquarters there was also residential accommodation – if it could be so called – for six constables. This was quite appalling. It consisted solely of one dormitory and a kitchen-dining room. The dormitory contained six iron bedsteads with the minimum of bedding, and behind each bed there was a coat hook on the wall where a man could hang his suit ... There were no chairs and no covering for the floor. In the kitchen the only furniture was an old wooden table and two backless forms, while the plates, cutlery, pots and pans were such that I quickly had them consigned to the dustbin. Conditions in the police stations throughout the county were not much better... many [rural police houses] did not have electric light or water closet lavatories...*

During the hostilities, many police stations were damaged by enemy action and temporary police stations sprang up in all sorts of unusual places. These were seldom properly equipped and it took all the native cunning of the officers concerned to make their new work place as comfortable as they could. When the gas was cut off from Millwall station, all meals had to be heated on an open fire in the charge room – not a very satisfactory arrangement. One day the duty sergeant saw four of his men walking towards the station carrying a coffin-like box which was obviously very heavy and, on approaching this struggling band of policemen, he saw that it was in fact a Kitchener stove, all blacklead and polish, the pride of every East End home. Deciding that discretion was called for the sergeant branched off to avoid meeting the approaching men and, on his return to the station some time later, found the stove happily installed in the Recreation Room where it stayed for the duration. Was this a case of looting? Probably, according to the strict definition of the law, but it is equally probable that, if left, the stove would have been destroyed in the subsequent clearing-up operations and the operation was no doubt regarded by the policemen concerned as a good and proper case of salvage of abandoned goods.

As far as is known, this rescued stove never gave cause for concern, unlike the chimney at Woolwich police station which one day caught fire through a well-intentioned officer putting a sheet of metal in front of it to help it draw. With smoke billowing everywhere, the already embarrassed policemen were further chagrined when a passing sailor poked his head in the window and cheekily commented,

'If our ship had made that much smoke getting ready to leave, you would have booked us.'

It is perhaps symptomatic of the times that this sailor would probably not have dared to make such a comment before the war and it nicely illustrates the relaxation of the 'them and us' attitudes which had previously prevailed. The war caused much stress and trauma but, so far as the police were concerned, it did have its positive aspects and probably marked a sea-change in relations with the public.

EUC 705

14. Looking to a Brighter Tomorrow

In the years between the two World Wars, a high level of unemployment, coupled with poor social welfare arrangements, meant that the police – a job with prospects and a good pension – could take its pick from the many applicants, most of whom came from the upper working class or artisan level. A very high level of physical stature and fitness was demanded, together with an above average level of education and literacy. This is not to say that recruits were all budding academics but they were certainly literate and numerate.

Not only could the police authorities demand a high standard from their recruits, they could, and did, demand a high standard of behaviour and imposed what was sometimes quite Draconian disciplinary measures. Where a constable was appointed acting sergeant to fill a temporary vacancy his chances of promotion to substantive rank depended very much on whether he had put some of his colleagues on report for some disciplinary misdemeanour or other. Since the same constable might well have to revert to his true rank without being promoted, or pending promotion, he was in a somewhat difficult position; if he failed to be strict, his promotion prospects were blighted, if he was firm, his popularity and standing with his colleagues would be at zero.

Tom Jones was a constable in the Liverpool City Police at the beginning of the war and remembers one sergeant tapping a certain pavement flagstone with his stick, saying that if the constable was not standing on it, he would be off his point and would be disciplined. On another occasion an inspector arrived at the scene of an unexploded bomb where three constables had been on duty for sixteen hours without any refreshment. Looking across at the mobile canteen which had drawn up at the scene, the inspector made it quite clear that anyone found partaking of refreshment would be put on a charge.

Bert Cavey, the Metropolitan Policeman, tells how, when he was on plain clothes patrol in Bethnal Green with another officer, he saw a brewer's dray, drawn by two huge shire horses, galloping towards them along a narrow cobbled street, out of control, with no one in the driving seat. As the street led directly into a major road where the bolting horses could do untold harm, the two officers grabbed the harness as the horses passed them and managed to divert them into the side where the dray rubbed against the wall and so stopped the runaways. The draymen came running up and said that they had been having a cup of tea when the horses had bolted. As it was illegal to leave such a vehicle unattended, the officers told the draymen to say that one of them had been with the horses when they bolted but that he had been unable to restrain them. A passer-by, having seen the incident, reported it to the police station with a view to the constables' bravery being recognised and an investigation was begun with a view to the award of a medal. Unfortunately, the draymen decided to tell the truth when they were interviewed and, instead of being decorated, the constables narrowly avoided being disciplined for neglect of duty, on the grounds that they should have reported the errant draymen.

In the Metropolitan Police, the previous Commissioner, Lord Trenchard, had introduced the controversial 'Trenchard Scheme' for the accelerated promotion of what he regarded as young 'high-flyers' to the rank of station inspector, and ultimately to the very highest ranks of the police service. Many of them did so and a number of the chief constables in post-war Britain were 'Trenchard men'. As might be expected, the scheme was not an overwhelming success with the lower ranks, many of whom saw their promotion prospects diminished by the installation of these young, inexperienced men over them. Many tales were (and still are) told of their incompetence, most of which are probably apocryphal, although most undoubtedly have a basis in the truth. Bert Cavey, a wily and experienced motor patrol officer, tells how he stopped a lorry containing a load of old car batteries which the driver claimed to have picked up from various garages. As all the batteries were of the same make this did not ring true and so he arrested the driver on suspicion. At the police station the young station inspector was going to refuse the charge on the basis that the man's story *might* be true. The constable responded that, in this case, he would follow the lorry until it left the sub-division when he would rearrest the driver and take him to another police station. Luckily, the more senior sub-divisional inspector arrived on the scene and agreed to accept the charge, thus avoiding a degree of unpleasantness, and the lorry driver was in due course convicted of receiving stolen property. On another occasion the same station inspector asked the driver of a patrol car in which he was being given a lift why they were keeping to the back streets, rather than using the quicker main road. The driver pointed out to him that, since criminals tended to avoid the main streets and prefer-red to stick to the quieter side roads, that is where the police should be. This rather naïve inspector eventually gained experience and wisdom and went on to become the chief constable of a county force.

Duties were demanding and any shortcomings were dealt with harshly. Special Sergeant Frank Butler described graphically the arrangements which existed at Cloak Lane police station in the City of London at the beginning of the war and which reflected those which had been in use for decades :

> *Mostly about 60 men paraded but there could be double that number. They paraded 20 minutes before duty, in three lines relating to sections. The station sergeant stood at the desk and called out the number of a constable and the duty allotted to him. It was necessary to be very attentive... The order would then be 'Truncheons and armlets' and each man would lay his truncheon across his armlet and the station sergeant would pass down the lines verifying that each man was properly equipped..*

Although the men already on patrol could not go off duty (and were in fact not supposed to leave their beats) until relieved, they would quietly make their way towards the station and lurk in dark doorways. As the reliefs marched out of the police station and passed them, they would softly call out the number of the beat they were still supposed to be patrolling. When the relief allocated to that beat for the next eight hours heard the whispered number he would stop and be briefed by the man he was relieving. The relieved (in more senses than one) constable then returned to the station where he would report to his sergeant for permission to go off duty. Given the time taken reporting on and off duty, the official eight hour tour of duty was seldom actually less than eight and a half or even nine.

Despite the strict discipline, policemen always seemed to find a way in which they could get a cup of tea or a pint of beer to relieve the monotony of their work. Sometimes they employed quite ingenious ways of escaping from supervision for a few minutes such as the group of City of London policemen who created a small 'rest room' for themselves in the ruins of a bombed-out building. A small fire was kept burning inside to ward off the cold winter weather and the constables would recline in salvaged armchairs for a chat and a smoke, out of sight of their superiors.

The uniform worn at that time had changed but little over the preceding half century. Constables and sergeants usually wore the traditional helmet, although men on rural beats and the comparatively rare drivers and motor-cyclists commonly wore a peaked cap, as did the more senior officers (albeit of a somewhat different design). The tunic was done up to the neck in the 'dog collar' manner in the case of the lower ranks while inspectors and above wore a tunic modelled on the military service dress with a belt and four large pockets. The rural men in some forces wore breeches and puttees to make riding a bicycle easier. In wet weather a heavy serge cape was thrown over the tunic which merely succeeded in diverting the flow of rainwater onto the knees and calves of the unfortunate and miserable policeman. The proliferation of uniforms during the war caused many to look more closely at the police version and the *Police Review* received a number of letters in 1942 suggesting changes, usually advocating some form of battledress, which was seen as being much more practical than the existing uniform. Since the Special Constabulary was still in many cases without any uniform all, blue battledress was also suggested for them. The Cardiganshire Standing Joint Committee considered this suggestion but decided to postpone a decision on uniforms for the Special Constabulary for three months 'because the war might be over by then.'

Wartime conditions highlighted the problems which a large number of independent and autonomous police forces posed when matters of national importance were concerned. Tradition and sentiment militated against the creation of a national police force but it had long been clear that some of the smaller forces were not as efficient as they might have been, simply through lack of resources. The question of amalgamating the smaller forces with their larger neighbours was by no means a new issue. Such mergers had taken place in the past and the Desborough Committee of 1920 had recommended the amalgamation of all non-county borough forces with the neighbouring county force. The Home Office decided against introducing legislation and actively encouraged voluntary amalgamations, but with little success; local pride was too strong! There was also the view that the smaller forces were good training grounds for the eventual occupants of major chief constable-ships. Leamington Spa was quoted as an extreme example, where there had been four chief constables in as many years, resulting in so many changes in practices that the ordinary member of the force was thoroughly confused.

Over the years further mergers were recommended but, even in June, 1940, the Home Office view was that there was no particular need for action at that time.

It was a problem which was not going to go away, however, and war-time conditions and the need for a concentration of policing powers in a single force where this was called for on military grounds became more and more apparent. At an interview with the representatives of the police authorities, the Home Secretary gave assurances that, so far as he was concerned, this would be a purely wartime measure. Regulations were therefore made which gave the Home Secretary the power to make Orders regarding the amalgamation of police forces if he was satisfied that the merger was necessary to facilitate military operations. Some of the police authorities were violently opposed to these powers and stirred up a lot of opposition. On 14 October, 1942, the House of Commons debated a Resolution praying that the Regulations be annulled but the Home Secretary reiterated his promise to restrict amalgamations to cases where the war made them desirable. When asked whether he would want to reestablish the small forces after the war, he replied,

'This is being done by Defence Regulations, it automatically comes to an end at the end of the war, but it is perfectly competent for the Government and Parliament of the time, if they so wish, to pass legislation continuing these measures and to provide for others. But I do not think I ought to prejudice that issue one way or the other', and the Resolution was withdrawn[1].

The views of the military were sought who plumped for widespread and wholesale amalgamations but the Home Office eventually decided to restrict these to the southern counties of Kent, Surrey, Sussex, Hampshire, Wiltshire and Cornwall. In the case of Sussex there was no one force which could be regarded as predominant and suitable to serve as the centre or headquarters of a joint force and the only practical solution was to unite the two county forces of East and West Sussex, and the borough forces situated therein (Brighton, Hove, Hastings and Eastbourne) to form a single new force. In Surrey, the Guildford and Reigate forces were amalgamated with the Surrey County force while, in Cornwall, the Penzance borough force was amalgamated with Cornwall county. Salisbury merged with Wiltshire while the Isle of Wight and Winchester forces joined Hampshire.

The most significant change occurred in Kent where no less than nine borough forces were amalgamated with the Kent County Constabulary (Maidstone, Rochester, Gravesend, Folkestone, Margate, Ramsgate, Dover, Tunbridge Wells and Canterbury city). The strengths of these borough forces varied from 40 (Canterbury) to 73 (Folkestone). This amalgamation was to take place as soon as a replacement had been found for the county chief constable who, as we saw in the last chapter, had committed suicide. In the event, Sir Percy Sillitoe, the Chief Constable of Glasgow was appointed to take over and organise the amalgamation (at a salary somewhat lower than that he had been receiving in Glasgow). Kent was singled out as a pilot project because of the long-range plans for the invasion of Europe and the amalgamation took place on 1 April, 1943.

These mergers were not without their problems. It was commonly alleged by county men that some borough chief constables promoted certain of their officers immediately prior to the amalgamation, thus ensuring that they had a much better position in the new force than they might otherwise have had. The county men were naturally aggrieved as this obviously affected their own prospects.

The pre-war depression which meant that police authorities had been able to get the pick of the labour market and yet pay them modest wages was fine as long as that situation lasted but the war brought greatly increased prosperity to the ordinary working man and the police, prevented from resigning by law, found their salaries diminishing in value. Average male earnings rose from 69 shillings in 1938 to 99 shillings in 1941, reaching a peak of 124 shillings in 1944. Private soldiers were on 15 shillings a week, 7 shillings of which was paid by married men to their wives (who also got an allowance for children) but they were clothed, fed and housed for nothing. Police auxiliaries were paid around 60 shillings a week, a sum similar to that paid the regulars although the latter had housing as well as uniform. In 1944, when the posts of chief constable for both Durham and Hertfordshire were advertised, the salaries were £1,450 and £1,000 a year respectively.

Police Regulations strictly prohibited the taking of other employment, although some took a chance and found themselves a part-time job. Constable Bill Cavey managed to build up quite a profitable window cleaning round in London towards the end of the war and was even employing three other men. Word got out, however, and he was called up before his superintendent who asked if he was in fact moonlighting. The constable naturally denied it and was told,

'Well, if you're not, you have nothing to worry about. But if you are, you'd be a fool to continue, wouldn't you?'

On the principle of a nod being as good as a wink to a blind horse, the part-time business was closed down forthwith.

As the war drew inexorably towards a close with the Allied troops advancing and liberating much of Nazi-occupied Europe, so a new police task began to make itself apparent. The policing of occupied Europe having been largely a matter for the occupying troops and the infamous Gestapo, their removal left a hiatus which needed to be filled, and filled quickly if these countries were not to become completely lawless. This was not an entirely unexpected event and a committee had been set up early in 1943 with the task of 'preparing a plan to control the civil population when the Allied Armies re-enter North West Europe.' Sitting on this committee and representing the British police forces and given responsibility for the police, fire, prison and civil defence services, under the umbrella name of 'Public Safety' was the 32 year old chief constable of Oxfordshire, Eric St Johnston – one of the contentious 'Trenchard' men.

Eric St Johnstone's first task was to try to assess the number of trained policemen who would be required to implement the as yet nebulous plans and an arbitrary figure of 500 was mooted. This was accepted by the Home Office which then invited serving policemen of all ranks to apply for posts in this new organisation. There was no shortage of volunteers and, initially, 20 chief constables and assistant chief constables were selected for special training at the Civil Affairs Staff College. The larger number of lower ranking officers was sent on courses at the Metropolitan Police Training School at Peel House. After training these officers were all returned to their own forces to await call up. It was agreed that those of chief officer rank would be appointed in the rank of lieutenant-colonel, while inspectors would be majors and sergeants would be given the rank of captain or lieutenant.

In the summer of 1943 a call was made for 60 police officers to follow the imminent invasion of Sicily and Italy. As they were needed quickly it was decided to take the whole number from the Metropolitan Police and the previously trained volunteers were quickly commissioned into the Army under the command of the chief constable of Leamington, Arthur Young, who was given the rank of full colonel. By the end of that year, the Police Review (24 December, 1943) was able to report that Chief Inspector Pollock of the Metropolitan Police, now holding the rank of Lt. Colonel, had been made the Chief of Police in Rome.

By April 1944 the full 500 police officers had been trained at Peel House and the time had come to call them up. They were duly commissioned and sent to holding units in various parts of the country, the main one being in the Grand Hotel at Eastbourne. It so happened that the Americans had very few professional police officers on whom to call for Public Safety work but when the plans had been made it was found that the British did not need the whole 500 Public Safety Officers for the British area of operations and so it was possible to supply British police officers not only for the Italian Theatre but also to join the American Civil Affairs detachments. Immediately after D Day in June 1944, the British were asked to nominate a British Public Safety Officer for the American detachment going into Cherbourg, the first large city it was expected to be liberated, and the chief constable of Accrington, W J H Palfrey, was appointed and did an extremely efficient job there. Later he moved to Paris where he was to act as the Allied liaison officer to the Paris Police.

As the war drew to a close, so the former policemen serving in the Armed Forces were gradually released to return to their old forces. At a meeting of the War Cabinet in February, 1944, the Home Secretary and the Secretary of State for Scotland had urged the early return from the Armed forces of any policeman not urgently required for operational duties. At that time there were some 15,000 policemen serving, 2,400 naval ratings and 800 officers, over 2,000 as air crew and 1,000 holding commissioned rank in the RAF and 9,000 in the Army. Meantime the regular police strength was 22,000 lower than it was on the outbreak of the war: the dilution with auxiliaries had necessarily resulted in some lowering of quality and their number, then about 27,000, would soon be reduced by a third and most of the remainder would probably want to leave the police as soon as they could.

A review of police establishments carried out shortly after VE Day, when the Civil Defence Services were being rapidly scaled down, revealed that the current state was as follows :

Regular policemen with less than 30 years service	38,739
Regular policewomen	416
Regular policemen with full service for pension	2,717
First Police Reserve	2,061
Police War Reserve	14,412
Full-time Special Constables	732
Womens' Auxiliary Police Corps	3,702
	62,779

The total strength was therefore not far below the pre-war establishment of men, 63,388 but, of course, the make-up was very different. Men and women in the last five categories were mostly retained unwillingly, especially the auxiliaries who had been conscripted and were serving away from their homes and were anxious to get back to their businesses. The potential loss in the near future might therefore amount to 15,000 men or more. Against this there was a similar number of policemen serving in the Armed Forces and it was expected that 8,000 would be released by the end of the year (1945). This would still leave a very large deficiency however, to which must be added natural wastage and so recruiting became an urgent problem.

Most of the policemen serving in the Armed Forces accepted the opportunity to leave and rejoin their peacetime occupation, although others chose to remain in the Forces where some had reached high rank. This was, in fact, one of the biggest problems facing the returning servicemen. Many former constables and sergeants had held commissioned rank, others had been fêted as pilots in the RAF and the thought of returning to the humdrum life of a constable was not always appealing. Freddie Pearce, who returned to the Devon force after over three years in the Army, describes the dilemma in which such officers found themselves:

... I found that, once hostilities had ended there was not the pressing desire to return to the force, that I had earlier anticipated. Following many varied experiences during the conflict and then many tasks connected with the military control of Germany ... I found myself being given tasks which, to some extent, had been influenced by my police background. This was followed by offers of a permanent commission with the probability of rapid advancement in rank. This compared, at first, rather favourably with the thought of returning to my force as a PC ...

The situation changed dramatically, however, soon after the defeat of the Churchill government in 1945. It soon became apparent that the new government envisaged there would be little need for a substantial permanent army and a three-year contract was then the most on offer.

If it was difficult for the policemen returning from the services, it was also difficult for those of their colleagues who had remained in the police force and had born the brunt of policing throughout the war. It is opportune to note the observations made in H M Inspectors' Report for the year ended 29 September, 1945:

As H M Inspectors we wish to avoid too fulsome expressions of praise for the police service ... but we should be doing less than our duty if in this Report we failed to pay tribute to the work of the police as a whole during the war. Virtually the whole of the younger officers were absent on active service, and many of those left were old for the arduous and uncertain tasks of a police officer, but they have borne their burdens ... with their customary faithfulness ... The public appreciation of the police has never been greater, the confidence that is placed in the police has never been higher and the relationship between the public and the police service was never better. For this state of affairs all ranks of the service – men and women, regulars and auxiliaries, part-time and whole-time alike – can take credit.[2]

These policemen felt that many of their ex-Service workmates had an inflated sense of their own importance, something which, as Freddie

Pearce found when he returned to Devon, they were not going to encourage:

> *When I did return to the force ... late in 1945, I soon found that*
> *there was no question of any of us being regarded as heroes by*
> *a fair proportion of the supervisory officers. There was some*
> *sympathetic reference to those who had unfortunately been*
> *killed on active service but little else. I was frequently*
> *reminded that, whilst away, the Home Front had been as*
> *difficult to maintain as the areas of conflict in which I had*
> *served. One rather dour and old-fashioned sergeant was not*
> *averse from making disparaging remarks about 'gentlemen*
> *types' from the Army.*

The lukewarm welcome was not made more cordial by the fact that some of the returning policemen tried to use their military rank in their title and wanted to be known as Major Constable Smith, or Squadron Leader Sergeant Jones. This idea was quickly quashed, however. Nevertheless, their wartime experiences had left their mark on some of the officers who returned to the forces they had left up to six years previously and this did not go unnoticed by their superiors. Quite a few received early promotion and went on to carve successful careers in the police service. Others (and not always those who had achieved some rank in the Armed Forces) found it impossible to adjust and left, some very quickly.

The problems of reintegration were aggravated by the serious housing shortage. Many officers had married in the time they had been away and, with no accommodation available for them within their police district, found themselves separated from their wives and families once more. When Constable A Roberts returned to the West Riding Constabulary after nearly four years on flying duties with the RAF, he found himself posted as a detective officer to Keighley where there was no accommodation for him and his wife. She had to stay with her war-widowed mother while he moved into 'digs'. Eventually he had the offer of a house in Harrogate, in a poor state of decoration and with no bath or hot water but, as Mrs Roberts was expecting their first child, he was persuaded to take it. He had to pay for his own removal and moved his few belongings on a flat lorry on a wet Sunday. The electricity and gas had been turned off and the newly-reunited pair had to wait until the next day for them to be connected.

Other officers in county forces applied for a rural beat, knowing that this would usually mean their being allocated a police house/office in pleasant surroundings. Dennis Vorley, another former RAF pilot, was delighted when he was posted to Boxgrove in West Sussex. Only four miles from Chichester, the beat included Tangmere aerodrome, Goodwood House and racecourse, a displaced persons' hostel, a German prisoner of war camp and a squatters camp.

> *The wide variety of work which this gave me as the only police officer covering the area was greatly to my satisfaction, even though my only means of transport was a heavy old Raleigh issue bicycle.*

One officer was informed by a colleague that an elderly man who had collapsed and died in the street had been contemplating letting part of his house. He rushed round there, arriving within an hour of the unfortunate man's collapse, only to learn from the widow that the rooms had already been let.

Those who had been away quickly noticed some changes. Tom Jones, who returned to Liverpool City (previously one of the most rigidly disciplined forces in the country) was astonished to see -

> *... the Bridewell sergeant, previously one of the most ferocious of men, leaning on the counter gossiping with three young constables. It was even more of a shock to find that I and one other were covering ground that was covered by two sections in other days, two and a half day beats which used to be five night beats. I think that, with the large number of men waiting to go on pension at the war's end, that the War Reserve Police were got rid of with indecent haste.*

Before the war recruits were told quite categorically that the force had no time for 'eight-hours-a-day men', the inference being that one did not go off duty as soon as a tour had been completed but stayed on at the station in case something came up. There was no question of overtime but this was soon to change and a system of 'time off in lieu' was introduced. Similarly, representative sport became regarded as duty and those selected to play for their force no longer had to arrange to be off duty to compete in a cricket or football match.

The ending of the war marked the closing of a brief but momentous chapter in the history of the police service of Great Britain. Never again would things be the same as they were a mere six years earlier. The amalgamations which had been enforced on a number of forces were retained in some areas, notably Kent, and those other forces which reverted to the pre-war position in this respect were to find themselves the subject of another, permanent amalgamation within the next two decades. The strict, military-based discipline imposed since Victorian times would gradually be relaxed to reflect the service role of the police, rather than the force aspect. No longer would policemen have to put up with antiquated and dilapidated accommodation lacking even the most basic amenities and police stations would be provided with appropriate refreshment and recreational facilities. The heavy bicycle would soon be replaced by the Panda car and the main roads patrolled by powerful cars and motorcycles.

None of this would take place overnight, of course, but the seeds were sown during the war and in the years which immediately followed it, which would bear fruit as time went on. Before many of those serving in the force at the end of the war had qualified for their pension, the police service would be very different from that which existed when those first sirens sounded. Heralding the outbreak of war, these noisome devices also heralded the genesis of the modern police service.

REFERENCES

Chapter 1 : The Storm Clouds Gather
1. J Waller and M Vaughan-Rees M Blitz : *The Civilian War, 1940-45* (1990)
2. Sir Eric St Johnston *One Policeman's Story* (1978)
3. ibid.
4. Andrew Rootes *Front Line County* (1980)
5. *The Folkestone Gazette,* 4 November 1953

Chapter 2 : Closing the Gaps
1. Johnston, op cit
2. H G Pullen *A Brief History of the Metropolitan Special Constab.* (1981)
3. *Home Office Circular* 815,056/63
4. Bolton Record Office, ABCF/23/48
5. *Home Office Circular* 826, 864/41, 22 October 1940
6. H M Howgrave-Graham *The Metropolitan Police at War* (1947)
7. Research & Experiments Department, Ministry of Home Security, in PRP, HO 199/453 (1942)
8. H F Grey, unpublished account of his experiences, in Imp. War Museum
9. S Ward, *War in the Countryside*, 1939-45 (1988)
10. Home Office file 820183/25
11. *Police Review*, 14 April, 1939
12. Johnston, op cit.
13. N Longmate *Air Raid: The Bombing of Coventry, 1940* (1976)
14. ibid
15. C Leon, "Special Constables in the First and Second World Wars" in the *Journal of the Police History Socy.* No7 (1992) p.28
16. *Police Review* 19 January 1940

Chapter 3 : Defence of the Realm
1. Sir A L Dixon, T*he Emergency Work of the Police in the Second World War* unpublished Home Office report.
2. *Police Review,* 11 June 1943
3. J Holliday, *It's a Bit Lively Outside* (1987)
4. B Wicks *Waiting for the All Clear* (1990)
5. R G Crane *Not One of the Heavy Mob* unpublished autobiography
6. Johnston, op cit.
7. N Longmate *How We Lived Then* (1971)
8. ibid

9. Ward, op cit
10. Longmate (1976) op cit
11. E S Turner *The Phoney War on the Home Front* (1961)
12. R Douglas Brown *East Anglia,* 1940 (1981)
13. Longmate (1971) op cit
14. R Ingersoll *Report on England* (1941)
15. A D F Gow *Letters From Cambridge* 1945
16. Angus Calder *The Myth of the Blitz* (1991)
17. Ingersoll, op cit

Chapter 4 : Waiting for Operation Sealion
1. Suffolk Village Report, Mass Observation Report No. 170
2. Barbara *Nixon Raiders Overhead* (1943)
3. P Fleming *Invasion* 1940 (1957)
4. R V Jones *Most Secret War* (1978)
5. Longmate (1971) op cit
6. B Collier *The Defence of the United Kingdom* (1957)
7. Grey, op cit.
8. Waller & Vaughan-Rees (1990) op cit.
9. *Police Review* 26 July 1940
10. Longmate, N *The GIs : The Americans in Britain 1942-1945* (1975)

Chapter 5 : Transports of Delight
1. A G Street *Hitler's Whistle* (1944)
2. Longmate (1975) op cit
3. ibid
4. D Taylor *999 and All That* (1968)
5. Ingersoll, op cit
6. Howgrave-Graham, op cit
7. Longmate (1976) op cit
8. ibid
9. P Chignell *From our Home Correspondent* (1989)
10. Howgrave-Graham, op cit
11. Letter from Mrs Agnes J Kirkwood (neé Cook) to the author
12. Letter from ex-Constable L Clarke to the author
13. Grey, op cit
14. Longmate, (1976) op cit
15. Nixon, op cit
16. Longmate (1976) op cit
17. Nixon, op cit
18. Longmate (1976) op cit
19. Nixon, op cit
20. Waller & Vaughan-Rees (1990) op cit
21. Longmate (1976) op cit

Chapter 6 : The New Partners
1. Sir Philip Game *Britain's Police in War,* article in the "American Journal of Police Science" reproduced in Police Review 8 December, 1844, p.594.
2. T H O'Brien *Civil Defence* (1955)
3. *Police Review* 15 December 1939
4. O'Brien, op cit
5. Angus Calder *The People's War* (1969)
6. O'Brien, op cit
7. Home Office *Dealing With Disaster* (1992)
8. Grey, op cit
9. Nixon, op cit
10. ibid
11. Johnston, op cit
12. Calder (1969) op cit
13. *Police Review* 9 August 1940
14. L Thompson *1940: Year of Legend, Year of History* (1966)

Chapter 7 : A Woman's Cause
1. *Mother & Home* November 1939
2. *The Vote* 28 August 1914
3. *Police Review* 30 January 1942
4. *Annual Report of the Commissioner of Police of the Metropolis for 1943*
5. *The First Hundred Years of the North Riding of Yorkshire Constabulary, 1856-1956* (1956)
6. A W Cockerill *Sir Percy Sillitoe* (1975)

Chapter 8 : Raiders Overhead
1. Thompson , op cit
2. Wicks, op cit
3. Holliday, op cit
4. Grey, op cit
5. F Harding "I Liked Being a Policeman" *Shoreline* August 1991, p.25
6. Grey, op cit
7. Howgrave-Graham, op cit
8. Longmate (1976) op cit
9. ibid
10. ibid
11. Wicks, op cit
12. Ingersoll, op cit
13. Broadcast by PC Bert Ayers, Kent County Constabulary, on BBC 1 o'clock news, 17 November 1940
14. Constable Arthur Marshall, quoted in Holliday, J *It's a Bit Lively Outside* (1987)

15. Harding, op cit, p.33.
16. Waller & Vaughan-Rees (1990) op cit
17. Marshall, op cit
18. Harding, op cit, pp.26-27
19. Marshall, op cit
20. O'Brien, op cit
21. Sam Hays, "My thirty years policing" *Constabulary Gazette* (Journal of the RUC), September 1967, pp.7-15.
22. Ingersoll, op cit
23. Harding, op cit
24. Wicks, op cit
25. Longmate (1976) op cit
26. S Rogers *More Gallant Deeds of the War* (1941)
27. R Howard, unpublished article prepared for the Police History Society
28. Harding, op cit
29. *Folkestone Herald* 23 November 1940

Chapter 9 : A Rapacious and Licentious Soldiery

1. Tom Harrisson, *Living Through the Blitz* (1976)
2. C P Stacey & B M Wilson *The Half-Million : The Canadians in Britain, 1939-1946* (1987)
3. Undated copy of a letter enclosed in Pearson to Crerar, 2 July 1940, Canadian Military HQ file 20/1 DIV/1, RG 24 vol. 12,714
4. W H Pilcher, JP, Chairman of the Godalming Borough Petty Sessions in remarks addressed from the Bench, 7 February, 1946
5. Longmate (1975) op cit
6. ibid
7. E Johnson in a letter to the author
8. Joan Salhurst in a letter to the author
9. Calder (1969) op cit
10. R Humphreys "Be my guest, said the gentle enemy" *Mid-Week Gazette* 17 November 1976
11. Arthur Street *From Dusk to Dawn* (1947)
12. Wicks, op cit
13. The Prisoners of War and Internees (Access & Communication) Order, 1940 (S R & O No 1389)

Chapter 10 : Wartime Crimes

1. Longmate (1976) op cit
2. Wicks, op cit
3. A Kendall *Their Finest Hour* (1972)
4. ibid
5. Waller & Vaughan-Rees (1990) op cit

6. ibid
7. P Lewis *A People's War* (1986)
8. Longmate (1976) op cit
9. J Mack & S Humphries *The Making of Modern London, 1939-1945 : London at War* (1985)
10. Nixon, op cit
11. ibid
12. Wicks, op cit
13. *The Times,* 24 July, 1940
14. *The Police Review* 7 June 1940
15. Turner, op cit
16. Street (1944) op cit
17. Lewis, op cit
18. ibid
19. Ward, op cit
20. ibid

Chapter 11 : With Felonious Intent
1. Central Statistical Office *Statistical Digest of the War* (1951)
2. Longmate (1975), op cit
3. *Leicester Mercury,* 1 June 1944
4. E Smithies *Crime in Wartime* (1982)
5. Longmate (1975), op cit
6. Longmate (1971), op cit
7. Smithies, op cit
8. Nella Last *Nella Last's War* (1981)
9. Crane, op cit
10. Johnston, op cit
11. CMHQ file 20/OFFENCE/1. The report appears as Appendix A to Report 119 Historical Officer CMHQ, 30 June 1944
12. *Birkenhead Advertiser* 20 February 1943
13. Stacey & Wilson, op cit
14. ibid
15. ibid
16. Nixon, op cit
17. *Police Review* 17 November 1939
18. *Police Review* 30 April 1943
19. Longmate (1975), op cit
20. *The Times* 5 August 1942
21. PRO, HO 45/20250
22. J L Hodson *Home Front* (1944)

Chapter 12 : *Morals, Manners & Mores*
1. Mack & Humphries, op cit
2. P Schweizer et al (eds) *What Did You Do In The War, Mum?* (1985)
3. Longmate (1975), op cit
4. ibid
5. Stacey & Wilson, op cit
6. S M Ferguson & H Fitzgerald *Studies in the Social Services* (1954)
7. Last, op cit
8. *Bath Weekly Chronicle & Herald* 5 February 1944
9. Longmate (1975), op cit
10. *Rochester & Chatham Gazette* 22 April 1942
11. *Police Review* 16 October 1942
12. *Police Review* 30 October 1942

Chapter 13 : *All Our Troubles & Adversities*
1. *Police Chronicle & Constabulary World* 29 March 1946
2. *The Kent Police Centenary : Recollections of a Hundred Years* (1957)
3. F Butler "City War Special - Reminiscences of Police Work in the Blitz" in *City, the Magazine of the City of London Police,* Aug/Sept. 1975.
4. A Marwick *The Home Front:The British and the Second World War* (1976)
5. Grey, op cit
6. Ingersoll, op cit
7. Lewis, op cit
8. Longmate (1976), op cit
9. ibid
10. Dixon, op cit
11. Stacey & Wilson, op cit
12. Calder (1969), op cit
13. Grey, op cit
14. O'Brien, op cit
15. Street (1947), op cit
16. Last, op cit
17. Grey, op cit
18. Commissioner of Police of the Metropolis *Annual Report for 1943*

Chapter 14 : *Looking to a Brighter Tomorrow*
1. House of Commons Debates, p.1734
2. Cmd. Paper (1946) No 168

SELECT BIBLIOGRAPHY

Belfast Telegraph, *Bombs on Belfast* (Belfast, Belfast Telegraph, 1941)

Bisset, I. *The George Cross* (London, MacGibbon & Kee, 1961)

Broad, R. & Fleming, S.(eds.) *Nella Last's War* (London, Sphere Books, 1981)

Brown, R. Douglas, *East Anglia, 1940* (Lavenham, Terence Dalton Ltd, 1981)

Brown, R. Douglas, *East Anglia, 1942* (Lavenham, Terence Dalton Ltd, 1988)

Calder, A. *The People's War* (London, Jonathan Cape, 1969)

Calder, A. *The Myth of the Blitz* (London, Jonathan Cape, 1991)

Central Statistical Office *Statistical Digest of the War* (London, HMSO, 1951)

Chignell, P. *From our Home Correspondent* (Beverley, Highgate Publications, 1989)

Cockerill, A. W. *Sir Percy Sillitoe* (London, W H Allen, 1975)

Collier, B. *The Defence of the United Kingdom* (London, HMSO, 1957)

Critchley, T. A. *A History of Police in England & Wales* (London, Constable, 1967)

Dobson, B. *Policing in Lancashire, 1839-1989* (Blackpool, Landy Publishing, 1989)

Ferguson, S. M. & Fitzgerald, H. *Studies in the Social Services* (London, HMSO, 1954)

Fleming, P. *Invasion 1940* (London, Rupert Hart-Davis, 1957)

Gow, A. D. F. *Letters From Cambridge* (London, Jonathan Cape, 1945)

Harrisson, T. *Living Through the Blitz* (London, Collins, 1976)

Hodson, J. L. *Home Front* (London, Gollancz, 1944)

Holliday, J. I*t's a Bit Lively Outside* (Sheffield, Yorkshire Art Circus, 1987)

Home Office *Dealing With Disaster* (London, HMSO, 1992)

Howgrave-Graham, H. M. *The Metropolitan Police at War* (London, HMSO, 1947)

Ingersoll, R. *Report on England* (London, The Bodley Head, 1941)

Johnson, D. E. *East Anglia at War, 1939-45* (Norwich, Jarrold Colour Publications, 1978)

Johnston, E. St. *One Policeman's Story* (London, Barry Rose, 1978)

Jones, R. V. *Most Secret War* (London, Hamish Hamilton, 1978)

Kendall, A. *Their Finest Hour* (London, Wayland, 1972)

Lewis, P. *A People's War* (London, Thames Methuen, 1986)

Livesey, A (ed.) *Are We at War?* (London, Times Books, 1989)

Lock, J. *The British Policewoman* : Her Story (London, Robert Hale, 1979)

Longmate, N. *How We Lived Then* (London, Hutchinson, 1971)

Longmate, N *The GIs : The Americans in Britain 1942-1945* (London, Hutchinson, 1975)

Longmate, N. Air Raid: *The Bombing of Coventry, 1940* (London, Hutchinson, 1976)

Mack, J. & Humphries, S. *The Making of Modern London, 1939-1945 : London at War* (London, Sidgwick & Jackson, 1985)

Marwick, A. *The Home Front : The British and the Second World War* (London, Thames & Hudson, 1976)

Nixon, B. *Raiders Overhead* (London, Lindsay Drummond, 1943)

O'Brien, T. H. *Civil Defence* (London, HMSO, 1955)

Pullen, H. G. *A Brief History of the Metropolitan Special Constabulary* (London, Metropolitan Special Constabulary Information Office, 1981)

Rogers, S. *More Gallant Deeds of the War* (London, Blackie & Sons, 1941)

Rolph, C. H. *Living Twice* (London, Victor Gollancz, 1974)

Rootes, A. *Front Line County* (London, Robert Hale, 1980)

Schweizer, P (eds) *What Did You Do In The War, Mum?* (London, Age Exchange Theatre, 1985)

Smith, G. *Bradford's Police* (Bradford, City of Bradford Police, 1974)

Smithies, E. *Crime in Wartime* (London, Geo. Allen & Unwin, 1982)

Stacey, C.P. & Wilson, B.M. T*he Half-Million : The Canadians in Britain, 1939-1946* (Toronto, University of Toronto Press, 1987)

Street, A. G. *Hitler's Whistle* (London, Eyre & Spottiswoode, 1944)

Street, A. G. *From Dusk to Dawn* (London, Blandford, 1947)

Taylor, D. *999 and All That* (Oldham, Oldham Corporation, 1968)

Thompson, L. *1940: Year of Legend, Year of History* (London, Collins, 1966)

Turner, E. S. *The Phoney War on the Home Front* (London, Michael Joseph, 1961)

Waller, J. and Vaughan-Rees, M. *Women in Wartime* (London, Macdonald Optima, 1990)

Waller, J. and Vaughan-Rees, M. Blitz : *The Civilian War, 1940-45* (London, Macdonald Optima, 1990)

Ward, S. *War in the Countryside, 1939-45* (1988)

Webb, E & Duncan, J. *Blitz Over Britain* (Tunbridge Wells, Spellmount Ltd, 1990

Wicks, B. *Waiting for the All Clear* (London, Bloomsbury, 1990)

INDEX